George Grant
Selected Letters

George Grant was one of Canada's foremost political and religious thinkers. In his published writings, Grant was a careful and guarded writer, but in his letters he was frank and spontaneous, expressing ideas and opinions he hesitated to convey in print. Grant's letters are remarkable for their continuity – about twelve hundred letters survive from 1923 to his death in 1988 – and for their quality. For more than fifty years, he favoured his correspondents with his observations about international relations, Canadian politics, religion, literature, and philosophy. William Christian has selected some three hundred letters, postcards, telegrams, and journal entries which reveal much about Grant – both the troubled man and the daring thinker.

His correspondence begins with the letters from his early years at Upper Canada College and his undergraduate days at Queen's University, followed by letters from London during the Second World War, when he struggled with the conflict between his pacifism and his sense of duty. The middle section includes letters that describe his life at Dalhousie University in the 1950s, his resignation from York University, and his hopes to create in the department of religion at McMaster University a kind of fifth column that would preserve a university within the multiversities he thought had taken over higher education in Canada. The later letters feature his remorseless attacks on what he felt were the perfidies of Trudeau during his long tenure as prime minister.

WILLIAM CHRISTIAN is a professor in the Department of Political Studies at the University of Guelph, and the author of *George Grant: A Biography*.

George Grant

Selected Letters

Edited with an Introduction by
William Christian

UNIVERSITY OF TORONTO PRESS
Toronto Buffalo London

© University of Toronto Press Incorporated 1996
Toronto Buffalo London
Printed in Canada

ISBN 0-8020-0757-0 (cloth)
ISBN 0-8020-7807-9 (paper)

Printed on acid-free paper

Canadian Cataloguing in Publication Data

Grant, George, 1918–1988
   George Grant : selected letters

   Includes index.
   ISBN 0-8020-0757-0 (bound) ISBN 0-8020-7807-9 (pbk.)

   1. Grant, George, 1918–1988 – Correspondence.
   2. Philosophers – Canada – Correspondence.
   I. Christian, William, 1945–   . II. Title.

   B995.G74A4 1996   191'.092   C95-932739-8

University of Toronto Press acknowledges the financial assistance to its
publishing program of the Canada Council and the Ontario Arts Council.

Contents

Introduction

'I would far rather live in the centre of the crisis.'
George Grant to his mother, 1939

In an age of the fax machine and e-mail, it is unlikely that Canada will ever produce another writer of letters of George Grant's calibre. He was a remarkable correspondent. His letters are direct, intensely personal communications with the individual to whom he wrote. Whether they were to a close friend, or to someone who had written him an interesting letter, if they deserved his full attention, they usually got it.

Mind you, a letter from George Grant, however pleasant an event, required more than a little effort from its recipient. His handwriting was difficult even when he was young, but after a car crash in 1970, which partly crippled his right hand, it became even worse. More than one person who sent me copies of the letters included in this collection kindly provided transcripts, although the number of words which remained problematic or simply illegible still remained high. When I asked Donald MacDonald, Grant's old friend from Queen's and former leader of the Ontario CCF and NDP, to read over Grant's letters from university, he generously agreed but was visibly relieved when I presented him with a printed version rather than the handwritten originals. Still, even though one could, at first reading, make out only about 80 per cent of the words (and a lower proportion of the proper names), it was worth persevering.

Born on the grounds of Upper Canada College in 1918, Grant began his epistolary career about the age of five, and about seventy letters survive from his childhood. That such a remarkable collection exists is the result of what Grant himself described as an 'Oedipus complex the size of a house.' From the time he set out for university in 1936 until his mother, Maude Grant, became too senile to make any sense of his letters, Grant wrote to her almost weekly. Maude saved his letters, as she did other family correspondence, and the metal filing cabinet at 7 Prince Arthur Avenue in Toronto, which contained her family correspondence, was one of her most treasured possessions. Her brother, Raleigh Parkin, made the collection of the family papers of both the Grants and the Parkins his hobby, and after his retirement, he worked at it very seriously. There are thirty-nine volumes of material in the Grant-Parkin collection in the National Archives of Canada. Grant's share of this amounts, in the charming way it is measured in the archives, to a foot's worth of shelf space. (I doubt he would have approved of metric equivalents; younger readers will have to figure out the length for themselves.)

Grant described his family as a gynarchy, but the more common term is matriarchy. The core of the family were Grant's mother and her sister Alice. Their father, George Parkin, was a New Brunswick farm boy who made good. Charming, intelligent, perhaps even charismatic, George Parkin made a brilliant career in education, serving as principal of Upper Canada College, a private boys' school in Toronto, before Lord Milner asked him in 1902 to take charge of the new scholarships which Cecil Rhodes had established to promote friendship between the British Empire, the United States, and Germany, the three powers Rhodes thought would dominate the twentieth century.

Parkin married Annie Fisher, the daughter of a successful New Brunswick merchant family. Four daughters and a son survived infancy. Lady Parkin (Sir George was knighted in 1920 when he retired as secretary of the Rhodes Scholarship trust) made sure that the family remained a Parkin affair. Her daughters made wise choices in their husbands.

Maude married William Grant in 1911. Grant was the only surviving son of George Monro Grant, who, as principal of Queen's University in Kingston, Ontario, from 1877 until his death in 1902, was one of the most important intellectual figures in late-Victorian Canada. William Grant, after proving himself an outstanding student of history and classics at Queen's and Oxford, taught at Upper Canada under George Parkin. However, he courted Maude, who was working as assistant warden of a women's residence at the University of Manchester, while he was a lecturer in colonial history at Oxford. When he accepted a history position at Queen's, he plucked up his courage and proposed. Maude accepted and they returned to Kingston.

In 1915 the structure of the family began to gel. Alice, Maude's elder sister by a year, married Vincent Massey, heir to the agricultural implements manufacturing family firm (Massey-Harris). Although well-to-do, Massey's later prominence came through politics and diplomacy. He served as Canadian ambassador to Washington, president of the Liberal party, high commissioner in London during the war, and later capped his career by becoming Canada's first native-born governor-general.

In the same year, Maude's sister Marjorie, nine years younger, married a Kingston lawyer, J.M. Macdonnell. Macdonnell's career was in business (he later became president of National Trust), but his passion was politics. He was one of the leading figures who held the Conservative party together during the bleak period of the 1940s, and John Diefenbaker rewarded the old man for his past service by appointing him to his cabinet.

This triumvirate – the Grants, the Masseys, and the Macdonnells – formed the core of the extended family in which George Grant grew up. The other two Parkin children were on the periphery. Grace married a British civil servant, Harry Wimperis, and lived in London. Grant was rather proud of the fact that Uncle Harry, out of a sense of honour, fought a prolonged battle with the British tax authorities, trying to prove that *he owed them* money. Raleigh Parkin, the baby of the family, served abroad in the First World War. The experience was emotionally shattering for the young man, and he spent a pleasant, but undistinguished, career with an insurance company in Montreal. However, he added an interesting leaven to Grant's circle of acquaintances, because he was friends with poet and constitutional expert Frank Scott and novelist Hugh MacLennan and, through him, Grant came to know something of the intellectual life of anglophone Montreal.

This web of Parkin alliances provided the broad context within which Grant grew up. In his immediate family, he was the youngest, and the only boy. His older sisters were all remarkable women with powerful personalities, and, when Grant was growing up, he felt rather overwhelmed by the world of women. His closest relationship when he was young was with his sister Margaret. As he grew up, he had a powerful and ambivalent relationship with Charity. Charity stood in no awe of her brother's intelligence. She had strong views on most issues, which she did not hesitate to express bluntly, and, since she rather disapproved of her brother's volatility, they eventually, in the late 1960s, fell into a prolonged family quarrel, which took some fifteen years to resolve. Margaret lived most of her adult life in Vancouver, and Alison, who married diplomat George Ignatieff, spent much of her life in Ottawa or abroad. As a result, Grant was not as close to his other two sisters as he was to Charity.

Outside the family, Grant's two great friends were men he came to know at Oxford. Grant met Peter Self when he arrived in Oxford in 1939 at the beginning of the war. Self was a pacifist, as was Grant, and Grant's admiration for Self's intellectual capabilities never diminished, although he regretted that Self devoted his career to public policy analysis, instead of more philosophical concerns. He could have been, Grant averred, the Kant of the social sciences, had he set his mind to it.

Few of Grant's letters to Self survive. However, Derek Bedson, whom Grant met when he returned to Oxford after the war to study theology, was more assiduous in preserving correspondence, and Grant's letters to Bedson are the second largest collection (by a long distance, after those to his mother). Bedson shared two of Grant's driving passions – religion and politics. Bedson was a Conservative and a Diefenbaker political adviser, who returned to his native Winnipeg, where he served successive premiers of Manitoba as their chief civil service adviser. In religion, he was a devout Anglican, although of an Anglo-Catholic bent of which Grant's more evangelical Christianity did not really approve. However, Grant felt comfortable confiding his religious concerns in Bedson, and he loved the gossip about Canadian politics Bedson was able to provide. He made his affection for Bedson clear when he dedicated his most famous book, *Lament for a Nation*, to him and journalist Judith Robinson.

In the later 1960s, when Grant was deeply involved in the opposition to the American war in Vietnam, he met Canadian poet Dennis Lee. The friendship was an immediate epiphany for Lee, who found in Grant's writings a conscious articulation of the deep matters he had intuited and expressed poetically, but had hitherto been unable to think through systematically. His strong sympathy with Grant's work was reflected in the rôle he played, officially and unofficially over the next twenty years, as Grant's editor. Grant's two brilliant collections of essays, *Technology and Empire* (1969) and *Technology and Justice* (1986), might never have appeared without Lee's prodding, and they would certainly not have been as effective or integrated. Grant so loved and respected Lee that he would willingly accept editorial guidance from him that would have sent him into a spluttering rage had it been offered from any other source.

Many of Grant's other correspondents in his later life were younger academics whom he thought shared his philosophic love (*eros* was the word he generally used), his driving attempt to understand what made the modern world he inhabited the way it was. In these he took an avuncular interest, literally in the case of his nephew Ed Andrew, figuratively in the case of people such as Joan O'Donovan and myself.

Grant's letters are remarkable for two reasons. The first is their continuity. From 1923 until his death in 1988, about 1,200 letters survive. In part, this volume of correspondence reflected his Scottish parsimoniousness, since he always thought of long-distance telephone calls as an extravagance. Inexpensive notepaper and a first-class stamp served him better, since he could set forth his thoughts with greater leisure. For over fifty years, he favoured his correspondents with his observations about international relations, Canadian politics, religious concerns, literary analysis, and philosophic reflections. His correspondence spans his whole life. It begins with the letters from his childhood and proceeds through his undergraduate days at Queen's, his great letters from London during the Second World War as he struggled with the conflict between his pacifism and his sense of duty, England's postwar reconstruction, and life at Dalhousie in the 1950s as he tried to build a socially critical philosophy department in the face of what he considered the philistinism and parochialism of Halifax. He set out in letters his reasons for resigning from York University and his hope that he could create, in the Department of Religion at McMaster, a kind of fifth column that would preserve a university within the multiversities which he thought had taken over higher education in Canada. Throughout the 1970s and the 1980s, he watched Canada fall increasingly into the American sphere of influence (as he had predicted in *Lament for a Nation*), and he remorselessly attacked Trudeau's many perfidies over his long tenure as prime minister.

The second reason for admiring these letters is their quality. They are not literary letters; Grant had no thought that they would ever be published. But what letters! Grant was always cautious about what he published. He had, early in his career, some bad experiences when he was too idealistic and too candid about the deficiencies he saw in some of the leading philosophers in Canada. He felt that he had paid a high price because of his forthrightness. He also wanted to wait until he could express his ideas clearly, and writing for publication never came easily.

In his letters, the freshness and the candour, the flashes of insight and the intellectual daring, are there in full force. The letters to his mother are perhaps among the strangest a son ever wrote. From the age of four to forty, she was his chief confidante. Although she was a woman who impressed everyone who met her with her grace and charm, Grant, even as a child, felt uncertain about her love. His letters were his way of trying to prove to her that he deserved to be loved. He sought and offered advice, talked about politics, told her his innermost fears and hopes. He even destroyed her letters, as he told her, so that she could be equally candid with him. Maude loved all her children, and she could never give him what he really wanted, a declaration that she loved him best of all.

This relationship was the continuing emotional crisis of his life. However, his desire to live at the centre of the crisis was vindicated, often through his own actions. Soon after he wrote the letter to his mother quoted at the beginning of this introduction, he found himself in Oxford in the first months of the war. Feeling guilty in the aloof comfort of Oxford, he set out in the summer of 1940 to join an ambulance unit formed by fellow pacifists. When that plan failed, he took a post as an unpaid air raid precautions warden in Bermondsey, a poor area of south London. For a year he was at the centre of the German bombing of London, and he came out of the experience emotionally scarred and spiritually transformed.

After the war, the president of the University of Toronto offered him the position of warden of Hart House, a prestigious and lucrative appointment, but leading members of the board of governors, critical of Grant's pacifism in the war, blocked his appointment. For thirteen years, he served his apprenticeship in philosophy in Halifax, but he chafed at being so far from where things, great social and philosophic things, were happening.

He even toyed with taking a teaching post in California, because there he could be certain of being at the centre of the coming crisis for North American civilization. Instead, he accepted an appointment in 1960 at the new university in Toronto, York. Toronto might not be California, but the new civilization was emerging there too, and he could both observe and respond to it from there. Within months, and with a wife and six children to support, he had resigned over important philosophical and pedagogical issues.

He took a teaching position at McMaster University, and for a decade was reasonably happy there. He analysed and exposed the Canadian crisis in *Lament* and denounced the growing American involvement in Vietnam, taking an active role in teach-ins and peaceful demonstrations. In the 1970s, he slowly became disenchanted with McMaster, which he felt was suffering the homogenizing fate of all Canadian universities. When he resigned from McMaster in 1980, some injudicious comments in the press brought his resignation to national attention. He moved to Dalhousie, where his return provoked a series of minor crises within the university.

However, by that point, the crisis to which he had devoted his attention for the better part of four decades was not any passing personal or political crisis, but the intellectual crisis of the West. How could human beings live good lives in the modern world? Modern science, modern technology, had transformed the self-understanding of human beings. It had cut us off from the divine as an orientation for our lives. It had made us oblivious of eternity. Yet modern human beings did not understand that they were all now living in the centre of a great crisis, perhaps the greatest of all crises. Grant's mission, that of a prophet, was to warn that the crisis was coming fast. At his death in 1988, he was planning a major book, which would be his final refutation of modernity as expressed by Martin Heidegger.

Different people will find these letters interesting for different reasons. I find them compelling on three grounds. First, as a human being, Grant developed and changed enormously over the course of his life, more, I think, than most people change. His correspondence gives a good sense of this, and his letters to his mother are remarkable documents in almost every way. Second, Grant was famous as a philosopher, and his letters contain much daring speculation that he was reticent to include in published work. Finally, Grant's interest in politics was lifelong, and his brilliant observations on Canadian and world affairs span more than half a century.

Most readers will find many things to admire (and some to condemn) in these letters. Everyone, at different times, will be amazed, amused, shocked, annoyed, and outraged.

William Christian
Guelph, Ontario

Acknowledgments

The reader owes a large debt of gratitude, as I do, to Erica Lamacraft, who typed most of these letters over a period of two years. To have done so is a testimony to her intelligence and perseverance, qualities that will serve her well in what I anticipate to be a successful academic career. I would also like to thank the many people who sent me copies of their correspondence from George Grant (if others who read this have copies of Grant's letters, I would be very pleased to have them too). Sheila Grant cooperated fully and actively with this project from the outset. She helped with illegible words, identified people and events, and firmly, but kindly, corrected my mistakes. I would also like to thank Dennis Duffy for his patience in reading the letters and giving me his invaluable advice on editing them. Mark Haslett read the current selection and helped greatly with many details; he was, as usual, both generous and kind. Don MacDonald, an old friend of Grant's from Queen's, kindly helped to give me background on events during the late 1930s. Mary-Jo Gordon was enthusiastic, determined, and resourceful in identifying people and events mentioned in the letters. Tom Tytor helped me to finalize several of the footnote entries. I would also like to thank Mel Hurtig, whose *Canadian Encyclopedia* made everyone's job a lot easier.

I am grateful to the following, who provided letters or helped with the identification of people mentioned in the letters: the Department of Alumni Affairs of Queen's University, Dr Margaret Angus, Dr William Angus, Phyllis Bray, Mrs Clara Brook, Mrs Beatrice Corbett, Mr and Mrs Robert Crothers, Dr Michael Gelber, Mrs Margaret Gibson, Donald Grant, Mrs Sheila Grant, Jane Kaduck, Jan Liebaers, Peter Macdonnell, General K.H. McKibbin, Henri Pilon, Miss Jean Richardson,

Mrs Sheila Rounthwaite, Marian Spence, Mrs Susanna Wild, Steve Zoltair, and the estate of Howard Brotz. Matthew Christian helped to organize what had become a chaotic mess of letters all over his father's study and prepared the index.

Note on the Text

The letters in this edition come from the following sources: (1) the Grant-Parkin Papers in the National Archives of Canada (MG 30 D 59 vol. 38–40), which include all Grant's letters to his mother and his journal; (2) other family correspondence from the Massey Papers in the National Archives (MG 32 A1, vol. 55) and the Vincent Massey Personal Records in the Robarts Library of the University of Toronto (UTA B87–0082); (3) the files relating to the Canadian Association of Adult Education in the Archives of Ontario (CAAE papers F 1205 series B1); (4) the University Archives of Dalhousie University; (5) the uncatalogued Derek Bedson personal papers on loan to the Provincial Archives of Manitoba; (6) Grant's personal papers, which are still in the possession of Mrs Grant in Halifax; (7) George Grant file, Rhodes Scholarship Trust, Canada; (8) George Grant file, Rhodes House, Oxford; (9) George Grant file, Department of Religion, McMaster University; (10) various correspondents, letters to whom I have collected. The current selection contains approximately one-quarter of Grant's known letters.

In choosing this collection, I could have done either of two things: I could have excerpted what I considered to be the interesting bits from letters; or I could have reproduced complete letters. Both methods have their merits, but, wherever possible, I chose the latter, because I thought that it gave a better view of the texture of Grant as a correspondent. The exceptions are letters 83, 84, 128, and 303. I was provided only with extracts of these letters, and I have reproduced fully the material that was made available to me. I understand that the material that was withheld was of a personal nature.

Upper Canada College may have been a good institution for building the character of its boys; but, if Grant is anyone upon whom to base a generalization, it somewhat fell down at teaching penmanship. Grant's hand-writing began to decline about the age of six, when he moved from printing in block capitals to cursive writing. From the point of view of leg-ibility, Grant's letters ranged from a small number that were profession-ally typed and dated by his secretary at McMaster, Mrs Grace Gordon, through those he idiosyncratically typed himself, down to those he wrote by hand. At the bottom, stand those he wrote when he was particularly upset, or worse, writing on a train, or a bus crossing war-damaged Lon-don. I puzzled for a long while about why he would admire someone's (what appeared to me) hamster, until I twigged that he had written 'ban-ter.' Proper names were often extremely difficult, often just a scrawl, and impossible to decipher unless one knew who they were by context. I would be grateful to hear from readers who can correct names or spelling.

Erica Lamacraft developed a remarkable facility to read Grant's hand-writing. Her first recourse in the case of illegible words was to me. Those I could not read or guess at, I took to my wife, Barbara Christian. The final court of appeal was Sheila Grant. Words in the text enclosed in square brackets represent additions to Grant's text of two different types. First, some additions supply words that are missing but seem necessary to the sense. The second sort also represent editorial additions to the text in the sense that they represent reasonably confident guesses at Grant's mean-ing. When [ill.] is used, it means that none of us could hazard even a sen-sible guess that made sense of the squiggle on the page. Question marks in parentheses in the text are Grant's own.

Besides the additions indicated by square brackets, the text of the let-ters has been emended only to regularize some accidentals of punctua-tion and to provide certain other missing ones (question marks, periods for some abbreviations, hyphens, etc.); to correct misspellings; and to correct minor lapses of grammar when they interfered with the clarity of the intended meaning. The only excisions were (1) those made at the request or insistence of those who gave me letters; and (2) Mrs Grant's. Her great moral authority made such requests difficult to resist. Such excisions relate exclusively to Grant's comments on private matters of lit-tle or no interest or significance, other than to the individuals involved. Mrs Grant insisted that their privacy be respected, and she was right to do so. They are marked in the customary fashion with '...'

I have intentionally kept the introduction short, to permit the inclu-sion of the greatest possible number of Grant's letters. In terms of anno-tation, I have tried to identify people as they were at the time of Grant's reference to them. Although many went on to accomplish great things, I have not mentioned these unless I thought they threw light on the passages concerned.

I have attempted to provide a representative sample of the letters. There are letters from every year from the time Grant entered Queen's in 1936 until his death. I have also attempted to show a broad range of Grant's interests – theology, philosophy, politics, universities, literature, music. I have also included letters that throw light on his personal life and character. The current selection contains letters, telegrams, postcards, memos, a reader's report, and a piece of verse by George Grant to eighty-six different correspondents, as well as extracts from a journal Grant kept in 1942, when he wrote few letters. This journal has not previously been published. I have also supplemented Grant's letters with three letters not written by him: one from his father proposing to his mother; one from his grandfather; and one about him by Victor Morin. I believe that these documents add to the understanding of Grant's life and thought.*

---

*Readers who wish more detail might consult William Christian, *George Grant: A Biography* (Toronto: University of Toronto Press, 1993).

Correspondents

William Grant to Maude Grant 1[*]
Sir George Parkin to George Grant 2[*]
Victor Morin to the Rhodes Scholarship Trust of Canada 14n (George Grant file, Rhodes Scholarship Trust, Canada)

George Grant to:

C.K. Allen 73 (George Grant file, Rhodes House, Oxford)
Ed Andrew 251, 254, 264, 277, 286–7[#]
Geoff and/or Margaret Andrew 46, 72, 113[*]
Ian Angus 273[#]
John Arapura 291[#]
Dean Archibald 132 (George Grant file, Department of Religion, McMaster University)
Patrick Atherton 209[§]
Terry Barker 293, 302[§]
Derek Bedson 122, 125, 127, 129, 135–7, 140–4, 149, 153, 156, 160, 163, 178, 195–7, 200, 207, 223–4, 226, 247, 268 (Derek Bedson personal papers, uncatalogued, Provincial Archives of Manitoba)
Burgon Bickersteth 214[§]
Alice Boissonneau 75, 79–80, 88, 111[#]
Stephen Bornstein 173[§]

[*]Grant-Parkin Papers, National Archives of Canada
[§]George Grant personal papers, Halifax
[#]Collected by the editor

Harley Smyth 225[§]
Leo Strauss 157, 170[§]
Katherine Temple 303[#]
Murray and Anne Tolmie 120, 139[§]
S.J. Totton 155[§]
R.A. Trotter 32, 41, 43, 61[*]
Pierre Trudeau 169[§]
André Weil 145[§]
E.T. Williams 181[§]
George Wilson 92 (George Grant file, Dalhousie University Archives)
Grace Wimperis 3[*]
Paul Younger 188[§]

George Grant
Selected Letters

Prologue 1910–22

1910

William Grant's letter proposing marriage to Maude Parkin

1/ William Grant to Maude Grant

c/o Rev. C.M. Grant
Clury House
Kingsmere
3 August 1910

My dear Miss Maude,[1]
I came to Pitlochry[2] on Thursday to say something to you, and came away without saying it. So now I must write it; it would have been better said, but a drive downhill behind Donach, ending in a rush for a train, seemed hardly the fitting time.

Ever since we first met at UCC,[3] I have admired you more than any others and, in the last two years,[4] I have come to love you very deeply. There! It is said now, and nothing else makes much difference; but I must go on to tell you the whole story.

We all more or less plan out our lives, however badly we stick to our plan, and I had planned out a life of work, of work to increase learning, of work for Canada, work with which no woman was to interfere. Now you have come in, and my plan is either ruined or perfected. It is ruined if I do not win you, for then the spring has gone out of my years and, although I shall try to go on without you, I shall not run but trudge; it is perfected for, with you beside me, I know that we can do ten times as much for Canada, can ten times as well fulfil whatever purpose it may be for which we came into the world, as I could if alone.

This is a wretched way to put it, for it sounds as if I valued you mainly as a stimulus to my work. That is not so at all. I want you for yourself; I want you because I love you. But, if I can but win you, it is my good hope that, in winning the woman I love, I win the woman who can help me most.

I shall not talk nonsense about first love. I am thirty-seven[5] and only in the last two years have I really learned to love you. A man does not reach thirty-five without going through various stages of calf adoration. But I can say with truth that never till today have I asked a girl to marry me, to share my life. Besides, now I am a man grown, and love is a far more serious – you will laugh if I say devastating – thing now than it was in my 'teens and twenties.

I have little to offer you, neither money, nor good looks, nor position. I am a poor man, and in all human probability always shall be; but, after all, I have my salary at Queen's,[6] and a little money besides,[7] and I can offer you a home small enough but not mean. In spite of my age, I don't think I have yet 'set like plaster.' I have still a certain amount of give and take, and God knows I would try to make you happy. Some of our ideas we tend to share, unless I am very wrong, and I do not think you would find me so ill to live with.

I do not ask you to say yes to this at once, but I do ask for a chance to speak for myself. I have arranged to go south on Friday afternoon, but I can wait over if you will see me in Pitlochry; if not I will wait – not patiently – till you are in Manchester.[8] But unless you are definitely pledged to someone else, this much I think I deserve, a chance to speak for myself.

When I read over what I have written, it sounds so cold and a bit pragmatic. But there is nothing cold in my thoughts. My dear, whenever I think of you, when I speak your name, the pulses in my neck quiver and tighten, and all my blood seems to be in my throat. How shall I end? How shall I sign?

Yours always,
W.L. Grant[9]

1 Maude Erskine (Parkin) Grant (1880–1963), second child of Sir George and Lady Parkin
2 Tayside, Scotland. A touring centre for the Grampians, the grassy, heather-clad mountains that stretch across the Highlands
3 Upper Canada College, a private boys' school in Toronto. Maude Grant's father, George Parkin, was principal from 1895 until 1902. William Grant was an assistant master at UCC from 1898 until 1902.
4 William Grant was Beit lecturer in colonial history at Oxford from 1906 until 1910.

5 William Grant was born 2 November 1872, the only child of George Monro Grant and Jessie Lawson Grant to survive infancy.

6 Grant was to take up a position as professor of history at Queen's University in Kingston, Ontario, in the autumn of 1910. His father, George Monro Grant, was principal from 1877 until 1902.

7 Grant's father came from a farming family and had little money. His mother came from a family of prosperous Halifax merchants. However, Grant had spent (and gambled) most of his inheritance away before he met Maude Parkin.

8 Maude Parkin was assistant warden of Ashburn Hall, a women's residence at the University of Manchester.

9 They were married 1 June 1911 at the Church of St Thomas of Canterbury, Goring-on-Thames, outside Oxford, where the Parkins lived.

1922

Sir George Parkin was a distinguished educator who dedicated his life to turning the British Empire into a political unit which would promote British justice and decency around the world. However, his injunction to his young grandson to serve his king and country was a great burden as Grant grew to manhood.

2/ Sir George Parkin[1] to George Grant   17 April 1922

Dear George,

A few days ago I was walking along the street in London, and I saw the picture of King George, which I am sending you with this. It seemed to me that your own name was George, and both your grandfathers were Georges and, as I knew you had at the College a picture of St George, you also might like to have King George in your room – so here it is. I have talked with him several times, and he is so cheerful and pleasant that I am sure you would not mind having a chat with him yourself, if you should happen to meet him. And when you grow up you will be expected to work for your king and country. The name George really means a farmer or earth-worker. So, when you do some gardening like you did last spring, you are really doing what your name means.

I was delighted to get that nice picture of our jolly little picnic at the shore.[2] How nice those oranges and bananas were, to say nothing of the bacon. I am quite sure the other girls and boys wished to be with us. I wish mother could bring you over to England with her, so that we could have another picnic here. This week I am going down beside the sea with your three cousins – Barbara, Elizabeth and Virginia.[3] We are going to stay at Swanage,[4] but expect to go over often to Studland,[5] which I think Leo[6] and Margaret[7] and Charity[8] will remember. Grandmother is sending me off there to get me out of the way while the house here is being cleaned. I expect to have a good time with the girls.

Give our love to Father and Mother, Leo, Margaret, Charity and Alison.[9] Grandmother sends you lots of kisses.

You must learn to spell and write as soon as you can, so that you can write me letters. I shall be a proud grandfather when I get a note from George P. Grant.

Your very loving Grandfather

1 Sir George Parkin (1846–1922), secretary of the Rhodes Trust, 1902–20, and one of the leaders of the Imperial federation movement

2 During the summer of 1921, Sir George and Lady Parkin vacationed with their family at Cap-à-l'Aigle on the north shore of the St Lawrence River in Quebec. The event was significant in George Grant's life because his mother believed that Grant was destined to carry on his grandfather Parkin's educational work. Sir George Parkin, who had been knighted for his services to Imperial education in 1920, died 25 June 1922. 'That picture of me on the beach – you know that story was told to me a thousand times – how he had asked for one child to stay with him on the beach and I was the one at the age of 3 who volunteered; and Mother would tell me ... my destiny was to carry on this work ...' (George Grant, interview with Raleigh Parkin, 13 September 1972).

3 Grace (Parkin) Wimperis (1882–1960), two years younger than Maude, married Harry Wimperis (1876–1960), an English scientist who helped invent radar, and spent her adult life in England. Barbara, Elizabeth, and Virginia were their children.

4 A resort town on the English Channel, near Bournemouth

5 A beach near Swanage

6 The Grant children's nurse, Mrs Don Leo ('Leo'). She had served with Maude Grant at Ashburn Hall before Maude's marriage, and came to Canada with the Grant family in 1917. She retired from the Grant's service about 1926 to the village of Allerthorpe in Yorkshire, and the Grant children regularly visited her whenever they were in the United Kingdom.

7 Margaret (Grant) Andrew (1912–82), Grant's eldest sister

8 Charity Grant (1913–), Grant's sister

9 Alison (Grant) Ignatieff (1917–92), Grant's sister, the closest to him in age

Childhood 1923–36

Grant's father studied at Oxford and later taught there. Grant's mother, a McGill graduate, had worked as deputy warden (assistant dean of women) at the University of Manchester. Her sister, Grace, married an Englishman, Harry Wimperis. As well, they had many friends in England, and they visited the Mother Country as often as they could. When possible, they took their children.

1923

Grant visited England with his parents several times when he was young. This early postcard recalls his visit to the London zoo.

3/ To Grace Wimperis   [probably 1923][1]

Dear Aunt Grace,
I have picked out this card for you specially. We have a lovely rabbit, and four goldfish, and Mac.[2] And they are all my pets. We went to the zoo and saw two India sacred cows and some little wallabys, and the little bear which was brought in an aeroplane and Jumbo and Baby Stella and a pelican and other animals. GEORGE

1 The letter is handwritten by an adult but signed in childish block capitals
   GEORGE. It would therefore seem to have been written in 1923 or 1924 at the
   latest.
2 A dog

1924

Maude Grant, like many of her class and generation, felt free to travel and leave the children in the care of her servants.

4/ To Maude Grant   8 June 1924

Dear Mother,
I hop you are well when are you cuming back I hope you cuming back soon by coss I am very lonseme with out you. I hop you are settled yet. I am get ing on with my writing is getting on but my speling is bad yet. We went to the school fate yester day and I wun a cocnut at the cocnut sire.[1] Billy has a new baby sister. He got it on tuday. I have not seen it but I saw billy at the fate
with love from Alison
OOO leo sends her love and george to ooo xxx

1 Coconut shy, a throwing game

1928

Another trip to England.

5/ To Maude Grant   Allerthorpe, York
                                                    27 May [1928]

Dear Mum,
I got on the 10 train and so should have arrived at 1:33, but on account of the floods, we arrived at 2. After seeing you off we went to the Tower [of London] and St Paul's [Cathedral] where I [for]got my hat which was found a minute after I left. We[1] then went to the Tower which was glorious. We then set out for Olympia[2] which was so thrilling I can't describe it. I like the King better than the Queen. Going up to York I was in the same [railway] carriage as a lady from Rhodesia who was just like cousin Mary. Mrs Stanley Baldwin[3] was in the next but one apartment [*sic*], I love Leo and her beautiful cottage. We saw Mr Rhodes Brown[4] last night at a meeting. When are you coming up here if ever? We both want you very badly. Thank you awfully for the letter. Heaps and heaps of love,
                                                            George
                                                            XXXXXX

1 Alison and George
2 Probably a visit to the Royal Tournament, held annually at the great hall in Olympia in west London
3 Wife of Rt Hon. Stanley Baldwin, prime minister 1923, 1924–9, 1935–7
4 A prominent neighbour of Leo's, later Lord Mayor of Birmingham, who owned property near Allerthorpe

1931

Lady Parkin, Grant's maternal grandmother, was seriously ill this summer. He spent part of the summer at friends' cottages.

6/ To Maude Grant   Pickerel River

Dear Mum,
I hope you are not tired and hope daddy [is] well. Yesterday 11 a.m. to 12 p.m. we paddled to the Recollet Falls on the French River 20 miles 10 each way. This is the next day. Tomorrow we are going to the Georgian Bay. There and back is 40 miles we are staying out over night.

Thank you ever so much for the lovely letter you sent me. The letters will come in batches because of the posting of letters. What is the family going to do through the summer. The Recollet are very beautiful because of the wildness of the place.

Yesterday we deported a porky[1] because we can't leave any on the island on account of Peter, the dog. He is the nicest dog I ever knew. As a matter of fact, he has been licking me all evening and still is. I have caught 3 pike and 3 pickerel all ready. It is a great disadvantage having to bring up worms. I have discovered a lovely present for mum's birthday[2] a special can opener.

Love, Heaps of love,
George

1 Porcupine
2 14 September

7 / To Maude Grant   23 August
Pickerel River

Dear Mummy,
I am terribly sorry about dear Granmummy.[1] I got daddy's telegram

before your lovely letter, and therefore could not write. I am coming home Wednesday morning and will love to see you again. Dear Granny was so good and loving.

Love,
George

1 Lady Annie Connell (Fisher) Parkin died 20 August 1931 of renal failure.

1932

8/ To Maude Grant

Wednesday
Sourvanis, Minnicoganashene

Dear Mum,

I hope all the family are well. I am sorry that I couldn't come home on the 26th, but Mrs Watson[1] didn't force me, but she did all but and I couldn't refuse. So I am coming on the 28th.

Edward Wallace (6 ft 4 in) who was up at the Foulds' told me that, if I read *Mutiny of the Bounty*,[2] the part you read to us was the worst. So I am reading the book. It is marvellous. If ever I wanted to call someone the same as when I called you 'J.M.'[3] I would call them Capt Bligh. He is the worst man I have ever read about. When I am reading about him I feel like hitting him I get so really mad. People talk about British Justice, but since I read this book I don't think there is such a thing. It is strange to think that in so few years the whole British navy has turned into something decent, something wonderful, from what it was in those days. The book itself is wonderfully written and very vivid and some of the descriptions of Tahiti are marvellous. I hope you are having a rest while I am away. Give my love to Father and the girls.

Lots of love,
George

P.S. The reason the postmark is Barrie is because a Mr Clarke up here promised to post it there.
P.P.S. There *isn't* any ink.

1 Mother of Grant's friend, Alan Watson
2 Likely Sir John Barrow (1764–1848), *Mutiny of the Bounty* (1831; 2d ed., 1914)
3 Jim Macdonnell

1934

Grant travelled to England again with his parents and stayed for a long period with Mrs Buck,[1] who acquired a pony, Rob Roy, for him to ride.

9/ To Maude Grant   24 August

Dear Mother,

I am having a simply wonderful time here. I have been to Old Kempley Church. It is full of 12th century wall paintings. St Anthony was on the wall. I thought of you. In the chancel the painting is very clear. We have been to Little Malvern Church where [there is] the only known picture of Edward V. One day everybody went out except Mrs Buck and I. She brought out the sketches of your trips and we went [over] the four trips that you had been [on]. She loves you ever so much. Miss Wallas[2] has been staying here. She is a dear. Mr McDougall[3] is here and Mr Andrew[4] and Mr Biggar[5] arrived yesterday.

We go to Tintern [Abbey] tomorrow. I am looking forward to that ever so much. Thank you for Grandfather's bible you had it done wonderfully.

We went to the last night of the Malvern Festival to see *A Man's House*.[8] We sat in the same row as Bernard Shaw.[7] Mr McDougall and I tried to make him step onto our toes. The play was very wonderful for the 1st two acts but it rather fell down in the last act. It is about a family in Jerusalem in the time of Christianity and crucifixion. It was too bad, because we did not realise that the main basis of the plot was a blind girl who is very bitter but who, in the end, receives her sight. Mr McDougall did not seem to mind.[8] Mrs Buck is much better and goes to different places in the car. Jones[9] is wonderful with her.

Aunt Margaret[10] told me a wonderful story of the wonderful trip when she went to the opera in Vienna. She went in with tickets got in and found that her tickets were for the next night. She stayed on. Her seat was not hers. Some other people came for their seat and she said, with a choke in her voice, that this was the opera she had wanted to see for years and it was her only chance to see it. They squeezed over and gave her room. Give lots of love to Father and lots of love to yourself.

Love,
George

1 Marian Buck was an admirer of Grant's Grandfather Parkin and a friend of Grant's parents. At one point she proposed, in effect, to adopt Grant, make

him her heir, and train him to carry on his grandfather's work of forging the British Empire into an effective political unit.

2 Not identified

3 D.J. McDougall (1893–1969), a family friend; taught in the Department of History, University of Toronto, 1929–62

4 Geoff Andrew (1906–86), a master at UCC, who later married Grant's sister Margaret

5 J.H. Biggar (1908–83), UCC history teacher, educated at University of Toronto and Oxford. He taught history with a great emphasis on current affairs. He had been a Parkin Scholar, a scholarship established by Mrs Buck to promote the views for which Sir George Parkin had stood.

6 John Drinkwater (1882–1937), *A Man's House* (1934)

7 George Bernard Shaw (1856–1950), British dramatist, music critic, and socialist theorist

8 McDougall was blind.

9 Her chauffeur

10 '[Margaret Beith] is the grand-daughter of a distinguished Scotch minister, sister of the well-known writer and dramatist Ian Hay Beith, and was Aunt Marian's adopted god-child ... Soon after Noverings became Aunt Marian's home, Margaret was invited there for a long visit and proved such a welcome congenial companion that she was urged to stay on ... and is now its inheritor' ('Aunt Marian of England,' typescript, Grant-Parkin Papers). The Grant children often referred to distant relatives and close family friends as 'aunt' or 'uncle.'

1935

William Grant died 3 February 1935, when Grant was sixteen. Because the family was living in the principal's residence, they had to find new accommodation. George Grant became a boarder for his final year at Upper Canada College, while Maude Grant went to England to stay with friends and relatives. A federal general election was held on 15 October 1935. The Liberal party, led by Mackenzie King, returned to power, and Vincent Massey was rewarded for his services by his appointment as high commissioner to the United Kingdom.

10/ To Maude Grant   Upper Canada College

Dear Mother,
You may probably already have heard of the election at the College. And that I am head of the Liberal Committee. As last week the fortunes of

the Liberals in Canada were going down, now I think they are going up gradually, although a lot of people think that no party will have a majority. That would be disastrous. Mr King, 8 Provincial Premiers, Uncle Vincent,[1] Mrs Thorburn[2] and Mrs Joe Fulford[3] are speaking at the Maple Leaf Gardens to-morrow night. I asked Mr Parlee[4] if I could go. He refused. Which I think was a very foolish thing to do. He infuriated me beyond measure when he wouldn't let me go. Even when the Masseys and Arthur Slaght had asked me. One result of being a boarder? Also Mr A. Slaght KC[5] asked me if I could go up to Parry Sound for the election. Of course I can't go.

Aunt Margie[6] told me to-day that she was going to vote Liberal because she thought King was a sound man. And more likely to give parliamentary government. Don't pass that on. Mr A Slaght KC said that Stevens[7] was a crook and gave a very good instance. Stevens said he would bring libel action. Slaght said that Mr Stevens couldn't buy some legal trick and came out of it much the best.

The Conservatives will get in at School, because most of the boys' fathers are small industrialists. Dr Peskey CCF[8] is the only one who has spoken. Fewer CCF people left in school after him. Hand, Reconstruction, to-morrow night. Lawson next day. Elmore Philpot, Liberal, Thursday. I am ashamed that you have not stayed in Canada to cast a vote for freedom and good government.

Mr MacD.[9] is a great success. Couldn't be nicer. Could you tell me where all the records are? I can't find them.

I went down and had tea with E.R. Peacock[10] to-day at the Macdonnells'. He was the nicest I have ever seen him. Absolutely at the top of his form.

I have just been reading some more about the Liberal Rally. It is going to be a wonderful affair. Lionel Conacher[11] the hockey player is going to be there speaking for the Liberals. Damn Mr Parlee for not letting me go. Curse him. I am simply furious. Why shouldn't I go? It wouldn't do him any good and me any harm. He is a Conservative he told me. Why can't I go? Bah! Bah! Bah! Hart asked me specially. How are Mrs Buck and Aunt Margaret [Beith]? Give them my love.

Heaps of love,
George

1 Vincent Massey

2 Not identified

3 Josephine Fulford, wife of G.T. Fulford, Liberal MPP, 1934–7

4 M.K. Parlee (1888–1966), mathematics teacher and senior housemaster of

Seaton's House, 1930–6, where Grant boarded during his last year at UCC
5 A.S. Slaght (1877–1964), Liberal member for Parry Sound, 1935–45
6 Marjorie (Parkin) Macdonnell (1891–1975), Maude's sister
7 H.H. Stevens (1878–1973), former Conservative cabinet minister, who led the
   Reconstruction party in the 1935 election
8 Cooperative Commonwealth Federation
9 T.W.L. MacDermot (1896–1966), a Rhodes scholar and history professor from
   McGill, who succeeded William Grant as principal of Upper Canada College
10 Sir Edward Robert Peacock (1871–1962), Grant's godfather, had taught at
    Upper Canada with William and was best man at his wedding. Peacock subse-
    quently went on to a distinguished business career as a director of the Bank of
    England, Baring Brothers & Co. (a bank), and the Canadian Pacific Railway.
11 Lionel Conacher (1902–54) played professional hockey from 1925 to 1937.
    He also excelled at boxing, lacrosse, football, and track and field. He was
    elected to both provincial and federal office as a Liberal.

1936

Grant spent the summer of 1936 in Quebec, the first student to take part in Upper Canada College's Visites Interprovinciales. He spent the first part of the summer with the family of Victor Morin,[1] and then as a paying guest with a Roman Catholic priest at St-Basile-le-Grand.

11/ To Maude Grant   7 July

Dear Mother,
Today has been incredibly hot and I have lain in the sun and got nicely brown. Oh this is a marvellous place, but I wish there were a place to bathe.
   Please do not take the idea of paints seriously and, if there aren't any in the house, don't buy any.
   What is Uncle Burgon's[2] address?
   Everybody comes and goes here for a day or for a week or for a fortnight. There are very few long stayers.
   Tell Charity that I have at last discovered what she dislikes in me and will try to correct it.
   There is a young boy of twelve here who always thinks he is right. He is simply unbearable. I must be the same. But I hope not quite as bad, because this boy (poor thing) is tortured by 4 young aunts who simply

murder him as they think that he is spoiled. He loathes the King and
Queen, which infuriates me and everybody. He says for instance: 'Of
course there is no play in the world that compares with *L'Aiglon*.'[3] He has
just read it. He has made me read it (which is a good thing). But he has
never read Corneille, Racine or Molière, let alone any foreign plays.
Immediately when he makes such a statement all his aunts, uncles and I
come down on his head.

The other day we were playing chess. He suddenly leant across the
table and asked me if I believed in transubstantiation. I was dumbfounded. Thought quickly and said 'No.' He said 'Why' (all in French)? I
was now rude. 'Because I don't believe in mysteries.' He started to shout.
I have no idea what he said.

All the others are very nice about my non-RCism, ask me if I wish to
have meat on Friday and are generally magnificent. That is the only situation that has been difficult. All other times it has been taken for granted
that I am Protestant and they are R.C.

I do not like their attitude that Mussolini is right because the Pope has
sanctioned the war.[4] Naturally I haven't said anything, but it is a complete
ban to my ever becoming R.C.

Thank you for your letter and for Mrs Buck's.

Heaps of love,
George

Love to Charity et tout le monde (Macdonnells).

This letter is enclosed with another as it is cheaper and the 'bureau de
poste'[5] is a mile and a half away – it is a very hot and dusty walk.

1 Victor Morin (1865–1960), Quebec lawyer, businessman, and author. He married Fannie Coté. His children were Lucien, Marc, Gisèle, Claire, Marie, Renée,
  Roland, Guy, and Roger.
2 J.B. Bickersteth (1888–1979), warden of Hart House, 1921–47, and a close family friend of the Grants
3 Edmond Rostand (1868–1918), *L'Aiglon, Drame en six actes, en vers* (1900)
4 The Italian invasion of Ethiopia
5 Post office

12/ To Maude Grant   St Urbain Street, Montreal
                                                          24 July

Dear Mother,

I have been dancing a lot in the evenings and having a magnificent time.
Yesterday I saw *Crime et Châtiment.*[1] It is a masterpiece. Even the Morins
have seen it six times. Pierre Blanchar, who plays the role of Raskolnikov
(student), makes Lorre[2] look like a second-rate ham. It is a magnificent
performance. Harry Baur as the inspector is entirely different from the
American one and, if anything, is greater than Blanchar. When those two
are on the screen together, it becomes incredibly magnificent. But I think
that the greatest part is the music with the film.[3] The whole thing makes
the American version look crude and amateurish. (With it there was a
musical comedy.) Everyone is so nice here. Today I went up to see Aunt
Louise and Elizabeth. A. Louise has had an operation. Elizabeth was all
excited about a picnic that she was going on and I didn't see very much
of her.

Oh dear, [the] heat must have been terrible. I do hope you get out in
the country sometimes. Tomorrow, I return to the country for good, to
go on with my sketching and tennis.

There are quite a lot of good records here and at the mountain. Today
I found some Chevaliers.[4] And at St Bruno there is a magnificent record
of Jascha Heifetz[5] playing 'Ave Maria' and a magnificent double record of
'Rhapsody in Blue.'[6]

I have just heard Dr. Townsend[7] on the radio. Impossible.

I think Quebec will stay Liberal under Godbout.[8] All the farmers like
him and I suppose that is the deciding factor. He seems to have no connection with Ta[schereau][9] at all. T. is the forgotten man of Quebec. No
one speaks of him. And if I did no one would think it polite. Duplessis[10] is
quite awful, I think. I heard him on the radio. He is just cashing in on the
Taschereau scandal.[11] He has no great qualification to be premier of a
province.

I hope you are not having too difficult a time with Mrs Peacock. Is
E.R.P[eacock]. coming to Canada?

I hope you aren't completely burned to pieces by the forest fires, which
all the papers say are simply terrible.

Love to everybody.

                                                          Heaps of love,
                                                          George

I discovered a book of El Greco[12] here. Someday I will go to Spain and Madrid and Toledo. Then I will walk into the Prado and see all those pictures. Until then I must be content with reproductions. But after all, Pegi Nicol[13] has never been to Europe; so I should be able to wait, as I am not an artist. Do go and see *Crime et Châtiment* if you get a chance.

1 *Crime et Châtiment* (1935), directed by Pierre Chenal and starring Pierre Blanchar and Harry Baur

2 German-American actor Peter Lorre starred in Joseph von Sternberg's *Crime and Punishment* (1935).

3 The music was by Arthur Honegger.

4 Maurice Chevalier (1888–1972), French comedian, singer, actor

5 Jascha Heifetz (1901–87), Russian-trained violin virtuoso who lived in the United States. He ceased to perform in public about 1970.

6 George Gershwin, *Rhapsody in Blue*, Op. 2

7 Dr Francis E. Townsend (1867–1966) entered politics at the age of sixty-six and was co-founder of the Union party in the U.S.A. He ran for president in 1936. Townsend was a leader of the movement for old-age pensions.

8 Joseph-Adelard Godbout (1892–1956) was premier of Quebec in 1936, and later from 1939 until 1944. Both he personally and his government were defeated by Maurice Duplessis's Union Nationale in 1936.

9 Louis-Alexandre Taschereau (1867–1952) was Liberal premier of Quebec from 1920 to 1936.

10 Maurice LeNoblet Duplessis (1890–1959) was Union Nationale premier of Quebec during 1936–9 and 1944–59.

11 Taschereau was driven from office by scandals involving his brother and certain government officials.

12 Dominico Theotocopuli, called El Greco, Spanish painter (1541?–1614)

13 Pegi (Nicol) MacLeod (1904–49) was a Canadian painter. She painted in Toronto during 1934–7 and designed stage settings for Hart House Theatre.

13/ To Maude Grant

Dear Mother,

I left the Morins' yesterday. I was never so sad to leave anywhere. Two of the girls told me I was going into the Catholic camp. (They are very bitter, I have discovered, against the Catholic domination. By 'they' I mean the psychologist and biologist and secretary.) They are right. I am right in the centre of Catholic rigidity. No more sunbaths. Up at 7:30 o'clock, no tennis, no water, none of the free and easy and delicious Morin life. I suppose that the following month will be a spiritual one.

I have never had such fun as I had on the last few days at the Morins. It was positive heaven. We went to two parties. I slept, painted and went on wonderful long walks. I had long talks with two of the girls who are definitely anti-Catholic, except as a religion to go to Church. One said, 'If we only read that which we were allowed, we wouldn't read very much.' Practically all psychology is banned.

I suppose I will get to like it here. But it seems very dull and formal after the Morins'. Conversation a good deal more limited than at St Bruno. Although this is impossible, I am dying to ask M. le Curé for Zola.[1] I would love to see his face. He has given me *Thomas More*[2] which talks about, in French, 'the devious and underhand ways in which the Lutheran heresy tried to undermine England.' He does not realise that it is best to start reasonably with a would-be convert, as Thomas More is liable to put my back up.

This letter is rather nasty. But he seems so flat after Morin. His intellect I don't think compares with Morin. I think I am mainly angry because I have to wear a coat and tie. I will try and get out into the country. But St Alexis is bigger than one would think. There is no water, no mountains for four miles. Give my love to everybody at home.

Someday you will come with me to see the Morins and I am certain that you will like everyone of them in the same way as I do. Madame Morin is magnificent. This July has been one of the most perfect months of my life.

Heaps of love,

George

1 Émile Zola (1840–1902), French novelist, famous for his involvement in defence of Dreyfus
2 Possibly Émile Dermenghem, *Thomas Morus et les utopistes de la renaissance* (2d ed. 1927)

14/ To Maude Grant

Dear Mother,

Since Father's history arrived M. le Curé and I have been having a grand time looking for mistakes in G.M. Wrong's history[1] and the history of Father's.[2] We have found many more in GMW's. One very big and important one which I would like to show Mr Wrong. We verify the mistakes in 3 or 4 other books and with documents. I have grand fun.

Yesterday the Morins called for me and we went for a glorious ride in the Laurentians [St Donat]. Marie Morin has given me *Marie Chapdelaine* in French, a most beautiful edition. M. le Curé has given me *Montcalm,*[3] *Washington et Jumonville,*[4] *Thomas More. Washington and Jumonville* proves conclusively that Washington was a murderer and that he assassinated Jumonville. It is proved without a doubt with documentation. M. le Curé likes Father's book. Especially struck with 'the saddest scene in Canadian history' as a description of the expulsion of the Acadians.

Tomorrow we go on a three day expedition 1 day to St Michel des Saints (the farthest civilized place in the Laurentides) 2 days at a camp where M. le Curé has installed his sister & two little nieces.

This is just a note to let you know that I am still alive and think of you.

I got a grand letter from Mrs Buck. Another terribly nice from J.H. Biggar.

> Heaps of love,
> George Grant

If you see J.H. Biggar, tell him that M. le Curé is certainly not an anti-climax. (He said he hoped he wasn't.)

I wrote to him from an early stage of being here after the Morins. Did you get my biology book?[5]

1 G.M. Wrong, *Ontario Public School History of Canada* (1921)
2 William Grant, *Ontario High School History of Canada* (1914)
3 Georges Robitaille, *Montcalm et ses historiens: Étude critique* (1936)
4 Georges Robitaille, *Washington et Jumonville: Étude critique* (1933)
5 To: La Société royale du Canada   [autumn 1938]
   I am in receipt of your letter of the 22 instant informing me that Mr George Grant is a candidate for a Rhodes Scholarship this year and asking me to send you a frank and confidential statement of his qualifications as itemized in your circular letter; I take pleasure in answering as follows:
   (1) I have had frequent occasions of discussing literary and scholastic questions with George Grant, and I have always found him a bright, intelligent young man, well versed in these questions, and eager to learn. He shows quick comprehension of such questions and discusses them intelligently.
   (2) As to qualities of manhood, truth, courage, devotion to duty, sympathy for and protection of the weak, kindliness, unselfishness and fellowship, I may say that he has lived with my family during the summer vacation two years ago, and

we have all been highly pleased with his high qualities. In fact, my wife and children have all kept the best remembrance of his sojourn with us and of his amiable qualities, and we are always pleased to meet him. During his stay with us, he has acquired a good practise of the French language and has observed the characteristics of French people around us.

(3) Exhibition during school days of moral force of character and of instincts to lead and to take an interest in his schoolmates. I know that George intends to devote his career to political diplomacy, and he knows what qualities are required in order to succeed in this difficult branch of politics; my impression is that he will succeed. As an example of his force of character, I am aware that he engaged his services during the last vacation on a transatlantic cargo [boat] in order to earn his passage to Europe, which he wanted to visit in order to increase his circle of knowledge, and he worked for his expenses. I saw him on his return, and I was highly pleased with his appreciation of what he had observed and criticized during his voyage in the fields of economics, art and literature.

(4) I have no knowledge of his outdoor sports.

I may add that George Grant is an orphan. He had the misfortune of losing his distinguished father who was a member of the Royal Society a few years ago, and his mother is now the warden of the Royal Victoria College in Montreal. He is a nephew of Sir [*sic*] Vincent Massey.

Hoping that these informations will be satisfactory, I beg to remain

Yours very truly,
Victor Morin

In September 1936 Grant followed his father and grandfather to Queen's University in Kingston, Ontario. Still a relatively small university, it had a core of excellent faculty. However, the choice of Queen's was probably a mistake, because Grant felt smothered by all the family connections both at the university and in Kingston.

1936

15/ To Maude Grant 30 Sydenham St, Kingston
10 Dec. [1936]

Dear Mother,

Please do not think that in this awful time I have been supporting Edward VIII.[1] Please realise that, as soon as I saw how serious it was, I wasn't 'mawkishly sentimental.' It was pretty awful what happened today. Anne[2] broke down and cried poor dear. It has been pretty terrible, but I think the best thing is now to support George VI and forget completely Edward VIII who I blame 100%. Baldwin's speech in the Commons was rather fine and, unlike most, I think he acted in the best possible way. After all the people should know what their paid officials are doing. I only hope that they do not give Edward some fabulous sum, as he is working no longer. I think York[3] & *his wife* will be perfect and I feel (although others don't seem to) that he can live down this stain. (Did you notice that Baldwin mentioned Canada as the Dominion which had been particularly shocked.[4] As I said, I don't like Baldwin for Ethiopia,[5] but I think he was A1 here.)

Could you get 2 tickets (Anne & I) for *Ma Claire* on the evening of the 23rd please.

I have got an invitation for the 22nd. As I finish on the morning of the 22nd, I can make it, but, as you know, it would mean buying waistcoats and ties here. May I? Could you write to tell me, as I have to answer the invitation? The boys here dress very properly and they said they would advise me on the right thing.

Mrs Buck's present was A1. It is sent. What is Joan's address?[6] Leo and Aunt Grace are done. Alison, simply money I think. Aunt Lois[7] here, flowers. Aunt Lois is a wonderful person. I can not see her just now as she has bronchitis.

For my own Christmas you asked me. Have we parts of Spenser (*Fairy Queen*) at home? Otherwise anything at all.

Heaps of love,
George

P.S. Did you notice there *The Week* suggested that Baldwin only wanted to get rid of the King on any pretence. Baldwin is glad.

1 Edward VIII abdicated the throne to marry 'the woman he loved.' The Abdication Act was passed 11 December 1936.
2 Anne Macdonell, Grant's cousin
3 The Duke of York became George VI when he ascended to the throne.
4 'I told his majesty that I had two great anxieties – one the effect of a continuance of the kind of criticism that at the time was proceeding in the American Press, the effect it would have in the Dominions and particularly in Canada, where it was widespread, the effect it would have on this country' (Stanley Baldwin, 'Speech Delivered in the House of Commons, 10 December 1936').
5 Mussolini's fascist government invaded Ethiopia.
6 Joan Arnoldi (1879–1969) was a close family friend. She became national president of the Imperial Order of the Daughters of the Empire in 1920.
7 Miss Lois Saunders, librarian at Queen's, and godmother to one of Grant's sisters

1937

Grant spent part of the summer as a paid companion to Professor D.J. McDougall, reading to him and taking him on row-boat rides.

16/ To Maude Grant   Pine Grove c/o MacD

Dear Mother,

Thank you very much for both of your letters which were both very welcome and very nice.

Life continues here with *Sir T. More* by Algernon Cecil,[1] which is so vitally Catholic that it loses some of its power by a continuous sense of attempted justification not of More (which is not really necessary), but of the dissolute and wholly immoral clergy; and especially on the point of the murder of Hume(?). The book takes every chance to get in a stab at modern institutions which do not fit in to the autocratic RC doctrine. More, who was undoubtedly a great and moral man in an age of petty and immoral men, is given a portrait which is shrouded by a continual attempt at lauding dissolute Catholicism. And certainly the light of More would help Catholicism better than the murky darkness of Wolsey or the Italian popes. This sounds like a sermon, but, really, this is very important as I am being inculcated by such an amount of propaganda.

C. Cochrane[2] and Dan MacDougall annoyed me the other day by criticizing Burgon for nervousness. I wanted to [tell] MacD that, if he was as good as Burgon with children, this house would not be in a state of spankings and tears. Mr MacD scorns so much: Cody,[3] Carlyle,[4] all liberal historians (his examples are Macaulay,[5] Trevelyan[6] and Fisher[7]), Wagner (I partly understand), Tchaikovsky, all motor cars – in fact everything except the intellectual and medieval quiet and cold worlds that I want to tell him that there is something of change in the world. He prefers Aristotle to Plato (of which I know little except that, to me, one has a greater belief in advancement). He believes in the local feudal village, and even uses logic on his children and believes that mankind marches in concentric circles rather than straight lines. But, through all this, I like him, because he is so coldly logical and very fair. He would never allow himself to make a grandiose statement and weighs evidence as fairly as a biased opinion can under RC circumstances.

The two Mrs MacDs are dears, both patient and understanding.

I had a game of golf with Uncle James because Mr MacD had indigestion. [Hunt M] says something about using her house at the end of August while we move. *I cannot send the desk to the Fitzes*[8] *in Kingston, because my rooms are full in the summer* and that would mean that it would be necessary to move it out and in. But I will write to her about it. There are plenty of things in my room and cupboard which I would rather you didn't touch, as I will have time and *will* know what I want to do with them.

There is one of Mr MacD's young nieces down here of about 14 or 13 years old who has reached the giggling stage, which infuriates Mr MacD, but, all the same, I imagine everyone has to pass through the giggling stage and she is an angel with the children.

I hope that I am passing through the supremely selfish stage which has been enveloping me and that this job, which entails doing exactly as I am told very cheerfully will do me good.

It is proof that war should be avoided at any cost by the loss of Mr MacD.'s sight, which I know he misses so terribly. I do not understand how you can say that deafness is worse than blindness. Mr Holland seems to me to suffer infinitely less than Mr MacD, from my account.

My love to the Fords[9] and thank you again for Tadoussac and remember that I love letters of whatever you are doing, whatever you are thinking or reading, or of whatever you are planning.

This is a very sententious letter, but it contains

Heaps of love,
George

1 Algernon Cecil (1879–1953), *A Portrait of Thomas More, Scholar, Statesman, Saint* (1937)
2 C.N. Cochrane (1898–1945), later professor of classics, University College, University of Toronto. Grant very much admired his *Christianity and Classical Culture* (1940).
3 H.A. Cody (1872–1948), Canadian historian
4 Thomas Carlyle (1795–1881), British historian and social critic
5 T.B. Macaulay (1800–59), British historian
6 G.O. Trevelyan (1838–1928), British historian
7 H.A.L. Fisher (1865–1940), British historian
8 The Misses Fitzgibbons with whom Grant lodged in Kingston
9 Cousins

1938

In September, Grant returned to Kingston to continue his studies.

17/ To Maude Grant   30 Sydenham St, Kingston

Dear Mother,
I am listening to a Town Hall of the Air.[1] On one side Dorothy

Thompson[2] (the superb woman, wife of Sinclair Lewis)[3] speaking in most superb and moving language, language that is extremely beautiful. Sticking to her colossal ideas on foreign affairs, saying that U.S.A. must seek allies on her own terms to keep certain regulations for international law. She says that peace has always been enforced and that the democracies are just scared and that they are being bluffed.

She was replied [to] by a man who made the most incredible speech for isolation. Senator Nye.[4] The questions are now in progress and is Dorothy Thompson winning. All along the line she is winning and Nye is evading the questions.

She is a superb orator and realises that international fascism is going to stick together.

Freud seems such a stupid incident.[5] Why can't they let great men alone? They said he had hurt German nationalism by his psychoanalysis.

And then Franco[6] keeps on advancing with the Catholic Church right behind him.

My life was changed by the Senate of Queen's University when the number of comprehensives for next year was reduced from 5 to 2. I don't know what it will mean, but I think it will probably hurt rather than help me, as I would like to write comprehensives. But that is far away. By the amount of work I have done I should do better this year than last, but terrible doubts assail me. *I must do better.*

God, that wonderful England is represented by Chamberlain[7] I sing a hymn of praise that Eddie[8] is here. Dorothy Thompson was wonderful tonight. [He is] getting over RMC[9] very fast. Only an intelligent person could.

Dorothy Thompson said the newest weapon in war for gain is revolution.

Love,
George

Wonderful weather. I loved JAG's [Alison's] remarks.

1 Begun on 30 May 1935 from New York, and moderated by George V. Denny, Jr, the radio program sought to place two basic positions in opposition to one another.

2 Dorothy Thompson (1893–1961) was expelled from Nazi Germany in 1934 because of her anti-Nazi statements, and began a thrice-weekly column for the *New York Herald Tribune* in 1936.

3 Sinclair Lewis (1885–1951), American satirical novelist, author of *Babbitt* (1922)

and *Elmer Gantry* (1927). He was the first American to win the Nobel prize for literature, in 1930.
4 Senator G.P. Nye (1892–1971), senator from North Dakota (1925–44). Nye became nationally prominent in the mid-1930s by leading a senate probe into the size and influence of the arms industry, which he blamed for entangling the United States in the First World War. He was a leading isolationist.
5 Sigmund Freud (1856–1939), the founder of psychoanalysis, a Jew, fled Austria after the Nazi takeover in 1938.
6 Francisco Franco (1892–1975), leader of the fascist forces in the Spanish civil war
7 Neville Chamberlain (1869–1940), British prime minister, 1937–40
8 E.E. Campbell, a close friend from UCC who had gone to the Royal Military College in Kingston.
9 Royal Military College

18/ To Maude Grant

30 Sydenham St., Kingston
13 March

Dear Mother,
I got your letter this morning and in truth Europe is going up in smoke. Fascism is on the march in truth and all these people around here who were so sure of everything going so perfectly are now crying, 'Oh dear, oh dear, what are we going to do?' Some of the army people around here have simply medieval ideas on international affairs. Their argument is that we should have squashed Germany in 1919, so that she could do nothing. They have those quaintly amusing ideas that something they don't like can be stamped out, that a country can be completely [held] in abeyance. Of course, they went to RMC and what can you expect where the strongest person physically bullies and teases the weaker ones physically, so that they can assert their own stupid egos? They are very nice, but they are narrow.

Thank goodness Eddie does not believe the myth of keeping Germany in submission. But he seems to believe along with the rest that all foreigners are dagos and emotionally unstable [and] that the English are perfect. Oh, how I wish Eddie *hadn't* gone to RMC.

I just sit and worship Dr Trotter[1] in class because he is so magnificent. He doesn't know I worship him because, when he looks my way, I try to take the cow-like adoration off my face and substitute intelligence if possible.

Please don't write to him about seeing him because that would seem so businesslike and as if you wanted to discuss – which I wouldn't want you to do. How do you know that he wanted to see you? I am interested to know, not that I doubt but that he would be very interested to meet you. We can arrange it when you get here.

I am looking forward immensely to seeing you here. At the moment my life centres around 19–27 April. What momentous days they seem to be. Would you bring some Toddy down with you? I would have done better on my exams last year if I had been able to sleep and I think I will make myself Toddy before the exams, so that I will be able to attempt to sleep anyway.

Our literary supplement came out on Friday – some good poetry – some lousy short stories and I had an essay in it on propaganda.[2] I have tried to work quite hard and on Friday at 2 a.m. I finished my last essay.

The next is going to seem terribly silly and studentish to you. But I am doing it because anything must start somewhere. A group of us got together by accident and decided it was stupid just to get together and are trying to make ourselves vocal about what is happening. Stupid, but I think necessary in that now I see no real reason for any of us to have any hope at all in a world that is drifting from crisis to crisis without anything being done. We are a drop in an enormous ocean, but you have to start somewhere. I have to go now to the meeting, which I am trying to get people out of their complete placidity because they should be the people who count in the next Canada as citizens.

Heaps of love,

In great haste
George

1 R.A. Trotter (1888–1951), professor of history at Queen's from 1924. He retired in 1950.
2 George Grant, 'Art and Propaganda,' Queen's University *Journal,* Literary Supplement, March 1938, pp. 6–7

Maude Grant arranged for Grant to spend the summer of 1938 in England. As a travelling companion she decided on Alan Watson, whom Grant had known at Upper Canada College.

19/ To Maude Grant   30 Sydenham St, Kingston

Dear Mother,
Alan[1] went through on the train yesterday; I am getting sceptical now. For

he said, 'This will be my first trip over and it's England I want to see.'
'How about a week or ten days in France?' I was polite, but it was a far different impression that I got from your original letter. My dear, I don't
want to go traipsing around England on a bicycle and then spend 7 to 10
days in France. I thought of France as a country of dreams – as the mecca
of my voyage, as the raison d'être of my journey. When I was on the continent for the first time we might get even to Italy. We might get to Paris for
the whole of the 7 days or the 10 days of the trip. But to spend about 2
days in the Paris of *Danton, Robespierre*, [Madena], Rolland,[2] *Voltaire*, Mirabeau,[3]Richelieu,[4] Louis Quatorze, Mazarin,[5] Marie Antoinette, Marat,[6]
Zola,[7] César Franck,[8] Jean Jaurès[9] would be for me a heart break. Everybody tells me France is going to be a disappointment. France the country
of civilization, of hope for the world, France the country that England has
just betrayed and France has to follow England away from all the idealism. France that is all that is fine and noble; it may be dirty, but France is
individualism. I can't even think of going to England at all if that is the situation. I would rather hitch-hike around North America.

From your first letter I had no idea this was the idea of Alan and
wouldn't have written such a letter back. I would much rather go alone
and see Europe, because although everybody in the modern world is
afraid of being alone, I really like it in its independence.

Alan said he didn't know anyone in England. That would be OK as he
would be a nice person to show around. But I couldn't tell him and his
father last night that I love England and I admit I have seen very little of
it, but I want to go somewhere else. I am not going this year to London as
a sight-seer. I am going to England to see the people who queerly enough
want to see me. It is in France that I want to sight-see.

Please tell me what I should do. Because it wasn't knowing the situation
that I wrote you a letter. I would never have minded to go alone although
everybody seems to think that being alone is such a terrible fate. I can't
see that myself, as I like being alone. Everybody says, 'Oh, you must get a
companion.' Why? I would have loved to have Alan as a companion, but
oh if it is to be 'a week or ten days in France' I did not understand that.

Eddie has been in the hospital with flu. (You have to go to free hospital
here. Do not tell anybody who might get it back to his mother.) I and two
others in the house have been fighting colds as hard as possible. I think
today that I have lost the battle and that I am going down to defeat.

Gladstone & Disraeli were titans, absolute titans. I started with a great
bias for Gladstone, but now I have absolutely no idea whom I prefer. I
read four of Disraeli'snovels[10] and one of his political writings; the great

life (abridged slightly) by Monypenny & Buckle.[11] I think for a while Disraeli was the great Victorian statesman and Gladstone the highly limited and bigoted politician. Then I read something about Gladstone and I say he was the colossus, he was the great statesman who dominated England with supreme greatness; then I think Disraeli was a crafty opportunist politician. *What giants* they were. Colossuses. I practically burst into tears when I read the story of Bismarck at the Congress of Berlin in 1878 and he turned to someone and said, '*Der alte Jude, der ist der Mann.*'[12] A superb story.

But then the polemic of Gladstone on ideals and Armenian massacres. Ideals rather than necessity and selfishness in foreign policy. Ireland and his conscience. Power and the Midlothian campaign.

Then Disraeli laughs (oh so humanly) at the utilitarians who tried to form society around a formula, a principle. Philanthropic Disraeli.

No one would feel the same disgust if Disraeli had done what [Neville] Chamberlain had done. Because you could *hate* Disraeli as a great man, but God, that second-rate commercial chancellor of the exchequer, the son of his father.[13] Scaring the house through second-rate melodramatics, giving way to a blackmailer and a bunch of thugs.[14] Admitting that idealism has to be given up in a crisis, but it is in a crisis that idealism is most vital. With his policy there will probably be war, and why not fight for an ideal anyway rather than a commercial share? We have glorified middle age at the expense of viable youth and strong old age. We have gone back to power politics of the 19th century. Gone back to the thing that caused the last war. We have made France give up her ideals and then to think Chamberlain is saying that the volunteers must leave Spain. Well, I wonder if he succeeds. I hope he does for Spain's sake, even if I loathe that mealy-mouthed, white-blooded party leader. (This is all the hate I would love to pour out on someone else.)

And now heaps and heaps of love and I am sure you were a great success at the Carnegie affair.

My love,
George

Please write.
Oh, Mrs Gray told me that Aunt Lois is very ill and could you write her a note, as she doesn't think she will recover?

1 A.G. Watson (1919–), a student at McGill while Grant was at Queen's; later a partner with Peat, Marwick, Mitchell & Co.

2 Romain Rolland (1866–1944), French musicologist and author of lives of
  Michelangelo (1906) and Gandhi (1924)

3 Honoré Gabriel Riquetti, comte de Mirabeau (1749–91),
  French revolutionary politician. Elected president of the assembly in January
  1791, he died of natural causes.

4 Armand Jean Duplessis, Cardinal Richelieu (1585–1642), one of the leading
  French statesmen of the seventeenth century

5 Jules Mazarin (1602–61), born Giulio Mazarini, Catholic cardinal and statesman, advisor to Louis XIII and Louis XIV

6 Jean Paul Marat (1743–93), French journalist and revolutionary, murdered in
  his bath by Charlotte Corday

7 Émile Zola (1840–1902), French novelist, famous for his involvement in
  defence of Dreyfus

8 César Franck (1822–90), Belgian-born French composer

9 Jean Jaurès (1859–1914), French socialist politician and co-founder of
  L'Humanité. He was assassinated in July 1914.

10 Benjamin Disraeli (1804–81), 1st Earl of Beaconsfield, author of *Conningsby,*
  Contraini Fleming, Lothair, and *Sybil, or the Two Nations.*

11 W.F. Monypenny (1866–1912) and G.E. Buckle, *The Life of Benjamin Disraeli,*
  Earl of Beaconsfield (1910–20)

12 'What a man the old Jew is.'

13 Joseph Chamberlain (1836–1914), British Radical and Liberal Unionist statesman who advocated tariff reform giving preference to colonial products

14 Hitler and the Nazis

*In the summer of 1938, Grant worked his way over to England on a cattle boat to
visit Mrs Buck and travel with his friend Alan Watson. It was not a meeting of
minds, and Grant eventually abandoned his friend to travel to France and Italy
with his cousin Hart and his sister Alison.*

20/ To Maude Grant   Hôtel Roma, Milano

Dear Mother,
I have been slow writing, but there has been so much to do and it has all
been perfect. I have never seen such wonderful things and, above all, *you
must not miss Chartres.* Paris, however wonderful, *must* be given up for a bit
to see Chartres, as it is the most wonderful man-made thing I have ever
seen, even after Geneva (marvellous), Switzerland & the mountains, the
lakes and Milan. I think I loved Chartres best. Even rushing through
France I realised that it was far in a way not a foreign country but *home.*

Italy & Switzerland were foreign, but every expectation of France has been achieved even in two days and I will see more.

Milan is a lovely place and this morning we set out sightseeing the 'Last Supper' etc. Then on to Venice via Verona and Brescia. It is all magnificent. The life the colour the heat.

Now, I must go.

Heaps of love,
George

Charity – if you find in the flat the Queen's (Course List or something of that name) Calendar for 1938–39 please keep it, as I am lost without it.

21/ To Maude Grant

Venice
Monday evening

Dear Mother,
My letters so far have been non-existent, really, and I am sorry, but time goes so quickly. Now, I have time.

Venice is an amazing place and I have been fascinated. Above all, I have got the impression that Venice is very much a temporal city. Commerce as its all engrossing element has left it no mysticism. It is a secular place and in many ways completely Babylonic. It is sensual and pleasure-seeking and yet remains a relic of the past. The queer mixture of the old Byzantine Venice, mixed with the Renaissance that came late, gives a queer impression.

Unfortunately, my digestion went back on me this afternoon, but I am recovering fast.

Last night there was an enormous drawing of a lottery in the piazza and we sat there for hours in a square so packed with Italians that one could hardly move. It was wonderful. Grant Allen[1] I find immensely helpful, although the other two sneer saying I look too much like a tourist, but then I am. So that is the answer.

Verona was lovely on a Sunday morning in its cool way of laughing at the sun and yet not baking, so that the glare cut right at one's eyes. It was far less full of noise than other places.

This is the most superb trip and I have the feeling that it is so marvellous that there is no reason for me to have it – I do not deserve it at all. Sometimes I am overcome with the wonder of being here. I never dreamed I would, but here I am.

I was depressed about my prospects about ever doing anything at all worthwhile after everything, but now at least there will be this marvellous trip to look back on and think about.

My love to CLG and especially to you.

George

Today we saw the other statue from our front hall.

1 Grant Allen (1848–99), *Venice* (1898)

After returning to Canada as a paying passenger, Grant returned to Queen's for what was to be his final year. He still lived at 30 Sydenham Street, but, as his letters show, he became increasingly disaffected with his fellow lodgers. The high point of the year was winning a Rhodes Scholarship.

22/ To Rhodes Scholarship Selection Committee   9 November 1938

Dear Sirs,

Apart from my academic work my main interest has centred in the discussion of public affairs and more particularly Canada's international relations. This year I am President of the International Relations Club. Other activities have included the Dramatic Guild where I have taken parts in three act and one act plays; a private club for the discussion of artistic subjects and occasional journalistic work in the form of articles and reviews for the Queen's *Journal* and its literary supplement. On the whole most of my free time has been used in general reading, more particularly plays, biography and French literature, an interest that was stimulated by a summer with a French family in the Province of Quebec. My athletic activity has comprised golf and tennis in the summer months and skiing and badminton in the winter.

If I went to Oxford I would spend two years in taking a B.A. in jurisprudence and, if granted a third year, would use it in taking a B.C.L. with the ultimate object of practising law in Canada, preferably Ontario.

Yours truly,
George P. Grant

23/ To Maude Grant

Dear Mother,

Tomorrow I go to Toronto[1] and I don't think I have a chance.

Life has progressed steadily around here. One of my best friends got a grand job of lecturing in England & Canada for good Anglo-American relations. Wansbrough[2] of Lower Canada is the Montreal Secretary. The name of the chap is Don MacDonald[3] and we have been great friends. He is 26, very forceful and full of blazing energy. Completely self-made and about my best friend. He has given me more heart about this thing on Saturday than anyone else. Today at noon Anne Macdonnell told me I didn't have a chance of winning it; so I was depressed. I had told Anne because somehow Aunt Marjorie (who knew) mentioned it in her presence. Well, naturally Anne's remark depressed me (though, of course, I took it with the pound of Macdonnell gall I must always expect), but Don at least put heart in me; so there it is. Well anyway, Don is grand and tell anybody that you see, indirectly, if you hear about it, that he is terrifically good and you are glad, etc.

Today has been one of my least successful days. I am getting farther & farther away from the people of this house and they make me madder & madder (except for Eddie). Last night I just didn't have time to go to an Upper Canada dinner with exams & this trip and anyway it would have bored me stiff. None of the nice things about it. Only the worst side. An awful person, Douglas, was speaking. Recently, on the other hand, I have found many, many new and awfully nice friends who can be clever and intellectual and amusing and who are *students*. They came to university to *find out*, not only through the classroom, but every way. The others, who don't do that but fritter away their time in any way, are so stupid and are wasting society's money.

Yesterday, I went to lunch with a young friend of mine & his wife. They spend three dollars a week between them on food, live in one small room. But yet, that chap has enough guts to take an honours course in philosophy before theology, because he wants to be educated. He is the only theology person here who isn't an ass or sentimental or pretending that he isn't in theology. He is straight ahead with lots of strength yet great sensitivity. Yet there are people here who don't even work at all and who spend 20 times as much money. This couple, I must impress, are not proods (however you spell it) in their tiny little room; we cooked a good meal and had lots of fun. In all that lack (eating two meals a day) they are full of fun and work like niggers, yet never let it get the better of them. Next week I am going to take them to the B. American[4] with a couple of others. I must. I have got a motivation every time anyone says anything and I instinctively agree, to make things easier, and my awful desire to be liked comes up. I say 'To thine own self be true.'[5] It is marvellous. In three days I am improving

a little bit. That is going to be my motto, because it is the motto that I
need most.

On Saturday, afternoon and evening, pray for me, but it won't do any
good, but at least I will realise that there is one person who is behind me,
wishing for me.

Heaps of love.
George (Grant Esq.)

'To thine own self be true'
Isn't that good?

1 For the Rhodes Scholarship interview
2 V.C. Wansbrough, headmaster of Lower Canada College, Montreal
3 Donald C. MacDonald (1913–), later leader of the Ontario CCF-NDP, 1953–70
4 British American Hotel in Kingston
5 Shakespeare, *Hamlet* 1.3.80

*In spite of his worries (and his lack of sports), Grant was successful and won a
Rhodes Scholarship. He was not particularly popular at Queen's and his success
caused a lot of gossip, with many people suggesting that he had been successful only
because of his contacts and his grandfather's role in establishing the scholarships.*

24/ To Maude Grant

30 Sydenham St, Kingston
12 December

Dear Mother,
I got home last night and I am pleased as anything. I can't help it. I try
not to show it openly, but I can tell the truth to you. I am pleased for
father, I am pleased for Mrs Buck, I am pleased for you and I am pleased
for myself.

Anything that I ever have done completely & utterly depends on you.
Not only physically, but mentally. I depend on you.

The thing that I must remember is that this is only a beginning. This
was luck and I must justify this luck. A Rhodes S. is no claim to fame in
itself; it is what it produces. I hope it is something. This doesn't mean that
I am being stupidly & hypocritically modest, but this is not the end of
one's existence at all. It is a help towards the end.

When I realise that all the pleasure I am getting is completely related to
you then I want to thank you again for my whole existence.

Heaps of love,
George

Dr Graham[1] is pleased, I hope.

1 Gerald Graham (1903–90), history professor and family friend

1939

25/ To Maude Grant   30 Sydenham St, Kingston

Dear Mother,
This is written from my sick bed where I am convalescing from flu and where my only consolation is your note, which was so cruel. I waited and hoped to hear something from you. Eddie I cannot answer for. I know nothing of his conduct except that he was in bed with the flu practically all last week. He put so much store in the Constantine's[1] dance and then missed it. E.J. Hartnett[2] is in hospital with pneumonia. There is talk of completely suspending the university for a week as everybody is sick.

My unforgivable mistake was that I thought that when I went to Montreal I was going home rather than going on a visit to see someone to whom I was a guest. It was a stupid mistake to make under the circumstances. And I must remember that I have no home in Montreal. When I am merely a guest I must write a really nice thank you note. Here it is.

'Dear Mother,
It was sweet of you to put me up for a delightful weekend. You are the nicest of hostesses. My trip home to Kingston was quite uneventful, but since then I have developed influenza.

Yours,
George Grant'

I am glad that I realise what you want now, for after all, having some permanent anchor is a quite unnecessary appendage and of you I was asking something quite impossible. I am terribly sorry to have ever thought of such a thing.

Do you think it will be possible to come and visit you in May, or will that be a very bad time for you to have a guest? It would only be for a few days.

Perhaps, from a long existence of having some place to go, I developed some unnecessary sentimentality for the home, or was it the natural disruption that comes from your becoming modern and a career woman? Anyway, it was nice of you to state your case so lucidly because it removes from my mind all doubts as to what you want. Your definition of a son would be a trifle cruel, no doubt.

Alison and Margaret are safe because they are independent, but please do not think it won't be hard for Charity when she comes home. She, like myself, has the Victorian neurosis of desiring an anchor.

Heaps of love,

George

They accepted me for Balliol.[3]

1 Major-General C.F. Constantine was commandant at RMC during 1925–30 and commander of the Kingston Military District in 1939. He had three daughters, Doonie, Anne, and Evelyn.
2 Not identified
3 Balliol College, Oxford, the college that Grant's father attended

Grant became a pacifist while he was a student at Upper Canada College. In this he was influenced by his father and by Beverley Nichols's Cry Havoc *(1933), an extremely influential book.*

26/ To Maude Grant

Dear Mother,
Although I did not mean to write again, I have to because I am finding that my whole convictions about everything are changing with recurrent crises. My ideas seem green and distracted, but perhaps if I put them on paper they will be clearer.

War is becoming more supreme. Evil is completely predominant if you look anywhere. Force is being used on every side and everyone is hopelessly lost. Perhaps (although this is impossible for a government) force should be given up. The crisis comes, of course, not here in Canada; so perhaps we have no right to express the opinions I am going to.

If one is a Christian one must be forced back without doubt that one can never fight. Force cannot vie with force. Christ could have called on the angels to tear the temporal power of Jerusalem into ten billion fragments, but he didn't because he realised that, by passive resistance, he won in the long run, because he realised that even if he let tyranny, stupidity and foolishness be destroyed they would crop up again. But, if he made the permanent protest of non-resistance, in the end he would create a far greater victory in his example. Of course, the world has not accepted the example, but it still stands unflinching. Therefore, if one is a Christian, one cannot fight. Of course, if one isn't, there is no reason in the world why one shouldn't fight. This theory, of course, is very easy to propound when one lives in Canada rather than England. And sometimes I am simply furious that I live in Canada. I would far rather live in the centre of the crisis.

But, of course, when war comes one must not only say 'I won't fight, I won't fight.' One must propagate at the expense of one's life, so that other people won't fight. I don't think it is nearly enough to just sit still and be killed.

Of course, again if you say that Christ was not divine, then the whole argument is broken through. All I say is that, if Christ was right and inspired, then one is breaking divine law if one fights, *however* just one's cause is. Because Christ's cause was just, but still he wouldn't fight force by force.

Of course, this does not mean you cannot fight with word and deed reaction and oppression, that you cannot even risk your life under a dictatorship for the sake of asserting your cause.

Yours,
George

I hope you don't think this is adolescent craziness inspired by the ease and comfort of college life.

In the summer before he set off for England, Grant, his mother, and his sister Charity set off on a western trip. They drove to Edmonton, where they stayed with friends, then to Vancouver, San Francisco, and back via Chicago.

27/ To D.R. Michener[1]

Royal Victoria College
McGill University
Montreal
25 September 1939

Dear Mr Michener,
I am sorry to have been so long in making any decision, but there were several things that I had to find out before I could decide. I have decided to go to Oxford for various reasons, which are not worth describing here.

I also enclose the form that you sent me last week. I finally finished at Queen's;[2] so it was not until then that it was any use sending it to you.

I believe you said that you notified Dr Allen,[3] but if there is anything that is supposed to be done from this end, I would be glad if you would let me know.

Thank you very much again for all the trouble you have taken.

Yours sincerely,
George Grant

1 D.R. Michener (1900–91), former Rhodes scholar and Toronto lawyer who served as secretary to the Canadian branch of the Rhodes Trust; later governor-general of Canada, 1967–74
2 Grant had to complete the compulsory first-year philosophy course. It was the only formal philosophy course he ever took. He got a 'B.'
3 Sir C.K. Allen (1887–1966), legal scholar and warden of Rhodes House, Oxford

28/ To D.R. Michener   Royal Victoria College
McGill University
Montreal
27 September 1939

Dear Mr Michener,
Thank you for your letter, which arrived this morning. I will try and get in touch with some of the people you mention.[1]

The negotiations are all but completed to sail by S.S. Manhattan on 4 October. It seems very wrong to patronize a non-Canadian boat, but yet it seems much safer.

One point on which I am not certain is whether we are to be in Oxford by 15 October, or whether the pre-war arrangements still hold, and we must be there by the 12th. It would seem obvious that such things as a freshman dinner (the reason for the early arrival) would be called off in a time of so great emergency.

Thank you for all you have done in making things clear in a changing situation.

Yours sincerely,
George Grant

1 Michener had informed Grant that only two of the scholars-elect had decided to take up their scholarships – Grant and W.H Feindel (1918–) of New Brunswick.

War 1939–42

Grant's sister, Alison, was living in London at 231 Sussex Gardens. She shared a house with Elizabeth and Mary Greey, two Canadian sisters who were friends from Toronto. Vincent Massey was high commissioner, and Alison served as Alice Massey's ('Aunt Lal') unofficial private secretary. As a consequence, Grant had a place to stay whenever he was in London, and had good connections with people like Lester Pearson, who was first secretary at the high commission and a frequent visitor to the house.

1939

29/ **To Maude Grant**   Balliol

Dear Mum,
This afternoon I arrived at Balliol. You can't guess where I am staying. Chez the master at the Lindsays.[1] Everybody has had to double up as Chatham House[2] is in Balliol and the master has taken in several undergraduates. I am one of them. I share a room with a Scottish boy, Barbour.[3] Nice person. But instead of rooms, everybody has two in a room. As a matter of fact, it seems as if we had a good place. We have good plumbing &, anyway, he seems a very nice man. Mrs Lindsay seems nice.

Alison, as you can see from the first part of my letter,[4] is in fine form.

Lady Wylie[5] just rang me up and asked me out to lunch tomorrow, which was very kind of her. I was feeling so low; that is swell.

Piles of Love,
George

P.S. I think of New York & the smorgasbord & *The Little Foxes*[6] all the time.
P.P.S. This may seem a strange hope, but I pray that we will not meet, as it is better to be in Canada than here just now. I am sorry about this stationery, but there is just now a shortage of Balliol stationery, as the Common Room has just decided to change to a new & cheaper firm.
I wonder what is the news of your new book.
P.P.P.S. It is funny how we can write and talk of small things and individual things when this outburst is everywhere.

1 A.D. Lindsay, later 1st Baron Lindsay of Birker (1879–1952), master of Balliol College, Oxford, philosopher and Labour politician
2 Royal Institute of International Affairs, whose London headquarters were in Chatham House, St James Square
3 Rev R.S. Barbour (1921–), ordained to the Church of Scotland ministry in 1954
4 When Grant arrived in London, he stayed with his sister and wrote a letter to his mother. Presumably he sent them together.
5 Wife of Sir Francis Wylie (1865–1952), first warden of Rhodes House
6 Lillian Hellman's drama *Little Foxes* opened at the National Theatre 15 February 1939.

30/ To Maude Grant   Balliol College, Oxford
6 November

Dear Mum,
Well, the weeks go by and I don't get as much done as I should, but other interests have been getting in the way. There are certain things that I am doing that one just has to do. Not to do them would show, not high moral scruples, but absurdity. In the first place I get up at all times day and night to listen to American newscasts, so that I can interpret them for Chatham House. Ridley,[1] who has been very nice, asked me and it would have been absurd to refuse. Secondly, I am in an auxiliary fire service, which takes time. Looking at these glorious buildings I have no scruples whatever about doing something to defend them, although at the same time it may indirectly help a war one doesn't like. It is as if someone attacked Chartres; well, what the hell, you just couldn't sit still. Chartres, and that day last year when we were there, seems to me to be one of the perfect days.
   So with these extra things plus games, boy am I hearty (as they say here) and then talking and parties etc. My work is not flourishing, but, that which I do, I adore. It is really tremendously interesting reading cases, although it seems dull.

From Margaret's constant letters and yours, which always come oddly enough in one batch (3 at once), I seem to feel that Canada is more warlike than here. Perhaps it is frustration. People who never had 'a cause' in peace time now feel they can fight with as yet little sacrifice if they are Canadians. People like Lionel[2] make the sacrifice to the jaded emotions of their older relatives. You are so kind you let me think for myself and be for myself and I think our family is closer than all the others. But probably Uncle Jim (whom I wrote to the other day) will, in masochistic exaltation, throw Peter as a sop to his conscience. Aunt Lal has done that to Lionel.

The master is really a fine man. Exalted about the war refusing (in a speech he made in the Sheldonian) to answer any socialist argument, but still a fine character from the short sermons he makes in Balliol Chapel on Sundays.[3] Really fine, there is no doubt. Whatever unreasoning principles he has he is like a prophet. The only thing is that, like Uncle J[im], (but more logically) he does not think in terms of economics. He still is living in the idea that politics are attached to how men make their living and that political ideals are generally a result of economic self-interest.

I went to the Howes'[4] on Saturday lunch. I like them both immensely. They are so simple still and yet take their position with natural dignity.

Do show this letter round as you wrote in your last letter. I met Uncle Burgon's nephew and hundreds of others.

I must go to church now.

Heaps of love,
George

Mrs Fould's sent me *Jean-Christophe*.[5] Blackwells[6] reminds me of Wilde's dictum that 'The only thing I can't resist is temptation.'[7]

1 M.R. Ridley (1890–1969), fellow and tutor in English literature at Balliol. Ridley was said to be the model for Dorothy Sayers's Lord Peter Wimsey.
2 Lionel Massey (1916–65), the Masseys' elder son
3 Grant regularly attended Lindsay's sermons, both during 1939–40 and when he returned to Oxford after the war during 1945–7.
4 Not identified
5 Romain Rolland (1866–1944), *Jean-Christophe* (1931)
6 Celebrated Oxford bookstore
7 'I couldn't help it. I can resist everything except temptation' (Oscar Wilde [1854–1900], *Lady Windemere's Fan* [1891], Act 1).

31/ To Maude Grant   Balliol College, Oxford
                                                              22 November

Dear Mother,

I got your letter last week for my twenty-first birthday. Thank you ever so
much for your letter and for your present. It cheered me up as it was the
first letter from Canada I had had for ages. Today I got marvellous letters
from Geoff and Charity and Margaret for my twenty-first birthday and
some kind of pomposity from Aunt Marjorie. As an effort to cement the
family feeling I had written to her and Uncle Jim against my better judgment. This 'most charming' of notes on my twenty-first birthday made me
realise that it was against my better judgment.

I am having a perfectly marvellous time here, but I never get a spare
moment and am tired as anything.

I feel I have written to you about Christmas already, but, anyway, here it
is again, as you will forgive. I hope you have a nice time and I am sure you
will in Toronto.

From all accounts Canada is more bellicose than here. At least the *Daily
Worker*[1] hasn't been shut here, as it has in Toronto and Cleveland.
Cockburn[2] keeps pouring out his vitriol in *The Week*. It would be easier to
make a protest in Canada than here. Peter and all the sweet people working in the COTC[3] for seven hours a week when they don't even do that
much here. That kind of insanity makes me realise that probably our
hope of life (at least mine) will be in the U.S.A. or in some place like that.

Lately I have been reading Nietsche(?). To say that he is completely
misunderstood by most people would be an absurd understatement. To
say that he is the forerunner to such bestiality and cruelty as the Nazis is
absurd. 'I love he whose soul is deep even for wounding and whom a
slight matter may destroy.'[4] 'Pity is the cross upon which he is nailed who
loveth mankind.'[5] That kind of thing is not like what he is supposed to
be. He uses the theory of 'the blond animal'[6] in utter derision; yet people
say that that is the basis of Nazidom.

It certainly is the work of a true liberal to ban the *Clarion*.[7] Uncle James
and his ilk will be fighting to save democracy so they can slaughter it at
home. Have you read what Mrs Roosevelt[8] (in her tremendous sanity)
said about the communists? The *Manchester Guardian*[9] quoted it the other
day as a truly great statement it was. Sanity, clarity and a heart.

A Czech friend of mine[10] here has just found out that many of his best
friends were shot in Prague. He, as head of Labour Youth, just escaped
miraculously. He is not feeling as Uncle Jim feels towards the war.

Give my love to the Parkins. Could you get something for Elizabeth for me? I enclose a card to put in with it.

A sweet letter from CLG. Tired from her work, but marvellously triumphant.

You may not know, but I have not got any mail yet for 3 weeks except airmail stuff. It is strange; you probably get as little from Alison and I.

Heaps of love,
George

Enclosed several Montreal bus, street and car tickets. Also, a ticket for Saturday afternoon to the Palace Theatre – use it.

1 Communist party newspaper
2 Claud Cockburn (1904–81), editor of *The Week*
3 Canadian Officers Training Corps
4 Friedrich Nietzsche, *Thus Spoke Zarathustra*, 'Zarathustra's Prologue,' section 4.
5 Ibid.
6 Friedrich Nietzsche, *Genealogy of Morals,* I, 11
7 Not identified
8 Eleanor Roosevelt (1884–1962), American humanitarian and wife of Franklin Delano Roosevelt (1882–1945), president of the United States (1933–45)
9 British newspaper of a traditionally liberal slant
10 Karl Johannes Newman (1913–), later professor of international relations, University of East Pakistan, Dacca

1940

32/ To R.A. Trotter   Balliol College
                                                                  18 January 1940

Dear Professor Trotter,

Today your letter arrived from London with its picture of your country place. Although each must have its own splendour for the owner, it is near and in the same terrain as ours; so I can understand how beautiful it must be.

It gets stranger and stranger here. Several of the friends I made last term have gone to the war. One whose metier was history, a brilliant Edward I scholar,[1] a strange person who stuttered & held himself in with tremendous efforts even at the ease of Balliol. The army one feels will be the end of a person like that and so many people for whom it would be possible to stay here.

This is all very first person singular present indicative, but it is from particulars that one gains the unhappiness that must be in England.

Law is mentally precise in its structure, detailed in its application, mixed with a kind of unproductiveness &, today, what an unreality.

This may seem heresy. Perhaps it is mere lack of courage, but it seems that if there was a chance of an early peace that had sure elements of hope in it, it would be better to have that then, rather than wait till we are tired and bitter. Certainly, when one hears Americans or even Canadians say one must fight to the finish, it is infuriating, for it is their people who will really suffer, not us.

It is hard to work here at academic subjects. What with being a fire-man some afternoons & listening to the American radio some evenings for Chatham House the reason for us being here is inclined to be neglected.

The sun and the frost has made the country around here shining and bright, with people skating. I haven't been able to because of a sprained ankle. But any person who talks of the unpleasantness of English winters seems crazy. They keep us in perfect comfort, in fact luxury.

You say that truth and right are hard to come by and that one despairs. At the moment there can be but despair and the search of which you speak is difficult to keep up. Yesterday there was a book I was reading by a Frenchman Rimbaud[2] called 'Une Saison en Enfer.'[3] It is intensely subjective; yet it is typical of the restlessness, the constant desire for doing, that is here. Not at all the feeling of tomorrow we die, but of tomorrow as unknown. All through that atmosphere, the parasitic civilian sits aloof, an unnecessary appendage.

G.M. Brown,[4] a Queen's man you may remember, is a fine person here. It is impossible not to respect him and like him too.

I am sorry to burden you with these subjective ravings, but your letter of this afternoon came so welcomely and full of hope & clarity.

My regards to Mrs Trotter.

Yours sincerely,
George Grant

1 Possibly C.T. Stratton (1919–)
2 Arthur Rimbaud (1854–91), French poet
3 Rimbaud's prose poem (1873) symbolized his desire to break from the past.

4 G.M. Brown (1916–77). Brown was awarded a D.Phil. by Oxford in 1940. He
served with the Royal Army Medical Corps and, after the war, returned to
Queen's as a professor of medicine.

33/ To Maude Grant   25 January 1940

Dear Mum,

Your letter depressed me, as really I have written often & definitely a good
deal longer than generally. But more than depressed me, it thrilled me, as
I had been on the verge of telegraphing you, as I had not heard since
before Christmas. It is, in both cases, the product of war.

To keep this personal, rather than public, and to keep it on the false
assumption that the world may be relatively the same place after the war
as before, I am going to write about myself. Mixed with a hopelessness,
intellectually I feel my desires are becoming more concrete, my energy
more directed. I would like to write a good deal; already there are several
titles to academic works that would thrill me to produce. Perhaps this may
not seem to you very worthwhile in the world at the moment & probably
it is not. It is probably merely a reaction from the number of people
around here now [who] are losing any [end in] existence. One has so
much of that feeling that perhaps it is better to have a limited & circum-
scribed end than no end whatever.

My room mate has just come in & has said in the news tonight there
was something about a Canadian election this winter. My instinctive
thoughts were (1) political move (a) on one side, to crush Hepburn-
Drew[1] move (b) crush, on the other side, any more radical elements that
may not approve, that is, moderation will try & kill both extremes. Whatever in that policy are goods & evils. But whatever, it is not statesmanlike,
but a good sound political move. Will he get burned like Duplessis?[2] I
doubt it. If he gets burned, it will be from the left or right.

At the moment I feel intensely clear headed. One alternates between
terrific emotionalism when one writes bad poetry & clearness when one
works or writes prose or letters.

It is late at night now and, in a few minutes, it is my turn to go on a shift
for Chatham House.

Today I read a book by the English modern, Christopher Isherwood,
called *Mr Norris Changes Trains*.[3] Technically it is exquisitely written; yet it
seems to me one of the most sterile, horrid books I ever read. So unproductive. Pornography without any point. Neurosis. Clear tragi-comic
description of 1930–3 Berlin, but with an infertile pointlessness, a death.

What one could describe as a whited-sepulchres attitude. The brilliant talent of the writer spent on producing *that*, instead of what he could if he tried. God knows, it's depressing to think that is what our civilization is doing.

Well, this is very invective-ish, but the uselessness of it attacked one & the brilliant Englishmen who I talk to love it, think it great art. Degeneracy. Like Watteau[4] or Boucher.[5]

'Pourquoi battons-nous?'[6] is a question one cannot ask, as the answer is, 'Je ne sais pas de tout.'[7] One dare not say it, as it would be cruel to people who are suffering like these people. I could ask it out loud at home, but not here. Only when the Englishman makes wild statements about others do I contradict them. You would be surprised how quiet I am. A good article by Mrs Lindbergh[8] (1) The English are suffering; the U.S.A. is not. Therefore, the U.S.A. has no right to yap for blood like the crowd at a gladiatorial show. (2) Never discourage an early peace, if it is possible. But if one does not ask here, I would like to ask of Uncle Jim & his ilk, 'Pour *quoi* battons-nous?'[9] These people here (who I am getting to like) – from what he said, Uncle Jim never liked them. Why does he want to throw them to Moloch? He urges on youth to do what here youth is not sure whether it wants to do or not. Somebody ought to arise like Zola & j'accuse to write 'Pourquoi battons-nous?'

Alison comes to Oxford this weekend. I promised I would not tell you & have restrained throughout this letter; she has not been well, but is getting better.

I write the Parkins, but never an answer, except Uncle Raleigh,[10] once.

Heaps and heaps of love,
George

1 Ontario Conservative leader George Drew combined with Liberal premier Mitch Hepburn to condemn Mackenzie King's federal government's war effort. King used the occasion as a pretext for calling a federal general election, which he won handily.

2 Duplessis called an early Quebec provincial elction in 1939, which he lost to Godbout's Liberals.

3 Christopher Isherwood (1904–86), *Mr Norris Changes Trains* (1935)

4 Antoine Watteau (1684–1721), French painter and engraver who specialized in country scenes

5 François Boucher (1703–70), French painter specializing in mythological scenes

6 'Why are we fighting?'

7 'I have no idea.'
8 Mrs A.S.M. Lindberg (1906–), 'Prayer for Peace,' *Reader's Digest*, December 1939. Reprinted in pamphlet form by the British Ministry of Information (1940)
9 'For *what* are we fighting?'
10 Raleigh Parkin (1894–1978), Maude Grant's brother

34/ To Maude Grant   Balliol College, Oxford
                                                                      Sunday

Dear Mother,
This week a letter from you came with spring like a voice of hope. Thank you ever so much.

Well, life is good. It is the vacation and at the moment I am at Balliol, not only working at ordinary work, but getting some good strong education from such books as Felix Frankfurter (you know the American Supreme Court judge)[1] *Labor Injunction*[2] and his brilliant *Holmes and the Supreme Court.*[3] Frankfurter for a year taught at Balliol and always sends his books here for the library – with his name in – they will become treasured possessions. Frankfurter is a *great* man in the U.S.A. like Lindsay is here, only far more acute intellectually. But, however acute he is, he realises always as all must who are lawyers that [Oliver Wendell] Holmes[4] is *the master.* I remember when Holmes died, Father came down the stairs feeling (as was true) that one of the geniuses had died. I asked him if it was the man who wrote the hymns.[5] It took all of Father's patience to answer me in kindness. The other day I was reading what Laski[6] writes of Holmes. He thinks he is the outstanding man of American life in the first 30 years of this century. That claim, large for most, seems absurdly small for Holmes.

Before I came back here I went to Mrs Buck's for a week. Compared to other times it was, beyond words, difficult. Because I was refusing food, Aunt Margaret sent for the doctor against my express wishes and he found (as I knew) that I was in perfect health. Mrs Buck has aged terrifically over Mrs Hollins and, with the aging, has come a terrific preoccupation with politics. A most strange thing she said just as I was leaving: 'You will never desert this England that you have seen, for if you do, you lose not only her, but us.' I just smiled. Mrs Buck I love, but not as a teacher in politics; I cannot change for her. Neither can I, or do I, mind that semi-threat. Yet, I do not want to give her up.

While there Lady Helena Glachen and her sister promised me to have me meet Axel Munthe – ever since *San Michel*[7] – that would be a joy.

Alison is coming down today and we are going out to lunch and then to tea with the Lionel Curtises.[8] He has been a million times kind with his wisdom and his charm and just plain niceness. A really fine man.

Sometimes I have an overwhelming interest in my work, sometimes in poetry which I write. Anyway, the spring has brought a surge of intellectual activity and interest that sweeps one on and on. Laziness, my *worst vice,* is going for the first time. Although I have heard that you have been asked to stay on at McGill and, although they need you, think of yourself for a while and give it up and live wherever you want. You will soon be sick of your children, but remember that this one is never, and can be never, sick of you.

Next weekend I am going to the Beetons', both houses, and then on to London for a Hudson's Bay Banquet.[9] Then back here for next term, which is going to be dull as my subject is that driest of objects, the land law.

Anyway, always my love.

Love,
Grant

Love to Constance and Mrs Drury.[10]

1 Felix Frankfurter (1882–1965)
2 Felix Frankfurter, *The Labor Injunction* (1930)
3 Felix Frankfurter, *Mr Justice Holmes and the Supreme Court* (1938)
4 Oliver Wendell Holmes (1841–1935), associate justice of the Supreme Court of the United States, 1902–32
5 Holmes *also* wrote hymns.
6 Harold Laski (1893–1950), British political scientist and economist, a committed socialist who later became active in the Labour party
7 A.M.F. Munthe, *The Story of San Michel* (1930)
8 Lionel Curtis (1872–1955), public servant and scholar. Curtis was an associate of Lord Milner and one of the founders of the *Round Table* in 1910. Through this connection, he became friends with the Parkins and the Grants.
9 Sir Edward Peacock was a director of the company.
10 Dorothy Drury (1889?–1987), the Grants' cook until 1935

On 8 April 1940 German forces overran Denmark and landed in Norway. Norway surrendered 9 June 1940.

35/ To Maude Grant   Balliol College, Oxford
9 April

Dear Mum,

I am writing to you on this paper because this may turn out to be a long letter and the other paper is so small.

Well, today the war seems to have spread again – Norway and Denmark. Denmark is no war; it is merely a march-in. What will happen in Norway seems to be absolutely impossible to say. Lots of signs here seem to say that the war is going to start. Some people (bored) here say they want it to start; I pray every day that it won't. Anyway, this last thing looks as if it was the beginning.

Over the whole thing it seems so depressing that I thought I would come home this summer. This is put very weakly, but, as it is time for bed, my brain doesn't seem to be turning over. The argument goes like this (1) Here I am at Oxford, learning, doing well, working, reading, [living] economically with a very high standard of living. (2) To some people, particularly my great friend Menzies,[1] that is all right. He is [staying] here till he is wanted; then he will be called up in two years when he gets his degree, but for sundry reasons, which cannot be catalogued here, there seems to me no chance of beginning to feel, to want to feel one ought to fight – it is not completely altruistic – it is probably selfish. The reasons are not for the post. (3) Granting these two premises, has one any right to go on being here when the ratio of unhappiness in England is going to soar, so that one's conspicuously easy position will increasingly grate on people's nerves? Then there are other reasons, which because of their technicality one cannot explain, but [I] will try to clarify them. Here the essential fact is that, unless poetry intervenes, my future is definitely as a lawyer (1) practising (2) using one's skill in the government (3) an academic lawyer. No. (2) definitely appeals to me the most. The thought of working for the government, being a cog in a well oiled machine, appeals to me immensely, especially as the lawyer is one of the people who probably does a lot of the oiling.

Well, if one is to be a lawyer in Canada with my views as to Canadian constitutional & common law principles, one must be practically trained as a lawyer in Canada. That means that one must either join the English bar here and then, from that, the Canadian one. The objections to that would be (1) terrifically expensive (2) again it is not a practice that appeals to me either as a means of being a good Canadian lawyer or as an adequately paid one. The other alternative, which seems to be the only one is to go to a law school at home and then be called to the bar. That would not have to be at all immediately; it could wait till I could save some money. In the meantime I could be working on law primarily as well as having an ordinary job. Because whatever else I have failed to do this year, I have learnt (probably at the expense of general education) the basic way of legal thinking. You may think that this all sounds grand, but I wouldn't have enough guts to tackle an ordinary job. That is where I hope I have developed in courage this year. It won't be easy to face people at home in the position of not being in the army, but it will never be easy. The difference between now and last September is twofold although (1) I have my end in view (2) I have the means to satisfy that end.

It will be a heartbreak to leave Balliol, but what will be the point of staying if, after being here, I will have to start anew in Canada to get enough money to go to Osgoode.[2] The work of next year here such as Roman Law, jurisprudence and some equity, I will miss, but without doubt I know most of the jurisprudence now. The Roman Law, however useful, (1) I will get some of at home (2) It is definitely not as a classical legal historian that my future lies.

This year I will never regret; it has been happy, at moments deliriously exciting and stimulating beyond measure. I have got what I want and, except for the actual degree (one of which I will have to get in Canada), I have drunk deep in law.

As to the obvious question about what the Rhodes and Balliol people want: (1) They want some to stay, but it is always on the assumption that it is eventually the army; as yet that assumption I cannot concede to. (2) More and more dons our going to war work naturally; the place is getting smaller and I feel we aren't wanted very much. C.K. Allen[3] I have talked to, but as it was not a propitious moment, in a party; he was vague. I will go again.

I know you are busy and often cannot read my letters thoroughly, but, *please* this time, do read this thoroughly as it seems to be vital in my life and, although it is difficult to realise any importance in one's own life, it is harder not to.

So please answer this completely & soon. You are my anchor and without your advice I drift. You are the *sine qua non*[4] of my life; therefore, how you equate the equation means a tremendous lot in my life. Please even among your terrific busyness take a few minutes to think the thing over, and please try and keep this premise in your mind: that I believe I can now stand up to more than when I went away.

Sorry this is so full of troubles; it is ghastly for you. The other day two letters from you arrived. I am sorry about Sheila's books and have written her an apology. As to your other letter, it was glorious beyond measure – really it was like a deep rich wine – only it was not temporary stimulation, but has been a long lasting comfort.

Tonight in the paper it was saying how, in Washington, there were lights in the White House at 4 a.m. It is funny how my immediate reaction was, 'Why weren't they blacked out?'

Good things from Uncle Raleigh were cheery and you can imagine how I gloried in 3 glorious letters from CLG in a week. Grand, hard-hitting letters of straight thought which were another mental tonic.

Alison was up here on Sunday. We went to the Lionel Curtises' for tea. She is a grand woman and so kind. What I like is, never having met Alison before and me only once, she begins with you assuming all the obvious remarks of getting acquainted and one goes right through to friendship. He is the same, although not quite to the same extent. English people are either supremely good, or else very bad, at that.

This weekend I am going to both Beeton ménages and then up to London for three days before term. Then back to real property[5] and Oxford in the glorious spring when the world is going to pieces and one can hardly remember it with the sun and the blossoms and the air and kind friends and pretty girls and interesting work.

My last letter gave my opinions as to you staying at McGill; so this is just a repetition in sentiment.

Love to Constance and Mrs Drury and to Aunt Louise Pottinger and Margaret Reid.

Heaps of love,
Grant

P.S. Please do answer this; it is the largest piece of advice I ever asked you for and very important for unimportant me. So as to eliminate anything that wasn't objective from this analysis, I have not mentioned anything to do with the clouds unfolding, of seeing you again; so, perhaps, it is best for me to try to look at it coldly.

A thing that isn't quite explained in this letter is that, when I say working at law in Canada, I mean only in my spare time. Your answer truly justified is that I never worked before. But there never was anything that *gripped* me before like this. There is a lot of work one can do in my spare time, for after a year of law I know where to look.

1 Duncan Menzies (1919–43), an Australian Rhodes scholar and war hero, tortured to death by the Japanese in Burma
2 Osgoode Hall in Toronto, the institution that trained lawyers in Ontario
3 Warden of Rhodes House
4 Absolute necessity
5 Law dealing with the ownership of land

In the Easter vacation, Grant went on a bicycle trip with his American friend Ray Cline.[1]

36/ To Maude Grant

Chichester
Tuesday

Dear Mum,
Here we are on our bicycle trip. Just dried up in Chichester after a long ride from Winchester when it rained all the time; so now we are settled down.

We started out on Saturday at 4 p.m. on the oldest bicycles; mine is so bad that it hardly gets round. All else that I had was a raincoat, a change of socks, the various accessories and a pair of underwear.

We rode from Oxford to Newbury[2] the first night and stayed at a nice place in the back of a shop. The next morning we went to Winchester,[3] spent the afternoon looking around the cathedral and as it was Sunday we went to a service. I met Brigadier Crerar[4] in the cathedral. The inside of Winchester is glorious, soaring – belief in what they were building.

We stayed that night in the youth hostel. Then we went the next day to Salisbury[5] & Stonehenge. Stonehenge is disappointing, but one feels the primitive urges that are part of it swinging up and holding the place. All the strangeness of man that stays with him. Salisbury is beyond words. The exquisite greyness of its outside against the blue sky & the green grass. All of one form, it piles force on force, in a lightness that I don't remember seeing in any other English cathedral. The medieval world had their end discovered and their goal charted. We build skyscrapers as a means – democracy as means – socialism as a means. This was the medieval end; they built this as their goal. We have no goal like that, no ends, and yet we cannot take theirs. We are hungry; yet we cannot eat their decayed meat. We must find something different. Anyway, Salisbury was glorious and the sun shone.

It is rather awful to have this shelter from the war and be able to go on a bicycle trip like this. Next week back at Oxford for the rest of the holidays, except for Easter[6] weekend at Mrs Buck's. I think my work is improving. My tutor[7] (in the interview that you & your tutor & the master have) said that there were glimpses of a first, but that it was as yet only glimpses. Still that is a beginning, because I had to learn a whole new technique – law.

For what I am learning it is crazy to say, wild to dream, if it is any use or any purpose.

Brooke Claxton[8] is cheery. I hope like anything he gets in. It is too bad [if] it is Cahan,[9] for he has more points than most of the Conservatives.

I wrote to Alison about the £70 today and will send it to her.

All my love. Don't work too hard in your last weeks.

You ask for letters of facts – two reasons you cannot get them: (1) Some facts are not for letters. (2) I am not leading a factual existence except in its widest sense.

Anyway, please write as everybody but you, CLG and MGA[10] seem to have forgotten.

Heaps of love,
George

1 Ray Cline (1919–), from Terre Haute, Indiana; later, to Grant's amusement, with the CIA
2 About 48 km
3 39 km
4 General H.D.G. Crerar (1888–1965); became chief of the Canadian general staff 1940
5 24 km
6 21–4 March
7 Sir Theodore Henry Tylor (1900–68), a blind law professor who understood the main purpose of law as the resolving of cases, not the rationalization of the legal system
8 Brooke Claxton (1898–1960), McGill lawyer, first elected to the House of Commons as a Liberal in 1940
9 C.H. Cahan (1861–1944), Montreal Conservative politician and cabinet minister in the administration of R.B. Bennett, 1930–5
10 Margaret Grant Andrew

37/ To Maude Grant   Balliol College, Oxford
                                              Sunday evening, 19 May

Dear Mum,
This has been a most ghastly week and I suppose one must expect that

worse will follow. Optimism can hardly be in order. Total warfare has
started in truth. The poor Dutch just seem to have been opened up &
swallowed – a terrible massacre.[1] England is no longer fighting for liberty,
but for her life. The whole atmosphere here in the last week has been
tense even in the most glorious spring week in Oxford's history. Nothing
had touched this place really before, but now it has come.

About coming home, I hate to make you 'bitterly disappointed,' but
this week has convinced me. All the people I trust most here of the dons
say it would be not worth staying either selfishly or altruistically. With
England preparing for total warfare, this place is folding fast. Last week
my best friend of the dons went to the Treasury; this week another goes
to Supply.[2] My tutor will stay, but his number of pupils has doubled as he
has to take other colleges' men. He gives us an hour a week from 9–10
p.m. when he is so tired from teaching all day that it is hardly worthwhile.
Oxford, *you must realise*, is just ceasing to exist. It is a luxury commodity
which England cannot afford if she is to win the war. None of the people
here can really want us to stay. For the time being this sort of life will just
have to stop. I don't know if you realise how serious the situation looks
here. To put it mildly '*It is bad.*'

One thing I must beg you and make you promise *not to do* is to write *to
the master.* Everybody is fearing a breakdown for him here; he is on his legs
day and night. Really, I could not forgive you if you wrote. This is deadly
serious.

Just lately I have suddenly been seeing quite a lot of the Adamses[3] who
knew you and Father. The Warden of All Souls – a really fine man with a
sweet Irish wife – who asked specially to have her love sent to you. They
are a sweet [ill.] couple.

Alison came down today and we had a glorious day, sitting by the river
and in Balliol quad. After the ghastly winter, it is evidently the most beautiful spring anyone can remember. Life is pleasant, pleasant, pleasant,
physically beyond words.

Really this year has been glorious. It has been exciting; I never
dreamed it could be half as good. I have had far the best part of the law
course, met the few older people up here, have [been] given more advice
than I dreamed possible from people just out of school, have made a lot
of permanent and good friends. None of these things can, or will, exist
next year.

Lionel [Massey][4] [is] going to France; everybody else asking what
one is going to do is another impelling force. Not only selfishly would it
not be worth staying on, but it also would not be altruistically. It is not a

question of letting anyone down by going, certainly not Balliol or
Queen's.

I hope that you will forgive this decision that is, of course, conditional
on [the world's] events and may change as they change. I only wished you
agreed with it. Nearly everyone I know here does absolutely.

Do tell me what your plans are? I have written to ask a thousand times,
but the last developments have slowed up the mail as no Canadian I know
has had mail for a couple of weeks. Probably it will all come at once.

The new government seems sound.

One argument I agree is valid for having me stay here is Alison, but,
although it enters as a factor, it does not outweigh the rest.

Sorry this is such a personal letter, but, if you asked for news, I would
merely say that there is none that is not personal about friends you do not
know or else that you must have gathered from reading the morning
papers – or that you would know as representative of Oxford life.

Heaps of love,
as always
George

P.S. For a while I may work here on a farm during harvest work this summer.

Monday morning –
This morning when I went down to breakfast your report of the Crane
Foundation was there. *Thank you beyond words for sending it.* It is like a
credo to any lawyer and it should be shouted in the ears of nearly every
lawyer in Oxford. One of the reasons of academic disappointment at
Oxford was that they taught no public law and, secondly, that the law they
did teach was a technical instrument, but not one to be used as a means
for a social end. That is the kind of training I would love someday after
years of other work. At the moment it is, of course, impossible. Coming
into this world, where only a few great men like the master can still think
calmly (I suppose Halifax too)[5] it came like a breath of fresh air to be
remembered.

Sitting in the sun with Alison yesterday somebody jokingly, as I enjoyed
the quad, said 'There goes the disintegration of a social conscience.' Let's
pray it isn't true.

Mother please believe: (1) That the work in Oxford is not worth doing
in war when the other benefits of Oxford are not here. (2) That it is
extremely selfish and stupid to stay here in the present state of affairs.

Menzies, my Australian friend, who thought I was an ass before the Dutch business, now thinks it is pointless to stay on.

1 Germany invaded the Low Countries 10 May 1940. The Netherlands surrendered 14 May.
2 D.G. Kendall (1918–), experimental officer with the Ministry of Supply, 1940–5; later professor of mathematics at Cambridge
3 W.G.S. Adams (1874–1966), warden of All Souls College, Oxford, 1933–45
4 Lionel Massey served in Greece, where he held a commission in the 60th Rifles. He was wounded, taken prisoner by the Germans, and moved to Athens. He was not repatriated until May 1944.
5 Edward Frederick Lindley Wood, Lord Halifax (1881–1959), British foreign secretary, 1938–41

38/ To Maude Grant   4 June

Dear Mum,

Mrs [Bone] says she will take this home to you.

The day after I had written to you saying I had decided to come home, your marvellous telegram came. Let me tell you the developments here first. The whole trend has been that *there will be no Oxford* next year. The master called an extraordinary meeting in hall. The warden of Rhodes House (when I went to see him this morning about going home) said, not as I expected, 'Oh yes, you better go home now in the summer,' but said, 'Don't even stay to the end of term; go right away.' He made me promise (against one's better instincts) to go and see the master at lunch. As usual the master was his glorious self. He advised me to go home right away unless I could be of use here. So I have written to Pearson[1] to see if temporarily they want anyone at Canada House, if they are short handed. Also I have telephoned this afternoon to London to ask Alison. The master said that nobody could or should want to stay on at Oxford at the moment. I agree with him.

What most I would like would be to bring Alison home too, but then that is impossible as here she wants to stay. Perhaps when I get home I will try and join up – something *non-military*. Not for a moment do I feel any differently towards the horror of this thing, or as to the evil that must come in its trail, but one cannot stand aside from it. If one is to stop such corruption it must be from the inside not from a holier than thou attitude. As to what one can do it is so stupid to ask and perhaps it would be better as Peter[2] says, to keep oneself and one's friends out.

I will continue this in an hour when I have heard from Alison, but probably it will be necessary to send it off before one hears from Canada House as Mrs [Bone] must have it by Saturday and mail now is not very certain.

All my love. It would be better to write of other things; of glorious weather etc., of Lord Wright[3] of [Dunley], of a ghastly hayfever this week, so that one feels like the wrong end of a broom, so full of dust and [streaming], but the last developments in the war are the only things that are real. God knows, whatever happens now, hundreds of people are going to get massacred to pieces. The hate and the waste that has been unleashed can't be covered by any insurance policies now. Nothing points to how much will go down the drain.

I have just had an evening with Lionel Curtis and Arnold Toynbee. Toynbee[4] is the colossal kind of person who makes one feel that even if civilization goes down now, it is merely temporary as there is something essentially a part of God in man's make up.

My alternatives are to stay here & join an ambulance unit or else to go home and get a job. It is a hard decision as any attitude to the events of this world that I had when leaving home last year has been strengthened rather than weakened by viewing this place at close view.

All my love to everybody and to Charity particularly. Tell her (but without mentioning that I told you to) that I mentioned her in this letter and how sweet she is.

Love Love

George

1 Lester Bowles 'Mike' Pearson (1897–1972), first secretary of the Canadian high commission in London; later secretary of state for external affairs, 1948–56, leader of the Liberal party, 1956–68, and prime minister, 1963–8. Pearson and his wife, Maryon, were family friends.
2 P.T. Clarke (1919–), a friend from Balliol who went to jail as a conscientious objector during the war. After the war, he farmed at Quainton, Buckinghamshire, and married Grant's cousin Anne Macdonnell.
3 R.A. Wright, Baron Wright (1869–1964), lord of appeal and jurist; chairman of the Law Revisions Commission, 1935
4 Arnold Toynbee (1889–1975). His ten-volume *History of the World* (1934–54) was an attempt to synthesize the principles of world history.

Grant, still anxious to be at the centre of the crisis, joined a group of pacifists who had decided to form an ambulance unit. For the English, it was an attempt to

avoid compulsory military service by showing their good faith that they were pre-
pared to serve in a non-combatant role. For Grant, it was a way of doing his duty
to king and country, without compromising his pacifist principles. During the hot
summer of 1940, while events on the Continent were still unclear, he trained with
his fellow Oxford and Cambridge students.[1]

39/ To Maude Grant   Hawkspur Camp

Dear Mum,

Last week a letter from you that was glorious – a wonderful letter. The
thought of you and Constance (thinking I was coming) made me so
homesick I could have cried, but at the moment I read it I was cooking
the lunch, so that there was nothing to do. Someday I am going to take
you to Otter Lake for two weeks and you are not going to have to do any
of the cooking or anything. In that way I can make up a small measure of
what you did. Never before have I realised the work of cooking for 22
people with the help of two different people a day. Today, Sunday, is my
day off.

From some remarks you made, I hope you aren't going to see Wendell
Wilkie[2] as a good substitute for Roosevelt. Do you remember that test we
did last year going out west? One of the questions was, which of the following businessmen have fought Roosevelt? Answer – Wilkie. Well, this
year, I read his brief as head of Commonwealth and Southern before the
supreme court trying to convince them that TVA[3] was unconstitutional. It
really revolted me. Every man has a right to plead his selfish case, but not
to say that that case is in the national interest. If he got in, it would be a
return in part to that pre-1929 businessman morality of aggression that
Roosevelt has tried to stop. The internal issue comes doubly clear with
Wallace as vice-president, as he was the initiatory of the AAA,[4] which
although ruled out in 2 years (in the Schecter case),[5] did enough before
that to coordinate industrial and agricultural prices. As for foreign policy,
Hull[6] and Roosevelt are far more competent than an untrained man like
Wilkie. But the essential issue seems to me to be between a progressive
democracy and a conservative businessman's heaven and a return to
speculation, fights against labour, etc.

Well, all goes well here – busy, busy, busy – and yet nothing has happened – no invasion, nothing; but, by the time this letter gets to you, perhaps it will be different. This unit is in a strange way. It was meant to go to
France, so that now it is rather at a loose end. The normal needs of this
country being well supplied. This only being needed in an emergency.
Thus, rather than sit around and do nothing, if by 15 October or there-

abouts, nothing has happened I will come home. In the meantime, if one can be useful with the harvest etc.; that will be increasingly good. Last night we heard quite a few of the moaning, droning German planes, but no bombs dropped near enough to wake us up. Around here the air is just never silent; there are planes coming and going. Of course, where to or from, one neither knows or says.

I have wondered if you still will be busy with many evacuees now that the scheme seems quietly to have folded up or whether now you will be able to get back to Otter Lake. Remember on no account are you to take on too much work. I wonder of Joan Arnoldi – have had no answer to my last letter. I imagine she is frightfully busy. The people outside the family I get pretty regular letters from are Ernie Stabler,[7] Sheila Wallace[8] and Bill Goulding,[9] an occasional letter from Philip, but few others. I wrote to Eddie Campbell, but have never even had an answer.

Alison seems in good form. She forwards letters with an occasional cryptic note. She adores London and is so nice to so many kinds of people. The Greeys are angels; please, if you ever get time, send them a letter or a present or something. They are so incredibly sweet. I try and do as much as possible, but they would really be touched with a letter from you. You are wonderful about people, but these are ones that have done so much for your family – Alison, Charity, George. Although you owe them nothing, they so adore you and Aunt Lal is sometimes frightfully, excruciatingly tactless to them, not recognizing them, etc.

There are some nice people in this unit – Hallam Tennyson – a great grandchild of the poet – awfully nice, but ineffectual. Many many others of varying standards of niceness and efficiency, of strength and weakness. There is one nice person called Fox. Half Spanish and of gigantic physical proportions, he lumbers round, clumsy, but effective, a superb European brain – different from the ordinary English kind. But to see this gigantic figure stumbling along on a route march with blisters on his feet, a frown on his face and disertating (in hushed whispers) on André [Gide][10] is really a good sight. Most of his family were destroyed by Franco.

I am getting quite expert at first aid. How one will stand up if something happens is another matter. Not badly I hope.

As for money, I still have a Rhodes sum left. If I stay here, it will be on a paid job; that will be OK. If eventually I come home, I also won't need the money.

The French fleet[11] has caused a great deal of heart searching. But why? Given the situation, what else was there to do? It seemed to me, granting all the premises of war, so natural.

Otter Lake must be glorious; it is the right place for you to be. After so many and hard stormy seas, one must find a port. Thank God Margaret and Geoffrey are there. Quiet and a sense of arriving. Everybody writes of a not very rosy future in Canada. My God, we must build the future; it is not inevitable. If other things collapse they will hurt us, but we must at least keep ourselves together. I got a letter the other day from the new Mr and Mrs Neilsen. There is the courage that one needs. Not the stark courage that Uncle Jim writes of, but the gallant, powerful, joyful courage of expectation and of anger. The courage of Roosevelt in 1936, when asked to back down from the New Deal, he made his 'we've only begun to fight' speech.[12] But not the courage of unknowingness – lift other people's evil into oneself – steep oneself in their wickedness and in one's own.

Oh how I long to see you. I think of you so often, of things we've done, of afternoons in Paris and in Chartres, of that meal Chippy and you & I had in San Francisco.[13] But often of how, in my *laziness* and selfishness, I let you down; that won't happen much again. When the crisis comes, it clears one of a lot of futility.

The other day the most brilliant inspiration came to me. Chippy and I will write a book together. I have written in detail to her of it. Do not tell her I have told you. Let's hope she will accept. Although we fought, I feel deep down she is the person of my sisters who one will know, because she is the one I need the most and she probably more than the others needs someone.

About six weeks ago, in packing to leave Oxford, I packed at the bottom, with the help of an Indian friend and a Canadian, that Madonna from Chartres. Like a wave, it flooded all over again. That memory of things past remains as the nicest of all gifts.

The way they began to pack for me was amusing. I was taking this Indian girl[14] out to lunch when I met this Canadian called Collins[15] (brilliant & nice – he just got a first) from China. They bet me I couldn't eat a Chile hot double at the Indian restaurant, without crying and in ten minutes without water. If I did not, they got a free lunch; if I did, they packed. I ate it and reclined all the afternoon in a chair on Sunday telling them where to put this and that. The Indian girl is so excessively clean and neat that even your superb packing looks like a laundry bag beside hers. You must meet her someday. A sad person, engaged to a stupid Englishman who will neither marry her or give her up. She has been one of my best friends. If she goes home through Canada and the States, she must stay with us. She is only 4'6" and like a nice monkey, a relation of Bose[16] who has just been imprisoned.

Love to everybody you meet I know and to you a thousand loves and conversations

George

1 Extract from letter written about 1984:

[Dear Mr Currer-Briggs,]

A pacifist friend at Balliol in June 1940 gave me Vaughan Williams's address at another Oxford college, and I went to see him and he accepted me. I was glad because I did not want to return to Canada at such a striking moment. As a Canadian citizen, there was no question of an English tribunal. When I had come to Balliol as a Rhodes Scholar in 1939, my attitude to the war had largely been determined by a certain inchoate sense of what harm the earlier war had done to Canada, and, therefore, a rather vague North American isolationist sense vi-à-vis Europe's conflicts. That is political and I was an entire secularist. I was deeply moved by a group of pacifists I met in Balliol in 1939 so that by the time of the UAU [Universities Ambulance Unit] you could say my motives were religious. After the UAU I went to Bermondsey, which was being heavily bombed, and gradually came to be in charge of certain shelters under the railway arches, and stayed there, very intensely, till the Russians came into the war in 1941 and the bombing of England lessened.

In 1941 I joined the merchant navy, but soon they found I had tuberculosis, and in 1942 my family had me shipped home to Canada where I was put to bed.

My chief impression of the camp was what delightful and cultivated human beings they were. Let me illustrate what I mean by the word 'cultivated.' On one of the marches I found myself next to Hallam Tennyson, who I had never met and he talked to me of worlds of art and thought which just enraptured me. They were worlds in which I had lived in earlier reading, but which had been entirely private because I took for granted they were not serious because my contemporaries at school and university had not taken them seriously. I had gathered something of the sort in my first year at Oxford, but was enchanted by it in the members of the UAU. I was, of course, meeting directly contemporaries from a society which had some history from before the age of progress, who took the worlds of religion and art and morality seriously. Intoxicating.

A rather ambiguous memory which has always stayed with me – political. One evening Ian Crombie put on a charade of [British prime minister Neville] Chamberlain meeting [Italian fascist dictator Benito] Mussolini on a balcony. It was intended to ridicule Chamberlain. I could hardly believe it, because I assumed that Chamberlain had been trying to maintain peace in

Europe while trying to keep the U.S.A. and the USSR out of Europe. It seemed to me strange for a group of pacifists to be ridiculing him. But this was a minor ambiguous note in the midst of my enchantment with the niceness of the English.

2 Wendell Wilkie (1892–1944), a former Democrat and president of Commonwealth and Southern Corporation, a public utility. Wilkie broke with Roosevelt over the New Deal and ran as Republican candidate for president in 1940.

3 The Tennessee Valley Authority was created in 1933 for a variety of purposes, which included increasing electric power, flood control, and reforestation.

4 The Agricultural Adjustment Act (1933) created an agency designed to raise commodity prices.

5 *Schecter Poultry Corporation v. U.S.* (1935), the American Supreme Court's decision that the National Industrial Recovery Act (1933) was unconstitutional

6 Cordell Hull (1871–1950), Roosevelt's secretary of state (1933–44), and winner of the Nobel Peace Prize in 1945

7 A friend from Queen's

8 Sheila (Wallace) Woodsworth, daughter of Queen's principal R.C. Wallace

9 William Goulding, a UCC friend, later an architect

10 André Gide (1869–1951), winner of the Nobel Prize for literature, 1947

11 On 3 July the British seized all French warships in British ports. Fearing that the French Mediterranean fleet at Oran would fall into German hands, the British demanded its surrender on 4 July. When its commander refused, a British force under Admiral Sir James Somerville opened fire and, in the ensuing battle, destroyed the majority of the French fleet.

12 'I join with you. I am enlisted for the duration of the war [against the royalists of the economic order]' (F.D. Roosevelt, June 1936).

13 During their western trip, summer 1939

14 Dorothy Bose

15 R.E. Collins (1914–), a Rhodes scholar, 1938, and graduate of the University of Alberta; later with the Department of External Affairs

16 S.C. Bose (1897–1945), Indian politician and leader in the fight for independence

On 10 July 1940 the Battle of Britain began. Paris had fallen three weeks earlier. On 13 August the Luftwaffe began mass attacks on British airfields, factories, and docks; 7 September marked the beginning of the London Blitz.

40/ To Maude Grant   231 Sussex Gardens, London W2
                                                       31 August

Dear Mum,

Your letter of August 1st arrived today. Thank you very much. It was an interesting letter. It was strange that it should come a week later than one you posted on August 16th.

First as to plans here. Cooking went on and on. We were trained and nothing happened. So I lived in camp but took a forestry job chopping down trees at 8/6 a day. Terrifically hard physical labour. But it is coming to an end. Also, nobody will take us as a unit as it is composed of all manner of objectors. It is nothing to blame; it is just to be expected. It is disappointing that there is nothing to do. When this job is over I will do some farming and then come home.

What you say about Roosevelt and Lewis Douglas[1] is interesting. In the wonderful speech accepting nomination in 1936 – the 'We've only begun to fight' speech – he made this quotation. These men 'have conceded that political freedom was the business of the government but have maintained that economic slavery was no one's business. They granted that the government could protect the citizen in his right to vote but they denied that the government could do anything to protect the citizen in his right to work and his right to live.' There is where Roosevelt stands; the case seems so one-sided as few elections are. I can't see the ordinary man in the U.S.A. turning him off for a man of Wilkie's calibre who could do what he has done in his belief in complete business freedom from economic interference. How can a fairly liberal person like 'Mike' Pearson say that he doesn't care – as long as the U.S. foreign policy is right, to hell with their internal policy?

On Monday last we had a tremendous experience. Walking in the woods, suddenly all hell broke out above. We saw two planes crash. One only about a field away. So we rushed, I wondering what I would do if I met a German. But before we got there a parachutist came down about a hundred yards away, very fast, so we ducked down behind the trees. The yokels got so broad in accent I couldn't understand a word. Then we waited but the big, white thing didn't move; so we went forward. The German was dead – broken – the flaxen hair blowing all over his quiet face but his body smashed. Then we went on to the plane, but strangely it was English; the pilot was all burned up and all the bullets went off. Eight Germans came down in parachutes all round. One man had been at

Cambridge for eight months. Then last night and this morning they attacked a nearby objective.
[page missing]

1 Lewis Douglas (1894–1974), director of the budget under Roosevelt and later deputy war shipping administrator

France had fallen on 22 June 1940. It slowly became clear that there would be no need for the UAU's services in the near future, and its members hotly debated their future course of action. Eventually, most decided to become unpaid Air Raid Precautions (ARP) wardens in the poorer parts of London. George stayed with his sister Alison and then went to Bermondsey, a working-class district south of the Thames, near the docks and warehouses. It was to be one of the most heavily bombed parts of London in the following months.

41/ To R.A. Trotter

In shelter, London
18 September 1940

Dear Professor Trotter,
An air raid is on and the guns are going. Work has stopped and it gives me the opportunity to thank you for sending the copy of your article from the *Quarterly*.[1] I was doubly glad as it had been mentioned in two letters from Canada. Second-hand accounts make one want the real thing. It came one afternoon and that evening, the first of the Blitzkrieg here, I read it. What a contrast between its sanity and the noise and shakings. Canada, as part of the world, will, I hope, go on giving its particular contribution but (although this may be cheek to mention to you) are small national units possible any more? It makes me mad over here sometimes to see such violent Welsh, Scottish, Czech, Polish nationalists never thinking in larger European terms, but always stressing their national existence. There is no thought that the national existence may not be the best way of achieving happiness for Europe; [for them], it is not a means but an end. One notices the Dutch and Belgians here (with whom I happen to be thrown at the moment) never stress their nationalism but rather their own identity as part of Europe. To draw an analogy (that may be false) mustn't Canada be only part of a larger whole? Whether as part of the empire one just has to wait; but, if not, the U.S.A. This may be completely off the point and, anyway, natural deficiency and the raid noises make it very badly expressed.
    You must have heard it so often you are sick, but the fact of the Lon-

doner's courage is impressive. We have had to deal with quite a few of the less severe casualties and occasionally give blood to the [men] and one never sees anything to make one doubt them. There are lots of funny stories and a lot of sad ones, more of the latter unfortunately, but through it all work just goes calmly on.

Do you ever hear J.B. Priestley[2] on the radio? He seems to express the whole thing. Through the whole thing, the pervading waste of everything is appalling. The design of a shell cap outside our door the other day was a product of a fine brain. The loveliness of all the search lights in the sky. All the skill and energy of people being thrown into destructiveness.

The guns have stopped; so back to work.

Afternoon -
Another raid gives me time to finish this. Our ambulance has folded up, as we were trained for France and so perhaps, after this particular part of the war, I will come home.

Sorry to bother you with so lousy a letter.

Yours sincerely and again many thanks.
George Grant

1 R.A. Trotter, 'North America and the War,' *Queen's Quarterly* 47 (Summer 1940), 133–46
2 J.B. Priestley (1894–1984), British novelist, playwright, and critic

The centre of Grant's life in Bermondsey was the Oxford and Bermondsey Club (OBC). Founded by evangelical Christians from Oxford, it was a combination of soup kitchen and social club, which sought to provide social and physical nourishment in a Christian setting. It was across the road from the Raven and the Sun, the pub which George consequently frequented. Through the OBC, George met Mrs Lovett, a middle-aged woman with a large family, who became a sort of surrogate mother to him.

42/ To Maude Grant   Oxford and Bermondsey Club
Tanner St, SE1
21 December

Dear Mumps,
Well, dear mumps, how are you?

Two weeks ago I wrote a letter that everything was going well and settled down. I went out and posted the letter and, half an hour later, our biggest all night do started, but having [just] written to you all quite amazed me.

Lovely letters come from you. Thanks ever so. We dawdle towards Christmas – 7 September till 7 December raced so fast and so did one week in December, but now the days commence to dawdle as the terrific excitement gives way to tiredness. One just can't live beyond a point at a trying emotional pressure for so long without suddenly getting a reaction. Every happening or smallest incident was taken at such a high pitch that I need [restringing].

Yesterday sent down from Canada House was a lovely parcel from you, with a sweater and socks, tea for Gran and some mitts. It was an accident that yesterday afternoon was the first time I had been able to see Gran in weeks. So I trundled along there with that and some dolls and sweets for a grandchild. She loved the tea. The sweater will be most useful; a woman in our shelter knitted me another one for under a coat. And this one does for [ill.]. It is wonderful and a good thickness. Thanks ever so much.

Well, it is nearly Christmas now. The papers are full of an invasion scare again and rumours fly hectic. There was tremendous calm as to rumours in those worst months of bombing as the bombing was so all engrossing, mere, ordinary life was not good enough.

Dec 27th Well, Christmas is well over. It comes but once a year, thank God. I have been to eight parties – drank consecutively (not too much) for three days – danced, kissed at least 200 people under the mistletoe and generally rushed around as I have never rushed before. This autumn I have often thanked God I was your son, but never as over this Christmas. One just has that energy from you that can turn on and keep a party from turning into a brawl or keep a party from getting dull. Some amazing moments. One. I was in the wonderful place where all my friends go called the 'Raven & the Sun.' A man and his wife came up and said to me you must come & see the Irishman. Well, I thought that 'the Irishman' was probably some queer Bermondsey expression, but I went, not knowing the people. It turned out I had held the woman's hand when a bad air raid was on & got her to shelter. But we marched over. The woman was expressively a Londoner. Her husband was a lisping man who talked Irish & the Irishman really was an Irishman. An old devil in bed with two bottles of Irish whiskey. My God, what a performance. We talked like a surrealist dream. The Irishman would say something, the Cockney woman would then translate and the kind lisping Irishman would say 'Sure and he can understand an Irishman better than a bloody Cockney' & the fight would start. After two drinks I knew that I had had enough and then the argument started. 'Sure the lad's not going to disappoint us' 'But you don't want to give him a drop too much.' Well, I departed. It was the most amazing experience – like a one act play. I will probably never see them again; yet there that little episode stands with no beginning and no end.

2nd The Mayor of Bermondsey [McHenley] is swell; he is a railway man with a real public sense. Comes to an occasion, not as a visitor to the zoo, but really to enjoy himself. At our dinner he came and made a speech at the serious point of which one of my friends – a very quiet elemental woman called Mrs Hunt who has really suffered, but never complained of the bombs – was quite overcome and collapsed helpless on the table. Christmas with a few drinks and not being at home and her boy home on leave just let go all the pent up feelings of months of this life. This woman of 60, the height of wonderful calm, suddenly just gave way.

Granny Peck was just bombed out a second time. It was too much. She sat by the fire, but I knew she was dying; so I sent for the doctor. He got an ambulance and Granny put on her wonderful black bonnet & her cane & her bag of treasures – her whole life of wonderful things of all kinds. She walked down with me. We lifted her into the ambulance. I kissed her and said 'Goodbye, Gran.' All she said was 'Don't say goodbye; it's just au revoir.' She looked so calm & lovely – and a week later she died. This isn't sentiment, but some of them take one's breath away with that tremendous tranquility that knowledge of what is that I could never find. Small, poor people pushing a package of cigarettes in one's pocket or a flower or a drink, people so thankful for the smallest kindness. God, I have learned more about living from these people than from any others.

But most [of] all the children – dancing, racing, stamping, shouting, laughing, coy and finally on Boxing Day completely tuckered out – just finished sleeping – going wild eating, drinking, crying and laughing.

Yesterday morning early I went up & saw Al. We had a lovely boxing day. We went & saw Bette Davis & Charles Boyer in *All This and Heaven Too*.[1] Naturally, since the Blitz, films haven't meant too much, but this stirred me as only that woman can. It is her dignity. She acts here with that restraint that leaves me [taut] to the end. Yet, behind her dignity, her breathless calm, one feels a power, a restlessness that is really divining. We loved it. Then in to see Aunt Lal; then back here.

Don't forget Aunt Lal has outdone herself for me this Christmas and in helping my people. Yesterday I was most touched when I described to

Aunt Lal and Uncle V. how I felt. How interested they were. Aunt Lal has given me so much. Do write and thank her, as you mean a great deal to her.

This letter has been interrupted by a long talk with a chap just going back to the army. He has never had half the chances I have had; yet he is twice the person. Strong mentally and physically, straight. Let's hope he is England's future. If his type is, one cannot be afraid. One of the nicest things of this job is meeting people who are [encouraging].

It is people that pull one out of defeatism. They haven't given up, why should oneself? Self-pitying, not caring, one gets often, but it just isn't good enough.

Well, goodbye. Be good.

Look after CLG and look after Elizabeth Greey. Really never forget that of all people in England, Elizabeth looked after your chickadees.

Love, love, love, love, love,

George Grant

P.S. Since finishing your letter I picked up two articles by that American Ralph Ingersoll[2] that you sent to me a week ago. I don't know about the rest of London, but about the 'East End' he is abysmally ignorant. One statement he makes about no shelters having been hit is just one big lie. He can't understand the English at all. He writes a lot of the Dorchester[3] life, but as far as I can see he did nothing, but live it with an occasional visit to the 200's down here. There doesn't seem to me anything more dangerous than viewing this as a super spectacle or a football game. He has seen shelters on ordinary quiet nights, but not when all hell is loose outside. Neither has he been outside on an expedition.

1 Directed by Anatole Litvak and based on a novel by Rachel Lyman Field, *All This and Heaven Too* (1940) starred Bette Davis and Charles Boyer. It was the story of Henriette Deluzy-Desportes, who was accused of conspiring with the Duc de Praslin of murdering his wife. It remained Grant's favourite movie.
2 R.M. Ingersoll (1900–85), publisher of *Time*, 1938–9, and author of *Report on England, 1940, Top Secret*
3 An allusion to the Masseys, who had left their house and installed themselves in the luxury Dorchester Hotel (which they thought safer) for the duration of the war. Although living in comfort, they still were subject to the dangers of German bombing.

1941

43/ To R.A. Trotter   42 Tanner Street
                                                          Bermondsey, SE1
                                                          23 January

Dear Professor Trotter,

I hope you will excuse this kind of paper and a pencil, but in the hurly burly of this shelter of about 1500 people the social amenities just go.

Your Christmas card finally reached me. Thank you very much for it. I loved the woodcut. Whatever the mystery connected with that particular woman and her child, these last months make me believe that children are something in which there is hope; and seeing the way in which these East End mothers have withstood this compared to the men makes me realise in crisis who holds the family. There are a woman and child here, of that dark Irish strain which came with the 1832 famine from Ireland to build the Southern Railway, who I wish you could draw or paint. She holds her family calmly together through all the troubles of losing two homes, sickness, etc. which is the East End's lot at the moment.

It would be exciting to be at Queen's for the next Canadian-American relations conference. So much has happened in the way of detail that it must be well-nigh impossible to pull together an agenda. I wonder if LaGuardia[1] will be able to be there. From mother's stray remarks, he seems to be a success, a good executive as well as a good talker and publicity man. One personal thing in his favour is that he isn't weighted down with his own solemnity. That is one of the things that make my friends here love Churchill. He doesn't let down the public dignity of England; yet he isn't always keeping up his own pompousness. Whatever a lot of these people think of his politics, they like him as a man. It seems silly to make any remarks about American relations, but everybody here asks me about [Lord] Halifax. Will he go down in the U.S.A.?[2] He is so unpopular in the East End that it is hard to explain to them that he may be a success there. Although they obviously haven't decided on their foreign policy because of an ambassador, the technicalities of what is wanted, I suppose, make it a big job. (This is very bad, as it is noisy and interrupted here.)

It is [so] nice to have someone to write to about something other than Bermondsey politics & bombs that one forgets that one is writing to a busy man.

One thing I hope that is understood in Canada & the U.S.A. is that whatever England can take (and here she has taken as much as anywhere else and taken it splendidly), there are certain kinds of things which one has gathered from our warden's training no flesh and blood can take, such as continuous gas. Sometimes the black and white complacency with which one sees England's courage talked about, as a kind of political tool, makes me mad.

Give my regards to any mutual friends at Queen's and particularly to your family.

Thank you very much again.

Yours sincerely,
George Grant

1 Fiorello LaGuardia (1882–1947), mayor of New York City
2 Lord Halifax left the government to become British ambassador in the United States.

On 17 February 1941 one of the shelters for which Grant was responsible, and whose residents he knew well, was bombed by the Germans and suffered some three hundred casualties. Grant was emotionally shattered by the event.

44/ To Maude Grant   42 Tanner St, London, SE1
                                         22 Feb. [1941]

Dear Mother,
How are you? I am sitting down listening to Grieg's superb piano concerto;[1] it is a magnificent lyrical work.

Margaret has written to me asking me to be the child's [Ed Andrew's] godfather. I have written back saying I don't know whether I should or not, but will write soon.

Tomorrow I traverse town to meet Alison; it will be fun.

Everything else there is to say seems to relate only to one thing and always to one thing. I have tried to keep it out, but it just comes back so insistently that nothing one can do will change it. My railway arch was hit and most of my friends in Bermondsey were eliminated or in hospital; so there it is. I was out, but came back to find it after it had happened. I thought I had seen the worst, but this was the end. On Saturday night Uncle Burgon and I had been all through it, seen all the people. He was particularly impressed by a group of sweet fourteen year olds with whom I had formed a boxing club. The whole thing has had a profound influence on Bermondsey in what seems to be a sensible way, in my opinion.

But why these people should have to pay for other's ignorance & selfishness is beyond me.

What I will do now is beyond me. It just somehow leaves one impotent to pick up again. What an awful debt of ignorance and selfishness there is to be paid off. The dead are dead, but the maimed remain and in a way worse than the maimed are the families of the lost. Some so stricken that they are half dead. Poor mothers haven't anything to put trust in except their children. In fact the whole of poor families are the same. Someday – someday. The trouble is that, [after] the last war, one could honestly believe in the idea that this was never to happen again. It is supreme optimism to believe that now; yet there are glimmerings of that belief everywhere.

Now, heaps of love
George Grant

1 Grieg, Concerto for Pianoforte and Orchestra in A minor, opus 16

45/ To Maude Grant   42 Tanner St, London, SE1

Dear Mum,

Mr Pearson says he will take a letter back for me to Canada to you; so here it is.

You mention you have been reading *Lotte in Weimar*.[1] In the long reaches of the night I have been reading it bit by bit, step by step, and have found it of such interest and charm that one marvels at the solidarity of the man's genius. Lotte – well of Lotte one can only say she is of such dignity that she does not seem at all small as compared to Goethe. As for Goethe the restlessness and the questing is beautifully mixed with the arrival and the sureness of him. Compared to the only other book I had read, *For Whom the Bell Tolls*,[2] it stands certain and measured and real. One of the last great Europeans shows up an American writer hands down. Lotte is about smaller events, written with smaller tread and for a smaller purpose. It does not pretend to give the world a credo or a faith, but it has, in its small cameoish way, the marks of greatness, which Hemingway never reaches.

The other day I bought a record of Marian Anderson[3] singing 'Softly Wakes my Heart.' She is Ceres and Aphrodite rolled into one, that glorious liquid passionate confident voice moves me as no other singer does. Flagstad[4] doesn't sing as well. Gigli[5] sings better, but without that tremendous sense of assurance.

Without a doubt most people in Bermondsey are selfish, brutal and dull and, worst of all, stupid. I have never been able to worship the working classes of this country as a whole. To me, faith in democracy does not come as an outcome of a belief that the mass is always right, but from a belief that more chance of being right is found in numbers. Canada has a hate of aristocratic people. By that, I don't mean the aristocrat of birth, but the aristocracy of character. Last night, I had my weekly talk with an old gentleman of Bermondsey. He is in a sub-post of the ARP, so old that he cannot be out, but sits there as a kind of dean of good worth. He is a big man who has lived a full life and [has] an easy salty tolerance and a fine observational power. He tells me stories of his observations of birds and small interesting details he has noticed of wild ducks. He details in the same way his remarking of the curious traits of his wife or neighbours. Amused, aloof, yet full of understanding and real cynical loving kindness. He goes into details of the enjoyment three of them got for twenty-five years going for 21 days to Deal on the East Coast for fishing holidays. He is a friendly old man, pipe in mouth & we exchange tobaccos. In this same sub-post are the toughest, roughest crowd of courageous people, who have worked at their ordinary jobs all day and at ARP all night, since September. They would save any man's life & steal any man's property. My greatest pride here is that I can melt into them & sit there & they are natural.

Well, this is about a week later. I have missed Mr Pearson; so here it must go just ordinary and take a long time.

I have a friend from Oxford called Brown. You heard his father[6] deliver [a sermon] at Chalmer's Church [in Kingston]. He is an extraordinarily balanced and nice Canadian whom you may have heard about from Alison. He is a physiologist and an extraordinarily brilliant one at that. He won the Rhodes Scholarship from Queen's the year before me. Bit by bit we have become greater friends and if we both get back to Canada he will be a mainstay and a prop. I am glad I have come to England, but often wish I could get back, good and soon. Then I will build the finest ivory tower the world has ever seen and will set it up and live in it, only to issue from it on the most extreme provocation.

Well, my dear look after yourself. Have a good time and don't work too hard.

Love,
George Grant

Why can't they leave us alone? Last night was worse than before.

1 Thomas Mann (1875–1955), *Lotte in Weimar,* trans. H.T. Lowe-Porter
  (1940)
2 Ernest Hemingway (1899–1961), *For Whom the Bell Tolls* (1940)
3 Marian Anderson (1902–93), American contralto and first black singer at the
  New York Metropolitan Opera (1955)
4 Kirsten Flagstad (1895–1962), Norwegian opera singer; made her triumphal
  debut with the New York Metropolitan Opera in 1935
5 Beniamino Gigli (1890–1957), Italian tenor celebrated for his renditions of
  Verdi's and Puccini's operas
6 Rev. G.A. Brown

46/ To Geoff and Margaret Andrew   42 Tanner Street
                                                      London SE1

Dear Geoff and Margaret,
The other day I wrote you a long letter, but since then a parcel of chocolates arrived, which is so like a gift from the gods that I must thank you both. It was more than generous; it was inspired. I love chocolate and one day I said to Alison I couldn't decide what to do when reaching Canada – either chocolate or scrambled eggs with tomatoes. So you know how much I am grateful. I was going to make this letter only a letter of thanks, but something Herbert Morrison[1] said caught my ear: 'Rational living is here to stay.' However fair, however equal, however noble, my God what a world – life brought down to mediocrity, everybody lowered or raised to a dull, middle-class, robot class. It overcame me with a sense of, however bad it may have been, Florence, with its colour and its vitality, is better than the perfect equality. It is heresy, but it is what one can't help feeling.
    Tonight, with the news.
    Ronnie Knox[2] gave a very well-phrased talk about Chesterton.[3] He didn't say much, but it gave one the knowledge that here was one man greatly influenced by another.
    This morning I walked around a church yard to inspect a D.A. weighing one and a quarter tons.[4] I had heard that they finally got the detonation caps out. I prodded it, kicked it, stuck sticks into it, all amidst the skulls that had been dug out with it – only to find that it was still alive. Never have I seen so large a one still not gone off. They throw entirely grand things around.
    Again, many thanks. My love to Alison & Edward and to you both.
                                                      George Grant

Of course, I would love to be a godfather, now that I have thought about it & so let me know what your plans for the summer are.

1 Herbert Stanley Morrison (1888–1965), Labour MP and cabinet minister in Churchill's national government
2 R.A. Knox (1888–1957), British religious writer and critic
3 G.K. Chesterton (1874–1936), British poet and religious writer
4 A delayed-action unexploded German bomb

47/ To Maude Grant   42 Tanner St, London, SE1

Dear Mother,
Here is a page of a letter I sent you last week, leaving the page cold, stranded in the back of the pad, not knowing what to do with itself. So I send it along to go with the letter for without it it is nothing.

Well, how are you? The war progresses towards some incalculable destination, 'That undiscovered country from whose bourne no traveller returns.'[1] It is like death, the strangest feeling of not knowing (apart from the obvious short[-term] military situation), where England over a long period of time has the advantage, but where in the immediate future Germany seems to have the advantage. Certainly the world, if it be the traveller, can never return to the destination whence it started. The wheels are set in motion down the hill and the car is gaining velocity and going faster and faster. Whether it is going to crash or not depends on whether there is anyone strong enough to put on the very worthless brakes or to control the obsolete steering gear. Oh what a crash. It would be tremendous and sudden like a car. It will be bump, bump, bump, till the car falls to pieces. I see only blackness from Germany and Italy cooperating and although pleasant for all of us Anglo-American capitalism would wreak havoc on the rest of the world. All I care now is that not too much of what I love is pulled down to ruins.

The thing that depresses me is the trust a person like Margaret has in the TLC [Trades and Labour Congress] and Bevin[2] and Morrison. I do not know the ordinary people of this country except in London, but I can see no brave new world coming from them. The Labour council of my borough is corrupt to its very roots and the people in it are either ineffectual or they have lost any sense other than desire to get on, through having to fight so hard to get where they are against snobbishness. The Labour party leaders have a less realistic view of England's position than the Conservatives. Labour does not understand the paradox of its position. It is the Labour movement in a country whose life is based on the incoming dividends into the country from the exploitation of other countries, sometimes by force as in India, sometimes by the threat of force. The Conservatives say, 'We are honestly going to continue that rule by hook or crook.' Labour can't decide whether it believes in economic imperialism and, if it does not, how is it going to support this country without this influx of money from abroad? What is the solution?

Altogether the solution deepens and the only thing is to pursue one's own life to the best of one's ability and let the creature world go far away.

I am reading *The Pickwick Papers* at the moment, a fascinating thing to read when one is living so close to a lot of the world Dickens knew. They are really amusing and it is the only book that has given me any good, friendly laughs. At night now, in the early hours of the morning, I get two to three hours for writing. Do you remember how one laughed at the woman losing her head and the hand still carrying the sandwich? By the way, what did happen to you and Aunt Marjorie on the dock that day? It would be frightful – the worst ignominy of death – to be killed without knowing that.

One of the most fascinating speculations I know is the wondering at the way a bomb can descend &, in the space of a second, destroy even the most intricate, delicately balanced human personality. Not only is the beautiful mechanism of the body torn, ripped, masticated by the tiger-like violence of the high explosive, but the existence of the person knitted with his thoughts, passions, ambitions, inhibitions is destroyed. For a long while the one possibility about the war I could not envisage was the destruction of my own self. It came from a belief that God just wouldn't have the nerve to let my personality [suffer] that. I had [ill.] that was not anything more or less than the world and or me. Yet, now I feel much more objective.

There is a beauty in the country so arresting, so physically compelling, that its colours and shapes are the most wonderful things. If we could only on this June day hunt the cypredium[3] – wander across the rough farmland of near Toronto, Ontario to reach the woods and go across the marsh and through the mosquitoes feeling one was finding more; then suddenly – lovely pink and tall – quiet in the green with an occasional flicker of sunlight making the green enchanted into light.

Today suddenly, before one could guess it, summer had arrived. The sun was out and it was warm and the surprising thing was that everybody was dressed in winter or early spring clothes, instead of the loveliness of girls in summer dresses. Oh, by the way, since Sunday, clothes are rationed. Could you send me for the summer my brown linen jacket and a pair of shoes with crepe soles? It may sound selfish to ask for these; but, where this place was very cold in the winter, it is extremely hot in the summer. The brown linen jacket is the important thing; so please send it as soon as you can.

This letter is dull, but some day we must live again. These last ten months have taught me how to appreciate leisure and comfort and I will never again be the spoiled darling I was before.

Love to Chip and ever more to you.

Love Love Love
George Grant

If it wasn't heretical to write German at the moment I would say that Goethe's '*Kennst du Das Land*'[4] runs through my mind about Otter Lake so often – never will I argue with you that it is not as effective as the French 'Connais-tu le pays?' You as usual are right – it expresses the mood a thousand fold more fully.

Oh, today when summer is arriving, I want to turn once more to Canada, like a silly fluttering bird caught in the cage of his own making wants to fly north to nest in the spring. I wish I could be a scarlet tanager, but one is only a floppy sparrow. Do you know the poem 'L'Invitation au voyage'?[5]

It is amazing how one is attached to one's family. The only long letters I write are to you & Charity & Margaret.

Dear Chip. As I got a letter from you today, I continue.

It reminds me of a quotation: 'This church was built by X in 1653 at a time when all things sacred were being destroyed and profaned throughout the land. X *whose singular praise it was to do the best things in the worst time and to hope for them in the most calamitous.*'

There has been a rather silly book published here called *Black Record* by Sir Robert Vansittart.[6] The accusation, so general against 80,000,000, whoever they are, seems to me absurd. But against a country that in the last hundred years has produced the three great contributors to human thought of the time – Marx, Einstein and Freud – apart from all the rest of its contributions, it seems absurd. The growing misunderstanding of the reason to fight seems to me disastrous.

The thing that this country must learn if it is to survive (one might say if Europe is to survive) is that it is not heaven-endowed to run the world. Even these poor people who have not had the real fruit of the products of empire still have received many of the benefits. Instinctively they believe that they are entitled to run the world. The English have a real belief that they are the salt of the earth. The same belief seems to be growing in America. I hope it doesn't grow, so that the Americans become too self-righteous. There is no consciousness in this country of sins that have been committed as a society; India is just taken for granted. Liking the English so much, it is this quality that I find most depressing.

Goodbye again,
George

1 Shakespeare, *Hamlet* 3.1.79–80
2 Grant wrote 'Bevan,' which would point to 'Nye' Bevan (1897–1960), British Labour MP, in opposition to the government throughout the war. However, I think the reference is to Ernest Bevin (1897–1951), the general secretary of the Transport and General Workers' Union, who entered the government as minister of labour in 1940.
3 In retirement in Nova Scotia, Grant took great pleasure in hunting for these flowers.
4 'Kennst du das Land, wo die Zitronen blühn?
... Dahin! Dahin!
Möcht ich mit dir, o mein Geliebter, ziehn!
[Do you know the land where the lemon trees bloom?
... There! There!
I would go, O my beloved, with you.] (Johann von Goethe, *Wilhelm Meisters Lehrjahre* 3.1.5–6)
5 Grant reproduced the poem in his letter. See Charles Baudelaire, *Les Fleurs du mal*, ed. Yves Florenne (Paris: Le Livre de poche, 1972), 73–4.
6 Robert Vansittart (1881–1957), British diplomat, *Black Record* (1941)

48/ To Maude Grant   42 Tanner St, London, SE1

24 June

Dear Mother,
All news must necessarily be dwarfed by the unbelievable news of the invasion of Russia by Germany. I was coming off duty in the morning when somebody told me and what immediately sprang to my mind is the quotation of Danton's 'C'est nécessaire d'avoir de l'audace et de l'audace et de l'audace et encore de l'audace.'[1] And what audacity those men have. He [Hitler] is a genius of death and hate. Looking at it impartially, he is without doubt one of the few great geniuses of brute force Europe has known. It is useless to try and predict what will happen as even the

most astute political observers, here at least, are gasping. Two things
interest me particularly. One was that Molotov's[2] proclamation to the
Russian people was not based at all on international communist lines, but
completely on old fashioned Russian lines – nationalism openly appealed
to. It is the bug that pervades us. It is, rather than anything else, the driving force, the power that leads us to sacrifice. The second thing that interests me, How are certain elements in this country and in the U.S.A. going
to respond to Russia as an ally? Churchill has never liked Red Russia and
the U.S.A. went mad over Finland, who are now fighting with Germany.
The intelligent working class here, who are good solid British left, are
jubilant, saying it is a people's war at last. The nationalist ones are merely
frankly glad the two dogs are fighting amongst themselves. Since it happened I have not retired to the middle class world and so don't know
what the other people are thinking. I find that generally they think more
clearly than Bermondsey people, but that they think within their own
basic premises and do not go out of that congested area. But the whole
business is so immense and so tragic; yet one is so engulfed by it that all I
do is giggle.

Since writing to you Alison, learning of how much I was interested in
Thomas Wolfe at the moment, gave me, when we met the other day, *Of
Time and the River*.[3] Now that [Hitler] is dealing with Russia, I imagine I
will have time in the nights to get into it. The sad interdependence of the
world is that Odessa's or Moscow's loss is our gain. Since the shattering
blows of May we have had peace and we wondered why. This Russian
manoeuvre is the explanation, but not a satisfactory one.

Well, this is a couple of days later. I have started to read *Of Time and the
River* and how interesting it is, full of the mountainous fault of repetition
and repetition and repetition over and over again. The clichés come back
over and over again, sometimes about the same person, sometimes about
different people. But yet the torrential flood uncontrolled and poured
hectic-wise over page upon page has ten times the lust for life – ten times
the power – [of] the realism of smaller books. It is a great piece of writing. He throws aside other writers' stupid pretensions that they are not
autobiographical and is frankly so. Why hide it then under a false aura of
objectivity? Why afraid of oneself, when it is the end and the beginning, the middle and the substance of all reality?

One myth that I hope someday will be destroyed is the myth I find
everywhere, even in the cool confines of your letters. The myth that the
ordinary man – the working class – the masses (what you will) are the
blameless stooges of selfish scheming. You say, 'Thank God, we are fight-

ing for Bermondsey.' I like to believe that we are fighting, if possible, for the eradication of the hypocrisy of all classes of people. The working class of this country are just as corrupt as the people above them. If they were on top, they would be, in the majority of cases, just as brutal and savage. The saddest thing about Bermondsey people is their ineptitude for true leadership. All their lives they have been ground down and bossed by governor and foreman, [so] that when they have a chance, they get their own back in more than good measure. A friend of mine was, about two months ago, put in charge of a gang near here and, since then, any basis of niceness goes. He is losing all his friends. He admits to me he indulges in all the worst forms of petty [theft], his attitude to everything changes when power is in his hands. Intellectuals & artists believed (you see it in Hemingway) that where life in the industrial world had corrupted those on top economically, those who benefited less materially had not been corrupted. My God, what idealism; here at least it goes too deep. Of course, I only know of a certain type of working class in one country, England; but I know them, in all honesty, very well. Perhaps again it is the perpetual paradox of the English world, that it has been based primarily on exploitation not at home but abroad.

Well, my dear, all my love. I am glad Sarah has gone to the Hellmuths, as it is obvious how much she loves it there.

Again always love
George Grant

1 'It is necessary to have audacity, and audacity and audacity and still more audacity' (George Jacques Danton [1759–94], French revolutionary). In the face of the Prussian army's advance, Danton declared, 'Pour les vaincre, pour les atterrer, que faut-il? De l'audace, encore de l'audace, et toujours de l'audace' (2 September 1792) [To defeat them, to gain ground from them, what is necessary? Audacity, still more audacity, always audacity].
2 V.M. Molotov (1890–1986), Soviet commissar for foreign affairs, 1939–52
3 Thomas Wolfe (1900–38), American novelist, author of *Of Time and the River* (1935)

49/ To Maude Grant   42 Tanner St, London, SE1
21 August

Dear Mum,
Today, down here, a letter came from you – then I went to Alison's to help her in some of the moving business of getting out of 231 Sussex Gardens.[1]

I got one to her. By far the most wonderful news was the pictures from Margaret of her [children], Alison and Edward. Alison is one of the exquisite children of the world. Such lovely exquisite blondness and health and vigour. The way she walks in the picture is so full of independence and so full of strength. Edward, of course, looks more like Geoff than most children look like anything. There is no question that Margaret ever liked the milkman or the grocer's boy. It is Geoff's child with that amazing shaped head. He will be very clever.

Thanks for both your letters. I love them, particularly the part of you being chairman at the civil liberties meeting, and your description of the Greeys.

I am sorry about my letters being cynical and distrustful, but surely the attitude is right. It is: 'We would like to see you, but you oughtn't to come.' Cynicism is not very important. It is, I am afraid, so ingrained that it can't be resisted. It must be the whole basis of one's life. For instance, I am going to try to get into the Navy or the Merchant Marine next week, even though I think it is one of the stupidest, most useless, basest actions I have done. But people expect it; so there one goes. My only revenge (a puritan always needs revenge) will be the privation, frustration & bitterness of the world. It is the strange product of one's life. As Rembrandt once said, 'One is a slave of one's baptism' (my favourite quotation). When young one was given the most luxurious of lives, a fine chance and education, and now one pays the piper, as one has to do futile and terrible things. As to 'spiritual integrity' that is a thing that just doesn't count. One should have realised it ceased to count when the war started.

One thing that is happening that may interest you is what is taking place in Alison. Her whole being is being metamorphosed. She always was a grand person, but she is being so sweet and so kind and more & more feminine.

Several days later –
Yes, the more I think about it, the great regret is not the loss of one's spiritual integrity, but the loss of constant being with one's natural environment, which is the great hope, the only fertile ground, of an artist. In a letter, Elizabeth [Greey] said you once said to her that a Canadian in England is neither 'fish nor fowl nor good red herring.' For me that is not sad. The sad thing is that I am getting accustomed to Bermondsey; it is part of me. My whole being is in the process of metamorphosizing. My God, there is no connection with Canadians when I meet them. I am English; yet within one lurks the Canadian background, and only from

that can anything decent spring – only from that can one live – mess-of-pottage-less. I am becoming part of England and with that becoming one is lost for [the] purpose that one is made for. It is the beginning of a terrible emotional impotence that will eventually leave one sterile and useless. This process is already in progress and yet one cannot prevent it. Yet, you ask for no cynicism.

You now think that this sounds depressed, but to the people here I am a dream of optimism, which is very necessary at the moment, as after the great optimism of the first days of the German-Russian war, there is now a wave of great pessimism. The common person is such an incredible fool; he goes up to the height of happiness over one success or advantage, then down to a too great despair over some loss. There is no sense of balance. They are in the main (and with notable exceptions to the contrary) very unintelligent. There are many good qualities among them and I like many of them, but they are not overpowered by the virtues of the mind. That is the sad plight of this country.

Next day. I have just heard Churchill's magnificent report of his meeting with Roosevelt.[2] He was at the very top of his form and his form is top at any time, but this speech is certainly the best since last summer – these 'Blood, sweat and tears' speeches – and in my opinion the finest of the lot. He doesn't move me as Roosevelt does, but this was once when he was the top of his authority. Apart from the strength of the oratory, what he said was worth saying. He said openly – we – America and England [are] to govern the world after the war and such a government must naturally & obviously be based on force. We set ourselves the task of telling the world how it is to act. I am glad he said this, as it needed saying. The League idea has failed; the Germans are attempting an alternative. We say, and say unequivocally, this is our alternative. I like that spirit in Churchill. Of course, the dreadful difficulties that stand in the way of that government are immense, but what interests me more is – On what basis is that government going to be founded? An interesting piece of political data told me by the person who directs the Indian propaganda in the U.S.A. is that Roosevelt has intended to shelve the great problem of India till the war is over – to forget its difficulties – to forget its implications even more. That seems to point to the fact that he intends to get the job done and then bring up the difficulties. That has its obvious advantages and its less obvious, but just as deep-rooted, disadvantages. Anyway, I prefer to have England and the U.S.A. govern the world than Germany, as long as they do it passably, do not ask too high a price, and do not ask me to govern or help enforce that government when the war is over.

Uncle Burgon is interesting in solving the problem of that depressed young man, George Grant. He wants me to join up – which I am – but he also wants me to send you a cable saying 'Have consulted Alison, Burgon. Am joining up.' The points that stand in the way of such an adequate solution are (1) Alison says she is interested in it, but would not have the presumption to advise me. (2) It doesn't seem important enough to cable – although naturally one adores and longs for one's family – a two year enforced parting makes it all a trifle distant and aloof. In fact, a cable sounds so dramatic over nothing. And how can you possibly advise or be interested as we do not know each other any more? But it is sweet and rather touching to see kind, tolerant Uncle Burgon trying to fathom the neurosis of this young man.

Well, after that complacent gasp, I must say farewell.

Love, as always
George Grant

Please do not write to people that I am depressed. Here one is superficially in perpetual good spirits. Anyway, it is a bore to be always considered depressed.

1 Since both Mary and Elizabeth Greey, whose house it was, had returned to Canada
2 Churchill met with Roosevelt off Placentia Bay, Newfoundland. Their meeting produced the Atlantic Charter, outlining the principles of any peace settlement.

50/ To Maude Grant   42 Tanner St, London, SE1

Dear Mother,

I got a letter from Sheila[1] today saying that she was not sending me food as you said that I can get it from the Red X. Well, I tried and failed; of course, I can't. Your attitude seems to me frankly stupid or else disgraceful. I hope it is only disgraceful.

Yours ever
George Grant

P.S. You seem to have enough for Alison.[2]

1 Sheila (Skelton) Woodworth
2 Reply penned on bottom: 'Regret stupidity about food. Alison's parcel's for

you too. Cable us what you want and where. Parcels now restricted but longing to help. Love GRANT'

51/ To Maude Grant   c/o Mrs Massey, Canada House

Dear Mum,

Yes, it is now nearly two years since we parted on the dock at New York. Two years lying like a long field that one has crossed – parted for two years of such wild events we can hardly know each other again – two years – yet it isn't very long. Sometimes, when I am talking to Alison of you or Charity, I can remember every gesture and it is as if a mere week had passed and, other times, it is as if I remembered you out of some distant past that is gone and which will never be recaptured. Two years so dreadfully long for they are so full, so overflowing, ten times as long as three years at Queen's, a thousand times longer than all my previous life. If the impossible dream materializes and someday, through some odd coincidence I was settled in Canada, then I would never cross the ocean again. Yet, I would not forswear all the friends that I have here now – would not want not to have lived through what one has lived through. Yet, that must be true of everybody – [one is] so made from the life one has lived that one cannot really imagine one's life as taking any other channel.

A letter from Philip [Foulds] the other day. There is no greater cruelty than that of tolerance, patronising and dogmatic in its attempt to be fair. Saying that it would be nice to talk [over] the whole subject of the war. He obviously thinks that it is merely some inane idea about killing that holds one back, not realising that to kill for a purpose seems to me utterly justifiable. The whole subject is so part of all that one has met that his letter is unanswerable. He is a fine, clear, honest person; let's hope he meets with no river of fire to turn him inside out.

Thomas Aquinas once said '*Ad pulchritudinem tria requiruntur – integritas consonantia claritas*'[1] and, although it is easy to form the *integritas* [and] to find the *consonantia*, the *claritas* is the escapable thing, the spark within the beauty that diffuses it with life and power, the motivating force of 'genius.' Perhaps it is the one excuse for beauty.

You wouldn't think that it would take such an infernal amount of difficulty to become a ship boy on a merchant vessel or anything they want me as, but that it does. And heaven upon heavens, it looks as if I may not make it. It had seemed such a perfect glorious means of hiding myself from all eyes till the war is over, a place of hard work and laager from excitement, but a place above all like Douglas's Island where few troubling winds could appal.

I have written so often to you of this, but please remember Aunt Lal's intensely sweet kindness to me, kindness not only of material kind, but of real human, helpful kindness. She and Uncle Vincent had me to lunch today à trois before they started northward for ten days hectic inspection. It was sweet. Both of them were not only feigning interest, but really warm. Aunt Lal has taken real trouble and real thought. It is easier for her to do that for Alison (as she admires Alison), but with me, it is from the bounty of her heart and her love of you. Whatever may happen, I will make that debt up to her and in some small wise return her warmth. They have had a report from the Red X, at last, showing Lionel is well now, but telling how much worse he had been than any of us had guessed. She said to tell you that her letters will be scarce till this term is over, as it will be hectic.

I came across a strange outdated quotation from a speech by Roosevelt in 1936: 'If war should break out in another continent, let us not blink the fact that we should find in this country thousands of Americans who, seeking immediate riches, fool's gold, would attempt to break down or evade our neutrality. They would tell you and, unfortunately their news would get wide publicity, that if they could produce this and that and the other article to belligerent nations, the unemployed of America would find work. It would be hard to resist that clamour. It would be hard for many Americans, I fear, to look beyond, to realize the inevitable day of reckoning that arises from false prosperity. To resist the clamour of that greed if war should come, could require the unswerving support of all Americans who love peace. At this date with the wisdom, which is so easy after the event, were it possible to trace the tragic series of small decisions which led Europe into the Great War of 1914 and eventually engulfed us and many other nations. We can keep out of war, if those who watch and decide make certain that the small decisions of each day do not lead to war and if, at the same time, they possess the courage to say "no" to those who selfishly or unwisely would let us go to war.'[2] Oh, brave new world – or did you read it?[3]

London is an amazing conglomeration of desires. It has no unity; yet a great cohesion that binds it together, so that each section, each atom of each section, is bound up to all other atoms. The terrific organism, which had no purpose, which showed itself only in queer kaleidoscopic pictures gradually settles itself as one gets to know it better into an enormous formless heart, so that the streets of Chelsea are connected with Russell

Square and the squares of Mayfair, even with the courts of Bermondsey. Yet, if one judged a city by the standard of integration, London would not be large. Only small sections of it are integrated; yet the whole is pulled together not by the river, not by a thought, not by a road, but [by] a terrible economic purpose that lies subconscious in most Londoners' minds. This city is the capital of a great empire and it serves that empire efficiently, sometimes even wisely, and it is not a beautiful luxuriant centre of the world. Rome, Paris, New York are imperial cities. London (though I like it best of all) is not. I often wonder if the city would and ever will bear the terrible disintegration of industrialization. I am not one of those futile, bloodless creatures who preach a return to the middle ages. Economically, we have taken industrialism and we can't support a half of the world's population [without it]. But we certainly haven't learnt to control it. The boys and girls I know in London whose work has no coordination with the rest of their lives (who, after a tiring day in their factory, seek escape in the movies, or alcohol, or the less productive experiments of sex) are merely typical of the fact that there has been no kind of adjustment to keep the individual in line with the changes of the industrial world. The family has been broken up as an economic unit, but there is little communal unity. It is a strangely savage and sordid city at the moment with our fellow countrymen leading the bacchanalia around Piccadilly, with all the furies of a war-torn country heaped on top of one another, so that they could not miss the eye. Yet, with this new fury, the old charm remains. There are still ducks in the park – still stately, grey houses and lovely trees – still the even measured tread of the ordinary, middle class clerk – the backbone as usual. Yes, it is a strange city and I like it, but not in the way that we like one's own. Not with that knowledge that one gets that this is [a] place you do not possess, for it possesses you. Without it you are a sounding brass and a tinkling cymbal,[4] a creature who echoes against nothing. Very rarely does one feel it. Yes, many look for it, far from where they were born, wanting it so imperatively that they spend their talents and their life to find it. I don't think women do want it in the same way as men because women make their home where they are in that wonderful acceptance of things, but men can only feel, or not feel, that their home is there. This is not all foolishness. Take, for instance, when driving through England, Alison and Mary Greey could say, 'I would like to live there,' dreaming of a family in a house, a fine husband and a full life. It just wouldn't strike me for, however glorious a wife, whatever peace and calm, I just wouldn't dream of living there.

You always say, write of what I do. How can I? Doing, to me, is always in relation to people and you do not know the people that I know. You cannot conjure up the intimacies and thousand knowledges of some people who I know so well. In this interval, I write all morning and all afternoon, read in the evening or else roam these long, dark, blacked-out streets wandering, talking to strangers, prying into new corners; or else go to see a friend and wander with him through the city. The fact is that the wandering supplies a natural curiosity, and also exercise, after the life of sitting at a desk all day. Who are my friends? Somehow some of my best friends are in London at the moment. One young lad of nineteen, waiting in London to be called up in the artillery, is being a statistician at the Ministry of Works. His name is Lance[5] and he is a man of Kent to his very stolid, patient backbone. At the same time, he is one of the most brilliant economists Balliol has ever had. Another is Richard Ghiselin, whom you helped pick, working at the Ministry of Mines with one of my old professors. Ghiselin – charming, erudite, hard working, but unfortunately much lamer than he was, having to go into hospitals with increasing pain in his thigh, but a civilized human being, in the vanguard of the Morrison movement. We have one thing in common by being joint sufferers at Noverings. He tried hard and loved a great deal and did a lot, but once when he was down there he went for walks and talked late with a girl staying there at the same time (perfectly innocent) only to get a shattering letter of Mrs Buck's, probably dictated by Aunt Margaret, saying things about that was not the kind of conduct they would have expected from a Parkin Scholar – quite naturally dumbfounded, it naturally helped knock the props out of any affection. Oliver[6] came to town for a week's leave. He is a Balliol and Eton boy (whose father[7] is an armament king – before and during the war). Oliver should have been a guard's officer but instead is a tough little private having refused a commission; he is one of the radical organizers in the British army. He knew he couldn't accomplish anything as an officer; so he is a private. It is hard for him, naturally, to be bossed and bullied by his inferiors, but takes it without a word. Then, as well, there are Alison's friends, whom I see occasionally. Alison is so kind, so sweet – so [lambkin presh] – a source of such warmth.

   Strictly confidential (not to be mentioned to a soul, not even our beloved Charity). Mary Greey wrote terribly disappointedly, almost in tears, of Elizabeth's inability to grasp at all the love and affection that had brought her home. Feeling that Elizabeth wanted her not to be in her way and that Elizabeth thought Mary was dodging the war (instead of the fact that it killed Mary to leave her life in London). But (and here is the more important thing) Mary obviously will turn more and more upon Mike [Pearson]. All I want to say is, understand and try and help. If you have ever seen Mary and Mike together you would know how absolutely suited they are for each other and how each adores the other. They are both far too fine to ever let it interfere with his children and wife, but please try to understand it and make it a natural easy thing. If you mention this to anybody else, may you be doomed to an earlier demise from dropsy.

All love, my duck. Remember always to remember Aunt Lal. Love to the family.

As always,
George Grant

I do not mention the war in Russia. It is a cloud, as the whole war, which stands over us all. At the moment the horror is not here, but do not think us insensitive if we do not write of it.

1 'Nam ad pulchritudinem tria requiruntur. Primo quidem integritas, sive percetio, qaue enim diminuta sunt, hoc ipso turpia sunt; et debita poroportio sive consonantia; et iterum claritas, unde quae habent colorem nitidum pulchra esse dicuntur' [Beauty must include three qualities: integrity or completeness, since things that lack something are thereby ugly; right proportion or harmony; and brightness. We call things bright in colour beautiful] (St Thomas Aquinas [1224?–74], *Summa theologica* 1a.39,8).
2 F.D. Roosevelt, 'Address at Chautauqua, N.Y.,' 14 August 1936
3 Aldous Huxley, *Brave New World* (1932)
4 St Paul's discourse on charity, 1 Corinthians 13.1
5 The name is very unclear in the letter. It *could* be Ronald Louis Peverell (1922–), from Bromley, Kent.
6 Oliver Wrightson later held a commission in the Coldstream Guards.
7 Sir Thomas Garmondsway Wrightson, Bt

Under remorseless pressure, especially from Mrs Buck, to do his duty to king and country, Grant buckled and decided to join up. His options, as he saw them, were the Royal Navy or the Merchant Marine. Either, in his view, represented a betrayal of his pacifist principles. He opted for the Merchant Marine because he thought that he was most likely to serve there with the kind of people he had come to know and love in Bermondsey.

52/ To Maude Grant   c/o Canada House
                                                          [November 1941]

Dear Mum,

Well, here I am, having left Bermondsey and about to go into the merchant navy. It is strange how suddenly one is out of one thing and into the
next. I was terribly sorry to leave Bermondsey, but that is over now; so one
goes on to the next. Life carries on from the first stage and to the second;
yet the first disappears before one arrives at the second. Anyway, I believe
that the merchant navy may carry me to Canada, which would be terrifically exciting. If it happened that one was to land in Montreal, or some
place like that, I would telegraph you and we could meet. It would be
overwhelming and let's hope it comes off. At the moment I feel as if one
will never see Canada again and it is like a dream to find that one may
find it a lot sooner. If I do land on Canadian soil, we must try and meet
for however short a moment, for ever since we said goodbye on that dock
in New York I have longed to see you. People who say they have seen you
drive me almost crazy with jealousy. I have a lovely cigarette case Aunt Lal
gave me for my 21st birthday and in it I used to keep a picture of F.D.R.
and the matches case from the Swedish restaurant, now only the matches.
My political faith may waver, but never my individual.

Passing a book shop I saw a small book of John Dewey[1] on education.
They are a collection of his essays written about 1900 on education.[2] As
they are general, they still bear reading as a creed for progressive liberal
education. I meant to read them and then send them air to you, but find
that one can only send books direct from a book shop. The first essay on
'His Pedagogic Creed' is the complete justification written well of
Father's life. In general, it is a fine and clear expression of all that Daddy
worked and strove for. As Dewey says, the educator is the greatest of all
artists. When I was younger I often wondered why Daddy gave up a brilliant academic career for teaching. This is the answer, and coming on top
of work in Bermondsey; it is the complete answer.

The book of Canadian poetry you gave me interested me a lot, but disappointed me more. Except for some of E.J. Pratt's[3] lines the rest of the
poetry was weak. I love and admire cynicism and doubt and disbelief but
dislike pessimism. Why should the poets of a young expanding country
like Canada be pessimistic? Why do they ally themselves with the defeatism of Auden[4] and Eliot[5] of this country instead of the hope of the
U.S.A.? Their tradition should be that of Sandburg.[6] Frank Scott[7] derives
his from an American poetess of the 19th century called Emily

Dickinson[8] to an almost unbelievable extent, but his form of thought is European. His poems are pleasant, but not much more.

Without forcing myself to be North American, my whole mental being is caught up in that tradition. In philosophy, my favourite philosophers are William James[9] and John Dewey, Frank Lloyd Wright[10] in his buildings or writings stirs me. Thomas Wolfe or Faulkner[11] in writing move me. Robert Frost[12] or Hart Crane[13] in poetry. It isn't a feeling I push upon myself; it is one that just seems to come. I hope that I survive the war to be able to contribute to that tradition & bring Canada more into line with it, but that is something one will just have [to] wait and find out.

Young people are fools; we always have to learn each lesson for ourselves. You and Daddy had taught me good lessons about drink and I am only now learning how good they are. Last winter, after one was sometimes dog-tired, I would go into the pub to get some whiskey, so that one would be bright and gay for the rest of the night, something to carry me over the hard events. Since the difficulties ceased I continued the practice and came rather to depend on it, not to any dangerous extent, but just something that was an enjoyable escape. Now, I have decided to call a halt. The exaltation that it gives one is too transitory, too incomplete and deprives one of real natural mental exhilaration.

I am glad to hear what you and Margaret write of Hugh Slaght. If he has chosen what he is to be, I am glad; he is going to be good at it. It isn't my choice. It doesn't seem altogether to be a wise choice but, anyway, he seems to be doing it in a big way and an interesting way. If we are going to have big capitalists, let's have good ones and let's have people who don't putter around on the edge, but are either in or out. I like the fact that Hugh is going to do it well. It makes me respect him where I will have little respect for the friend who putters around on the edge, making a good living, but hardly his own master and hardly competent enough to be more than a stooge. I can think of so many of my friends who will be small time. Hugh won't be that. He knows, to a far greater extent than a lot of the boys, what he is after; so more power to him.

Russia – Russia. Russia is on everybody's lips here. Their entry into the war and their present continuance in the war are having profound effects on this country. It is far too premature to estimate or weigh these effects, which will depend a great deal on what the Russian resistance continues to be like, but even if they don't hold out already the feeling is enormous. Yesterday I was at Hyde Park speaking grounds for the first time in ages and every political speaker (that is every speaker with a large crowd) was talking about Russia. Russia all the time. More and more it seems to me that the key economic strata in this country at the moment are the lower and median middle class and I know very little about them. Up to now they have solidly (except for a negligible fringe) backed the upper middle class, but are they going to continue to that seems to be the crucial factor that will continue throughout the coming years. There are so many currents such as empire and foreign affairs – markets and individual leaders that bear on the subject that it is premature to more than touch the subject, but it is one of vital importance.

My great gloom of August is gradually shifting and my way and potentialities seem clearer. One moves ahead. Discipline and steadiness of purpose are needed and let's hope I have the chance to get them.

The other day the nicest letter come from Minnie Gordon[14] – so sweet of her to have written it – one from Ernie and one from the beloved Cline. He is a boy from Indiana who worked his way through Harvard [and] won a scholarship to Oxford, where we were great friends. He is a short, tough, bear-like creature. He was the only American I met at Oxford who had the rugged American strength combined with real depth. His letter in the spring was depressed, as he thought he would have to give up teaching to get a more lucrative job to support his mother (as his father had died), but his latest was jubilant, as he had won a junior fellowship at Harvard, could support his mother and had also got married to his beloved girl. So that was swell.

Now, my love this dissertation must stop as it is well past midnight. Alison in swell form; so love and love and love and more love.

Yours as always,
in saecula saeculorum,
George Grant

Perhaps we may see each other. Oh clouds unfold.[15]

1 John Dewey (1859–1952), American philosopher and educational theorist. Grant later attacked his views on progressive education.
2 John Dewey, *Educational Essays* (1910); Dewey was also author of *The School and Society* (1900).
3 E.J. Pratt (1882–1964), Newfoundland-Canadian poet
4 W.H. Auden (1907–73), Anglo-American poet and essayist, author of *The Dog beneath the Skin* (1935), *The Ascent of F6* (1936), and *On the Frontier* (1938)
5 T.S. Eliot (1888–1965), American-born poet, author of *The Waste Land* (1922) and *The Hollow Men* (1925)
6 Carl Sandburg (1878–1967), American poet, winner of a Pulitzer Prize (1950)

7 F.R. Scott (1899–1985), poet, professor of constitutional law at McGill, and one of the founders of the CCF; a close friend of both Louise and Raleigh Parkin

8 Emily Dickinson (1830–86), American poet whose lyrics were often spiritual

9 William James (1842–1910), American philosopher and psychologist. His philosophy was called pragmatism and emphasized the relative nature of truth and the importance of human freedom.

10 Frank Lloyd Wright (1867–1959), American architect; creator, among others, of 'Falling Water' outside Pittsburgh

11 William Faulkner (1897–1962), American novelist and winner of the Nobel Prize for literature in 1949

12 Robert Frost (1874–1963), American poet and professor of English, winner of Pulitzer Prizes in 1924, 1931, and 1937

13 Hart Crane (1899–1932), American poet

14 Professor Wilhemina Gordon, Department of English, Queen's

15 William Blake, *Jerusalem*

When Grant finished his training, he presented himself for a physical examination, preparatory to joining his ship. The examination revealed tuberculosis, a disease that was often fatal. Elizabeth Greey had returned to Canada suffering from the same illness. The following letter describes his disappearance but does not mention the TB, likely because Grant wanted to spare his mother the news. He ended up working on a farm, in part because without a ration card, it was the only way to get food. One morning, a few days after the Japanese bombed Pearl Harbor, Grant was riding his bicycle along a country road early in the morning on his way to perform his farm work. He opened a gate to walk his bicycle through. By the time he had passed through the gate, he believed in God finally and irrevocably. It was the defining moment of his life.

53/ To Maude Grant   13 December

Dear Mum,

It is a long time since I wrote to you, probably the longest time ever, but there is a reason and it is better to tell the long story.

In October of this year – it seems completely like another life it is so long ago – I was accepted for the merchant navy & for two weeks was on a training ship learning how to be a sailor – well you may not know it, but the way it is worked in the merchant navy is that you have your medical exam just before you sign on for a ship – well, that is what happened to me and, after being trained & said goodbye to everybody & having been given scarfs &

having bought oilskins & everything, I was turned down medically. I couldn't go back; so I just went to Liverpool & tried to get a ship unofficially & got a temporary job on demolition through some friends whose son had been at Oxford with me. My evenings spent haunting the docks & everything; of course, it was impossible in war time – so I gave up at last & now have a job on a farm – when I am strong and well again I will try again. That is that, from beginning to end a completely uninspiring story. Of course, I did not understand that people would be wondering where I was, but last night I came to London & saw & told Alison. The strange thing to me is as always the fact of how far one travels. Three years ago I had just won a Rhodes scholarship & was in Toronto having a good time. It is not a journey that one could call up or down; it is merely to a different plane of existence. Spiritually, it has been so far that it is as if it wasn't the same person who started out. (Please do not write to Alison or the Masseys or say to anyone in Toronto, particularly not the Macdonnells or Andrews that you are worried about me. There is no fear for my mental health, as just recently I feel as if I had been born again.) Gradually, I am learning there are unpredictable tremendous forces – mysterious forces within man that are beyond man's understanding driving him – taking him along courses and [over] which he has no or little control. Sorry to write much of myself, but to whom would I write it to but you? There, for instance, is one of the mysterious forces in action. Though mentally & in experience & mental understanding one or two of my friends over here have much more in common with me than you have – yet there is some unpredictable bond between us that makes it, so that I would throw the whole wonderful lot of them overboard for any of my family at a moment's notice.

I really have a very remarkable lot of friends in England. One[1] I have never described to you & who is an interesting specimen I will describe to you now as his father is very much in the picture at the moment. He is the son of Sir Somebody Self.[2] The father is Beaverbrook's absolutely No. 1. A businessman, but like what I imagine Morris Wilson[3] is – a man who is more interested in the necessity of intelligent argumentation than in his immediate profit. He started at 10/- a week & has got to the top taking time off to become a doctor of theology & a cultivated human being. His son, whom I got to know at Balliol, is tall, like a crow as I remember him in his enormous billowing gown & undoubtedly the mental giant of any of my friends, English or Canadian or American, terrific in the facility he can tackle any problem & with the quality of thoroughness that so often doesn't go with facility. He & the other boy[4] (who was my greatest friend in England the one I told you about who is in Wandsworth prison) were so much ahead of me intellectually that it was funny when we spent long hours living 'in triumvirate' as one might say. The only possible thing I could contribute was a kind of intuitive sense that came from too highly geared feelings.

Well, the whole world is in it now. We gave the Japanese western industrial civilization &, heavens, are they using it. It is very much the clash of two great spheres of economic power clashing head on, but one's mind & heart can only be on one side. The people for whom I have the greatest admiration at the moment are the Russians. They tried for ages to keep out of the war, but now they are fighting with the kind of tenacious courage that always seems to me most deserving of belief. The thing in Tolstoy that always stuck out for me was the old general Kutuzov who stuck out & saved Russia far more than the Europeanized tsar. What we all forgot about Russia (& particularly the writers pro & con forgot) is that they are *sui generis*, that the standards of our civilization just don't apply to theirs, that our ideas of the world moving forward in the liberal way just don't mean very much to them. They have their own that are as valid for them as ours are for us.

Chippy's letters are of great interest. I suppose the reason I feel closer to her now than Margaret is that like myself she is still in a state of becoming while Margaret has become (strictly private).

Before the merchant navy episode, I saw Peter Macdonnell. I admired him immensely although we have little in common. He lectured me on what the English people were really like. It is the kind of audacity of laying down the law left & right that only the extrovert has. I made a few qualifying remarks to some of his general statements, which he didn't listen to. Yet, when he was talking about Canadian politics, which he knew something about, he was extremely intelligent.

I went out to see the parents of my great friend in prison. They are the most middle of the middle class & so fine. They are stunned & uncomprehending of what has happened, but he is their son & they are proud of him. The old man who worked from 14 onwards & has founded a milk distributing centre for the suburbs is bewildered & sad. Yet, with a tolerant & triumphant pride that won't do anything, but stick up for a son he doesn't quite understand. Gosh, I admired the parents & saw the real nobility of them as I never had before.[5]

Look after yourself, don't work too hard, don't worry about me & let's hope that everything may yet turn out.

Love,
George Grant

It must seem to you that being alone & being solitary for two months nearly has made me verbose. Sorry.

During the time alone I have been thinking over the lessons of what I experienced in Bermondsey & the main lesson it seems to me was the fact that, although we have created a great industrialized world, it hasn't become positive for many. The boys & girls I knew in Bermondsey didn't see much connection between their work & their lives. There was a boy I knew intimately – a regular down & outer – tough, dishonest – thieved, couldn't keep a job. When he went into the RAF he found something to which he could apply himself & when I saw him on leave he had become a good fellow. He had found in the war something to put his heart into he had never found in peace. This country will just have to find it after the war.

Alison is an angel; that is the only word for her, so kind & sincere. The girl, Kay Moore, who lives with her, is in the midst of some trouble & she told me that Alison is the person who makes life possible. She has certainly been so fine to me that words are useless to describe the debt of love I owe her.

1 Peter Self (1919–), a lifelong friend, later a journalist with the *Economist* and a professor of public policy at the London School of Economics
2 Sir Henry Self, KCB, KCMG, KBE
3 Morris Wilson (1883–1946), Canadian businessman, president of the Royal Bank of Canada
4 Peter Clarke
5 Peter Clarke credited Grant's visit with reconciling him and his parents.

1942

54/ To Maude Grant

c/o Mrs Massey
Canada House
Trafalgar Square, London
3 January

Dear Mum,
Alison forwarded me a note you had sent – it was lovely. It is ages since I had a real letter from you and if you have time I would love it, as there are

none I would rather get, and I remember the wonderful, fat ones that used to come.

There was one phrase in your letter that appalled me and it is probably owing to what it stirred in my brain that you get so prompt a reply. The first stricture I must make is that, do not say to others, 'Oh, George wrote me such a critical letter,' because that is false and creates such a nasty impression. The phrase was 'You will have been thrilled, despite yourself, by the entry of the U.S.A. into the war.' The only words to describe that it seems to me is that you must think I am a fool or else I must have turned my face away from God. If you want to know my sensations they were the following. For three days I really almost was on the point of suicide, certainly nearer than I have ever been or ever hope to be. It just didn't seem worthwhile to struggle for that spreading of the war almost guaranteed in my mind the triumph of all that I had hoped would not conquer. The Japs have gone mad. To substantiate what I have said would take reams of paper & a lot of time. I haven't either, but someday I will give you a book on it, *deo volente*.[1] The saddest part of the phrase is, of course, that it is indicative of the fact that we have not seen each other for too long.

12 January. This letter has lain in the writing pad for nine days and reading it now I understand how badly expressed it is. Let me try again. Obviously the entry of America into the war makes it almost certain on top of the tremendous resistance of Russia the elimination of the evil power of Hitler's military might, but in doing that it brings 130,000,000 more people into the war, an experience which will only create greater ill will, greater misunderstanding that will take them farther from the face of God. It may [help] (in fact, it is almost certain) to establish the Anglo-American *pax*, but will that be much nearer to God than the other alternatives? Some kind person sent me the report (as I told you previously of the report of the Canadian-American conference). That seemed to me a fine conference technically, but did practically anyone understand what other parts of the world would feel about the establishment of Anglo-Saxon civilization? We have just presumed that our standards fit others that ours are the best, that other people can find their God through our way of life. We have created God in the image of our own wills. As some great man said, 'We have made Him a tame confederate of our petty adventurings.'

Well, how are you? I have no idea what life at Prince Arthur Ave must be like, as Ernie wrote to me he met you and you said you were doing nothing except – and then you catalogued a million interesting things. What about Sarah? Do you ever see the Attlecks or Mrs Drury or the Mac-Dermotts, Miss Arnoldi? What about Terry? How are Margaret and Geoff? How is Chip, whose letters are a great joy?

Whenever I think that I am a complete rat, I remember what nice friends I have and it makes one think one may have something in one after all. Malcolm Brown, for instance, who got the R.S. from Queen's the year before me (and whom I never even knew at Queen's) is now as intimate as anybody I have ever known. Interestingly enough (and very very confidentially) he was engaged to Mary Mundle who Alison lives with at the moment. He is a brilliant physiologist and has the leading job (as far as I can gather from outside jobs) that Oxford has to offer for young medicos. Yet, so unlike most Canadian doctors, he has a profound interest in politics and does what so few doctors do applies mental discipline in thinking outside his work as well as in it. But more important he is interested in beauty and the good life. We both agree that the first R.S. from Queen's, Gordon Davoud,[2] is a burden, but Brown is tops and will be a great Canadian. Tell that to any Rhodes choosers that they chose the tops. His father is the minister at Chalmer's church in Kingston.

The fate of the third R.S. they chose is at the moment slightly in limbo, but out of all the confusion of the autumn I have risen newer and surer. One grows and at least out of all the terrible confusion that the world has experienced for fifty years & which one has experienced; at last some gleam of understanding, some power seems to appear.

Don't be worried about Mrs Buck. Of course, I will write to her and have written; it is just without feeling. I bequeath her to Peter. Cynically, may he do as well as I did, without the hurt on both sides.

'One loves not as one wants, but as one must.'[3]

Give my love to everybody who might possibly he interested.

Love, as always,
George Grant

P.S. It is fascinating to think of Philip [Foulds] married. Let's hope they will be as happy as they deserve.

1 God willing. Grant would sometimes abbreviate it as 'dv.'
2 J.G. Davoud (1916–); graduated from Queen's in 1937 and received his D.Phil. from Oxford in 1941.
3 Possibly a reference to Christopher Marlowe: 'It lies not in our power to love, or hate, / For will in us is over-rul'd by fate' (*Hero and Leander. First Sestiad*, ll 167–8).

With the help of Vincent Massey and Edward Peacock, Grant secured passage on a ship and returned home to Canada and his mother to recuperate from his tuberculosis and his emotional strain.

1942

55/ To Maude Grant

87 Forest Hill Road[1]
Toronto
[autumn 1942]

Dear Ould and Gentle Heart,

How was the journey? The pretence must be kept up, as I have lied black and blue and had a serious conversation begun by Aunt Marjorie about how far you were going on your gas and then, worse for worse when I tried to leave a gap open, saying that it would be nice to take gas in a can 'Oh you can't do that, just can't do that these days.' So there it is; it must be locked up, squeezed from all openings etc. You would be spat on as a moral leper if the story was told.

How is O'Hara? Why say more, enumerate, list out a series of questions that can be summed up in that one sentence?

How foolish, how unutterably foolish we were to think that staying was possible. How ghastly we are in our tragic misconceptions over family as if we had been spawned (as it were, thought of, conceived, born, baptised, weaned and grown up) upon hopeless, tragic, silly misunderstandings of situations. A kind of blind (not optimism), but just not premeditating enough, so that one is in the situation before one knows what it is and then one is left there not in terribleness, but just the unutterable wrongness.

If I had given it but two minutes thought, I would have known it was just unutterably wrong to have come here. But I didn't and, therefore, it is here and one must spend hours, first of regret and then of trying to get out of it.

Of course, the thing is that one is living in Toronto sans you, which is sans everything.

Don't be discouraged however; I really am enjoying it here.

Yesterday, absolutely terrible news came through. My beloved Mrs Lovett and her son have been caught stealing. Their sentence is not [pronounced] yet; they were out on bail. The husband would not support her and she found her expenses mounting. I have been criminally negligent not to have sent her any money. Do you know anything I own I could sell? That is saleable? Nobody seems to want my mind; so perhaps the only alternative is my body.

This is a gloomy letter, but we seem doomed for gloom. This war, this war and we sit here thinking we can have a war and not pay for it. Do you realise this woman with her family have been smashed by the war? The people who never got anything from the peace are destroyed in every way by the whole process of war and the high and mighty, the propagandists, the safe, can get up and say: 'Oh war, oh wonderful for freedom.'

You know that family is in my heart, for they proved one thing to me that you can't help loving people, if they love you.

This is all round a very private letter, particularly about Mrs Lovett. So don't go spreading it around. The trouble is there is no responsible person to trust. Alison would just be a middle-class bitch about the whole thing. Aunt Lal aussi. I am writing to Burgon. God, when it comes down to a pinch how few people one can trust. Do write, if you can, of anything I can sell; the gold watch; Leo's gold sovereign; the Canterbury psalter; the few things I own. Because they mean absolutely nothing to me beside Mrs Lovett, who, quite truthfully, saved my life. They possessed me with their love, for it was just there, not wanting anything.

Don't talk about this, for Alison or the rest of the cheap minds would say 'Merely a woman who was George's mistress' or something as foolish as that. Not realising that love is quite a different thing, that we can love people without having the one relationship they feel is the real one.

Don't be distressed about the Macdonnells; it really is fine here. But do write of Mrs Lovett.

Love,
George

1 The home of the Macdonnells

Grant began to keep a handwritten journal. Like most would-be diarists, he started enthusiastically, but the entries eventually become fewer and peter out finally about Christmas.

56/ Journal Entry   21 October 1942

Last night in the interval of mental wandering before sleep I decided to keep a journal, partly for the sake of recording events, but mostly for the practice in permanence it would give me, the discipline. So here it is; I don't know what caused the mood last night, but it was as if suddenly the sickness that had enveloped me since 1940 was over. I knew that all the usual weakness of character – frustrations – etc. would continue. God, how can one conquer them, but that the utter sense of defeat was given? Was the mood temporary? What caused it? Was it sexual? Was it the people who had been in for the evening? Youth. One can ask oneself the next morning all the doubting negative questions about it, but at the time it was peace beyond peace, calm beyond calm. I looked out of the window at the Park Plaza[1] rising above us with its pattern of lights on the back & side – at the trees – blowing their leaves in the moonlight – the amber yellow chestnut leaves almost within reach out the window – all rustling so close. It was as if I hadn't looked out the window since early spring & then now it was autumn – all the slowness of change having not been seen – I did not see it, therefore, as something slow organic – inevitable, but the terrible change from life to the beginning of death. Well, anyway, it does fill one with a glorious sense of rest – of having thrown off the sickness – the first sane & peaceful moment since June 1940 – or I suppose May 1940, the first moment of life's overpowering worthwhileness since the February [1]7th episode 1941 – a year and a half to feel like that. Is it real, or is it a romantic stewing in the guise of one's sorrow to take so long to recover? Why does one learn to depend on a person like that? Was it that she gave me sexual peace & a sense also of real manhood for the first time & then to find it broken into by the shocking suddenness & worse completeness of death? Anyway, it was wonderful to think it is over as a destroying force, the part of one it has corroded into is still there, but it can corrode no farther. But what a bastard I have been in the last year, emptiness, sleeplessness, the grossest animalism, then even worse emptiness & finally a long illness. Really, if there was some way of recording one's thanks to older people? Mrs Lovett, Aunt Lal – Mother – Brown-Pooh. Sarah. Joan A[rnoldi], but, of course, 3/4 Mrs Lovett. On the other hand it is better not to record one's bitterness at the people who

have not fathomed one, who have just plainly let one down – Alison,
Peter, Morin, Margaret. Anyway, one is reborn & I hope it comes to something.

1 Grant's bedroom looked out onto the back of the Park Plaza Hotel at the corner of Bloor Street and Avenue Road in Toronto.

57/ Journal Entry   26 October

Have felt lousy all day, bad tempered, tired & headachy, interspersed with
periods of glory when all I could do was to chant the romantic theme
from the 2nd movement of Tchai. 5th. But a totally unproductive three
days; this had been just blank. One pays & pays & pays. But one learns. I
looked out into the garden this morning, a typical late autumn garden,
leaves everywhere and the beds full of foliage that was tired. But tomorrow I will & must wake to work, no thought of anything else. Mrs Agnes
Macd. in, *still* in widow's weeds after years & with the white – dead looking
skin of one who had fed on her grief. Mother is so different – her grief is
immense – she is always talking not only of Father, but what a bitch life
has been for her, but her grief has not acted like a fester within her –
amusing & beautiful letter from Mrs Lovett.

58/ Journal Entry   31 October

I read something about *War & Peace* by Eddie McCourt,[1] hopelessly inadequate, hopeless misunderstanding of its depth, talking of it simply as an
allegory of the present conflict. Even in English W & P is the greatest symphony in the world, the opening themes of society & the family at home,
weaving up to the early battles. The intricate personal themes woven in to
each other & woven into the whole. The crashing & the thunder of the
battles, the terribleness of the fall of Moscow. To me, the greatest theme is
Kutuzov[2] – the old – duty – novel-reading, old, old Russian – like the
earth itself – like the force that drives the Volga. Berated first by the talk-
ers because he retreats – berated finally because he will only beat the
enemy & drive them out of Russia, no farther. He is past pleasure & past
pain. The noblest portrait in literature. Of course, after the tumult & the
shouting, comes the wonderful peace of the family life – like a great
placid theme from Bach & then the end, the discourse on history, on
God, on history, on man in God – on life itself & more than life – the
most profound yet simple – beautiful, yet overwhelmed by the conscious-

ness of sin – optimistic yet founded on the rock of little hope. As he says somewhere in it, the point about life is to live it despite its misery & unhappiness, misery & unhappiness even if it is not one's own fault. Of course, it would be the master's[3] favourite book.

1 E.A. McCourt (1907–72), Irish-born novelist and English professor; he had taught at UCC during 1936–8 and was, at the time, professor of English at the University of Saskatchewan.
2 General in charge of Russian forces
3 A.D. Lindsay

59/ Journal Entry   1 November

One thing that is consistently forgotten among leftists of a certain class, the Anglophobe leftists, is that English imperialism is not the only side to the life of England, and that English capitalists have performed almost as great an exploitation within their own country as without, that the average Englishman has had little benefit from the empire other than fighting to maintain it, that the average Englishman (& by that I mean the average income group £3/10 etc.) has had little of the economic benefit of the empire. Take Joe Penney.[1]

1 A friend in Bermondsey

60/ Journal Entry   2 November

The bairns[1] were here today. Alison so excited with a pink dress. Before she had always worn blue; so today she was thrilled in pink. As soon as she came in she unbuttoned her coat except for the button at her throat, pulled the coat sideways and said 'Look at Kitten's new dress.' It is one of those small children's frocks that come up cottonish and is hard to keep straight. She was very proud of the whole business and was just like an older woman in her showing it off, except (one) she was much more excited externally and made no effort to hide her excitement (two) unlike older women, she was just excited about her dress, however it was, and insisted on her underwear showing down her arms instead of being hidden by the puff on her sleeves. I said 'Turn round and show me the back'; and so anytime anybody else – Mother or Sarah – wanted to see the dress, she would turn round, graceful and extremely feminine and her face smiling and expectant, looking over her shoulder to see how the admirer is admiring. They are such dear children because Eddie is so masculine and Alison so feminine, so intrinsically feminine. Ed careening around the room, pushing over everything, stumbling, wanting, with an intense physical want, to eat or to play. He will be an extraordinary child with this intense physical motivation and intensity of feeling. When he smiles his fat pudgy Russian face breaks into a smile completely irresistible, when he cries he really cries. He was playing behind the mirror with Margaret (who admires him) and there was a great deal of laughter from Margaret and him. 'Where's guffinkus, where's guffinkus?' and then roars of laughter. Then suddenly he banged his head, his fat face went blank for a moment, then began to pucker up, his underlip went forward on sadness and he went and laid his head against Margaret's knee for maternal healing. Kitten's smile so sweet and heart-touching its gentle feminineness, Ed's is like the sun; he just grins. Yet, although Ed is the more powerful of the two, Kitten will be the harder one to bring up. She is the moody one; she is the turbulent one emotionally: 'I won't, I want, I don't want to go here, I want to say goodbye.' Eddie's grief is less intense.

Listened to Toscanini[2] conducting the *Rhapsody in Blue*[3] with Benny Goodman[4] playing the solo clarinet – evidently asked by Toscanini to do it – an amazing performance – glittering – blatant, colourful – all the qualities that Gershwin wanted in it. It is strange that the best performance of such a wildly American piece of music should be given by a European, but, I guess, technique [ill.] he can just get what he wants from the orchestra. Beside it, the Brahms 4th[5] by the NY Philharmonic under Bruno Walter[6] was mediocre. Goodman was amazing on the clarinet – it was like a wild shriek of New York's triumphant life. What genius of Toscanini to ask him.

Last night England & particularly Bermondsey was deeply in my thoughts – Mrs Lovett & Ellen – it was as if I could have touched them. Also, the playing of [Anapola] brought back the memory of that girl, that squadron leader's wife – the luxuriant healthy English country one – so meant for complete physical life & with her husband away. I thought of her leaning against me in the night saying 'Stay' – a thick hot voice – war is brutal – I suppose I would not think of these things if I had started life again. It is the fact that one felt so intensely in those last months – everything was so tremendously heightened, so that one's senses were magnified. I dreamt the night before that I got a letter from Peter Clarke from Guadalcanal[7] & knew when I woke that he was very near.

1 Margaret Andrew's children

2 Arturo Toscanini (1867–1957), Italian conductor of international repute
3 George Gershwin (1898–1937), Piano Concerto in F Major, opus 2 (1924)
4 Benny Goodman (1909–86), American clarinettist and band leader, known as
   'The King of Swing'
5 Johannes Brahms (1833–97), Symphony No. 4 in E Minor, opus 98
6 Bruno Walter (1876–1962), conductor of the Berlin Philharmonic from 1919;
   became conductor of the New York Philharmonic in 1951
7 The American battle for Guadalcanal Island in the Pacific, November 1942.
   Peter Clarke was in England at the time.

61/ To R.A. Trotter   7 Prince Arthur Avenue
                                                     3 November 1942

Dear Professor Trotter,
You must have enough of the writings of present students, without being
troubled with a letter from an ex-student. The reason I write is because of
something that has worried me about the future relations of Canada and
Great Britain, and because you are an authority on our relations to the
Commonwealth. I hope you do not mind me writing.
    It seems clear that, after the war, the people of England and Scotland
will have to face their problems, particularly their economics ones, with
far greater power in the hands of the state, than they have ever granted to
it before. Collectivism has bad connotations, but it will apply, I think, to
England. I think they will be able to carry this out within the framework
of their past political institutions and will be able to do it without pitting
class against class. But that they will have to do this seems to me inescapable. The reorientation of a war economy to one of peace – the necessity
of planned building for the considerable bombed areas, the loss of much
of their foreign capital both in foreign countries like the United States
and Argentina or in countries like Malay or India that they controlled
politically. (On this point, it always seemed a shame the way the U.S.A.
made England give up all its capital invested in the U.S.A. before it would
grant Lend Lease.) But for whatever reasons, all the signs point toward
this new economic planning. Sir William Beveridge[1] or Archbishop
Temple[2] would not have spoken out for it, irresponsibly.
    On the other hand, we in Canada and in the U.S.A., for a host of rea-
sons (not least the fact that we have not been geared to war as completely
as the English), will probably want to continue with our economic institutions that gave the individual an almost free hand. What seems to me the
danger is that those elements in our country, who believe strongly in an

uncontrolled economic life, may so distrust the new England economically that it will find expression in antagonism to the continuance of our free relationship with England. Already in Toronto I have heard the early symptoms of such an attitude.

This would seem to me a disastrous attitude, for my interest in the maintenance of our connection with England has never been because of its advantages in terms of power, but of the very practical, if intangible, advantages of a North American country freely keeping in close cooperation & friendship with a country on another continent. If our relationship will not stand the test of England's changing status, then it does not seem to me to be 'founded upon the rock.' This may seem very idealistic in a world where power seems to play the vital part.

If you have got this far, please do not think of answering this, as I know how busy you must be, and lying in bed I have all the time in the world.

Yours sincerely,
George Grant

1 Sir William Beveridge (1879–1963), later Lord Beveridge, author of the famous Beveridge Report (*Social Insurance and Allied Services: A Report*), which laid the groundwork for the British welfare state
2 Archbishop William Temple (1881–1944), author of *Christianity and the Social Order*, published as a Penguin special in 1942

62/ Journal Entry   5 November

'God sees the truth but waits'[1] – what a phrase that is. The whole tragic futile benighted sublime ridiculous grandeur of our lives is there. We sow & sow & sow without heed and not caring – &, God, in his infinite wisdom & perfect power just damn well waits & then with that irony of all ironies we reap what we have sown. So many people will say 'but, but what nonsense.' A poor person does not reap what he or she has sown – yes they do – reap of all that they have been & everybody has been. So many have taken 'as you sow, so shall you reap' as a moral warning – it is not moral in the sense of right and wrong – it is the pitiable & wonderful truth – & that is the point. God sees the truth but waits. Personally, it is a great emotional discovery – the discovery of God – the first glimpse of that reality – not amateurish or kind – not sentimental or moral, but so beyond our comprehension that the mere glimpse is more than we can bear. God, not as the optimist – nor as the non-mover, but, God, *who sees the truth but waits*. God waited through the selfish nationalism & ignorant self-seeking of the nineteenth century. God waited through the struggle of the first war, & through the continuance of our sloth and greed & our ignorance from 1918–1939, he saw the truth – he saw what the policies that we were following would mean. He saw that each individual sin multiplied in countries & continents would bring us down to this – yet he did not intervene, he waited.

Of course, the approach to God is, I know not how. For me it must always be *Credo ut intelligam*;[2] the opposite of that is incomprehensible.

Who wrote another great title for a short story – 'Nothing Breaks but the Heart'?

1 Title of a short story by Tolstoy (1872)
2 St Anselm, following St Augustine: 'I believe so that I might understand.'

63/ Journal Entry

Reading Uncle Burgon's letter from England one realises the old guard is still in power in the most important places.

Jim George married today.

Art is wonderful – it is part of all – it is the beauty that gets us nearer to the final and ultimate reality, but the reality of living is greater, nobler than the art itself. The depth of one's own feeling is deeper than any art one could produce, and I think this raised to the highest degree that the tremendous understanding of Tolstoy was greater than anything he did in Art from *War & Peace* to *Where God is Love is*. It is because the medium, however well it is used – used to the full – yet not even cramping as in the case of Bach or Beethoven; still it is a medium – & not the person. How much more wonderful to have been Emily Brontë's lover than to have read 'Last Lines' – or whatever that last poem[1] – for then one would have touched the very source of the fountain – felt the depth of that driven personality. Or is this all muck I write – made from too great a dinner & too emotional a day? After all, depth of emotion is greater when one has fed well; that is why it is so limited.

1   Emily Brontë (1818–48), 'Last Words,' edited by Charlotte Brontë in 1850:
    Those eyes shall make my only day,
        Shall set my spirit free,
    And chase the foolish thoughts away
        That mourn your memory.

64/ Journal Entry   18 November

The attacks on Wilkie here seem to me to be very misguided. The point
they seem to forget is that Wilkie has made no attempt to castigate the
British Commonwealth but *imperialism* of the old school in whatever form
it is. Of course, what Americans do not understand in my opinion is that
Churchill does not represent England's views as to a world of peace,
merely the war years. They seem to equate imperialism with England, as
Canadians do. The result is the picture here is we like the empire, we like
Britain. They do not like imperialism in leftist circles in the States; there-
fore, they draw from that a conclusion as to England.

65/ Journal Entry   4 December

Time passes into time, but I am progressing fast, perhaps there is a
chance that if I get over my mixture of sloth & sensualism I might turn
myself into something.

Mrs Crooks[1] with her hands curling over the arm of the chair like tal-
ons, her ugly black dress hanging on her great body, her awful black hat,
her voice slow and methodical not because she was dull, but because she
had trained herself not to say anything, her face quiet but neither from
time calm or boring placidity, but again based on this terrible restraint.
Also, nothing on her in the way of ornament except thick gold and dia-
monds, as remembrance of her wedding. Think of the story. Mrs Crooks
remembering her son,[2] her beloved son sent away from home because of
the scandal that broke around old Crooks's head for swindling – going to
England, to the RAF. He crashes and now how she hates her husband –
proud and controlled – somehow unable to see any but the kindest of
neighbours, but hating her husband. Is it true? Does she hate him? I
doubt it.

1 A friend of Mrs Grant
2 David Crooks, a friend of Alison and Charity's, was killed in the war.

66/ Journal Entry   13 December

'Take what you want said God – take it and pay for it.'[1] What a tremendous
truth for men and societies – with the individual he or she can choose to
be cruel – to want power – to be oversensual – to be decadent – to be (like

myself) slothful – he can take any or all of these things. He can take them, but will pay for them. Also with nations – they can take empire – or power or wealth – or on the other side isolation & irresponsibility – they can take them but will pay for them. These people who believe that 'as you sow, so shall you reap' as merely a moral little lesson to be learned for the good of all & that if one doesn't learn it one is a bad boy, but nothing much else – are fools. As you sow, so shall you reap is the terrible & furious pronouncement of the law of human life. It is not an improving aphorism; it is the truth. Sow violence and you get violence – sow greed – you get greed. One pays and pays and pays for everything. Right now we are paying for the greed, selfishness, slothfulness & irresponsibility of the past years – and we are paying for it in an easy way, however strange that may seem. We never faced up to the issue, but gave over to the arbitrament of force without thinking, therefore, after the war we will pay for this.

In *All This & Heaven Too*, war is described as the same kind of action as a man who burned down his house because there were rats in it.

1 In the preface to *Technology and Justice* (1986), Grant describes this as a Spanish proverb.

1943

67/ To D.R. Michener   24 March 1943

Dear Mr Michener,
This is an extremely late note to thank you for the trouble you took to give me the information about law. It was very generous of a busy man to spend time over such a thing.

For the moment at least I have decided to postpone the law training, so as to earn some money.

Again, many thanks.

Yours sincerely,
George Grant

As he recovered from his mental and physical exhaustion, Grant began to look for some way to occupy his time and earn a little money. He found a position as secretary to the Citizens' Forum. It was part of the Canadian Association of Adult Education, a body that his father helped create. The Citizens' Forum followed the experiment of the Farm Forum. It originated radio broadcasts, which formed the basis for discussions organized in small groups across the country. It was Grant's job to organize this experiment in the educational use of public broadcasting. For a history of the Citizens' Forum, see Isabel Wilson, Citizens' Forum: 'Canada's National Platform' *(1980).*

68/ To D.R. Michener

National Citizens' Forum
198 College Street
Toronto, Ontario

Dear Mr Michener,

Hearing that you were just on the point of going to Great Britain, I have not wanted to trouble you with an interview, and have, therefore, put this in the form of a letter.

I would very much like to go back to Oxford after the war, if it is considered that I have a right to do so, by the Trustees. However since the war and because of the situation in Canada I would like to return and study theology rather than law. From all I can gather the United Church would accept that here.

I hope that the conference is as successful as it should be and that you have a wonderful stay in Great Britain.

Sorry to bother you with this, when you must be so busy.

Yours sincerely,
George Grant

69/ To Maude Grant

Ma Chère Ould,

Isn't the news fantastically good?[1] Though, of course, it is not clear yet what it means; it cannot mean bad it seems to me. Churchill's speech sounded as if he was leaving the way open for a compromise with Bagdolio[2] and it seems to me the advantages to be gained are so enormous that it is the right thing to do. (1) It is not right to risk lives of our armies. (2) Any compromise that would save Europe from another winter of war seems to me worthwhile. At least one will be able to fight people like Bagdolio when war is at an end, and the replacing of Mussolini is a stage in the right direction. With Giraud[3] there was a sound alternative [to] de Gaulle, and the American compromise seemed to have been a useless one, but here it would not be useless. Whether they would take the same kind of compromise from conservative Germans will be interesting. What will Uncle Joe[4] think?

Life goes on here at a mild and pleasant rate. I feel really surprisingly better and am losing the slightly traumatic hysterical note that assailed me since January 1942.

No news from Dr Trotter.[5] I am going to write to him again.

Keep some vegetables.

Love from the Parkins, and more from me.

George

1 The Allied successes in Italy
2 Marshal Bagdolio replaced Mussolini at the head of the Italian government. Roosevelt supported the liberals who wanted Bagdolio out of office, but between March and June 1944, Churchill continued to defend the marshal.
3 General H.H. Giraud was Charles de Gaulle's rival for the leadership of the free French forces.
4 Stalin
5 Grant had written in the hope of finding a teaching position.

Grant spent much of the summer of 1943 at his Uncle Raleigh Parkin's cottage in North-Hatley in the Eastern Townships of Quebec. Frank Scott and Hugh MacLennan[1] were neighbours there.

70/ To Maude Grant   [summer 1943]

Dear Ould,

Your letter of this morning was quite a surprise. Mild interest at the apocalyptic events in Italy,[2] fascinated interest in the Ontario election.[3] You sound as if you didn't expect me to be interested in the news from Italy. The potentialities of it are simply so amazing that your comparative lack of interest seemed to be out of character for you. On the other hand, the small importance, even for Ontario itself as to which of the three alternatives get elected, makes your supreme interest there equally surprising. This is not meant as a rebuke; it is merely a question of interest.

The Mussolini affair seems to me fascinating. The whole fabric of future world affairs seems to be there in full; the replacing of the fascist world by the conservative one when they are far enough away from Russia to pull it off; the Anglo-American people pretending to want unconditional surrender, and the gradual way they will come to terms with the conservative royalists. Of course, as far as Italy is concerned, I think they are very foolish not to come to terms. There is no alternative in Italy as there was with Giraud & de Gaulle[4] & and anything that will save Europe from another winter of war & prevent the dissolution of everything is worthwhile.

This was started about 4 days ago. Since then there has been a weekend of interest.

Yesterday we motored over to Magog for probably the last public appearance of Henri Bourassa.[5] He was speaking for the Bloc Populaire[6] in the Stanstead by-election. Aunt Louise, Mrs Curzon Dobell, Aileen Ross, Mason Wade,[7] Hugh MacLennan, Dorothy Duncan and myself. Mason Wade is an American Catholic up here on a Guggenheim studying French Canada. Through his work for the recent life of Francis Parkman[8] he became interested in Quebec as part of his ideal Catholic America. He is no fool and knows what his religion means and entails. Evidently he has got nearer to the heart of Quebec than any outsider. He is like an austere young Jesuit in civilian clothes. His knowledge (not merely a compilation of unconnected facts) of French Canada is amazing. He emotionally comprehends their racial business and their Catholicism.

Well, we drove into Magog through the wonderful township country with the hills all around. Glorious countryside in the two essentials; it is lived in, fertile & with the mark of man's touch and at the same time it is powerful, strong & wild. Magog was a typical French town, recently industrialized, enjoying its Sunday. (The townships that used to be 3/4 English, 1/4 French, are now 80% French.) We had an ice cream cone & then went to the meeting. The platform was on the steps of the main RC church with microphones planted in the west windows & the Bourbon fleur-de-lis & cross everywhere & the tricolor draped around the front of the platform. The priests looked on (six or eight of them from the upstairs gallery of the presbytery next door). A large crowd spread around and out into the street – a crowd of both industrial workers & farmers. A lovely gay French crowd, with its humour and stupidity, its highly respectable farm women and its tart-like industrial ones. Well, first the candidate from Montreal-Cartier spoke, then Choquette[9] for Stanstead – both dull and short. Then Barré,[10] the head of the cultivateurs au Québec, got up. 'Je suis un cultivateur comme vous.'[11] Opening with an attack on the agriculture policy of King, then on to the main body of the speech. 'J'aime les Anglais, j'aime l'Angleterre, mais après le Canada et les Canadiens.'[12] The gift of millions to England – oh how terrible and best of all – the fat pompous Bennett[13] lining his pocket and filling his purse – then saying 'I am going home.' Roars from the crowd. Barré spoke as you would never hear (or at least rarely hear in English Canada) with humour, wit at first, then gradually bringing it all up to a climax –

far better than we can do. Then, suddenly, in the middle of one of his rising polemics, a honking of horns & in an open car – the old man [Henri
Bourassa] arrived. Against all my judgment it was the most moving
moment I have ever had in Canada. The first feeling of being a Canadian
since returning from England. He stepped from the car – the old man
helped along by a young man. His fine Gallic face – white beard – and
the crowd – not very excited up to that – going wild – & wild with a feeling that this was their man & they really loved him. He walked down the
centre aisle – shaking hands with an elderly cultivateur here & another
one there – and as he reached the platform they sang (&, mind you,
everybody sang O Canada, deeply moved). Compared to the fat King or
the pompous Bennett, this really was a man. He was not only a leader of
a party – who had kept power, to whom power was the end. This man
had an idea. A bad idea, a pernicious idea, but at least an idea. He was
something in the realm of morality, not merely a man whose end was
office. Woodsworth[14] was the only other Canadian who has ever given me
that feeling & these people believed in him. He represented in some
basic way the aristocrat of 'leur pays.'[15]

A young man got up to introduce him. Here was a danger. A young fellow called Laurendeau,[16] editor of *Action Catholique*, bitter, Catholic, the
real fascist, evidently the brains behind the Bloc. Far too urban, too
smooth, too passionate without solidity, for the agricultural audience.
Obviously deeply moved at the last meeting of the grand old man of their
movement.

Then Bourassa. Again wild cheers. An old man's voice – 'Je viens de la
camaraderie de vous voir'[17] – tired, but what a show – up and down the
platform – gesticulating – and humour. Magnificent entertainment. King
being seduced by the Queen – feeding her cognac, but being duped. 'Je
respecte le roi – mais le roi du Canada – pas le roi d'Angleterre.'[18] The
Queen departs, bored stiff, with poor old King a real royalist, etc., etc.
King is only an expert on farming with the sheep he has in Parliament.
[ill.] wild, great cheers, the biggest of the afternoon other than
Bourassa's arrival. Then 'ce brave Paulliot' – what scorn. Then back to
King. He had a grandfather, I had one – 'Louis Joseph Papineau'[19] – wild
cheers. King has deserted his grandfather. I have remained loyal to mine.
Foreign policy, for years dictated by G.B., 'mais maintenant plus servant à
Washington.'[20] (Solitary cheers from GPG.) King going to London via
Washington, to Washington via London, but '[pour] le Canada jamais'[21]
etc., etc. Then suddenly and very effectively from melodramatic humour
and exaggeration to dramatic seriousness – quietly and with terrific force,

'I have never lied to my people.' Wild cheers. We must look to our rights – we must be Canadians etc., etc.

Then, he sits down amid prolonged applause – we left hastily.

I think because this particular county is 40% English they stressed the Canadian nationalism rather than the French-Canadian. But what impressed me most – this was a show – a mixture of a festival in honour of the great man and a circus for entertainment. This was alive, real, vital. Whatever party wants to get anywhere in Quebec, it seems to me, must put on such a show. Thirdly where the CCF were allowed to rent the RC parish hall for their candidate, who is the RC mayor of Magog, these people had the steps of the church with microphones from inside.

All in all, they think the pleasant Davidson, the Liberal candidate, will get in; the English are determined to have an Englishman. He has gained much sympathy locally by having his barn burnt out.

We are all well, a pleasant weekend here.

As always my love
GPG

1 Hugh MacLennan (1907–90), novelist and professor, three-time winner of the Governor-General's literary award for fiction, and a friend and neighbour of Raleigh Parkin

2 The arrest of Mussolini and the formation of a new government under Marshal Bagdolio

3 4 August 1943

4 Churchill and Roosevelt wanted Giraud to supplant de Gaulle, but they were thwarted by Anthony Eden, the British foreign secretary.

5 Henri Bourassa (1868–1952), founder of *Le Devoir,* federal MP, and one of the main early influences on French-Canadian nationalism

6 Quebec nationalist party, which ran candidates in federal elections

7 Mason Wade (1913–86), American historian and director of Canadian studies at the University of Rochester

8 Mason Wade, *Francis Parkman* (1942)

9 J.-A. Choquette (1905–), president of the Union catholique des cultivateurs; elected to the House of Commons in the Stanstead by-election 9 August 1943 for the Bloc populaire canadien

10 Laurent Barré (1886–1964), farmer and politician, first president of the Union catholique des cultivateurs (1924)

11 I am a farmer like you.

12 I like the English; I like England, but only after Canadians and Canada.

13 R.B. Bennett, later Viscount Bennett (1870–1947); Conservative prime minister, 1930–5

14 J.S. Woodsworth (1874–1942), clergyman, social worker, and leader of the CCF from its founding until his death

15 Their country

16 J.-E.-A. Laurendeau (1912–68) became provincial leader of the Bloc populaire in February 1944 and was elected to the Quebec Assembly. In 1963 Lester Pearson appointed him as co-chair of the Royal Commission of Bilingualism and Biculturalism.

17 The French text is not clear. Probably Grant means: 'I have come to you out of friendship.'

18 I respect the king, but the king of Canada, not of England.

19 Louis-Joseph Papineau (1786–1871), leader of the 1837 rebellion in Lower Canada against the British. Mackenzie King's grandfather, William Lyon Mackenzie (1795–1861), led the rebellion in Upper Canada.

20 But now more in Washington's interest

21 Never for Canada

1944

71/ To Maude Grant   Christmas 1944

To Mother,
    To wear a nightgown and to greet the grocer
    Is for a matron, not considered fun.
    The menial might want to hug you closer
    And on Prince Arthur, that is never done.
    Perched tranquil in the bath, or on the closet,
    The raucous bell, from back or front may sound
    To fetch the laundry, or to pay deposit
    For Eaton's parcel or Campagna's pound.
    So we decided, both in love and fear
    To quickly end your incommodity.
    Never again need you half-clothed appear
    To some strange butcher, a mere oddity.
    Girdled, black-swathed and neat we hope you find
    Within this housecoat, God's good peace of mind.

1945

72/ To Margaret Andrew   [early 1945]

Dear Margaret,
Without putting one's own pessimism into the field of general speculation about Canada and the world, I am now somehow suddenly scared.

Historically, that is looking at what has been, to try and determine what
should be, I have a feeling that man, faced suddenly with the problem of
industrialism and all that it entails – urbanism, new forms of work, leisure, tremendous power over nature – has started (as is quite natural)
badly; and, as he does it and makes these mistakes, he starts naturally to
look for blame, and will probably blame the wrong things & then will
eventually say & do: 'We must have a saviour to pull us through this. It's
too bloody difficult.' Of course, the saviour may do a lot of good and
build us *sensible cities*, modern organizational structures, etc., but we will
certainly give him the right to make our decisions.

Of course, historically, there is proof that there is something special in
mankind, supra animal, more than material, that will make him eventually pull up his socks and be on the way up again; but at the moment, this
colossal, material change of industrialism has been too much for our
great tradition (really a remarkably thin veneer) of personal responsibility, the dignity of the individual. Do teach Kitten, Ed & Caroline personal
responsibility & the ghastly, difficult thing that God has put upon them of
being free. I am always willing to surrender my bloody will to anybody.

This is a ghastly particular letter. Not meant to be. Just is. Love to Kitten
particularly. I hope her ear is better. Of course, also to Eddie and Caroline & Geoff. The story of Ed & Caroline going to the store tore everybody's heart strings.

> Yours with endless and endless love,
> George

*Grant decided to return to Oxford after the war to study theology. He needed to
know whether he would be allowed to take up his Rhodes Scholarship.*

73/ To Dr C.K. Allen   7 Prince Arthur Avenue
Toronto, Ontario

Dear Dr Allen,
Mr Michener told me, on his return from England, that there is a possi-

bility of returning to Oxford in the fall. I wonder if you would be good enough to tell me what you think of this and whether you would consider it advisable. Since the war, as for everybody, life has changed a great deal and, if able to return, my plans would be to study theology instead of law. Would this mean that I might return to Balliol, or would I enter another college? My natural inclination would be, of course, to go back to Balliol if it was at all possible. Also, would it be possible to get a degree in theology at Oxford in two years and would I be able to have my scholarship for two years? From your knowledge of Oxford, do you know who it would be good to study theology with? As a member of the United Church of Canada, I am, I believe, what is called in England a non-conformist, but would like very much to take my theology, if possible, within the great Church of England tradition.

I am sorry to put such personal plans on your busy shoulders, but we are so far away here that it is difficult to know what the situation is. Naturally the thought of returning to England is an extraordinarily exciting one.

My best regards to Mrs Allen and the children.

Yours sincerely,
George Grant

God and Marriage 1945–50

Grant returned to Oxford, uncertain of what kind of studies he would undertake, but certain that it would be something in theology. What he really wanted to do was to 'explore the universe.'

74/ To Maude Grant   Balliol College, Oxford
[September 1945]

Dear Ould,
Just a line having arrived in Oxford and in the winds, a bit of a gloom after the pleasantness of London. London seemed real and vital and alive; this place seems drab and self-centred and populated with unintelligent, opinionated schoolboys.

Of course, everybody was away on arrival, the Master and Mrs L. in Ireland, C.K. Allen too busy to see me. Not a single old friend up and around. In fact, except for some scouts[1] who remain good friends, it was singularly lonely and depressing. Nathaniel Micklem,[2] however, was superb, gave me some very good advice and some pleasant talk. Really, he couldn't have been nicer. What a swell person he is. Warm and intelligent at the same time. He advises me not to take formal theology, but to try to get the university to let me take a D.Phil. in some subject mixing theology and law. The prospect appals me because a D.Phil. is one of the most difficult degrees at the university; it is of higher calibre than a Ph.D., although much the same thing. If not, I can try for a B.Litt. in the same way, which is a much weaker and less intensive degree. Micklem says a D.Phil. is a colossal degree in the academic world and would be useful. He says, if I took undergraduate theology, I would have to spend too much time on techniques and not enough on what I want to do – explore the universe, yet be narrowed down.

At the moment this decision rests till the master returns at the weekend and till I have seen C.K. Allen. It will be a superb help to have Micklem's backing and encouragement. His mind appealed to me immediately – the right blend of 'non-conformity' and Catholicism. A real liberal. What the master will say, God knows – whether the university board will let me, God knows. Whether Allen will dish up the dough, God knows.

Really, the few days in England increases my respect for them. The difficulties of ordinary living after Canada are large and I would imagine far harder for a family than an unhampered individual like myself. Yet their vitality and gutsiness continues. In Bermondsey, the impression of real drive and love of life is unmistakeable. After the varied and intense difficulties my friends have lived under for years such ebullience and zest makes one feel that decadence in England is limited to the less important quarters.

In fact, that is what the Labour victory[3] meant, it seems to me: that new and more vital elements in the population, with creative ideas and free enterprise (if you will) have come to power. As for controls by the state, the rigidity is essential. England is living on such a borderline regimen that if there weren't controls they could never get through this period. Patriotic business understands this well, I would imagine, and will respond to Cripps's[4] pleas for hard work. As one realises the tight corner England is in and the difficulty it will have getting out of it, only this disciplined work will get them out.

Life has been plagued with complete digestive collapse since arriving in England. This is partly caused by the smallness of the diet and my habituation to richer and larger amounts of food, i.e. plain hunger, but also to the change in diet which results in peculiar fermentation in my stomach. Your Enos are a saving grace.

If you ever can send food (but for goodness sakes don't worry much) fats (e.g. butter) are the things I would like much. Of course, for goodness sakes, remember that Europe and Ch[arity] G[rant] are in so unspeakable a state that any to me must be fractional compared to the latter.

Tell Alison I helped Mary move. That Charles and Kay[5] are changing, the former exceedingly fine.

Ch. G. I hope will be coming for leave soon; it will be glorious to see her.

The Wimperises are with John at the moment and very excited. How swell.

Blessings to tout le monde – J.A.G. especially and to you as always my very best and dearest love from one who will have to work [to] not be hungry; and try not to get continual colds.

Love,
George Grant

1 College servants at Oxford
2 Nathaniel Micklem (1888–1976), a theologian; he knew the Grants because he had taught theology at Queen's. His children had stayed with Margaret and Geoff Andrew during the war.
3 Clement Atlee's Labour party defeated Winston Churchill's Conservatives in the 1945 British general election.
4 Sir Stafford Cripps (1889–1952), president of the Board of Trade in the Labour government, 1945–7; chancellor of the exchequer, 1947–50
5 Kay Moore, Alison's flat-mate during the war, married war-hero Charles Gimpel.

75/ To Alice (Eedy) Boissonneau[1]   Balliol College, Oxford
[13 November 1945]

My dear Friend,
A short note reached me from you via the fair hands of Isabel. How nice of you to write. Although many letters have come from Canada, yours is one of the rare ones that has any validity, for you can write so that what you are thinking loses no large part of its substance in the writing. Perhaps after all that is a mere product of the essential stuff in you as a person. And I think of you one night with your hair on top of your head, dressed in purple and with your eyes shining, sitting in that dingy room the Clarks call (with supreme effrontery) their drawing room, soft with your understanding (God knows why) of Canadian youth.

Again thank you for your letter for, although my admiration for this country grows apace and one has many good friends and an occasional amusing one, even beloved England is not my own country and I find myself sick for longing for one's own country.

To be sickeningly personal, the years in which you knew me were in their minor turbulences not easy and I am afraid that perhaps I was not always as pleasant as the occasion would have warranted. I felt tired and dead and unemotional after a plethora of emotion in the first years of the war. That is no excuse for any failure to as good and as kind a person as you; but, in its insufficient way, it is a reason. The well of poetic feeling on which I had conducted my adolescence was wasted and dried up and there was nothing very substantial to take its place.

Today is my 27th birthday. The first part of the day was filled with sadness and sick for home I stood in tears amid the alien corn.[2] Then for some reason two perfect things happened. First, I made a good friend. Second, my best friend pushed into my letter box a fine piece of music he had written for my birthday.[3] So God's goodness is indeed good. For what is better than friendship? Or what finer than to love and be loved?

God cannot live in mountains. Those romantic pinnacles surrounding Vancouver are strangely unmoving in their romanticism. Perhaps He lives in the foothills near Calgary. But, if there is a gracious God and if it is possible to find (and I am sure there is and I am sure it is possible to find him, even though he escapes and escapes and escapes because one is not willing to search), then there is no other that is God.

As for what you mention about finding him in books. You find many things in books, but not the living God. Although in one book I think you find him more than in others. Read the 40th chapter of Isaiah, eliminating verses 19 and 20,[4] and read some of the psalms.

This piece of paper has been slopped with beer from a party I gave last night for my birthday. Forgive it but can't write it out again.

As usual my love for what the English island [stands] for in the world grows apace: individualism, yet with respect for their fellows. Gentleness that does not go as far as softness. Sensitivity that is not weak. Those are the traits that are more common here than anywhere else I know. Already there are large movements of progressive people who say that the *extremely skimpy* rations here must be cut down so that Germany does not starve this year. That is good in any society. It is remarkably good with people who are tired and have to queue up for every single morsel of food they buy and you have no idea how much less food there is than Canada. In no way sentimentally they are an extremely moral people by and large. Oxford, of course, is not as pleasant, as any group of young people concentrated in the mind are apt to be difficult. In fact it is a loathsomely slow business getting settled down to work.

Anything you can get done in Vancouver to see that food can be got to Germany and Austria this winter would be to your credit in heaven. Particularly in the eastern zones there is evidently going to be untold misery. With every justification in the world, except the ultimate one, the Russians have evidently decided that Germany and Austria will be laid waste. The news that one gets here all the time is of a real Carthaginian peace. Of course, it is nothing like the organized perversion and methodical barbarity of the Germans; it is better than that. Still it is pretty barbarous. Of course, after what the Russians went through, it would be sloppy to expect anything else.

Never say that your book is going to be published only mythically. Of course, it will be published. It will be part of a great upsurge of Canadian life. It may even be not exactly like *A Tree Grows in Brooklyn*.[5] It will be fine. If it comes from your sensitivity and texture of feeling; it will be good for every crass member of our country to read.

Yes, Dr MacKenzie[6] is nice and friendly. He is also one of the shrewdest apples and fence sitters it has been my privilege to know. He will do superlatively well in BC and will be extremely popular. Don't pass on my cynical comments, as his Realpolitik is excusable and is on the whole on the side of the angels.

This is a dull – foolish – badly written letter. But it brings you my best love.

George Grant

Do look up Marjorie Smith Dept of Extension at the University. Really a sweet and sane person.

1 Alice (Eedy) Boissonneau (1921–), social worker and writer. She and Grant had met about the beginning of 1944 and become close friends.
2 'Perhaps the self-same song that found a path / Through the sad heart of Ruth, when sick for home, / She stood in tears amid the alien corn' (John Keats [1795–1821], 'Ode to a Nightingale'). Grant had *The Poetical Works of John Keats*, ed. H.B. Forman (1931) in his library.
3 Geoffrey Bush
4 'The workman melteth a graven image, and the goldsmith spreadeth it over with gold, and casteth silver chains. / He that *is* so impoverished that he hath no oblation chooseth a tree *that* will not rot; he seeketh unto him a cunning workman to prepare a graven image, *that* shall not be moved' (Isaiah 40. 19–20).
5 Betty Smith (1904–72), *A Tree Grows in Brooklyn* (1943)
6 N.A.M. MacKenzie (1894–1986), formerly president of the University of New Brunswick and president of the University of British Columbia, 1944–62. Grant's brother-in-law, Geoff Andrew, was MacKenzie's senior academic advisor.

76/ To Maude Grant   Balliol College, Oxford

Ma chère Ould,
Indeed, you must be exceptionally busy as, except for a short note and a
cryptic telegram, no news of you has been forthcoming. In the past years
we have lived rather intimately and I cannot call off the deep feeling for
other people and therefore thinking of you daily; one dashes to the por-
ter's lodge before breakfast to search for some letters, to find many from
certain people, but none from the person one wants to hear from mainly.
Although I adore England and am becoming more reconciled to Balliol,
my heart is in Canada and would like to hear of it.
    Naturally, of course, I recognize that you must be bust with Aid to Rus-
sia,[1] Alison and the many friends who make a call on you, but remember I
am your greatest and closest friend; so make an effort. Many or any of us
haven't heard a word. We haven't a clue as to what's happening nor have
we a clue about plans for the future. I find it rather disturbing to read of
Alison's engagement in the *Times*, to hear of these plans from a person
who happened to see Norman Robertson.[2] I think in fact you are really
letting our side down. (Don't pay much attention to this but some.)
    Gerald was up for the weekend. Mary for the day and my greatest
friend Peter Clarke came down for the weekend. Then Sholome[3] arrived.
Then Lionel. I was involved with other English friends so altogether it was
hectic. Sholome as sweet as ever. Gerald and Mary as always unbelievably
nice. Lionel, as I believe I have written, rather dim as he looked at 7 of my
friends who were in for tea as if they were rather dismal types, although
two were POWs, etc. But gave one the impression that we were all rather
worthless asses.
    Sholome arrived again today with 45 RCAF chappies who I showed
around Balliol. Chief argument was against Balliol having Germans on its
honour role.
    My overwhelming admiration at the moment is for Martin Luther.[4]
Erasmus[5] one agrees with more. Calvin[6] was a greater thinker and arguer.
But that great peasant with his feet set on the ground seeking with all his
heart and soul and need a gracious God, and at last out of great rough
tribulation finding him, is the noblest of the lot. Every charge can be
levelled against him except that of being an honest man in great need of
peace. Nothing makes me madder than the smirking RCs thinking they
have discredited this man and the Reformation when they go into the
details of his very happy normal relations with a nun and her children by
him. Even a supposed fine man like Maritain[7] goes in for such billingsgate.

Yesterday 2 November, the anniversary of Daddy's birthday, a letter from you arrived. How welcome it was. Nice to know news of Alison and of Geoff's splendid apartment, of the Masseys' visit and a grand letter from Arthur Meighen.[8] If my pamphlet[9] is out please send me some copies, as I would like to see it and to have it for friends like Gerald et al.

Today, 3 November, my permission arrived to write a D.Phil. As it was very much in the air, I have not mentioned much about it. But this gives one a go ahead signal. The actual title is 'The Concept of Nature and of Supernature in the Theology of John Oman.'[10] That means very little. It is a pin on which I can hang two years work reading Descartes, *Plato*, Aristotle, Calvin, Luther, St Thomas, Marx, Freud, and my beloved and, at the moment overwhelming, enthusiasm *Pascal*. Although for a series of reasons, I never could get it over to you, nothing on earth interests me like theology. If I had studied law I would have hated it and not spent much time on it and certainly not been able to contemplate two years at Balliol. Without being foolish and for a series of reasons that may be miasmic, my need of God is as overwhelming, perfectly in a realistic, practical sense you understand, but you know the quotation (not accurate) 'Surely I would have fainted had I not hoped to see the glory of God in the land of the living.'[11] I repeat what was said in Toronto, I do not look for God because I am disciplined, charitable and calm, but because I am undisciplined, uncharitable and deep rooted in sin. Anyway, literally, I can do not other and anything else would be my destruction. That you must believe, really and basically my destruction.

This is very badly put. Of course, two points are necessary to state: (1) a D.Phil. from Oxford is a very fine degree and will be of great practical use. (2) Be prepared for failure; it is extremely hard and they turn down a large percentage; so be prepared.

As far as Christmas goes, Mary has asked me to spend it chez elle at her new cottage in London. It will be swell. One complication will be the Massey-Greey relationship, which has been rather a bad one, namely due to the Masseys' neglect of the Greeys and Alison's inability to put her foot down over it.

I am sorry to trouble you about this, but as I am sure I am going to have to spend a lot of time in bed this winter, which means eating one's own outside supplies of food, could you send me some?

I saw Christina Bevin for a moment when she was in Oxford. What a dear person she is.

Mrs Buck I have not written to as yet, but will. Gerald says I must as she is very sad about not hearing.

Give love to all concerned and I hope all goes for the best 17 November. Love as always,

George Grant

P.S. One thing that might interest you was that Sholome told me that at a meeting he was addressing on Commonwealth solidarity a man (McDougall's) Lemay got up and extremely vehemently said, 'The greatest menace to Canadian unity and Canada itself is our connection with the British Empire' and a long rigamarole on that line. The growing RC appeasement and love of Quebec above all costs. Wouldn't Mrs Buck be pleased with her McDougall protégé she is so keen on!

1 A blue-ribbon charity in which Maude Grant was active
2 N.A. Robertson (1904–68), Canadian high commissioner in the United Kingdom, 1946–9 and 1952–7
3 Michael Gelber (1918–), a UCC friend who later became a rabbi and professor of religion at Columbia
4 Martin Luther (1483–1546), German religious thinker and founder of the Reformation
5 Desiderius Erasmus (c. 1466–1536), Dutch humanist and scholar
6 John Calvin (1509–64), French Protestant theologian
7 Jacques Maritain (1882–1973), French philosopher
8 Arthur Meighen (1874–1960), Conservative prime minister, 1920–1, 1926
9 George Grant, *The Empire, Yes or No?* (1945)
10 John Oman (1860–1939) was perhaps not quite as obscure as Grant imagined. The son of a farmer, he was born and raised in the Orkney Islands off the coast of Scotland. After philosophical studies at Edinburgh, his interest in theology took him to United Presbyterian Theological College in Edinburgh and then to Erlangen and Heidelberg in Germany and Neuchâtel in Switzerland. In 1907 after seventeen years as a minister in Alnwick in Northumberland, he became professor of systematic theology and apologetics at Westminster College, Cambridge. He was elected Moderator of the Presbyterian General Assembly in 1931 and became a member of the British Academy in 1938. He was regarded by his contemporaries as one of the most powerful and original religious thinkers of his day. *The Natural and the Supernatural* (1931), which was the focus of Grant's thesis, was his most admired work. Oman's theology stressed the freedom, worth, and dignity of the human personality, qualities which were endowed by God. He was regarded by his contemporaries as a man of high moral purpose and personal integrity, as well as a man of commanding physical presence.

11 '*I had fainted*, unless I had believed to see the goodness of the Lord in the land
    of the living' (Psalms 27.13).

77/ To Maude Grant   Balliol College, Oxford
                                                        postmarked 18 November 1945

Ma chère Ould,
Yesterday was the day of the wedding and how often I thought of you
and Alison and George.[1] Do send me a description of it. I went to
London for the day to see Mrs Clark (you know the [ill.] wife) who is over
here in charge of the Canadian delegation to the Youth Conference.
What a swell soul she is and how full of life and charm. I saw Gerald and
we drank J.A.G.'s health. I saw V and Lal and Lionel and we drank it
again.

Alhough Oxford is still not terribly pleasant, the one thing that makes
it really worthwhile is theology. It is just my subject. Never have I really felt
so completely alive in anything. After the years in Canada when I had
ceased to write I am now writing again, and which is better than writing it
is giving me the power to make myself a better and more effective person,
where the last years in Canada I had been going down hill. You may be
interested that one of the books I will really have to deal with will be
Space, Time and Deity by Alexander.[2] If you are sending any books, you
might send a copy of that. Do also send another copy of my pamphlet
and perhaps any comments there may be on it.

Please, please do not quote my letters. Aunt Lal said yesterday that she
quite agreed about C.K. Allen. You are the only person in the world one
can write to *not judgmatically*, so my loose and wild judgments please do
not pass on. Allen is not nearly as bad as I said. Just not adequate after
heavenly people like the Wylies whom I went to see two days ago and who
send you their love.

Uncle Vincent was evidently very, very cold to Mrs Clark; so please be
nice to her when you see her. Please, please keep in touch; without that
life will become unbearable. You don't know what a Canadian or U.S.
magazine or a copy of Uncle Jim's speech or something like that means.
So often it is a question of *sick for home, I stand in tears amid the alien corn*.
England is Heaven, but it is never Canada and it is never you. Don't you
understand that, compared to less close members of the family and even
your manifold other activities, you are an absolute necessity to Charity
and myself. Just because one does not cry it from the housetops, that does

not mean it is not true. Everybody else has somebody else, but we have only you; so please, please write.

If the movie of *Henry V* with Olivier[3] comes to Canada, don't miss it. It really is a splendid movie and one you would love. Whenever I am sad I read the last twenty or so verses of *1st Corinthians,* chapter 15.[4] What a superb thing it is. Also, so many of the psalms are becoming more wonderful than I could ever imagine. Love to everybody whom I know.

To you, of course, much the most

George Grant

1 Alison Grant married diplomat George Ignatieff (1913–89). Ignatieff joined External Affairs in 1940 and served in London, where he met Alison and George. He later served as provost of Trinity College (1972–9) and chancellor of the University of Toronto (1980–6).
2 Samuel Alexander, *Space, Time and Deity* (1920; the Gifford Lectures 1916–18). According to Grant, there was some slight romantic connection between Maude Grant and Alexander.
3 Laurence Olivier (1907–89), English actor, producer, director
4 'Now this I say, brethren, that flesh and blood cannot inherit the kingdom of God; neither doth corruption inherit incorruption. / Behold, I shew you a mystery; We shall not all sleep, but we shall all be changed / In a moment, in the twinkling of an eye, at the last trump: for the trumpet shall sound, and the dead shall be raised incorruptible, and we shall be changed' (1 Corinthians 15. 50–2).

78/ To Maude Grant

Dearest Ould,

Here I am in the country staying on the farm of Peter Clarke, one of my great friends, reading and trying to think & resting & walking. It is lovely Buckinghamshire country & a strange old farm house. Other friends come down for the weekend; so altogether it is a very pleasant life & one that is very healthy. It is made to recover the equilibrium I lost at Oxford this term. The terms of the Anglo-American loan[1] have come out and, although they probably will have to be accepted here, they are cruelly hard. The Americans have put the English over a barrel & have extorted every possible pound of flesh. Conservatives & Labour agree on this. As the *Economist* wrote, England, having put most into the war & being a moral creditor, is expected to pay out for the rest of the

20th century as well. Well, if they smash Great Britain, they may not find the world a pleasant place. The other depressing thing in the paper is the fight for the site of UNO.[2] The Russians want it far away from Europe, so that they can make Europe their preserve & UNO can be pleasantly idealistic or 'far from the madding crowd.'[3] I was thrilled to see that Canada had come out for a European site, a good move & a forward-looking one.

I have been reading Plato's *Republic*. What a book it is, what a superb book. One of the things that one had to do in one's life.

Your parcel with Joan's present et al arrived in Oxford just as I was leaving. Thanks a million. How lovely it was to get it.

I went down to the village today & went into the village church to look around and who should be there but A.L. Rowse[4] the English historian, at his most flutey & exquisite he talked to me in front of the yokels rather as Aubrey Beardsley[5] would have talked at his club, if he had one. 'Dear boy – this heavenly church with these divine rococo monuments – etc., etc. ruined by the too horrible horrible hands of those nineteenth century barbarians' etc., etc. Yet he writes so well & sensibly.

Theology alternates between being sheer mumbo-jumbo, interesting intellectual speculation and the most absorbing reality. There is so much dross in modern belief that must be swept away, & underneath [we discover] there is such glory & intelligence.

Still, no news of Charity & whether she is coming at Christmas. I hope she will. Is it true that George Ignatieff[6] is coming here for a conference? More & more I long for home, yet love to be here. Do you know the feeling? But I realise how completely my life is Canadian if I ever had any doubts. There are a great many people who I love & respect here. But the problems here just don't get me like they do in Canada. One doesn't feel in the same way, part & parcel, responsible for things. Where are you going to spend Christmas? In Ottawa? Tell me how Hart is getting along. The prospect of years at university would well-nigh appal me.[7] I find I am less & less the student type. Lionel's plans seem still uncertain, although probably he will be coming back in the spring. I hope he makes a good decision about a job.

Always love,
George

---

1 A government-to-government executive agreement in which the American government agreed to a long-term loan at a low rate of interest, but required the British government to agree in principle that it would abandon the system of

Imperial preferential tariffs, thus effectively opening up the British Empire and Commonwealth to American trade.

2 United Nations Organization

3 Title of a novel by Thomas Hardy, from Thomas Gray's 'Elegy Written in a Country Churchyard': 'Far from the madding crowd's ignoble strife, / Their sober wishes never learned to stray.'

4 A.L. Rowse (1903–), English historian, author of *Tudor Cornwall* (1941)

5 Aubrey Beardsley (1872–98), English illustrator and 'decadent'

6 George Ignatieff (1913–89), Russian–born Canadian diplomat; served at Canada House in London, 1940–4, where he met Alison Grant, whom he married 17 November 1945; later ambassador to Yugoslavia, ambassador to the United Nations, provost of Trinity College, University of Toronto, and chancellor of the University of Toronto.

7 After the war, Hart Massey studied architecture.

79/ To Alice Boissonneau   Balliol College, Oxford
                                                    23 December 1945

Dear Alice,

A parcel of stories arrived from you today. Thank you for them. They are beautiful and some of your feeling for people [bended] to me, feeling for Isabel,[1] etc. But a word of explanation is needed and now is the time. I thought when they talked of being born again that it happened quickly and also that there were only certain levels of despair. But from 1942–1945 I found that one could go on sinking and sinking into despair that was not exciting but just continuously depressing, in which one's awareness of the richness and intensity of life was gradually filtered away. You were kind enough to be a good friend in those years of despair, but it meant that you did all the giving and I the taking; so, sometime, let's meet again when it can be more evenly distributed. But enough.

At the moment I am staying on a farm with a great friend who owns and runs the farm. The whole point is to try and read some theology, a lot of which sounds to me like mumbo-jumbo while the rest is brilliantly alive and real. How much knowledge has much to do with living, and how much it is a trapeze trick you fasten on top of living is impossible to say. Anyway, when one has read such pure, clear nobility as Plato's *Republic*, one can have little doubt that really true thought is worth thinking.

In the meantime the post-war world seems more depressing than the war world. Germany is being starved so that thousands even millions will die this winter, are dying even as you read this letter. Russia has evidently decided on a Carthaginian peace and North America does not care enough to send sufficient food. The Anglo-American loan has come out. The Americans have extracted every drop of blood from this island and it is in such precarious state that it can do nothing but accept. Truman[2] seems to be falling into the hands of the worst type of capitalist and they are going to make the job of the great new government here as difficult as possible. The new government here is really good except for one or two weaknesses. Cripps is great and Bevin[3] goes on from strength to strength.

The digging to China over your new work seems swell. I hope that mere material necessities do not prevent you from writing and being free and happy. Do you love Vancouver? Where and with whom are you going to spend Christmas? May it be happy wherever it is and for goodness sakes go on writing and working at what you want.

How I envy you in Canada. Strangely this time in England although I like it and admire it as much as ever, I find one feels less part of it and a good deal of one's thoughts and hopes remain at home. If you ever have time again do write and again please remember that my inadequacies and futilities done are constantly remembered and perhaps sometime they will even be eliminated.

Till that great day with much love,
George

1 Isabel Wilson, with whom Grant worked at the Canadian Association for Adult Education
2 Harry S. Truman (1884–1972), vice-president of the United States, 1944–5; president, 1945–52
3 Ernest Bevin was foreign secretary in the Labour government, 1945–51.

1946

80/ To Alice Boissonneau   Balliol College, Oxford
[spring 1946]

Dear Alice,
Two or three weeks ago I wrote you a letter after my first wave of Henry James.[1] But it seemed too cold as I then felt wild and so have delayed doing it, till one was more sure.

Nothing that I have read in my life has influenced me more than James and only Dostoevsky has influenced me equally. I write of him to you because I believe that, quite apart from the fact of exquisite pleasure that he will give you, I think you could learn tremendously from him. That sounds as it were slightly wrong to say that to you, as so obviously one can only learn from oneself; but it is said as you know by one of your intensest friends and therefore is said in sincerity. His style, which he had to invent if he was going to say what he had to say, would be dreadful if imitated. One's style can only be one's own, but he does teach one the lesson: that, if one takes on the job of being a novelist, then the development of a style completely at one's command is one's first job. Of course, for me his style is the full revelation of beauty.

What he has done for me, above anything else, is that by his tremendous pessimism, he has shown one that, to whatever depths one sinks, one is not, as he so often describes his characters, 'a man without an alternative.' One cannot, in fact, for whatever reasons do what Milly Theale did in the *Wings of the Dove*, that is turn one's face to the wall. However much one may believe one is beyond the grace of the love of God, that is a mere romantic conception and one can never escape from hope.

Anyway, read him right away. Read the great novels *The Wings of the Dove, The Golden Bowl* and then read the great short stories like the *Beast in the Jungle* and *The Altar of the Dead*. They are of such greatness.

The feeling is pretty general here in left-wing circles that, where Bevin was absolutely right to do what he did at UNO,[2] Churchill was wrong and, perhaps intentionally bad, to make the speeches he has in U.S.A.[3] Quite frankly, if it is a question of U.S.A. capitalism lived up with the sinister Realpolitik of the Vatican against the totalitarian USSR, it seems to me hard to choose – but on the whole the USSR. But why the Russians did what they did at UNO is beyond me. They literally drove this country into the arms of the U.S.A. They had some real hope of friendship with the government here, if they really want it. Why did they attack this country when, in terms of power (if not of moral greatness), it is on its knees? The Labour Party here quite frankly does not want itself to be either a satellite of either of the two colossi and, yet, Russia by its actions at UNO drove it to the U.S.A. The Tories in this country have only one hope of survival that is by saying to the country, 'You are through unless you become a satellite of the U.S.A.' Any idea that the Russians may have that Bevin is just a new edition of Churchill is completely phoney. Of course, the capitalist press in North America doesn't report his socialist speeches or the socialist part of his international speeches, but they are surely read in Moscow. On the repeal of the Trade Disputes Act he made his greatest yet when he said 'You would take the bread from the mouths of the workers' families' to the Tories. Of course, equally having been in trade union work, he dislikes the totalitarianism and Russian imperialism of the communists.

The spy scare is it seems to me a grave pity, but oh what fools people like Raymond Boyer – Dave Shugar[4] have been. Nobody can blame the Russians for spying; but, if Canadians give oaths of secrecy to their own country, they should respect them. If their tougher loyalty is to Russia then they can only expect what they get. Of course, the effect it will have on Canadian life is deplorable and surely the men involved in it would see that it would revive every false bogey.

I am thinking very seriously of coming home this summer. As you know my respect and love for this country is very great, but it is never one's own and it never can become one's own. I can do the work I am doing just as well at home as here. This is as yet very tentative and I may very well change my mind.

Do look after yourself, my dear, and don't, under any circumstances, do anything foolish economically. I mean if you find yourself not eating or any extremity like that; appeal to your family. Starving (for all the romanticism of the nineteenth century) does not produce the good writer, but hard work, and one's best work only happens when one is well fed and has energy.

You are quite right about us being brought up as people who believed our dreams [should] come true. And it is very necessary for us to go down to the depths of pessimism. But, also, having rooted oneself in fundamental pessimism, one must then realise that life is good and that in the long run there is purpose and meaning in that life. Fundamental pessimism is a romantic and adolescent conception, only one stage better than the snivelling optimism of the Rotarian sort. Hopelessly said.

I came across a good tombstone in Worcestershire the other day, written at the height of the civil war in England when men were pessimistic.

'Here lies the body of Sir Robert Shirley Baronet of this parish, who did the best things at the worst times and hoped for them at the most calamitous.'

Love, Love, Love as always.

Sorry this is not a better letter.

George Grant

1 Henry James (1843–1916), American novelist
2 The USSR had condemned the presence of British troops in Greece, and Bevin asked the Security Council to rule that they were there with the full consent of the Greek government and that their presence did not constitute a threat to Russian security.

3 Churchill delivered his 'iron curtain' speech in Fulton, Missouri, on 5 March
  1946, in which he condemned Soviet imperialism and called for a fraternal
  association of the English-speaking peoples.
4 Dr Raymond Boyer, an explosives expert with the National Research Council,
  was implicated by Igor Gouzenko for his part in a Soviet spy ring. He was con-
  victed and sentenced to two years in prison. Dr David Shugar was tried and
  acquitted.

81/ To Maude Grant   Balliol College, Oxford
                                                    [spring 1946]

Dear Ould,
Here I am sitting in Hyde Park in the afternoon watching people pass
and writing you a letter. Over and over again, I have to say thank God for
such wonderful pleasure. I came down on Sunday by a seven o'clock
morning train and went straight for an all day performance of the *St Matthew Passion* at the Albert Hall. It was interesting to hear it quite uncut
compared with the Toronto one. There is also something in sitting so
high in the Albert Hall that everything orchestra, chorus and soloists are
mere impersonal specks at the end of so long a telescope. The singing
was superlative, particularly an alto who was even more noble than Eileen
[Low] in Toronto (also some of the cuts made at home are of some of the
unbelievably beautiful alto parts). But all the same it lacks the simplicity,
intimacy and reverence of the Toronto performance and was interested
that Christina Bevin, whom I met going out, felt the same.

   Am now staying with Mary for a couple of weeks. Your letters have been
a great help to her. She is so little the [designing] woman and is so much
the opposite even to the point of gaucheness. Also, remember that Gerald [Graham] has colossal qualities that only a real intimate can see. He
was so touched by your kissing him.

   Have just been at Aunt Lal's for lunch. Well, but tired, and Uncle Vincent is worried. They were worried about Hart and your telegram about a
small wedding.[1] Remember now that they are in a worried state and criticism worries them. They will need real love to buttress their courage. You
often think my judgment is bad – as generally the worst side – indecision,
bad temper and foolishness; you are the only person I could trust to show,
but do trust this. They need your love, uncritical love, now.

   I, on the other hand, need your critical love as never before, because as
one's strength and hope comes back, I am getting down to the necessary
business of improvement.

I have definitely decided to stay for another year unless something untoward has happened, but I am rather not announcing it and using it as a weapon to try and squeeze Rhodes House. You were quite right as usual.

Last night went to a dinner at Aunt Lal's of Harold Macmillan,[2] Lord Camrose,[3] R.A. Butler[4] and a young Molson[5] you know. The Lees (the present to Hart A) and an incredibly dull Mrs Bram (once Moira Bessborough P). Harold Macm ruthless, tough but brilliant, not warm enough for Conservative leader, but what a mind. It was so sweet of the Masseys to ask me. This is part of a letter as this morning a glorious letter arrived from you.

My dearest,
George

1 Hart Massey married Melodie Willis-O'Connor, whose father was later a member of the governor-general's staff.
2 Rt Hon. Harold Macmillan (1894–1986), Conservative MP; later prime minister, 1957–63
3 W.E. Berry, First Viscount Camrose (1879–1954), proprietor of, among other newspapers, the *Daily Telegraph*
4 Rt Hon. R.A. ('Rab') Butler (1902–82), Conservative MP, and minister of labour, 1945. Butler was one of the most important Conservative politicians of the twentieth century. Although he never became prime minister, he held all of the other senior positions in various Conservative governments.
5 Rt Hon. A.H.E. Molson (1903–93), British MP

Burgon Bickersteth had decided to retire as warden of Hart House and return permanently to England. He and University of Toronto president Sidney Smith[1] decided to offer the position to Grant. It was a plum appointment, but opposition began to build in the board of governors because of Grant's wartime pacifism.

82/ To Maude Grant   postmarked 1 August 1946

Dearest Ould,
This morning a nice letter came from Sidney Smith. The following extract I give verbatim as you must read it carefully. 'In surveying the field (that is for Warden of Hart House) Burgon and I have thought of and come back to your name. I have spoken to Mr Massey about the idea and to say the least he is interested although naturally he is concerned about the family

relationship. On that score I have assured him that if you were selected & if you accepted the offer, I would have no reservations. I know you well enough not to be concerned in that regard. The purpose of this letter is to inquire if you would be interested. You know the House, its traditions, what Burgon has striven to achieve, the variety & the standards of its activities. Perhaps you could have a little talk with Burgon before you reply.'

Well, my dear, you can imagine how that letter has knocked Kant & Bergson out of the window. There are so many things I want to say to you about it. But as there is limited space I put them very succinctly and, I hope, clearly. You will clearly not mention this to anybody, but Charity. Do talk it over with her, read her this letter and then if you both could write independently, *as soon as possible* it would be very helpful.

(1) Can I do the job? For the ordinary U of T boy I think yes – for the tough SPS & medical, would they think me a real intellectual? (2) Will the connection with Uncle Vincent seem too great. A certain amount of backbiting on that score one has to put up with. Will it be too widespread? (3) I can say this clearly: I am a much more integrated & steady human being than I was nine months ago. (4) I am not a dominating personality. When I know people closely & in small groups, by & large they like me. But in large groups I am not an impressive person. (5) As to theology I would have no regrets, as there could be no better parish in Canada than Hart House.

Please both you and CLG think this over carefully. Both your letters to me will be read over and over again. So write them carefully. No other advice will mean 1/10 what yours will.

Of course, you realize from Smith's words that it is not an offer, but only a sounding out but a very warm one.

All my love. Forgive such an exclusively personal letter. But you can imagine what a body blow this has been.

Love,
George

1 S.E. Smith (1897–1959), president of University of Toronto, 1945–57

83/ To Sheila (Allen) Grant[1]   Yorkshire, at Leo's
30 August 1946

[extract:][2]
The very kindly copied letter of H.J. [Henry James] came this morning.

Thank you most awfully for it has been so often in my mind, as also
have you. What a magnificent letter it is; in rereading it the cynical
mind wonders (as it must wonder in reading his other ones) how many
were meant primarily to meet the needs of the person concerned and
how many as 'The Letters of H.J.' and thus for posterity. For obviously
despite all his despair and pessimism about life, he never doubted of
his genius and was sufficiently a product of the sane Victorian world to
believe in the survival of a civilization that would recognize his genius.
Of course, he is right, but when one reads him one cannot help realise
that he will only really be recognized by people in times of civilization
that is old and full of the knowledge of decay, even if not perhaps recognizing that the decay must inevitably become universal (this last parenthesis put in lest any false Spenglerian connotations be added). But
quite clearly he is not the man for the pragmatic (?) Commissar or
industrial production engineer.

[extract:]
Well here I am in Yorkshire staying with my old nurse. Thank God, at
last getting some work done, walking through the flat farm countryside
in the afternoons, sleeping long, listening to the Promenade Concerts
and generally feeling utterly new in the glorious peace. Because, my
dear, you often saw the vigour and rather half-hearted extravertism of
me in the fall, you may not have known that without self-pity or exaggeration I was in a pretty battered state when I came back to Oxford in
October. The result was, of course, that I was far too deeply and selfishly concerned with 'the terrible algebra'[3] etc. Of everybody who suffered, as people inevitably do suffer, from such selfishness you have
taken the most. Please forgive that, but also do not use it to feed your
own love of being hurt or of drama. (This last not meant as a gratuitous
annoyance, but just to mean that my conduct has not been worse than
it has been.)

[extract:]
Well, I have been getting Kant over the barrel. This absurd attitude of his
to religion infuriates me to the pitch of constant annoyance. My dear,
please understand that I am in truth as catholic as all Christians must be –
as you are. On the other hand, the pretensions of the Church of Rome –
in the temporal sphere are so uncatholic and contrary to God's will that
they must be fought. The intemperate attitude to you has been quite
wrong, a product of nerves and adolescence.

I hope you are getting work done and generally having a pleasant time.

Always yours

George Grant

1 Sheila Veronica Allen (1920–), Grant's future wife
2 Sheila Grant provided only extracts of the letters addressed to her.
3 Henry James: 'the terrible algebra of your own'

84/ To Sheila Grant

[extract:]

Your emergency postcard came this morning; as is usual in England, it took longer than ordinary mail. I hope you didn't think it very bad not to come south for the Selfs, but work is work, and it means I can come for the end of the vac to see you in London.

Sin destroys what one loves best. I realise that the thing I admire most in the world is that direct and formal perception of the world that makes beauty. After the war and all the distortion of myself I can still think clearly and act fairly morally, but the ability to write poetry or to have that direct and objective perception of the world is gone. I can't write poetry or stories. It is the result of sin, for one is clogged into one's own self more and more, and less and less able to get out and be objective.

Now, for the Roman Church. There are two points to be decided, and they must not be decided scientifically by dividing up and only taking in the measurable, but by all that is highest and greatest in one's experience, and that means experience that validates itself. Also, any decision must be remembered as tentative – that is capable of being changed – yet intense – that is to be acted upon (more on that later). One is caught in the position that all knowledge is one's own and, to be knowledge, must be in one's head; and yet the experience of Jesus Christ on the Cross, whatever its theoretic explanation, is of such depth that we only glimpse, as it were, in the light far ahead and, therefore, although we must say, 'This is what Christ meant and this is why Christ seems to me of validity,' still, we mustn't try and explain what he thought by the categories of our experience. A balancing act to keep these two in order seems necessary.

1st Question. What kind of an organization did Christ intend to leave behind?

2nd Question. (Apart from all the other questions equally important about the kind of church) Has it to be an infallible church? And by infallible I mean a church that could lay down propositions of fact about the universe, and particularly about God and his acting in history.

3rd Question. Granted an infallible church, is it the Church of Rome?

Now, Derek as an Anglo-Catholic (strange position) says yes to 2 and no to 3. I say no to 2 and therefore by implication no to 3 and am at sea, as many liberal Christians, as to the answer to 1, but I hope to be moving nearer to an accurate picture.

I've only got Ronnie Knox's translation[1] here and can't find the quotation on Matthew. It is also in John.

What I was saying about John, which you take up so vigorously, was clearly in answer to question 2. In the Gospel narratives one has vague and distant accounts of what Christ was. All the very worthwhile criticisms of the texts must be honestly sorted out, and one can come to one's own conclusions on their accuracy. One fact that does stand out clearly is that Matthew, Mark and Luke are accurate and straight forward accounts. John (and this makes it no lesser) is a poem written through the eyes of Neo-Platonic philosophy, and using undeniably the whole symbolism of the Jewish year to express the life of Christ. That in no way detracts from its greatness. This complicated natural (?) and theological symbolism brings out the meaning of Christ's life in a way to me that the more direct accounts do not. But we cannot deny that it is more highly symbolic than the others. Although, of course, every word ever written is a symbol. I cannot see that to point that fact about St J's Gospel out makes, as it were, a thicker veil between Christ and oneself, or as far as accuracy of what he said goes, is a dishonest argument.

You see your remark about the Apocalypse and St John's Gospel are examples of a Roman attitude of mind.[2] There is a great deal of controversy (with which I am not sufficiently familiar to judge accurately) as to when they were both written [or] whether they were written by the same man. In Oxford for instance Lightfoot, a great Johannine scholar,[3] thinks they were written by different people. Farrer,[4] entering the ranks, now reverses this traditional Protestant line and says by the same man. But your attitude is this. You take as accurate the Biblical criticism written in such a way as to substantiate the Roman claims. The Bull of 1906[5] just said that any discovery that went against the faith just wasn't so. Now, if you accept the Biblical scholarships of this sort, of course, you will never come across facts that don't agree with Roman theology.

This letter is far too long, but it brings my love.

P.S. I want to add that an argument, to be effective, has to be listened to, and as soon as I open my mouth about the Roman Church your eyes get wild, your hair gets more untidy, and your tongue inconsequential.

1 *The New Testament of Our Lord and Saviour Jesus Christ, Newly Translated from the Vulgate Latin,* trans. and ed. Ronald Knox (1946)
2 Grant persisted in describing Sheila as a Roman Catholic to the end of his life, although she had left the Catholic Church before he met her.
3 R.H. Lightfoot (1883–1953), author of *St John's Gospel: A Commentary,* ed. C.F. Evans (1956)
4 Rev. A.M. Farrer (1904–68), Anglican theologian, fellow and chaplain of Trinity College, Oxford, 1935–60; later warden of Keble College, Oxford
5 Pope Pius X denounced the separation of church and state on 11 February 1906. In *Lamentabili* (3 July 1907) and *Pascendi* (8 September 1907), he denounced modernism.

85/ To Maude Grant   Balliol College, Oxford
                                                        14 November

Dearest Ould,
(Show this only to Charity) I went up yesterday morning to get my mail and there was your telegram, the definite one saying the appointment to Hart House was off. It was such a relief to get it, for your indefinite one the two days before had (though obviously sent for good reason of preparing me) had left life in suspended animation and my alimentary canal a small Gethsemane. It is good anyway that it is over and this morning; yesterday not being able to think as I had to be guest of honour at two large parties for my birthday and therefore not by word or gesture show that one was anything but at the top of the world. I just feel the last four months are over and get on with the next. I am so frightfully behind in my work, for you know me well enough to know that I am not the kind to work when my mind was on this (and, between us, I was oh so sure). That was a silly mistake, but my youth combined with Dr Smith's and Burgon's sureness, made me fall into that silly trap.

Don't ever mention this to Burgon because he has been so nice, but I think he and Dr Smith should have been old enough and mature enough to have helped me to miss that mistake. Please never breath this feeling to anyone.

In fact that brings me to what this letter is about. There must be no outward or visible sign from any of our family. As [Henry] James so beautifully says 'There must be no smell of drugs or medicine.' This sounds as if

I overestimated my own disappointment and underestimated your wonderfulness but it is the one thing I really care about the whole affair; so write it down.

Well, I haven't really settled down to knowing what and how I am going to spend the vac or anything. The almost and only real wave of disappointment comes when I know I am not going to spend Xmas with you and Chip and Margaret and the bairns etc. One counts, I repeat again, when one just shouldn't have counted. For this reason do try, however busy you are, to write often. Communication means so very very very much to me. More I think than anything else and not to have it cuts out the ability to do other things. Do also (mainly because it is a question sheerly of curiosity) write clearly and sequentially what exactly happened. Who were the men who objected and who, if anyone, organized them into objection? This, you can really take from me, is with no least thought of anger, for I completely understand and sympathize with their position and it is by no means [an] unnatural one, but I would just like to know to pack it away. One always loves to sit and wonder on the various facts of one's existence and my innate inquisitiveness just won't stand a picture of my own life which is incomplete.

This letter, my dear, seems so full of requests and assertions but you know my ambition and the rest of me well enough to know that this has been hard and to know only the most loved can one ask things from.

The last point is that I have spent money, not much more but a bit here and there over these last months that I wouldn't have spent, if I hadn't done this foolish counting. (In a crude Scots way, how I would like to ask the U of T to recompense me, but, of course, can't.) I, for instance, have ordered a suit (you know that in England now they cost £25). Well, I have to go through with it and buy it. (I will, by the way, find out which is cheaper – here with purchase tax – or over and back with Laval etc.) I, for instance, had the unheard of opportunity of getting a complete St Augustine whom, as you know, I am going to write a great work on someday, but it was extravagant £6. You know etc., etc. Could you lend me a little money to get me through this?

I don't think since childhood, have I ever had a birthday ... [pages missing]
You will, of course, know that this is just for clearness sake.

Do also, my dear, start to think what I should do when I come back this summer. The summer at home I am going to somehow try and finance somewhere in the sun finishing my thesis. But it must be with you in Canada in the sun. Silcox[1] (if he is seeable) is really the one man in his strange queer way who knows my thoughts and it would be lovely if you would talk to him soon about this.

Do get Chip to read this. For, although it is selfish, there are some people one wants to share one's inside with and its selfishness is mostly conditioned that here, even to my closest friends, and in Canada, even to Burgon and to S Smith, certainly I must take the high line, strike the clear note. And I repeat again – do restrain any unclear notes.

Love to you both and remember how I desperately and always count on you both; so do write.

My indigestion clears with the end of indecision and when it is sheerly a question of coping with one's own immature instincts.

Love,
George

The thought of hearing Austin Farrer next two terms and of the New Old Vic products make even the English climate somehow bearable.

Today the Micklems have so sweetly included me in a party for Niemöller.[2] What a thrill eh.

1 Edward[?] Silcox, a Protestant preacher Grant much admired
2 Martin Niemöller (1892–1984), German Lutheran pastor and outspoken opponent of Hitler, was confined to the Dachau concentration camp. After the war, he condemned the German churches because they had not opposed Hitler more forcefully.

86/ To Sidney Smith   Balliol College, Oxford
7 December 1946

Dear Dr Smith,

You must be wondering why my answer to your kind letter of 11 November is so slow in reaching you. Unfortunately your letter, although marked airmail, came by the ordinary channels and so only reached here yesterday 6 December. Now my reply will be caught in the rush of Christmas mail here. Transatlantic correspondence doesn't seem the most satisfactory method of settling a matter.

Thank you for such a long and pleasant letter. Of course, I see clearly the point about the impossibility of taking on such a job as the wardenship of Hart House under the circumstances and also indeed quite understand the fairness of the objections you mentioned. The difficulty, touchiness and great importance of these next years at the university would make it foolish to contemplate anything that might produce friction in the student body. Also men, who may have had sons in the armed forces could never feel happy about appointing to Hart House somebody who had not taken on that responsibility.

Thank you, therefore, for saving me from such a difficult position; also thank you for all your kindness since this business was first mooted. I hope you will have some rest and some fun over Christmas. How one longs amidst the drizzle of English December, for a white clean Christmas as at home.

I hope the delay over this correspondence hasn't been a nuisance.

Yours sincerely,
George Grant[1]

1 'I discussed fully last week-end with my good friend George Wilson at Dalhousie, the situation. You may know that in World War I, he even went to jail for his conscientious objections to bearing arms. I was gratified to get his testimony that it was fair for me to describe to you the actual situation. George is now Dean of Arts at Dalhousie and he is looking for a man to teach philosophy in that institution. He is wondering, I know, whether you would be interested in that post. It is my guess that you will be hearing from him' (Sidney Smith to George Grant, 14 December 1946).

1947

87/ To Maude Grant   Balliol College, Oxford

Dearest Ould,
A letter came from George Wilson yesterday about going to Dalhousie. It is not definite, as I must wait till I hear from the President (and therefore, of course, it is private) but it seems quite definite. It is for one year at $3000. If Stewart[1] will be going at the end of the year and then I presume that, if they have taken to me, I may be offered the job. This going for one year is just right. Your news the same day that Nick Ignatieff[2] was going to Hart House seemed just right too. Strangely enough when Burgon had me to Canterbury to ask me about going the person I had suggested as better than me for the job was Nick. (Even writing to you I am so afraid of getting I's and me's mixed.) I am quite honestly sure that he would do a really far better job than I ever would there. And God is good, for teaching Philosophy is much more my métier; for clear thought,

although I find it difficult, is my great goal. Every other part of my soul I would and have sold but not intellectual honesty – bad temper, laziness, etc. you know all too well. So all comes for the best. Oh Leo's is perfect. I write in the morning, walk, garden etc. in the afternoon, read, listen to the radio, write in the evening. It is the perfect place for that kind of emotional peace & quiet that one must have for writing & which the modern world never seems to offer. The thought of coming home is marvellous – after two years. The marvellous thing is that, after these years, I hope you will find me an easier person to be with. Poor Lionel now, when he has had so much to contend with (not only from the war,) but all that wealth may bring, should he have this to put up with. One feels it is so unfair. Mary G is back from Geneva. I haven't seen her. This summer won't be easy for her if Mrs G is coming over. People all seem to have their agonies.

My love to Chip and to Alison when she appears. Also to Peter and to Hart. I thought of them both during the boat race. I go to see Anne and Peter C for a few days at the end of the vacation. All my love – look after yourself and in July I will be home.

George

1 H.L. Stewart (1882–1953), educated at Oxford and the Royal University of Ireland; taught philosophy at Dalhousie, 1913–47
2 Nicholas Ignatieff (1904–52), George's brother, had taught history at Upper Canada College from 1934 until the war; during the war he served with the Canadian armed forces, rising to the rank of lieutenant-colonel. He was warden of Hart House during 1947–52.

88/ To Alice Boissonneau   Balliol College, Oxford
                                                          3 March 1947

My dear Alice,
As always in my life I have been hopeless about writing, but you know what life is like – one gets wound up into more and more people. You wouldn't know me since I came here. I have been reborn. All the energy and vitality that went during the war has come back. My mind is soaring again and, despite the agony of the world, it is good to be alive. You would find me a much more balanced person.

I always write the same stuff to you about self-disciplined writing, but I know that it is true. I was reading the other day an American publication *Partisan Review* that made out pretty well that writing was a phallic occupation, or at best a belly occupation.[1] Well, of course, the impulses of sex and of the body are finely important in writing, but *it is still* essentially an activity of the mind and more important of the creative *Will*; indeed mind and will are spirit and that's what makes us write and the animals not (the birds are suffering dreadfully from the cold here). American writing is degrading itself from its great past, by becoming phallic without anything great to direct it. Don't give up the great idea of self-disciplined dignified humanity.

The Canadian-American military agreement[2] makes me despair – so obviously against Russia. I know categorically that, in any war between the U.S.A. and Russia, the Christian must just not take part. The revolting-ness of the Roman Church in the U.S.A. putting Jesus on their banner against Communism, without attempting to understand the no doubt wrong, but great hope, of communism. Jesus didn't try and misunder-stand people who disagreed with him, but understand [them]. This sounds rather sloppy liberalism but I mean it at the depth of love. The people who try and condemn the USSR without attempting to see its qualities and its grave failings are so cruel; I guess I was guilty of that with you. Forgive me.

All my love. Look after yourself. Work and write with your mind and soul.

George G.

1 William Barrett, 'Writers and Madness,' *Partisan Review* 14, no. 1 (Jan./Feb. 1947)
2 An agreement between Canada and the United States for cooperation, coordi-nation, and planning, especially in the North.

89/ To A.E. Kerr[1]   15 April 1947

[cable:]
Accept with pleasure appointment in philosophy.

1 A.E. Kerr (1898–1974), a United Church clergyman who served as president of Dalhousie University, 1945–63

90/ To Sheila Grant   Allerthorpe, York
                                                        15 April 1947

Dear Sheila,
Thanks for your letter. Could I come on Saturday the 19th? On no account put off the ballet. I can go to some other theatre and then we can meet afterwards. I will get in from York somewhere about 2 in the after-

noon and will come on down to Blackheath, if that is convenient, and then we can come back to town for the theatre.

Could you possibly ask Francis King[1] if he is free on Saturday night and ask him what theatre he would like to go to and if you could book two tickets. He and I might go and meet you after the ballet. If he is not free, could you get me one ticket to *The Eagle Has Two Heads*.[2] Or if that is impossible, *Sweetest and Lowest*.[3] Otherwise anything you say, except an English drawing room comedy. I will pay you for the tickets when I arrive.

Could I stay till Wednesday the 23rd? Interestingly enough a cousin of my father's has written to me to spend a night with him on Wednesday. The last chance, as they go abroad in May. It will be interesting to meet a cousin of my father's as I have spent so much of my life with my mother's family. Could you not plan anything for Monday, so we could see some friends like Gerald and Mary.

Sorry my dear to put so much on you.

Have been reading an existentialist novel. If one wants that tough, fate cannot harm me, Byronic pessimism (which is a bore at the best) Faulkner and Hemingway and the Americans do it better. And it takes the dignity and discipline of the French to do it well. All we can say is that, as Pascal said of conquerors, he could understand a young man like Alexander being interested in such stuff – but for a grown up man like Caesar! So it is excusable to Russians and the U.S.A., but not the French.

Worse, I heard *Deirdre of the Sorrows*[4] on the radio last night – lush romantics. Death and passion and parting better than life and love and a productive life together. So romantic in a destructive sense.

I am going definitely (that is dv)[5] to Dalhousie University in Halifax, Nova Scotia to teach philosophy next year – good news, eh? Did you see in *The Times* that an absolutely smashingly good person[6] got the job I missed last autumn?[7]

It will be so good to see you.

1 Francis King (1923–), British novelist, short story writer, poet, and critic who was at Balliol with Grant
2 Jean Cocteau (1889–1963), *L'Aigle à deux têtes* (1946)
3 A review by Alan Melville and Charles Zwar; it played at the Ambassadors Theatre from May 1946 until April 1948.
4 J.M. Synge, *Deirdre of the Sorrows* (1910)
5 God willing
6 Nicholas Ignatieff
7 Warden of Hart House

91/ To Maude Grant   London, WC
                                                      postmarked 19 May 1947

[postcard – puzzle cup with sign of the mermaid, seventeenth century:]

We are just in town for the day and I have just bought Sheila an engagement ring. An eighteenth century ring with a sapphire. We bask in the
golden air. This cup is a cup of happiness.

                                                              George Grant

92/ To George Wilson[1]   Balliol College, Oxford
                                                      postmarked 28 May 1947

Part I
Dear Professor Wilson,
I have been hopeless about answering a letter of yours, but the last weeks
I have been involved in getting engaged to be married and never having
done anything of that kind before, have been as engrossed as a sixteen year
old. She is an English girl called Sheila Allen. I am sure you will like her. We
were going to wait till after the year at Dalhousie, but her family are making
such a possessive fuss that we are going to be married in June and make
the break. So she will come to Halifax in September. I hope you do not
think this is a mistake or that I should have let you know before. We have
known each other for a year but it was only two weeks ago that the light
dawned. Forgive me writing all this to you, but your letters have made me
feel we know each other better than the one meeting we had.
    James Doull[2] also tells me he is coming to Dalhousie. What good news.
Of all the Canadians of my generation he certainly has the clearest intellect of any I have known. Nothing I would ever have to say about philosophy will compare to his knowledge of it. How splendid it is that you have
got him back to Canada.
    This engagement business has completely driven out of my head
whether I ever answered your letter about a photograph. There is none
extant that makes me look over 12 and I am sure none of them would be
good publicity for the university. As I do look older now, if you want one I
can easily have one taken. I also believe you wanted some details of my
life; those I will put in the second part of this letter.

                                                              George Grant

1 George Wilson (1890–1973), professor of history at Dalhousie, 1919–69, and

dean of arts; author of a privately published nihilistic autobiography, *All for Nothing?* (1972)

2 J.A. Doull (1918–), classicist and philosopher, who became Grant's mentor and close friend

93/ To Maude Grant   Balliol College, Oxford
                                                postmarked 2 June 1947

Dearest Ould,

I am sitting in the Balliol quad on one of those unbelievable English May days with everything at its most luxuriant. Yesterday a wonderful letter came from you about money and getting married. The point is, I was already feeling badly about getting married just when I could let you have some money; so your letter made one feel ever more how goldenly generous you are. I don't think we will need any money over here as we have all we need. The only real extravagance has been an engagement ring, but it was so cheap. When you could loan us a little is in September to get to Dalhousie before a first pay cheque; but it must be a loan and not a gift. I have always taken so much more from you than any of the others.

All goes well. Sheila is taking her schools[1] in June instead of December which will mean she won't do well. She just is a far more deeper human being than I am. My trouble will always be not to ride roughshod over her and to be fine enough for her. She will be the kind of wife so that I will probably do less in life, but what I do will be much better than it otherwise would have been.

Since starting this a cable came from you. You must be up to your ears. Here we are in absolutely unforgettable June England and although one tries hard to work and to think one can't do much more than hang about in the golden air. The date seems to be the beginning of July. Then go to France. Then home, we hope, about the 20th. Sheila is full of devastation about not writing to you. But I surround her with a hundred and one of my friends. She hasn't even time for her own work. How you will love her as she will love you.

Always my deepest love,
George Grant

1 The final examinations for her B.A.

94/ To Maude Grant   London, WC
                                                 postmarked 21 June 1947

[postcard:]
We are up in London for the day getting a wedding dress. We yet haven't
heard definitely about a passage, but are hoping for the middle of July.
We both so deeply excited about seeing you. You will see how the gods are
with me.

                                                                George

95/ To Maude Grant   44 Mount St, London
                                                 postmarked 30 June 1947

Dearest Ould,
I am just at the moment waiting in Austin Reed's to have my hair cut and
washed. It is Saturday morning and, God willing, on Tuesday I will be
married to Sheila. It is a difficult time mainly as one has no place to go.
Sheila begged Mrs Allen to have me but she wouldn't. Dearly and sweetly
Aunt Grace has asked me to stay. As for Sheila, [it is she] who really has
the difficulty. Her mother is hopeless. Mary Greey has arrived from
Geneva but Sheila is having all the food, drink and flowers plus her
clothes to get. We don't want them (particularly Elizabeth Walker) to do
anything. Mary only here a few days is so deeply engrossed; Gerald – so
altogether. I never felt so alive. Sheila is really an angel to her mother ...,
who just give[s] her no affection and, when you meet her, I know you will
know how much she needs it. We all must give her a real feeling of family.
Of course, it has given her enormous strength for she has always had to
be the mother in her family.
    ERP simply wonderful in getting us a passage home. It is terribly diffi-
cult to get one just now and he has got us one on the July 16th passage of
the Empress of Canada. That will mean we will be home, if all is well, in
about 4 weeks. We land in Montreal and will come on to Toronto. Could
we go to Otter Lake almost right away. Sheila is just tired out and so am I.
Also, I have so much work to do in getting my lectures ready for next year.
    I hope you aren't exhausted. Oh, my darling it is almost unbelievable
that we are soon to meet. I just daren't speak of it for it is so exciting and,
of course, even more exciting for you and Sheila to meet. Your letters are
so full of George and Alison that I never know what Margaret and Charity
are doing. You know how wildly jealous I am. But it gradually goes.
    Oh, I never believed I could miss anyone as much as not having you

here at the wedding. The one consolation is that we will see you so soon. Think of us and remember how deeply always you are with us.

Love,
George Grant

With few formal qualifications, Grant began an academic career that would make him the most famous philosopher in Canada and one of the country's best teachers. His stay at Dalhousie extended from 1947 until he left in 1960. In 1980, he returned to Dalhousie and taught there again until his retirement.

96/ To Maude Grant   2 October

Dearest Ould,

The first lectures have been an amazing experience. To give oneself in them means three things which take all one's energy (1) A1 Preparation is necessary & often about subjects I am not trained in & this means extensive reading & thinking. This first year I am not going to be able to do much work but just prepare & give my lectures (2) preparation of stories, examples that, particularly in an elementary philosophy course of 125, is vital; (3) great emotional concentration at each hour of lecturing.

H.L. Stewart gives me a great advantage. Everybody at Dalhousie so clearly dislikes him that anyone changing his ways will be applauded at first.

Wilson is *the* great influence here, beloved by the best members of the staff even when they see certain weaknesses & beloved by the students. Except for too great quietism, clearly a very fine human being. Straightness & Decency. Page is a dear & we are both going the same direction. I would hope they would make him head of the department next year rather than me, if they raised my salary and status. He is fine educated Toronto United Church at its best ...

What do you think of asking the Masseys for a gramophone? For us music is the supreme pleasure & there is none played here & it will save us going out to the movies & it relaxes me after philosophy.

Love,
George

1948

97/ To Maude Grant   Dalhousie University, Halifax
                                           12 February

Dearest Ould,

Today a lovely letter arrived from you about the good news from Lionel and Lilias.[1] I am so glad for their dear sakes and for Aunt Lal's and Uncle V's immortality. I hope it all goes well. Are we supposed to know? Can we, that is, write to them?

Life goes well here. I went down to Lunenberg the other day. Didn't seem to me as pleasant as Sydney, [which] has that wild quality of untamedness that Canada should have at its best. Some of the students from there are simply wonderful. This week I have been getting some stuff back from my first year students and it really is so full of vigour and energy when they drop the artificial form that makes them believe that academic subjects are cut off from the life they lead. The one or two best students are interested in philosophy deeply. The difficult thing is that the growing technocrat civilization which, despite all the protests, is bound to grow, combined with the economic depression that is coming. It makes one (now that it has come to the Maritimes) wary of getting them committed to philosophy, which won't feed them.

Gandhi's death was a blow – but his being was of the quality that makes it possible for less clear lights like us to know where to go.[2] Poor old *Time* (even with its strong present day religious lights to combat Russian imperialism and as a useful instance of the American imperialism) could not face up to Gandhi – it compared him to Lincoln – a good firm democratic politician of the dying liberal world with this tremendous saint. What I always deplore in Nehru[3] is that he found Gandhi's civil disobedience wonderful because it was another successful instance in the political power world instead of its reality about human existence – succeed or fail. One thing I get from Gandhi is the great dignity of the imperial power of Britain he combatted and how he saw that. The British were truly civilization at its best – just, firm, caring only for this world and the bayonet used fairly. My God the Empires we are going to get now. The Russian, indeed, the most awful – but the American Empire – kinder certainly, juster perhaps – but not so different.

At the moment I am writing an article in spare moments – thought of this morning – on the sad fate of the Canadian liberal. Having preached isolationist humanitarian nationalist, they now, under WLMK, have to advocate our atom bomb saving of civilization. The Tories were always fair, straight and honest that civilization was only maintained by the bayonet, and rightly. Woodsworth and Co preached honest pacifism – redemption. Bennett or Woodsworth were both right – depending on what choice you make. Dafoe,[4] Skelton,[5] King were misguided whigs – who used the slick double-talk of liberalism and whose job must now be having refused to recognize the facts of life – prepare for atom warfare to spread the civilization of Hollywood.

We have to move out of the MacKays'[6] at the end of June. Should we get another furnished place or not? Arguments are (1) an unfurnished place easier to get (2) also cheaper – you pay for furniture which at the end you don't own. On the other hand the arguments are (1) furniture is expensive to buy at the moment (2) we haven't money (3) we don't want to get cluttered up with a lot of furniture in the insecure world we are going to be living in. What do you think of all this? Tell Chip to tell you the story of her looking at all the things here and seeing what we had gouged out of you. I feel [badly about what] we did [take]. We already own enough possessions. Too many. I want to keep everything to a minimum as I really feel that, in our lifetime, we may be called to the utterest precarious existence in a depression or another war. That is my firm feeling against buying or possessing furniture. I even dislike my own books. One's records one can easily get rid of.

Another thing Mrs Lovett, who is an old and deep friend in England, has asked me about getting one of her children to Canada. A boy of 17. All one has to do is to present him with a letter that you will meet him here and get him a job. I feel I owe it to Mrs Lovett (and more to England) to help with emigration which they need for survival. I know the boy well. He is the best of them and a keen one to get out of the slum life he has been brought up in. So I feel I must go ahead. It is another liability but it will be a charity and I won't give to others. Do write about this as soon as you possibly can.

You write of ISS[7] probably not knowing that I am the faculty adviser at Dalhousie and am doing all to help them. I don't know why they got me in – but am doing all that I can. By the way the Mrs Martin is Fred and Ross' mother in Hamilton. She sent us a lovely bowl.

As you see from this we are leading very full and happy lives. I have never felt so full of power and so integrated since I was born – but one is always chastened if one feels successful by the remembrance that all that can possibly do anything of any kind for the world is the depth of vision of the supremely great and humble and self-discipline and I haven't even

started on the beginning of the road to any of these. Gandhi's death sort
of stopped one up short and made one realise how utterly meaningless is
any accomplishment now but that of the depths, and that one sees no
prospect of such accomplishment coming from oneself. Everything has
been given to me in life – and without any false humility; as yet one is in
no way ready to pour out what one could.

Do write to us when you hear of Chip's job; we long to know. Give her
our love.

Sheila calls out her love to you. What with doing her English themes
every week – writing to her mother – writing an article on Gandhi she
feels guilty of not having written you. But this letter is as much hers as
mine.

Love
George

1 They were about to have their first child.
2 Mahatma Gandhi (1869–1948), a pacifist and one of the leaders in the struggle
  for Indian independence. Gandhi was assassinated by a Hindu fanatic on 30
  January 1948.
3 Jawaharlal Nehru (1889–1964), India's first prime minister after independence
4 J.W. Dafoe (1866–1944), editor of the Winnipeg *Free Press* from 1901 until his
  death
5 O.D. Skelton (1878–1941), professor of political science and economics at
  Queen's, 1909–25, and then under-secretary of state for external affairs until
  his death
6 The Grants had rooms at the MacKays'.
7 International Student Service

98/ To Maude Grant   6 Oxford St, Halifax
                                          31 August

Dearest Ould,
We know how wildly and strenuously busy you must have been getting to
Otter Lake and how hot it has been in Toronto and therefore know why
you haven't written – any more than we have. *All* that bothers us that you
might be angry about anything I wrote, for the thought of you in anyway
angry at me makes life difficult. The thought of you all at Otter Lake is
lovely, yet unbearable, as we would so love to be there. But it is without
doubt and always was an impossible dream. Anyway I am enough of a

Puritan to know that the very shape of the universe is grief and not least of the griefs is being so much separated from those one loves.

Here life proceeds. Tomorrow we go to the country for two weeks.[1] Its greatest joy is getting enough seclusion to write, as already the students are coming back and one can't get that environment of concentration which one must selfishly push for. A change will do us both good, as the thought of the year ahead of pouring oneself out, I do not face with even any excitement. I guess it will come. But there is such an endless sense of what one could do, in the marvellous opportunity, if one only had more singleness of purpose and unity of character.

Rachel[2] is her usual sweet self. Tonight was the first touch of autumn cold and so she got into her Gran's blue jacket. She looked very sweet. She has started to eat Pablum and is generally a vast mess after a session. But oh what dear hope. Who could not believe that beneath the surface there must be some meaning when something as dear as she is part of the world.

The lovely pictures arrived today. How nice they are. I prefer the Venice one to the Padua one. Although strangely, as a young child at UCC, I can remember thinking Padua was my friend, while Venice was stern and unfriendly. Perhaps it was the dark and the light. They were paid for when they arrived. *You must* let us know how much they were.

Kerr had me in last night and said that today he was going to have me made acting head of the department. So there it is. It means nothing, except perhaps sadness for Page and therefore wish it hadn't happened. He also said, as I did odd jobs for the University throughout the year, he would let $250 come my way, which is pleasant. It is a question of our high rent and he can't make a precedent of helping people; therefore, it is to be done this way. Don't mention it. I wish I could admire him. Oh he was so narrow and unseeing about his trip to England last night.

Well anyway, Drew[3]-Duplessis may be difficult, but they won't be worse than King and it will be good for Uncle Jim. I have at last boiled down my objection to WLMK. It is this. For his own purposes he always talked one way and acted another and thereby hid the real issues from the Canadian people and helped to keep the Canadian people at the level of political immaturity that we are at. Even the Americans are more mature than us, for they are faced with the exigencies of power. King helped to push that damned nonsense of the Whig myth and all its puttling liberalism so far in his talk, that Canadians really believe those are the issues.

But enough; I must turn out the light. Oh my dear I wish we were with you. It would be so lovely. But you are in our thoughts and on our tongues all the time. Let our love for you excuse our inadequacies – my inadequacies.

To everybody love.
Sheila – Rachel – George

1 At 'Owl's nest,' the Lauries' camp on the Grand River
2 Rachel Grant was born 25 April 1948.
3 George Drew (1894–1973), premier of Ontario, 1943–8; leader of the federal
  Progressive Conservative party, 1948–56

99/ To Maude Grant   6 Oxford St, Halifax
                                                           7 November

Dearest Ould,
This week I haven't stopped laughing since Truman's victory.[1] How much in the long run of policy it will matter doesn't seem to me the point, but that the polls and the papers can't push people around is glorious. On the whole farmers, labour and housewives seem to me better people than the American business community. What is wonderfully pleasing is that this may really scare the Republican Party out of the control of those Pennsylvania crew, who so obviously took Dewey[2] because he would make terms. Also, the fact that those men who believed themselves *experts* and above politics and wouldn't get out and fight like Forrestal,[3] now can toss away his political career, at least for a few years. The British and American tradition that the politician has to get out and fight if he is in a Cabinet, rather than be non-partisan seems to me a good tradition. Also, the fact that thousands of people have to come crawling to Harry S won't be so bad, as he is a humble little man. I stayed up all night on election day and just laughed and laughed and haven't been able to stop feeling happy ever since. So rarely these days can there be such pleasant events. Think how good it was that Ickes[4] got out and fought. A man of courage. I sent Geoff a telegram – Milton's

Oh how comely it is, and how reviving
To the spirits of just men long oppresst[5]

But have had no answer whether he got it or not.
Now to business and important business. I am sorry to always be trying to force letters and advice out of you, when you are so busy. But this is something I have to decide quickly and it is important.
I now plan, *unless* you are against it, to go to England next spring and stay there till Christmas, taking my degree at Xmas. That would give me

just the requisite time to finish it decently and to take the oral etc. (1) What makes this financially possible is that Sheila has just been left a legacy by an aunt which would allow us to live in England at that time. (2) What makes it necessary is that I must get this D.Phil., and thereby have some qualifications to teach and not to be utterly at the beck and call of the businessmen. Any university I will be at, I will be in fights over policy and I must have the solid basis of qualifications. (3) Anybody will tell you you can't do it while teaching. Philosophy is intense thought and one doesn't do it while one has to be intense about something else. (4) What adds to the necessity is I got two letters. One from Grensted saying it *had* to be in by June 1949; one from Dr Micklem saying he would fight for an extension for me. But he can only do that if I show I am working seriously.

As far as Dalhousie goes, it may mean the end or it may mean they will grant me leave till Xmas next year. I don't think I can worry too much about that. For, if I am to teach in Canada, I must so clearly have a D.Phil. Otherwise, the businessmen have you where they want you. Wilson recommends it, for as he says, he has had several inquiries about me and says I can probably get a job.

Now, another problem is if Kerr, when I tell him I am resigning, wants me to commit myself to come back. What would I do? There are many advantages here. I am head of the department; therefore, I can teach philosophy as I know it should be taught. I can say to you I am popular. Philosophy I this year, although not compulsory, is the largest class in the university. I get on awfully well with young N.S. and admire and like what they stand for. Of course, there are disadvantages. Kerr is for size and popularity with the public. That means science and applied science will be built up at the expense of education.

That is two questions I want answered, darling. (1) Should I go to England? You will have to present very strong arguments against this D.Phil. business, as I feel I must get it soon and know just what time I need. (2) What should my attitude be to returning here to Dal?

Please either write this week or, if you are too busy, telephone at my expense, as I must get my applications for extension off to England. One thing Sheila says over and over again is that she is against me going, as she doesn't want you to ever think that she is persuading me to go back to England. You, of course, recognize that it would be only temporary, as I have no interest in the least in becoming an Englishman. Never have since a week after I landed there in 1945.

As I write this a beloved soul is in her crib, blowing and cooing and rolling over and just being so angelic your heart would break. She is becoming more and more of a person everyday. She has an intense love of green beans and her vegetables and is full of all kinds of gurgling noises.

Otherwise life goes on at its hectic rate. One is simply a lecture machine and not a very good machine at that. But then one is very lucky.

Love to all,
George

1 Against Republican Tom Dewey in the American presidential election. Dewey had been widely expected to win.
2 T.E. Dewey (1902–71), governor of New York and Republican presidential candidate in 1944 and 1948
3 James Forrestal (1892–1949), American secretary of defence, 1947–9
4 H.L. Ickes (1874–1952); resigned from Truman's cabinet in 1946 following a political dispute
5 John Milton, *Paradise Regained* 1.1264–5

100/ To Maude Grant   24 November

Dearest Ould,
Dalhousie has come out for a graduate school. This is, of course, very ridiculous as they haven't got enough staff to give a decent B.A. & now they even talk of Ph.D. in the Maritimes. My department has 310 students with me the only full time teacher & they call that philosophy. The physics department has 8½ times as much spent on it as on philosophy barring equipment; so they can do graduate work while we can't even do undergraduate work in Arts. Well, this graduate school is sheer evidence, sans doute, that Dalhousie is going to be a technical college. So there is little hope of getting real philosophy done here. So it makes me want to go.

Love,
George

101/ To Maude Grant   6 Oxford St, Halifax

Dearest Ould,
When we wake up these mornings there is a little girl who is standing up at the side of the crib, smiling with such glorious pride at her great achievement, monarch of all she surveys. It is a great push and pull to get up and very wobbly when up, but oh what triumph. Last week she was not at all well and a little limp figure lay, just looking miserable and, when you

picked her up, instead of a lot of struggling and jumping, there was only a limp little girl. She is better, however, and we are relieved.

We want endlessly to pay for a trip down here for you, that is, if you feel well enough and don't think it would be too tiring. It will simply break our hearts to go to England for a whole year and not see you. We will send you a cheque, but only if you feel it wouldn't be too great a strain. If it were please tell us honestly. Why does life keep us apart? There are so few people that one longs for.

It looks as if we will be apart longer. From what I gather Queen's does not want me, at least not at a rank compared to what I can get here and the rank means the control over what you teach, which is the main thing, for most people still teach philosophy as if there were still a civilization in North America, instead of teaching it as if the old traditions were completely finished and we had to build new ones. The degree to which the scientific civilization has swept away Xianity is appalling. God sees the truth – but waits.

I didn't get the scholarship from the Humanities Council. I just heard that from Wilson yesterday. Too bad, but there it is. We will still go to England.

Since saying I was leaving here, there have been such comings and goings. First an unpleasant interview with Laurie[1] – what a fool. He thinks a university is a barracks and he can talk to teachers like NCOs. The next day a long and very pleasant talk with Kerr. So I am coming back here after Oxford, committing myself for a year to here. I think that is very reasonable. Heavens, nobody else offers me a job – they will give me a year's leave of absence. I can't bank on unknowns. (Private) The whole thing was complicated by Wilson who was away and who wrote me a highly emotional letter about not trusting a word Kerr said. I, as you know, find Wilson an impossible enigma. He won't fight Kerr, he won't resign as Dean; yet he is all undercover. He hates many of the things Kerr is doing; yet he always supports them in public – condemns them in private very strongly. What a strange man.

So as far as I see, I will stay here and build up the philosophy department. That suits me except for being so far away.

Well life goes on. No wonder the businessmen walk over teachers. Most of them are such ninnies.

Wasn't the Conservative victory in Quebec[2] amazing. I must admit the shakes it must be giving the Liberals is a pleasant and moving thought. Drew-Duplessis won't be worse than King, in fact perhaps better. A small and unimportant amusement was the look of wild, bewildered consternation on the faces of the oh so dogmatic Grits in this part of the country. You know the kind of people who idolize Hume and think Tupper a skunk.

This is a poor letter but life goes from one thing to the next. Always papers and if not then papers for philosophy and scientific clubs and sermons.

Love,
George

1 Lt Col. K.C. Laurie (1881–1967), a wealthy man from a distinguished Nova Scotia family (he counted a chief justice of Nova Scotia and a bishop among his ancestors), he was chairman of the board of governors of Dalhousie from 1943 until 1955. From Grant's point of view, Laurie's public-spirited desire to promote 'the development of Nova Scotia educational institutions' (*Halifax Chronicle-Herald,* 27 May 1943) was an unmitigated disaster for higher education in Nova Scotia.

2 Duplessis's Union Nationale, which many people considered the Conservative party in Quebec

102/ To Dr A.E. Kerr   Dalhousie University, Halifax, N.S.
                                              29 November 1948

Dear Mr President,
The announcement that there is to be a school of graduate studies at Dalhousie presents an opportune moment to put in writing to you my thoughts about the teaching of philosophy at the university. In the light of the multitude of your responsibilities, I hope you will forgive my writing at length.

There seem to me five main types of activity that can be carried out in the teaching of philosophy at a university, as they are constituted in Canada.

(1) The teaching of that mass of students who only need a single course in philosophy. This must of necessity be primarily a religious undertaking, to help the students understand some of the implications of our common tradition.

(2) The more extensive teaching of those students who need a wider background in philosophy, eg. theology students.

(3) The close supervision of those students who want to take an honours course in philosophy.

(4) The supervision and teaching of M.A. students.

(5) The supervision of Ph.D. students.

The question presents itself which of these activities Dalhousie wishes to undertake. The only one that would appear should be discarded on sight is #5.

At the present it would seem clear that Dalhousie has only staff to undertake #1 adequately and #2 passably. There is not the staff to undertake an honours course worthy of our tradition. A fortiori the supervision of M.A. students is quite out of the question.

This lack of staff is particularly evident in a subject like philosophy where (i) every teacher should be constantly enlivening his work with contemplation and reading and (ii) where different types of approach from teachers is of the deepest value for the students.

One solution to this dilemma would be to say that, at Dalhousie, philosophy would be considered as an unimportant subject and intensive work not carried on. Yet, of course, as a philosopher I could not be reconciled to such a solution. Neither do I believe that you as president would be reconciled to this either ... particularly in the light of what you so ably said in your inauguration address.

The reason why the formation of a graduate school raises this question so forcibly is that its establishment at this time can only be intelligible on the assumption that the university intends to go ahead with graduate work in some subjects, before it is staffed to do adequate undergraduate work in others. When one considers the staff in departments like Physics or Chemistry, and the fact that the number of students in those departments is about equal to one's own, one quite understands why they are willing to embark on graduate studies. However, you will quite understand that no philosopher, and certainly no Christian in this year 1948, could accept the assumption that the study of nature should be so disproportionately posed at the expense of the study of the deeper questions of human existence.

I hope for this reason that you will be tolerant of the frankness and length of this letter.

Yours sincerely,
George Grant

1949

Sheila Grant received a legacy from an aunt. Because of postwar currency controls, she could not bring the money to Canada. The Grants decided to use the legacy to finance a year in England, where Grant hoped to finish his D.Phil. thesis. They made the mistake of staying with Sheila's mother, Mrs Allen. At least, Grant reflected, it gave him practice in loving his enemies.

103/ To Maude Grant   Halifax, Nova Scotia
                                             9 January 1949

Dear Mumbles,

It seems dreadful to advertise one's own wares, but I thought you might be interested to hear my voice. It will be on the radio this Tuesday 11 January. I am not quite sure when – afternoon or evening – on a CBC program called *Points of View.* The question 'On Human Happiness.' I hope you like what I say, for it is one of those times where one can say something that one believes to be true.

We sail for England 15 May on the Furness-Withy line. Oh – oh – oh I don't know whether we will stay to finish my D.Phil. or just for the summer. The next month and a half will tell. By the way Uncle Jim wrote me such a nice New Years letter in which he said that he was glad 'I was going back to do some more work at Oxford.' *I hope and pray you or Charity did not imply to him that I was going* back to Oxford for next year; for then he might tell Wallace and then I would not get any offer from Queen's. Do read this to Charity. Because I haven't at all decided to go to Oxford and it would kill one's expectations. It may have been a merely general nice comment on Uncle J's part, or it might be difficult. As I have said to you before the only possibility of staying here and getting anything done, is not for them to think I am stuck here.

Life goes on at a great rate. Lectures have started. A new class of 210. A bad sore throat. Rachel looking and acting more like you every day. Happy, giggly girl, crawling over everything, gurgling about everything, grabbing everything, very determined and very sweet. Teeth have really appeared, although not in quantity yet. She really does look like you more than anybody else. She is long and large with a big head. The rattle you sent her is an enormous success for waving; the tree bear is still too big for her to manipulate.

It is thrilling news to hear CLG will be here; oh I hope it comes off. It will be glorious for Rachel to see her real aunt and godmother.

Sheila says to thank you for the photos you sent. I look like a very determined, and not very good-tempered child, even at that small age. It is a relief to know that, although outsiders often comment on Rachel's likeness to me, there is no great likeness between her and the photo of me on the sofa.

We are very lucky as some students have given us some very beautiful records recently. If there is anything that is a necessary drug, it is music. It is a question which is more necessary, tobacco or music.

Rachel is the wildest searcher for Eldorados, anything at the far end of the room, particularly a precious paper, will be sought with all efforts.

Love to CLG.
Always our deepest.
R, S, G.
XXXXXXXXXXXXXXXXXXXXXX

104/ To Dr E.A. Corbett[1]

63 Blackheath Park, London SE3
postmarked 19 October 1949

Dear Dr Corbett,

A good friend sent me your article on Dr Coady[2] in *Saturday Night*[3] and I just wanted to send you a line to say how much you brought his personality into colour and life, in my opinion. Apart from much else, what I have always admired is your ability to make adult education seem as if it was exciting not a tedious business that is only tried by those who have nothing better to do. You certainly made one feel all the zest and intensity of Dr Coady.

It was such a disappointment that it was that particular day that I met you in London last summer. For I was feeling full of my own troubles and hating England and therefore couldn't convey to you how much it meant meeting you and how much I wanted to see you again. There it is – just life – that sometimes those people who mean the most to one are the very people one just doesn't seem able to show one's warmth to. Forgive this outburst.

Sheila and I are getting on OK over here. Work is progressing and I hope that a Ph.D. will be the result to satisfy one's own worship of Baal and all the Baal worshippers around Dalhousie. Strangely both Sheila and myself feel very strange in England at the moment. However much one admires the country, and particularly a lot of what the new regime is doing, there is a big gap between it and Canada and the older one gets, I guess, the more the gap is apparent. Sheila is spending the year having another child, so if all goes well we should come back to Canada four. I don't know why one should bring more people into this world, but one can't stop with an only child.

My best regards to Mrs Corbett and to Joan and to Paul when you write. He must be thrilled with his new job. Also regards to Isabel Wilson. To you the best that a young man can say to an older whom he admires and loves.

George Grant

1 E.A. Corbett (1887–1964), director of the Canadian Association of Adult Education (CAAE) and a long-time friend of Maude Grant from their undergraduate days together at McGill
2 Fr M.M. Coady (1882–1959), first director of the adult education program at Saint Francis Xavier University in Antigonish, Nova Scotia, and founder of the Antigonish movement.
3 E.A. Corbett, 'The Man Who Changed the Lives of Nova Scotia Fishermen,' *Saturday Night*, 30 September 1949

105/ To Maude Grant   63 Blackheath Park, London SE3
                                            postmarked 25 October 1949

Dearest Ould,
A simply glorious parcel arrived from you today; the best parcel I ever saw in my life. Particularly the Klim and butter and bacon put us right back in the swim. Dearest Wo[1] was just thrilled beyond words, for she is a very skilled and fine cook, who loves having things to work with. Milk is in very short supply, so the Klim is as from the gods. Also that butter is wonderful to save for the ends of the week when so much is scarce. Also bacon is superb for breakfast and the steak and kidneys for decent meals on cold days.

Wo and Sheila are out tonight for the first time together since we came over. It has taken weeks of arrangement to get over Mrs A's jealousy. They both went out looking as if they were going to the circus. They are to see a comedy in London; so I had the exquisite time of putting a little girl to bed. So much laughing goes on, doing her little jobs and getting into her night clothes. She always goes down to sleep perfectly. She is so sweet, one wonders how there can be so much sweetness.

Between chapters I went down for the night to the Selfs' in Brighton. It really is always the nicest house to go to. Sir Henry is a tough old Cockney who is administrator of the Nationalized Electricity Board and also President of the Modern Churchmen's Union; a really modern theologian. What I like so much about the Self parents was that they were in the U.S.A. all the war. They loved it and admired it without ceasing to be really English and with real perspective of its faults and yet real understanding of its essential greatness and the hope that lies on our continent. *Confidentially* he is so shrewd about the difference between men like Morris Wilson and Hume Wrong[2] on the one hand and E.P. Taylor[3] on the other. Both Wrong and Wilson in their different ways had, he felt, real vision which transcended money and power. E.P. Taylor he made the remark of 'If those are the kind of men that you put your society in charge of, it will be not much better than the Russians, for they don't care for any value but their own money.'

Well, now back to another chapter. It is so strange not knowing whether one is doing good work or not. All love to you and Chip and so many thanks for such a lovely parcel.

From three Grants to the head of the tribe.

1 Sheila's old nanny
2 H.H. Wrong (1894–1954), son of historian Hume Wrong and family friend of Vincent Massey. Wrong became first secretary of the Canadian legation in Washington in 1928 under Massey. He became ambassador to Washington in 1946.
3 E.P. Taylor (1901–89), C.D. Howe's deputy on the Anglo-American-Canadian Combined Production and Resources Board during the war. After the war he formed Argus Corporation, a major Canadian holding company.

1950

106/ To Maude Grant   63 Blackheath Park, London SE3
                                              postmarked 18 January 1950

Dearest Ould,
Here I am on a very bumpy train to Oxford going up to see what the boys think of my thesis. Oh boy. Well, the election is on here. As you know I have less and less interest in politics, but in this one I am just 100% for Labour. I don't think the best of the Tories tell lies but the general penny press tells such dreadful lies that I find myself going around quietly propagandizing. The great lie is that shortages here are due to labour and not to the fact that the old ruling class led them through two wars. Also, as you know I don't believe in democracy and think there have to be rulers, however controlled by elections, but the English richer middle-class seem to be the last to rule. Their attitude, as far as I have been able to see it, is the state of England is [essential to] their privileges. So many of them talk as if the Labour Party had introduced class struggle into England, when my God the middle class have waged it for years. I do agree with the Conservatives that the manual worker has rather got the

bit in his teeth, but quite frankly I can't see the spoiled middle class as the disciplinarian and think Cripps, Morrison and Co. will do it better. The new up-and-coming lower middle class seem to have so much more vigour than the old soft one. But it's mainly the sheer crudity of the Tory appeal promises they can't possibly expect to keep, make me such a rip-roaring Labourite, far, far more than I would be CCF in Canada. As for Churchill, he's so good in the U.S. or Geneva, and then is not so good in England. Sheila sees more of the upper middle class of Blackheath and therefore is even more fanatically pro-Labour. I think the Labour will win; she, pessimist as always, thinks the Tories will.[1]

Well, I thought you might be interested in a bulletin about the elections. This letter includes little else except a great great deal of love. Pray for my clear head in the next months.

Always to you and CLG deepest love,
GPG

1 Atlee won a narrow victory in the 1950 election. He lost to Churchill in a general election the next year.

107/ To Maude Grant   63 Blackheath Park, London SE3
                              postmarked 18 January 1950

Dearest Ould,
I was up in Oxford yesterday and, in light of what I learned there, I am forced to make a change of plan. I simply cannot afford to turn my thesis in before 15 June and that means I have to wait in England through July for my *viva voce*,[1] so we can't guarantee to be home before 15 August. I hate having to upset your plans and, God knows, you know how deeply I hate not being with you in July. I am sick for home. But I can't afford to risk anything unnecessary over this thesis and not to take the extra month of rewriting would be risk indeed. As it is I am not now at all sure of getting it – in fact quite unsure. Life seems to be that way. What one wants most one can't have. I know you will understand just how sad I was to make the decision.

The decision was difficult for never have I felt so alien or foreign in England. The last two days in Oxford, I literally said I never want to see Europe again. That coldness that is there, that continual sense they have that they are the centre of the world and the way they think is the right way and the sure way, got under my skin. This makes it all the more tragic to have to stay in this country till August, but there it is. I guess as there is so little time from 15 August to 20 September when I will have to go to Halifax, there won't be worth the financial burden of you not renting Otter Lake. But I leave that, of course, to you.

This is a depressing letter and indeed for me this has been a depressing year. My confidence in myself has been somehow lost this year and my main feeling is a desire to crawl into a hole and escape from everything. The one redeeming feature and, of course, that is complete redemption, is the happiness and oh the fantastic luck of Sheila and Rachel.

My dear, my dear, my dear, sorry to write you a depressed letter, but it brings you oh such love.

George

1 Oral defence of his thesis

108/ To Sheila Grant

25 June 1949

[telegram announcing his successful defence of his thesis:]
George Grant Balliol Oxford
Gaudeamus et amemus O Carissime[1]

1 Let us rejoice and love, my dearest

109/ To Maude Grant

63 Blackheath Park, London SE3

Dearest, dearest Mummy,
Just a note about Aunt Lal's illness.[1] For you who have loved her all your life and who have looked after her, her illness must be dreadful. She has given so much to so many people. I can never say thank you often enough for what she did for me in the early days of the war. She was one of the rare people who didn't make me feel I was a leper. Also, her loveliness to Sheila when she came to Canada, the way she made Sheila feel at home was lovely too. I know what a wonderful strength you are to them now, but do save your strength and see that you get good rest. We will try to be as quiet as we can when we come out. You just decide about Otter Lake. We would, of course, love it more than anything else. But what matters far more is just being with you and CLG and it really doesn't matter whether it is in Toronto or in Otter Lake, and if OL feels too far away from Aunt Lal and too much a strain we will oh so completely understand. All that

will be good for Sheila is to feel she is with two people who are her family, for what is so awful about her mother is the fact that, if she had to choose between a cigarette and Sheila, she would choose the cigarette. You know Sheila well enough to know that she is of great tenderness and the lack of care of her mother ... has gone deep.

You mention getting a letter from Min Gordon. Unless she heard from Micklem she didn't hear from me. I said goodbye to Derrick Grant and told him as I have a very deep affection for him. He is sort of an image of Daddy. I told Peter Self, for he has meant more to S and me (close but no cigar)[2] than anybody else and was the only person who in a very busy life really helped me with my thesis. But otherwise I have told nobody, except to say that I enjoyed my *viva*. Don't think I was silly about thinking my work bad. Theology must be a study where one is surrounded by the dark. Nothing do I think of as much as 'But now we see as in a dark mirror, but then face to face.'[3] The glass of vision is for me particularly blackened by my laziness.

Practical plans. We sail on the Empress of Scotland on 1 August. Landing at Quebec 8th or 9th. The CPR cannot tell us about trains from Quebec-Montreal-Toronto exactly. I hope we will get an afternoon train from Quebec to Montreal and then an evening train to Toronto arriving in the morning. But keep in touch with the CPR about the arrival of the Empress about 8th or 9th and then you will gather about when the train journey from Quebec-Toronto is all done. We are sending most of our stuff from Quebec to Halifax. Cheaper than sending it from here to Halifax direct. Rachel is passing through a little more difficult stage; so do forgive her her trespasses when she arrives.

I got a nice letter from the President of Dalhousie making me Professor of Philosophy, to be a permanent appointment as soon as I am successful over my D.Phil.; so at last I have a decent job and can settle down. Although with Korea going on one just doesn't want to settle in an ivory tower.

I know you don't know Peter Self but you know what a wonderful friend he has been this year – indeed one of the best pieces of friendship I have ever met. He has just got engaged to a charming girl at the *Economist*. He has London at his feet, yet has always taken the time to see me this year. He has the gift of sheer zest and happiness as no other person I know.

Isn't Aunt Grace a remarkable and wonderful person? All the superficial difficulties are made up for by that remarkable perception of essentials she has.

We saw Uncle Jim. He came down with Anne and Peter for tea. Having people in this house is so nerve-racking and I found him not so easy as usual. How can one not admire that great directness and goodness but there is a certain lack of cynicism about him that makes him difficult to talk to in words that won't offend him.

This is such a silly letter coming to you when you must be tired out after Washington and now the added burden of Batterwood.[4] As Sheila said the other day, your ability to help people and to love people make us all look pretty useless. But you have taught me what real responsibility is.

Oh how exciting it will be for you and CLG to see Rachel and little Wimby.[5] It is going to be hard for me to be fair, as Rachel is so like me in character and Wimby looks like Sheila with his enormous sad eyes. He, I would imagine, is going to be a much subtler little person than Rachel. She has however this wonderful zest for life and is going to be hell to control. I can see her and Aunt Charity together no end, as Charity will be the only one strong enough and smart enough to out manoeuvre her.

In about three weeks we should be with you. Oh I can hardly wait. Give everybody at Batterwood my very best. To you and CLG always.

Love,
George

1 Alice Massey died 1 July 1950.
2 A signature phrase of Groucho Marx, which Grant used all his life
3 'For now we see through a glass, darkly; but then face to face' (1 Corinthians 13.11).
4 Batterwood was the Masseys' house, near Port Hope, Ontario.
5 Their son, William

Grant's examiner for his D.Phil. thesis was a man he profoundly admired, Austin Farrer, who praised the work Grant had done. He had confounded those who thought that he did not have the intellectual discipline to complete such a sustained piece of work. Even his bête noire, C.K. Allen, admitted he had been wrong. 'I am delighted to hear that George Grant has accomplished his task. As you know, I was always very doubtful whether he would manage it and I think that you shared that doubt. I am very happy to have been wrong about him' (C.K. Allen to L.W. Grensted, 30 October 1950).

1950

His degree complete, Grant returned to Dalhousie via his mother's cottage on Otter Lake.

110/ To E.A. Kerr   RR 2 Parry Sound, Ontario
                                         [August 1950]

Dear Dr Kerr,
I am sorry to be slow in answering your kind letter. It followed me back across the Atlantic.

First about business. It is good of you to have appointed me for a year, as it were on faith. I hope the result of my DPhil will not show that you were wrong. All that can be said is that before my oral I was not confident and after it have become more confident.

It was good to get news of Halifax. Both my wife and I long to be back there. Nova Scotia lives at a pace we both prefer to Toronto although I imagine your responsibilities do not allow you to taste the leisurely pace as much as some of us.

You mentioned before I went to 'the old country' that I might look around for somebody (preferably Scottish) to help teach philosophy. I came across nobody who seemed suitable. Indeed, the more I saw of young European philosophers the more I wondered how they would understand and fit into the Nova Scotian pattern. Science is so objective and certain that the background of the teacher is not of its essence. Philosophy, because it deals with such personal mysteries, does depend on the teacher understanding and sympathising with the background of his pupils. So many of the young English and Scottish teachers I met were able, but I doubted their ability to transfer that ability to a Canadian setting. This is not to say that I do not believe that Canadians have endless things to learn from the great tradition of European life and thought – but it does seem to me that somebody who was a Canadian and yet knew Europe would be better in the university teaching philosophy than somebody from the United Kingdom. Of course, if we heard of a really good man things would be different. I just didn't come across a really good man.

I don't know when this will reach you because of the rail strike. We are up in Northern Ontario and the strike makes us feel very cut off. This country is wonderfully beautiful. Although I love England, what one misses there is the wild untamedness of this country. Once one has been brought up amongst it, the polish and exquisiteness of the English countryside never quite satisfies.

I am doing a job at the moment that I thought you would be interested in. Father Lévesque[1] on the Royal Commission on Culture (etc.)[2] suggested there should be papers on the study of philosophy in Canada – English and French speaking. President Mackenzie of UBC suggested my name for the one on English speaking philosophy. Particularly they want to know why philosophy has never been of central importance to Canadians. It gives one great scope.

Excuse the awful scrawl of my writing. Please give Mrs Kerr best regards from my wife and myself. Also my regards to Miss Henry.[3]

Again many thanks for your letter and for your trust in appointing me in the dark.

Yours sincerely,
George Grant

1 Fr Georges-Henri Lévesque (1903–), dean of the school of social sciences at the University of Laval, 1943–55
2 Vincent Massey headed the Royal Commission on National Development in the Arts, Letters and Sciences, generally known as the Massey Commission. It reported in 1951.
3 Dr Kerr's secretary

111/ To Alice Boissonneau

My dear Alice,
This breaks a hideous and long silence which I hope you will forgive. This

year has not been easy for either Sheila or myself and the result has been that I haven't been able to do anything but just get through a series of routine matters as best I could. It is impossible to describe these states (which you know I am sure well). They seem so irrational and one should be able by sheer effort of will to rise above them, but I have never learnt and do not think I ever will. For me it has been the onrush of the dark around me and for Sheila the onrush of children and students around her.

Your lovely story[1] moved us both very much. What else is there to say. I find less and less about art that I want to say anything. That is perhaps that as a teacher of philosophy one spends too much of one's time explaining things and, of course, the heart of what you said is lost as soon as it is reduced to comments. We both loved it and just hope that life is giving you freedom to write more and more in which you can say what you have to say and whenever you feel like saying it. You are one of those people one knows will live triumphantly through life however desolating it is for you. So I know you will write, and if not write, something else done beautifully. Oh how I wish that I had your *claritas* and your immediate vision of what is the heart of the business. Sheila has that also in an exquisite way. My whole vision seems to be blurred by obliqueness and that easy loss of what is important for very trivial reasons. To have that direct vision is above all bargains and must make anything that you have to endure worth enduring.

What else is there to say except that this brings you love from us both. I could write and write about problems that hold my attention but would hardly seem important to you and indeed they hardly seem important to me. The one great hope is that I have started to write poetry again after twelve years. But that cannot be worth mentioning till I have sent you something that is worth sending. The children are dears. Rachel grows and expands and is lost in her particular daydreams. William[2] is a dear little boy – just that.

Anyway all kinds of thoughts and wishes from us both. Affection between people is too precious to waste; so I hope our distance doesn't mar that friendship. It will never mar the sense of wonderful respect we feel for you after reading a story. All the phrases are empty by this time of night but compassion is the very nature of reality.

Yours ever,
Sheila and George Grant

1 Alice Boissonneau wrote short stories.
2 William Grant was born 19 April 1950.

1951

112/ To E.A. Kerr   Dalhousie University, Halifax
                                                    8 March 1951

Dear Dr Kerr,
Here are some additions I have made to the questionnaire. I am sorry not to have spent more time on it, as I believe the report you have to make is probably the most important document being prepared in Canada this year.

You may think that the questions I ask are too frank and, therefore, not easy for you to send out to your fellow presidents. Nevertheless, pointed questions seem to me necessary if honesty is to be forthcoming. So often in the past I have seen statements by presidents in central Canada (about the religious life of their institutions) which could not but have had the effect of misleading the churches. That misleading of the churches by university people about what is happening in our universities, seems to me unpardonable because it is the churches that are mainly going to suffer from the fact that our universities are becoming secular technical colleges. If the questions are made specific, you may be able to catch some straight replies from the slippery old foxes who run the big universities in central Canada. I hope you will excuse my rudeness about your peers and my superiors, but I have found some of their statements that their institutions exist to serve Christian truth hard to reconcile with their building of an increasing number of mechanical engineering buildings while they neglect theology. Above all I must repeat because of my loyalty to the Church of God that nothing is more important than to awaken the ecclesiastics who are responsible for His work to the urgency of getting our students to think deeply about their religion and that only the Roman Catholics seem willing to spend the money; so this may be done. Frankly I think a general questionnaire will only evoke platitudes, although perhaps a more stringent one will bring out nothing better.

Lastly, I think it only fair to say that if you availed yourself of my suggestions it would be quite possible that some people who want to score off you would use my question eleven to make out that you were a narrow ecclesiastic. Nevertheless I think it is a very important question to be asked.

I take the liberty to enclose a copy of a report I wrote for the Massey Commission, which talks about the relationship of our modern universities to Christianity.[1]

Forgive my poor typing. It is just that much better than my scrawl by hand.

Yours always,
George Grant

1 George Grant, 'Philosophy,' in *Royal Commission Studies: A Selection of Essays Prepared for the Royal Commission on National Development in the Arts, Letters and Sciences* (1951), 119–33

When Leo died and left part of her estate to the Grant children, there was extensive discussion in the family about how they should respond. Grant wrote the following letter jointly to his mother and three sisters.

113/ To Maude, Margaret, Charity, and Alison   Dalhousie University
Halifax

Dear Ladies,

Terse executive circular letters are evidently the order of the day among the female members of our family (Alison excepted). Although I am sure they do you all credit, they leave the impression rather that Margaret and Charity are not sufficiently rational to maintain their generous impulses over a few weeks. Being male and maritime, I am neither so masterful or so moody.

Although you ladies evidently model your styles on the inter-departmental memo, will you bear with me while I write at greater length to give you the facts of the case? In recent years I am the only member of the family who has gone any distance beyond pious sentiment towards Leo. I am the only one of us who has spent any considerable time at Aller-thorpe, who has bothered to introduce his partner or has dragged the third generation over the tedious journey to that shrine. Therefore, I believe I know the state of Leo's mind and who among the natives had bothered with her in the last difficult years. Because of this knowledge of the facts, I thought we should do something for Mrs Lund, Mrs Ellsworth and Mrs Oxtoby. I wrote to mother to this effect and for her opinion on the matter. On receipt of that opinion, I was going to write letters to my three sisters.

Mother did not send me advice. She issued one of those powerful executive directives which I have been bred to defer to and which these days have the added sanction of being vice-viceregal.[1] I therefore, wrongly inferred that it had been declared *ex cathedra* that I was disqualified by age and sex from taking responsibility in a family matter. I also inferred that the whole matter rested in that so competent [a] quartet of hands at 7 Prince Arthur Ave. I believed I would soon be called on for a cheque and wrote to mother that £20, rather than £25, seemed more than adequate. (Clearly this last point was one for discussion – if I may use a term not widely understood among you.) My responsibility then seemed at an end. And not having executive inclinations, I do not covet responsibility.

The next event was the arrival of a circular letter from my eldest sister Margaret. This letter added nothing to the picture except to express her intention of generosity. It had some extrinsic interest as an example of her folksy style that is evidently a necessary expression of being adjusted to suburban Vancouver. I then received a well-mannered and competently written letter from my youngest sister Alison. It confused me by implying that she was going to send me her contribution.

Then today I received a terse order from my middle sister Charity. Let me make it clear that though my respect for mother is appropriate to the recipient, a suggestion from her I only consider as an hypothetical command, but from Charity such words are categorical.

Accepting that order categorically, therefore, and with no intention of 'taking a strong line' I send this letter merely as an apology. The long acceptance of slavery does not fit a man to take up freedom proffered by his masters. (I would use the word mistresses but it would be a case of an incestuously mixed metaphor.) But give me some clear opportunity on some other small matter and I will not fail you. *Excelsior.*

As clearly my confusion has been about the seat of authority and a central clearing house, would you ladies all decide how much and who is to do it and tell Charity? I hope that whatever method is decided upon, it will be remembered that I am the only person who knows how to distinguish between the five Mrs Lunds and seven Mrs Ellsworths who make their residence in Allerthorpe. This distinction appears important to me as I at least care about the money getting to the right persons. The danger of dishonesty is here increased by a considerable and unfortunate dissension among the female Ellsworths. (I add in parenthesis that this is caused by a classic example of the church and chapel question, at church Mrs Ellsworth having stated that a chapel brother-in-law was too notably 'randy' – I believe this was the expression used – to be a lay preacher.)

May I end with the hope that Charity hasn't chosen Mrs Anna Rosenberg as her ideal and by reminding you all that one of Leo's memorable phrases was 'More haste, less speed.'

As dear Colonel Laurie would say, Yours in God (be a streetcar, not a bus, man).[2]

George Grant

P.S. Dearest Mum please do not think I am brooding about you and Mr Wright.[3]

1 An allusion to the fact that Vincent Massey had asked Maude to serve as his chatelaine when he was appointed governor-general.
2 Laurie asked Grant, when he arrived at Dalhousie, whether he was a streetcar Christian or a trolley-bus Christian; that is, whether he was straight on the rails to our Saviour, or did he wander about all over the place.
3 A family joke of long standing was that there was a romance between Maude Grant and Mr Wright, the gardener.

1952

114/ To Maude Grant   200 University Ave, Halifax
                                                                6 April

Dearest Ould,
It was sad news indeed that you sent about Nicholas Ignatieff. He carried so much his fineness about with him and we need so much men like him that it is awful to think how harder and harder it is to replace his qualities in our society. Oh how the universities need men of his strength and gentleness. Aristotle has a word[1] to express the highest type Greek society could produce, a man who was so gentle because he was so strong. It must be a very great blow for you – friends like him are not replaceable. I know also how much it must mean to George.

I had heard but recently from Wilson that Sid Smith had written to tell him that N.I.[2] was going to resign. Oh the endless fights at universities. But we live under the continual tyranny of the rich – the oh so ignorant rich. It must just have worn his heart away. The only people who maintain any stand against the rich are the RCs and the scientists – because they both have the one factor the rich respect – power. And the corruption of the rich by their money grows. I have little sympathy for the democratic slogans – but when they become a cloak for plutocracy they are intolerable – anti-Semitic plutocracy here in Halifax.

Well, we have succumbed to plutocracy. We have bought a car. I don't know how long it will last as it is already 12 years old – a Chevrolet – but everybody says it is in excellent condition and that we made a very good buy. It will be lovely for the summer and we will put it away in the winter. After the extremely hard year and with Sheila with three children we thought a car would free us. Yet, we both feel guilty. A dark blue Chevrolet. Its greatest advantage is that it is a two-door so that R and W can be stuck in the back seat and can't get out or at us.

This is a boast of a proud father – but really Wimby is at the most scrumptious stage. I can't help thinking of 'Oh world be nobler for his sake.' He is very open hearted and innocent compared to the intense and fallen little Rachel. Our new house has made R's life quite new with endless friends. Elizabeth D[3] took R to her first play yesterday, *The Sleeping Beauty*. What a strange dream the child lives in. Little Wimby is the blond and the blue eyed.[4]

Well, our life goes on as usual. I live only for one event, the end of lectures, when I don't have to get up and open my mouth and when people aren't pulling at one for decisions a thousands times a day. It has been a wonderfully rewarding year, however, as last year I hated teaching and this year I loved it again and learnt a lot myself – particularly the infinite resources of Plato's thought. I feel I am reaching the point where I can put down with some clarity the grounds on which the non-Roman churches should stand in Canada. There is also a supreme chance for Protestants now. Both American capitalism and the RC Church are so willing to use each other in their very natural joint desire to attack the tyranny of Moscow. The Americans seem so eaten with pragmatism that religion is becoming useful to them and the RC Church with its history of political manipulation is willing to use American capitalism. In this situation Protestantism has a great chance of showing to the world that God is not an object to be used in economic and political battles when it suits our convenience – but He who sets the pattern and the only object that the Americans can't turn to their own ends. But I guess there is not much hope, as Protestantism will kneel to the rich and the technicians and the military as much as anybody. Did you read of Niemöller's trip to Russia? A strange report.

Give my love to Alison and George and to the boys. How is and what is Andrew like? How can one not say for them all 'Oh world be nobler for their sakes.'[5] And I do think somehow that however appalling are the forces of corruption in the western world, there are at last more and more people who see the situation more clearly and at least we aren't as foolish as the rich Europeans of the nineteenth century or of our continent in the 1920s. However hard and terrible the world may be, one's children won't be growing up in the superficiality of 19th century bourgeois England or 20th century America. That's for sure. I enclose a poem I sent to the *United Church Observer* for Good Friday.[6]

I know what you must be feeling about N. I. Your courage is so immense.

Always love

George

P.S. I saw in the newspaper that Lionel is to be Uncle V's Secretary. My thought would be how hopelessly unwise of Lionel and how selfish of Uncle V. Is there any better explanation? I hope so. Why can't V see or does he think it will be the best.? Do you know the story of Sir William Harcourt and his son? But then Sir W.H. was pretty great.

1 μεγαλοψυχια – greatness of soul, magnanimity
2 Nicholas Ignatieff
3 Elizabeth Douglas, daughter of the Douglases, whose house the Grants rented
4 Allusion to Thomas Mann's short story 'Tonio Kröger'
5 Laurence Binyon (1869–1943), 'O World Be Nobler'
6 George Grant, 'Good Friday,' *United Church Observer* 14, no. 6 (15 May 1952), 16

115/ To Maude Grant   Dalhousie University, Halifax

Dearest Ould,
Your lovely second letter arrived and so I will thank you for both of them at once and add news too. Sheila has not seen your second letter because I have not been home, but she said of your first letter that she thought it was the finest expression of human dignity she had ever read in a letter. Mine to you was pretty undignified, but one must be able to show pain to those one loves or else one will show it to others who will not understand and you so beautifully understood it. Your second letter was so lovely too. I never really meant that we were not intimate and I do know how wonderfully free you have left me. I know also how badly I have often acted towards you. All I really wanted to say is simply that to love you and be loved by you is essential to me like breathing. We now live far apart and, therefore, need to keep the bond. It is all part of the alienation and lack of communication one feels in all parts of society these days. What philosophy has to say to society is increasingly scorned and, therefore, one lives in a continual failure of communication. One of the saddest things for me is the scorn I have received from the United Church. Only the Catholics, with whom finally I have no connection, listen to me. In this continual sense of failing in communication, it becomes overwhelmingly important to keep open the lines to one's nearest and dearest. It was selfish to ask you to keep them open, but it was just asking you for faith. And your so beautiful letters just gave me faith. Another case of how you never fail.
     As for Fulton Anderson,[1] to hell with him. As Cochrane said over and

over, the philosophy departments in Canadian universities have surrendered their true task. They turned philosophy into technical work for the
few rather than a way of life open to all. Sureness is not necessarily dog-
matism and I know that it is not a question of Anderson not believing in
God and I believing. I know God exists. Plato shows to those who listen
that one cannot avoid that conclusion. The face of Anderson's scepticism
and secularism is all around the world. Life has been too long for me and
I had to learn at too great a price not to be frank about what one believes.
At the personal and practical level I am always unsure and confused; but,
at this level, I know I am right, not because of the 'I,' but because the
arguments are irrefutable. And nothing could be more important than
this because in the next years the future of the world is tied up with those
who have rational love of God. All I hate about it is the bitterness engen-
dered and the fact that good work may be prevented by that bitterness. As
to the controversy one cannot speak wrongly when one has Plato and
Augustine and Kant behind one. The issue is not really God but whether
philosophy is a practical study which can help men to live. I have not
done anything about the controversy except write two articles this summer (quite unrelated) one on Bertrand Russell[2] and the other on Plato,[3]
which will show even farther what I mean. I don't see why it was wrong to
get me to write it. It depresses me also that it will probably exclude me
from living in central Canada and therefore from you.

We had a short and charming ceremony for Cousin Dot. I have written
to Joan about it. The nicest thing was that the old man at the ceremony
quite well remembered Frank. A rather vacuous Anglican Dean read the
prayers as all the good ones were away for the synod. Don't tell Joan. The
prayers are, however, so beautiful. Paul's words are just perfectly the language of transcendence and that is what one wants at a funeral.[4] Altogether lovely.

Canon Andrew[5] rang up late last night to say that May[6] had died. I will
be at the funeral if I possibly can and will do all the right things.

I must stop now and get on with a terribly difficult paper I am reading
to a Maritime Philosophical Conference next week.[7]

Your letters I treasure so much, for they answered so perfectly the lone-
liness the whole incident awakened in me. It was selfishness to ask so
much from you and it was a wonderful expression of your loveliness and
unselfishness that you should take upon yourself the application of balm
around my heart. I hope that when the little creatures here are growing
up I will be one iota of the help to them that you have been to me today
and the last week.

(By the way Wimby is becoming the great wit of our family. At two he tells ridiculous jokes and roars with laughter. What a dear little boy he is. He just sparkles with good will and affection. Rachel has grown up immensely and is now a sweet and busy little girl. She is just a dear little girl. Bobby is a very good baby but too early to say much of him.)

A million thanks and a million expressions of admiration for your wonderful unselfishness. You have completely cured me of the whole incident.

George

1 F.H. Anderson (1895–1968), professor of philosophy at University of Toronto, 1917–19, 1934–62; head of the philosophy department at the University of Toronto, 1945–62; a bitter critic of Grant's royal commission study. See Fulton Anderson, 'Introduction,' *Philosophy in Canada: A Symposium,* ed. J.A. Irving (1952).
2 George Grant, 'Pursuit of an Illusion: A Commentary on Bertrand Russell,' *Dalhousie Review* 32, no. 2 (Summer 1952), 97–109
3 George Grant, 'Popper and Plato,' *Canadian Journal of Economics and Political Science* 20, no. 2 (May 1954), 185–94
4 1 Corinthians 15.20
5 Geoff Andrew's father
6 His sister
7 George Grant, 'Two Theological Languages'

116/ To Maude Grant   Dalhousie University, Halifax
                                                28 August 1952

Dearest Ould,

I want you to promise to destroy this letter when you've read it and I also ask you to read it only on condition you show it to nobody – not even Chippy – not only because of what it says (because it is an account of my pride and my inability to bring that pride under reason). It is also an account of a hurt and to account of that is weakness and I only write that to you because you are my mother and although you do not like me to be intimate with you, I would either have to stop writing to you at all, if I couldn't write to you as the person I class with Rachel and Sheila and Charity as nearest to my heart. I also ask you to take no action on the letter or to let your attitude to anything change or to feel that I have written it to get you to change any attitude. It is written simply because I have been hurt and I love you so much that the only way of getting over it is to communicate to you. I am aware, as I say, that you do not like me to be intimate with you, but I am not capable of anything else towards you.

When we got your letter about Uncle Vincent coming down we were naturally pleased and excited because we thought of the fun. We waited and waited for a word and none came. Then yesterday when they were here, I thought, the only thing to do was to pocket my pride and go up to the university, where he was to call in for five minutes. He spoke to all members of the Senate and therefore spoke to me and said, 'How nice, and how is Sheila?' That is the only communication of any kind we had with any of them. I saw Lilias in the party and smiled vaguely. I thought, when they found that we were not going to see them, Lionel would call. But not a word.

The reason I write is that I just don't know why it has hurt me so dreadfully but it has. I don't blame Uncle Vincent because he was having a long and difficult day, but the hurt from Lionel and Lilias I find pretty deep.

Now why? Why did it matter to me and why did it matter to Sheila? Sheila is a most unprideful person and a much less worldly person than I and yet she felt really hurt too. Of course, at a superficial level it is just one's pride, one wants to be part of the show and to get vicarious importance from it. That is a silly motive and one that I have very grave difficulty in overcoming. Of course, this is a motive that operates these days very deeply in teachers and particularly in teachers of philosophy (in the non-Roman Catholic world) because of the continual blows we get from the businessmen and the society of wealth, which pushes us around and from the democracy, which is so debased that it admires greed. But I do recognise that that kind of pride is bad and must be fought.

Of course, one is also hurt because of the Nova Scotians' inability to ask one. That comes very basically from their contempt for professors and such like.

But the hurt goes deeper; it is the relationship to one's past. I know that they were busy. I know that they probably thought we would be asked somewhere. But, when Lionel and Lilias found we were not, they should at least have phoned to say they were sorry. Particularly they should have phoned having seen me at the college. It is for me the need I suppose of that world of family unity which you and Aunt Lal and Uncle Jim and Aunt Marjorie and Daddy built up. It is probably always hard for one to grow up and for me life has been continually a process of remaking oneself and this, yesterday, was probably (and in a few days I will see it as such) the working of the wonderful mystery of God's providence, by which through hurt he leads one to know what is worth trust and what is vanity and pride. But the personal hurt is very hard. I suppose the hurt is at bottom a hurt in assessing my love for you. I have always felt the time and love you expended on the broader family was worth it, for even if it meant a less close relation between you and me, it meant that you beautifully bound a larger family together and that the particular evil was made well by the larger good. Now I suppose the sense of waste is deep in me, because I have been excluded from the larger family and have not had the intimacy with you. What I am doing in writing this letter is then really making one last beseeching request for love from you. I know you will consider this merely jealousy and I do not ask it in any sense as taking away all that Aunt Lal meant to you (I love and respect that). But I do not think it is jealousy. I will never admit to you that I am not making a fair request. To request love is always, of course, ridiculous because it is either there or it isn't.

Well, as you can see I was hurt and so was Sheila. In a way it is not serious because we are both too firmly set on our track. No earthly love for both of us can finally matter, for the love of God for us all is so infinitely great that what one learns on the way can only lead one to that. I think tragedy is for people who are hurt before they recognize this. Once that is recognised, the hurts that come one's way hurt for a moment and they show one one's own limitations and pride but they can never hurt one for long. Indeed I think that the sadness I felt yesterday is probably a good thing for it reminds one of one's complete dependence upon things that are not worthy of being depended on. You have so wonderfully known that in your life. We are only gradually coming to see it at all. Therefore, my request for affection from you is not really a request at all. It is really just a statement that this whole small incident just brought before me more than anything else how deep my affection is for you. I know perfectly well in my soul that you do care about me. But having been excluded from something that one's past life makes one think is important, I have a deep need to know that the real thing remains and that nothing comes between you and me.

Well, there it is. One lives and learns. Please believe that nothing I write is meant to touch your conduct. As Sheila always says it is wonderful the way you show love to the Masseys when you expect or want nothing in return. That is something that only a very great person like yourself would be capable of and my weakness should do nothing to interfere with it. All I want for my weakness and pain of putting the past aside is just the knowledge that my past vis-à-vis you need not be put aside.

All sorts of love and please promise not to show this letter to anyone or to discuss the business with anyone.

George

1953

117/ To Maude Grant   Dalhousie University, Halifax
                                            21 April 1953

Dearest Ould,
So lovely to get your letter and hear you were getting up. Please do not think of writing.

I have been reading Bell's *Life of Davidson*[1] – the Archbishop of Canterbury. What a strange generation that late 19th century and early 20th Anglican ecclesiastics were. At a certain level the deep sincerity and the Christian religion meant something to them; at another level great place seeking and an acceptance of privilege etc. which is [ill.]. One could sum up the biography this way.

p. 28. Letter to a Bishop.
'If I had my way I would, of course, stay here as curate of Boking-on-Tyre and centre my work among the poor, but much against my will God has called me to be Vicar of Mayfair.'

p. 158. Letter to Lord Salisbury.
'If I had my way, my only ambition would be to stay here among my beloved people of Rugby – but Edith and I have been on our knees all night and recognise that it must not be what we want, but what God wills for us, therefore I will become Dean of Windsor.'

p. 200. Letter to Queen Victoria.
'The Christian religion is never easy. All Edith and I would like would be to stay here in this simple life of the castle, but I grant your point that God has called me to the episcopate at Winchester.'

p. 300. His diary.
'I have been on my knees all week. I can find no escape from accepting Canterbury. I do not want it. It is not my will but His and I rest in His divine grace. So on to Canterbury.'

I don't think that Bishop Bell meant his biography satirically – but every time an ecclesiastical appointment arises, Davidson gives reasons to Queen Victoria why A and B and C and D would be hopeless for the job and then finally much against his will he moves to the appointment. No wonder the Anglican Church has bitten the dust, in the words of so many of the best English. It was just identified in Davidson's mind with a certain ordering of English society. What also amazed me is how all the top men were intermarried and what a closed corporation it was. Much the shrewdest of all the people who came out was Lord Salisbury. I am getting a greater admiration for the man all the time.

We are having an election here in Nova Scotia and believe it or not I am driven to vote for the Liberals. Angus Macdonald[2] is just a stronger man than Stanfield[3] and I think he represents Nova Scotia pretty well. Also in the Federal field I find myself quite close to voting Liberal because [of] how deeply I feel about public broadcasting and I don't trust the Tories not to fiddle around and cut away at the CBC.

Lectures are over and we are in the midst of exams. Also in the midst of a lot of fun with the children. The days pass quickly and we will soon be seeing your dear self. I just love to think of the children seeing you. William is just 'Strong Troy in vigour and in strenuity.'[4] Sheila and I may be decadent and lost – but he is not.

You are in our hearts all the time.

Love – so much love
George

1 G.K.A. Bell (1885–1958), chaplain to Archbishop Randall Davidson, 1914–24; later bishop of Chichester, 1929–58
2 Angus L. Macdonald (1890–1954), premier of Nova Scotia, 1933–40, 1945–54
3 R.L. Stanfield (1914–), Conservative premier of Nova Scotia, 1957–67, leader of the federal Progressive Conservative party, 1967–76
4 William Dunbar, 'In Honour of the City of London'·

118/ To Maude Grant   Dalhousie University, Halifax
                                           20 June 1953

Dearest Mum,
Well, here we all are back in the old rut again after a lovely holiday. We got home safely on Wednesday evening after a fascinating trip. We spent the first night at Iroquois as we couldn't get on to your place as for the only time on the journey the children were sick after Kingston. The next day we had lunch with the Moyses and then journeyed through Montreal and on just past Three Rivers. The next day we went on through Quebec by lunch time and then on down the south shore to a place called Bic just before Rimouski. Then the next day we cut inland through the Matape-

dia valley and then down through Campbellton, Bathurst and Chatham to a place called Buctouche (that was our longest day). We had a lovely welcome to N.B. that night for the old man who owned the cabins said he wouldn't charge a man for his children. Then the next day we drove on to Halifax. Just thirty-five miles outside Halifax a big bridge at Enfield (you remember the Truro side of the Lauries) had come down and we had to take a fifty mile detour up to Windsor. But we got home safely after a fascinating trip.

You were so wonderfully good to us in Toronto. We had such a lovely time. You were so lovely to the children. On the way home one day William in a flight of high spirits threw his colouring book out of the car which you had given him and Rachel said 'Don't tell Gran what he did; she would be so disappointed in him.' It was so lovely of you to send us off with a lovely lunch and all the lovely things for the journey and all the lovely things. Now we have looked at them I think the finest is the picture of Homer. It just is wonderful and we have put it up in our main room. It is as art even more wonderful than the Doge although for me not as filled with as many tones and quantities out of my youth. We have put the Doge over our mantle piece and the virgin[1] has gone on to a bigger wall which suits it much better. But Homer is the most moving and looks out so wonderfully in his blindness as if he saw behind all the shadows and imaginings into the truth.

As for the hundred dollars – all my sadness at leaving prevented me thanking you properly. It came at a wonderful time for us because through a series of misfortunes we were in debt. I am sorry we cannot buy something like Margaret did, but having had our children in a rush before we are established has meant a lot of difficulties and this will see us through. We were able through effort to keep the bond you sent us last year and not sell it but it has meant we have not caught up and this will help us catch up. Many many thanks. One thing I must not do is to start to earn money in the summers or I will become barren and empty of philosophy and then I might as well throw in my hand as a philosopher.

If sometimes I seemed strange in Toronto it was that it was all such a great impression to me. It is my job as a philosopher to try and see the industrial society as it is with all its virtues and its failures or else my philosophy will just be a barren intellectual game and you cannot imagine how overwhelming an impression the expanding society like Toronto is to an outsider. Of course, Quebec is even more an impression with the mixture of ugly and dogmatic Catholicism mixed with the industrial society, but then French Canada is not my responsibility the way that English-speaking Canada is. But I came back so shook up (in the best way) out of the rut that one gets [into] here and I felt I had really learnt something as well as having had the loveliness of just being at home. Corbett told me in Toronto that I should just become a happy agnostic, but that is impossible for the point in life is to see more and more and more and even if you are like me and find yourself surrounded by darkness and uncertainty still one must try and solve the mysteries for what else is there. Please never think I am a pessimist for I know that the highest virtue is charity, but the second highest is joy, and I never give up the effort to try and see the world as God's world.

This is a poor letter but it brings you so much love and thanks. We so wait for your time here. We have found that we can turn a room into a place for the children; so we are going to have more space and there will be lots of room. I hope you have a lovely time with Alison and George in August and a good time at the citadel. I hope your wishes come true and that the Conservatives do well. I think they will gain seats and the Liberals lose some but I am afraid the Liberals will keep their majority. Anyway a bigger and more organized opposition will be good. I am certainly going to vote conservative.

Give my thanks to the Macdonnells for all their goodness to us and to Charity. I will write in the next few days. Oh how I wish we lived closer. Perhaps we will.

Dearest Love and oh so many thanks.

George

1 By Fra Filippo Lippi

1954

119/ To Maude Grant   Dalhousie University, Halifax
28 January 1954

Dearest Mum,

For days I have been meaning to write to you about Hume Wrong – for I know what a break his death must be for you. As you say also for Alison and George and, of course, in a public sense the loss of a great public servant for Canada. Anyway his spirit counts in the world because he has taught many others the proper form of government service. Anyway I know, in some small measure, what his death must have meant to you and I know also the immense courage you have to endure such blows.

To go from death to birth. I am glad that you are glad that we are having a fourth child. For me the ambiguity is this. I am terrified at how proletarianised we are becoming. For you who belonged to an older world it was possible to pursue the life of education and not become proletarianised – but for us, it is impossible. Particularly in the field of philosophy there is no hope of earning that extra money which keeps professors going. And my philosophy is, I am afraid, so repugnant to the modern world that there is not going to be much success in it for me. Now the point of this is not for S and I who do not want money – the point is rather have you the right to bring children into the world when you know they are going to be proletarianised and when you know yourself that what one is going to say to the world is going to be unpopular. Of course, my great weakness is that I care tremendously for the pleasant things of civilised existence – not so much the material things as the civilised way of life that you so wonderfully taught us and I have a fear of what my children will be like without them. Of course, this is a failure in faith in God and yet that failure exists. Yet, I am caught because I do not think I could give up philosophy for other aspects of life that bring more money.

Of course, part of it arises from the loveliness of philosophic life. On the one side I very clearly see my dislike of the growing social democracy with its trust in psychiatrists and scientists to solve anything – on the other the *visible* Church and I have little in common.

Of course, it will be easier down here in N.S. where a simpler form of life still exists and, of course, the problem of proletarianism is made easier by the wonderful American machines. This automatic washing machine we bought is a wonder – it saves Sheila an hour a day and much energy.

How glorious it will be when you are here in June. We are just looking forward to it immensely. Summer never starts in N.S. till June and then it is lovely and we will be able to go on such lovely drives to places we have discovered and Bobby will be old enough to get around on his own by then. That is the only sad thing in N.S. that it is so far from you and we both feel so cut off from our past. Life becomes a mystery for me more and more – but a wonderful mystery. All one can finally say is that one is glad that one has had the experience of consciousness – it is such an immense experience.

Life has been pretty hectic. I had to address the medical students and the ministers this past week. I stayed up to 6 a.m. talking to the medical students about the relation of God to their work. I will send you a mimeographed copy of the paper I gave the ministers.

Sheila gave a paper to the philosophy club which I thought was simply brilliant. It meant that all her spare moments and energy were taken up with it – but not only for the youngsters but for herself it was marvellously worth doing. Because it not only got her down to thinking philosophically – but also made her once and for all admit that she had conquered her stuttering. We have also been busy (Sheila particularly) with Miss Lindsay[1] who had a bad fall. She is better now, but lame; anyway it wasn't pleasant. The kids are well. William as usual, to put it mildly, striving. His great interest is to learn to be a horseman – so we tell him that when he goes west he will be a cowboy. Rachel is full of life and Bobby at a difficult stage where he cannot quite yet speak.

Otherwise life goes on at a wild rate. Students and philosophy are our life. Entertainment pretty well nil – but we find it is less and less satisfactory when I spend so much of my life with people.

Of course, tell Charity our news and tell her that we are a social problem who needs some good adjustment to the country. And to her our love.

To you as always our best love.
George

P.S. After your letter we cashed your wonderfully generous cheque. It seems unfair to you – but it came at a glorious time and pays the 1st instalment on the washing machine.

1 Jean Lindsay, who had been a librarian at Dalhousie, became a close friend and a surrogate grandmother to the Grant children.

120/ To Murray Tolmie[1]   Dalhousie University, Halifax
29 March 1954

Dear Murray,

I have been meaning to drop you a note for so long, but the days go by and by this time of year they are like a cinematography – a string flickering by, in which one has no part. But then I heard a practical thing which might interest you. I heard that R.A. MacKay[2] was interested in you and would encourage you vis-à-vis External Affairs. This may bore you to tears or it may interest you – but anyway you should know.

I suppose it is my duty to say I hope you are working and I really do so hope, for at the barest minimum, there is a kind of unity and order in working that is a kind of happiness. Anyway I hope Cambridge is enjoyable and that you have found people you enjoy. For myself, people never fail – for sooner or later there is somebody whom one loves – but your consciousness I do not begin to understand and therefore I do not know if that loving is as, more, or less, important.

Life goes on here at its usual rate. For me the remarkable thing is what philosophy has done for me. Not being a person who would naturally (whatever that means) have turned to speculation – that is having been driven to it – I am simply flabbergasted to what philosophy has taken me. Just not at all the sort, of course, I expected. It is like setting out on what one expected to be a jaunt across the Arm – finding oneself shipwrecked time after time and yet knowing one has no alternative but to go on – moods of dereliction – moods of amusement and moments of joy – but above all sheer unadulterated amazement – I just could have expected anything of life – but not this.

Above all the dereliction is when philosophy is in direct conflict with ambition. For a variety of reasons my adolescence was taken up by the idea of fame as the *summum bonum*[3] and it is really shattering to me to have to face it for what it is. It is really perhaps only a sign of middle age[4] that the idea of the ravishment of sexual joy has been replaced by fame – with the question of money a sort of niggling extra like gluttony must be to the lecher.

As for the university here, God knows. Wilson's aesthetic mysticism and ruthless pragmatism leave him an enigma to me largely redeemed (for me that is) by his real care for people like you. He has not got Kerr out and they seem to have reached a modus vivendi – or a modus modi vivendi. James and Nancy flourish. I really think she is better.[5] Alan Macintosh[6] is like a ghost at the feast – etc etc. We expect our fourth child this summer – one cannot regret it. A strange spidery (physically that is) airletter from Carl Webber[7] appears often.

I hope we will meet in some real way in the summer. For me I am always diffuse because of children and abstracted because of work, while you seem to dream in some realm which is hard to know whether it is anguish or lyricism; but, anyway, I hope we make some contact. Of course, it is this damned philosophy which is the difficulty for me basically, because these continual shipwrecks leave one confused. No, that is not really the right metaphor – it is rather like a young (not quite) woman who has had a series of affairs and much alcohol with all of them and is so emotionally confused that she can't really remember whether her present love is the poet or the architect and only hopes to make the right response when called for. One must have some sense of being some place from which one can communicate.

Sheila sends her best. I really hope you are working and that the world is otherwise full.

Ever Yours,
George G.

P.S. This was written two weeks ago and not posted. The sun is strong.

1 Murray Tolmie (1931–), a former Dalhousie student, later a professor of history
2 R.A. MacKay (1894–1979), a political scientist at Dalhousie; he was Canada's permanent ambassador at the United Nations, 1955–8.
3 Highest good
4 Grant usually described himself as older than he was; at the time he was thirty-five.
5 Nancy Doull had developed TB.
6 Alan Macintosh (1929–), a Dalhousie historian, whom Sheila Grant remembers as somewhat gloomy
7 A former Dalhousie student who had gone to study at Oxford

1955

121/ To Maude Grant   Dalhousie University, Halifax
9 August 1955

Dearest Mum,
We have been terribly slow in writing to you about the parcel you sent us with such lovely things – but the last weeks have been hectic. First, we were out at Grand Lake with the Moyses (from Montreal) and although it was great fun it was extremely busy (as you can imagine). Then we had to rush in early to see Uncle Vincent and then the last week we have had all kinds of people here, including a young girl from British Columbia[1] who knows Geoff, living in the house. So you will have to forgive the slowness. Even now I am writing in bed with William on one side and Robert[2] on the other – as they are too wide awake to go to sleep.

Your parcel was just lovely. My socks were much appreciated and you will see them on me next week. Catherine's[3] socks are just lovely and so useful and Rachel just treasured her little dolls. The money for the children was much appreciated. William is saving up for a butterfly net and is putting his fifty cents towards that.

I really must give you a description of each of the children as they are a sweet crowd and I wish you could see them so often. Rachel has suddenly taken over reading in a big way and it is hard to get her away from books. She is a strange, frail little thing – but a pretty one. She lives in her own world. William has taken up natural history – so that his whole life is dominated by it. You can imagine what a pleasure Grand Lake was – snakes and snails and leeches and fish and deer and above all toads and beetles. His interest is really profound in it and I would hope it will continue. Robert is a gay, lovely actor – much the handsomest and very winning in his ways. Catherine is blossoming every day – a sweet lovely little girl with big blue eyes and full of life. Altogether it is, as you can imagine, very lovely living in the same house with them. Oh how I wish we were closer to you, so that we could see you often and they would have a sense of your dearness and all they could learn from you. Robert announced in a discussion of marriage that he was going to marry you – and was much confused by being told one does not marry one's Gran. As you so well know one cannot predict what will happen to one's children – but they are a diverse and interesting lot and you and WLG, I don't think, would find them unsubtle or unlively. I so often think that WLG would have loved Sheila. She has, what you have, so little care or belief that ultimately money is what rules the world.

We had a lovely time with the Masseys – a small dinner with the Lieut. Governor, Uncle V and his entourage and the Premier and his wife. The Premier (Henry Hicks)[4] is a man I like immensely and believe in. He has not got a good public appearance but I think has a good solid sense of Nova Scotia. A young man (40) and a Rhodes scholar. Uncle Vincent was as nice as he could be as was Lionel and Lilias. They were just as dear as they could be. I know this is thanks to you.

I had a long letter from Jim Ignatieff in Rome today about his son. I was so glad he wrote.

It is now ten o'clock and Bobbie is still rushing around the house – telling us strange stories about motor boats and the sea.

I am so interested in what you say about the papers and will be so interested to hear more about them in Toronto.

Well, it will be lovely to see you next week. Nova Scotia is lovely – but it is far too far from Toronto.

Best love to Charity and to you as always all the love in the world.

George

1 Anne Tolmie
2 Robert Grant was born 26 May 1952.

3 Catherine Grant was born 4 August 1954.

4 H.D. Hicks (1915–90), premier of Nova Scotia, 1954–6, president of Dalhousie University, 1963–80

1956

Grant had become increasingly unhappy about his membership in the United Church, and he wanted to raise his children within institutional Christianity. He and Sheila decided to be confirmed as Anglicans.

122/ To Derek Bedson[1]   Dalhousie University
                                                        31 March 1956

My dear Derek,

I just wanted to drop you a note that I am being confirmed in the Anglican Church today and that Sheila will be admitted.

It was so confusing that weekend in Ottawa, but always such affairs make me feel like a child at a party – quite wild. It was sad not to be able to get really down to talking about anything with you. But it is sheer honesty to say (as Sheila always does) just to see your smile and hear that laugh is to know how much we love you – however life may hold us apart.

We sail for England May 8th for 18 months. If by any chance you are there, you can get us through Mrs. Allen 63 Blackheath Park, SE3.

I hope your party is not, through Donald Fleming,[2] going to betray Canadianism entirely in broadcasting. If the Conservatives do that, they will gain the support of the private broadcaster – but they will be hated by the intellectual community in Canada. How can they in one breath talk of Canadianism in economic affairs and then betray it over cultural affairs?

I hope your work goes well.

Such love,
George

1 Derek Bedson (1920–89) and Grant became close friends while they were studying at Balliol during 1945–7. He became principal private secretary to Conservative leaders George Drew and John Diefenbaker from 1954 to 1958. In 1958 he became clerk of the executive council and secretary to the premier of Manitoba, a position he held under four successive premiers, both NDP and Conservative.

2 D.M. Fleming (1905–86), minister of finance in the Diefenbaker government, 1957–62

In the summer of 1956, Grant took his family to England for a sabbatical leave from Dalhousie.

123/ To Maude Grant   18 Morden Rd, London SE3
                                            2 November 1956

Dearest Mum,

This is the anniversary of dearest daddy's birthday and, so, I drop you a line in remembrance of what he was and what he meant to you and to us all. The older I get the more he is with me in all his wisdom and dearness of character. Whatever the four children have made of it, we started with a good beginning from you both.

The world is full of bad news at the moment what with the Suez[1] and Hungary.[2] I find my emotions very bound up with the Suez thing as Israel is one of the few causes I feel deeply about and [the] fanatic religious nationalism of the Arabs is pretty unpleasant. I am sorry that the English moved in – their only excuse being it seems to me the refusal of Eisenhower-Dulles[3] to do anything. In 1952 I hoped Eisenhower[4] would get in as I thought the Republicans needed office – but oh I hope against hope that Stevenson[5] will beat him on Tuesday. Above all I dislike the way Eisenhower has sold himself to the public relations boys and the general platitude gang.

As I said last letter Sheila is going to have her fifth baby in the spring. She has not been well in September and is now luckily better. It will mean a full and busy life for us both but we both see bringing up children as an important work in the world and an affirmation in the goodness of history and the hope of progress.

Monday is Guy Fawkes [day] and we will celebrate it with fireworks and a bonfire. William who passed through a bad time at another school is now going to a new school and is back to his usual form. He is a wonderful high spirited child and at low moments in life does much for my morale. My work is starting to go well. Brigadier Huxley of the Nuffield (whom you may remember having been at London House) and whom I think Burgon is not very certain of has been awfully good to me and speaks so warmly of you particularly through his brother Michael. He is not a particularly clever man but one of the good hearted country type English that I like. Often the English clever are pretty attenuated. By the way tell Charity that I got a letter from Silcox saying that he had heard my work was from her an attack on some phase of modern materialism. As the first chapter of my book is a hymn of praise to Karl Marx, as one of the supreme prophetic geniuses, I was rather stunned by her comment. I am moving into such fantastic views of the world that people will find my book difficult, but at last I feel I have broken entirely with the past and can see the future with some clarity. I look forward to hearing your comments more than any other.

Tomorrow we have Gerald and Mary and John Graham and Sir William and Lady Fyfe and Christopher to dinner. Christopher is a queer fish but I like him for he is so very much himself and so very broken away from the staid old English academic tradition. This week we also have Charles and Kay Gimpel to dinner. Oh I hope the fall and winter go well for you and Chip. And I hope you are not doing too much. I think so often of how lovely it will be to see you next year and to be able to talk of so much. I love England and the chance to do what interests me – but oh I miss dear old Canada. Such love from us all.

George

1 After Egypt nationalized the Suez Canal on 26 July 1956, Britain, France, and Israel agreed to attack Egypt. The invasion began 29 October, but the United States refused to support Britain and France and forced a ceasefire on 6 November.
2 A spontaneous rebellion against the communist government erupted in Hungary on 23 October 1956. The Soviet army invaded Hungary on 2 November 1956 to restore communist control.
3 J.F. Dulles (1888–1959), U.S. secretary of state, 1953–9
4 D.D. Eisenhower (1890–1969), Republican president of the United States, 1953–61
5 A.E. Stevenson II (1900–65), Democratic candidate for the presidency; defeated by Eisenhower in 1952 and 1956

1957

124/ To Maude Grant   18 Morden Rd, London SE3
3 January 1957

Dearest Mum,
This is to wish you a very happy 1957 and also to thank you for the lovely things you sent us at Christmas – the lovely presents for the children and the remarkably generous cheque to us. Sheila will write about the presents separately later. You are always so wonderfully good to us and never

has a cheque been so welcome, as there had been a holdup over our money and we lived over Christmas entirely thanks to you. We had a lovely Xmas, the children and ourselves acted out a quite elaborate 'Sleeping Beauty.' Rachel was very keen and adores charades etc. William was quite the most innocent wicked witch and profoundly uninterested. Robert loved it. We had Xmas with Wo and Tony and Mrs Allen at our house and after dinner Mrs Lovett and some of her grown children (old Bermondsey friends) came in. Altogether very pleasant.

Since Xmas we have been busy with minor details. William has the measles, Robert tonsillitis. Sheila knocked down the front gate learning to drive etc., etc. – all minor things but all time consuming. But we are so much better off as far as help goes and as far as space goes that it is much easier than in Halifax. Sheila is very well as far as the baby goes and her mother who was at last told yesterday has been good about it. Mrs Allen has gradually retired from life almost entirely, so that although we are five minutes away from her we rarely see her – but we see a lot of Tony and Wo.

Thank God the Suez business seems to be quieting down. I thought it was a great mistake on Eden's[1] part – but found a lot of the moralising about it irresponsible. I think the U.S. comes out of it well because having moralised they are going to take responsibility and one was relieved to see Hoover go and Herter come in. Canada, I felt comes out of it badly – a lot of moralising by the government without responsibility. To talk of colonial chore boys when this country is really on its knees is just unrealistic and I am afraid probably done just for votes. I see no reason why Canada should grow up as the U.S. has done – but the desire to be left alone to make money combined with general piety is not very impressive. To speak personally about a world crisis, what the Suez has done for me is to make me realise how profoundly I am committed to North American life. What I mean by this would take too long to explain here.

It will be good to see Alison and George and the children on their way through to Yugoslavia.[2] I know what a gap it will mean in all the family's life having them away from Ottawa, but it is splendid seeing them get a first rate job. You must be glad that all your children are doing things which interest them. Charity's last weeks must have been tragic and hectic. Again it must have been marvellous to do something about Hungary of a positive nature. I still hope that great things are going to come out from Russia despite the rulers. What has been done in Hungary was so horrible but one feels that it may have had some beneficial effect within certain classes in Russia. That is the best one can think of such tragedy.

This brings you oh so much love.

George

1 Sir Anthony Eden (1897–1977), prime minister of England, 1955–7
2 Ignatieff was Canadian ambassador to Yugoslavia, 1956–8.

125/ To Derek Bedson   Blackheath, SE3
                                                       13 June 1957

Dear Derek,
The wonderful news of the elections[1] filled Sheila and my minds with joy
not only in general but for you. What a wonderful victory and how thrilled
you must be. What a joy that the Canadian people were not so bemused
that they could throw the rascals out. I could hardly believe it. Positively
for you what I think is wonderful is that your having had the courage to follow your principles when the Conservatives were weak and when all the
young men who wanted prestige laughed at you, now will reap the reward
of that courage and loyalty. Sheila and I are thrilled at the victory particularly in what it means for you and for Uncle Jim. The chance for you to
be responsible and have authority. See that you use it. I just sing a quiet
'Te Deum' all day. Rarely in this life do the loyal and the principled have
their triumph in this world and Sheila and I are both rejoicing greatly that
it is in the case of two people we love as much as you and J.M.M.
    We have had a good year. Last month we had our fifth child Isabel.[2] A
big family is difficult financially – but if you are married we think it part
of our responsibility. I hope you agree.
    This is a poor letter. But our hearts are overflowing not only for Can-
ada in general but for you in particular as a triumph for loyalty, courage
and principle.

                                                       Hooray,
                                                       George

1 J.G. Diefenbaker (1895–1979), leader of the Progressive Conservative party,
   1956–67, and prime minister of Canada, 1957–63, led the Conservatives to a
   minority government, their first in twenty-two years.
2 Isabel Grant was born 23 April 1957.

*When Grant returned to Canada, he found that his mother was deteriorating. She
was beginning to show serious signs of senility. The Grants eventually found a
place for her in Homewood in Guelph, an institution with a fine reputation for the
care of the elderly. As a consequence, Grant's remarkable letters to his mother
ceased. By the early 1960s, when he visited her, she did not recognize him. She died
in 1963.*

126/ To Maude Grant   200 University Ave, Halifax
                                                        9 August

Dearest Mum,
It was lovely to get your letter of welcome. It is good to be back in Halifax
and it will be lovely to see you later on in the month. If it is convenient for
you, I would like to come and see you in the last week in August – arriving
around the 24th or 25th of August. From 2–8 September I go to an SCM[1]
conference at Bala.

Aunt Louise was so good to us when we arrived exhausted in Montreal
and we had such a wonderful welcome here from people. A small town
such as Halifax has its faults but it has great kindness. Rachel is happy to
be back with her friends and above all we are all thrilled to be back by the
sea in all its beauty.

It has been a great business getting unpacked as we had 29 pieces of
luggage – but we are getting gradually settled.

It will be lovely to see you in Toronto and lovely if you can come with
me back to Halifax. The children would just love to see you and Isabel is
such a sweet baby and as Sheila always says 'There is nobody who appreci-
ates a new baby as much as Gran.'

All seven of us send you our dearest love.

George and Sheila
Rachel, William, Robert, Catherine, Isabel
XXXXXXXXXXXXXXXXXX

The days go by fast and busily here but there is not a day when you are
not in our hearts and on our lips.
To Hell with the Roman Church.

1 Student Christian Movement

127/ To Derek Bedson   Halifax, Nova Scotia
                                                        28 August 1957

Dear Derek,
Just a note about the death of your father, of which I have just heard from
Aunt Marjorie. As a Christian, I know you do not take death as defeat –
nevertheless the mystery of separation from somebody one has loved, as
you loved your father, is still not easily borne. Even more it is hard for
your mother. Would you tell her how I have been thinking of her when

you write. The mystery of the triumph of God I understand less and less, but try and trust in more and more and I know your trust is very deep so that your present pain will be sustained in that mystery.

Love,
George

128/ To Sheila Grant   en route to Montreal
August 1957

[extract:]
I thought that I would spend the next few minutes trying to write out certain propositions about Marx, and instead of just writing them out I thought I would send them to you in the form of a letter. Then you can think about them and either send me comments or we can discuss them later.

(a) Human history has and is taking place and because of human freedom (not defining that word at the moment) it cannot be understood as a natural process. This is simply a negative statement – but true even if one does not know it and how it can be understood.

(b) The first question is then if – is the philosophy of history possible – are attacks such as Berlin[1] and Sartre's arguments back? On this Marx seems to take a rather strange position. He rejects Hegel's Gnosticism of the spirit yet he recognizes that if people are to know enough to act intelligently they must know what is going on in history, and that positivism must be rejected (Berlin's positivism is only possible because he assumes all sensible men know what should be accomplished). It is in this sense that Sartre is a Marxist. The issue here is the difference between Hegel's primacy of theory over practice and Marx's unity of theory and practice. I do not understand what he means by this unity – but that he is onto something of supreme importance I am sure.

(c) Let us say that the philosophy of history is possible – then I think one has to admit that Hegel is onto something prodigious when he says that history is the unfolding of freedom in the world. To say it is prodigious is not here to discuss its truth or falsity, but to say that it is what the modern consciousness is. This is what the mass of modern men believe and Hegel has expressed and universalised this progressive consciousness in a deeper and profounder way than any other. (i) Truer recognition of evil (i.e. abberation) than other moderns (ii) no rejection of the old theological tradition – but the attempt to bring it in to the progressive view of history (iii) a consummate knowledge of the intricate empirical facts of history.

(d) But above all it seems to me he failed (as I tried to say to James [Doull] the other night) and when I say failed I do not mean to imply anything about whether success is possible – although if it is not possible then we must just accept an impotence in a kind of act of acceptance of evil, which is what I think Hegel and James do and which is perhaps the true religious act – he failed to show how those who accepted his philosophy should act in the world – a supremely social philosophy ends up with an implied hiatus between philosophy and social policy.

(e) This is where Marx comes in with great force and cogency. He accepts the central proposition of the progressivist philosophy of history and says I can take it and make it explicit in terms of a livable social policy. Well, I stopped this at lunch on the train and have since been for a lovely day at Montreal with Louise, and then on [to] the absolute hell here in Toronto which I will describe on another sheet.

Mother's position is a real agony ... for a person who has considered control of life the end, the giving up of it is awful to watch.

I must send this off, so that you get it and I will write again more sensibly soon.

Love to Isabel
Love to Catherine
Love to Robert
Love to William
Love to Rachel
Love to you XXXXX George

1 Sir Isaiah Berlin (1909–   ), British political philosopher

1958

129/ To Derek Bedson　　　　　　　　　　　　Dalhousie University
2 April 1958

Dear Derek,

Congratulations – what happened on Monday must leave you certain.[1] The party will certainly need great wisdom now that such trust has been put in it. Last time I was glad for your sake that you were in a position of responsibility, now I am glad for the country. If ever there was a need of spiritual conservatism (I do not mean economic) it is now and you have it. I thought of what Milton wrote about Abdiel who was not moved by Satan:

'Among the innumerable false, unmoved.
Unshaken, unseduced, unterrified.'[2]
The people of character count so much in times of success. I am there-
fore so glad you are there.

You will be so immensely busy that my lazy heart goes out to you. I will
be in Ottawa next Tuesday evening April 8th and then again the following week (18–19 April). I would like to see you for a moment one of those
times. But will quite understand that these are hectic weeks for you. I am
going to be at the Chateau Laurier about supper time on Tuesday evening and will give you a call. If the week after is better I will call you then.

Sheila sends her best congratulations. Quite directly I hope grace will
be with you in the next so important years.

Ever,
George

1 John Diefenbaker led his Conservatives to a landslide victory 31 March 1958.
2 John Milton, *Paradise Lost* 5.893–4

130/ To Kenneth McNaught[1]

Dalhousie University, Halifax
1 December 1958

Dear Professor McNaught,
I hope you will forgive a letter from a stranger expressing the high admiration I feel at your actions in the present situation at United College.[2] It
always does the soul good to think of people acting on principle and with
such fine courage.

You surely know that there are many people in academic life ready to
take what action they can to stand behind you and your colleagues. So if
there is anything to be done – do let our Faculty Association know.

In writing I wonder whether you are the Kenneth McNaught I knew
many years ago? Whoever you are, this brings an expression of great
admiration.

Yours sincerely,
George Grant

1 Kenneth McNaught (1918–), professor of history, University College, Winnipeg, 1947–59
2 United College, Winnipeg, dismissed Harry Crowe in 1958. His case led the
Canadian Association of University Teachers (CAUT) to address issues of academic freedom for the first time.

1959

*When Grant returned to Dalhousie after his sabbatical, he felt increasingly restive
so far from 'the centre of the crisis.' He began to look around for other opportunities
and, since he was convinced that his quarrel with Fulton Anderson and the Canadian philosophic establishment had cut him off from Ontario, he considered the
possibility of going to the United States. Claremont College in California invited
him for an interview.*

131/ To Sheila Grant   Claremont College
                                                              10 June 1959

Dearest Girl,
First report. I have not seen Benson, who is away. But thought I would
send you a short report.

1) The town is ravishingly beautiful, just breathtaking. All the colleges
have gardens, fountains, vistas & really lovely Spanish style buildings. The
high azaleas and eucalyptus and olive and orange trees. Physically, it is
sophisticated in a way – in its own genre – almost as much as Oxford.

2) Los Angeles, which I only saw in transit, just seemed to me a magnified Toronto, but I think the thing around here is to keep out of it, as the
traffic is so difficult.

3) I think the heat is not too bad, cool in the evenings, but I think it
would require a major adjustment for you. For me, what would be
required would be a world without winter.

4) I admire the sophistication & charm of the Institute, but feel British.

5) What I love about it – the Institute – is being in a place where really
able people question everything I say and make me define. Even if the
job does not come off, it will be worth coming.

6) I have no idea of the students. The faculty seem very nice, decent
people and two of them, who obviously know of the possibility of my coming, have been very nice.

Of course, before Benson comes, nothing real can be said, except that
I have encountered nothing against & much for. Oh, perhaps against,
the idea of alien corn. But the whole place is obviously a very civilized
place & it is without question a very lovely place. Above all for me is the
fact that I would be with people who are interested in things I am.

The worst at the Institute is a professor from Oxford, who rages against
the welfare state. The best for me is an old-fashioned American, who talks
about liberty & freedom in a subtle & very acceptable way. In between is

a clever American professor of economics, who is philosophically positivist & rather frighteningly theoretical, but really quite left-wing. The members of the Institute are very good – several students of Leo Strauss[1] who just think he is God, which bodes well for the young [of] America.

Well, that is all at the moment, except deepest, deepest love. I love you more every day of my life &, for sheer selfishness, I would ask you to look after yourself. Love to all the children.

GPG

1 Leo Strauss (1899–1973), German-born American political philosopher whose works, especially *Thoughts on Machiavelli* (1958), *What Is Political Philosophy and Other Writings* (1959), *Natural Right and History* (1963), and *On Tyranny* (1963), profoundly influenced Grant's thought

While he was contemplating the possibility of Claremont, he received a letter from Murray Ross, who was president of the newly created York University in Toronto. It seemed to offer the possibility of returning to Toronto and teaching philosophy, something he had thought impossible. He accepted gladly. Thus began what was possibly the worst year of his life.

132/ To Dean Archibald   Dalhousie University, Halifax
17 December 1959

Dear Dean Archibald,
This is just to say that I am resigning from Dalhousie as of the beginning of the next academic year. My appointment at York University is confidential until it is announced from Toronto, but as various people seem to have heard of it from Toronto, I thought I should tell you without delay.

Yours sincerely,
George Grant

The Years of Lament 1960–70

1960

Grant accepted a position as chairman of the new philosophy department of York University in north Toronto. He expected to be able to create a philosophy department that could present an alternative view to the study of philosophy at the University of Toronto. However, he did not understand the arrangement between the two universities, which made York an affiliate of University of Toronto until 1965. When he discovered that his department would be subordinate to University of Toronto in its initial stages, and that he would not have control over the curriculum, he resigned; and much to his surprise and chagrin, his resignation was accepted. He was unemployed, with a large family to support.

133/ To Murray Ross[1]   27 February 1960

Dear President Ross,
I am sorry to bother you with a letter when you have so much to attend to.

Two weeks ago the registrar of York wrote to ask me for a paragraph about the first year course in philosophy. He enclosed the paragraph from the Toronto calendar and said we were going to teach the same course as Toronto. Knowing that York was going to be under the guidance of Toronto, but not knowing that we were going to teach completely identical courses, I wrote to Professor Anderson asking him about textbooks and describing the way I would like to cover the material. I also said that as ethics was cut from general philosophy at the U of T because of the collegiate system, I would like to include Plato's *Republic* in the first year. I remembered what you had said about getting youngsters to think about what makes a good life and the *Republic* has always seemed to me the greatest book on that subject (perhaps on any subject). Professor Anderson replied civilly, but forcibly, that the questions I had raised were not pertinent as York students were going to have identical courses with the U of T for at least four years and were going to write the same examinations. I write, therefore, to ask clarification about that identity.

Will the York professors have anything to do with setting the examinations at Toronto which their students write? Will we have anything to do with marking those joint examinations or will that be done solely by Toronto appointees? Identical is quite a word (and it could include York students listening to Toronto professors on tape or by microphone). Of course, what in fact matters is how these problems are worked out in a flexible and developing practice.

I quite recognize that one need of York in the next years is to have a cooperative association with Toronto and that all you do or say to anyone must turn around that need. I recognize that all your skill will be required to balance this against the need for York to be something on its own. You also may be quite confident that I will not get into any theoretical argument with the philosophy department at Toronto about how it is best to teach philosophy, and I will try to eliminate any acerbity in the dealings I will have with them. But I had understood when I accepted your offer that the York teachers were going to have some freedom in what they taught and how they taught it. The minimum condition of there being any freedom is for the teacher to have some say in the setting and marking of the papers of the courses he teaches. I blame myself greatly for not having discussed these questions with you in detail. My enthusiasm about the whole project meant that it just never entered my head that the new university would have the hand of Toronto so heavily upon it. To repeat, I recognize that what is important is not formulas, but how these problems are worked out in practice and how one sets out to make accommodations in good temper. But much hangs for me on how this relationship works itself out, for you can imagine that I do not relish the prospect of being *in statu pupillari*[2] to the U of T.

Please do not take this as a pressing letter as I recognize how subtle must be the job of guiding the new institution in these next months and years. Because of your burdens I have tried to make this letter short and practical and therefore have not raised questions of long range principle about the teaching of philosophy in Canada with the coming generation of youngsters. I am going to put in the mail some comments about these broader issues which you can read at your leisure (whenever that may be).

Yours,
George Grant

1 M.G. Ross (1910–), founding president, York University
2 In the status of a student; that is, as a subordinate

134/ To Murray Ross   14 April 1960

Dear President Ross,
This is just to say that after long thought I have decided it would be wrong on my part to introduce youngsters to philosophy by means of Professor Long's textbook[1] and that as there seems no alternative to such a procedure at York, I must with regret submit my resignation to you.

As this is an important matter of academic principle I would like to state my objections to this procedure. (a) Professor Long's textbook pretends to be an introduction to philosophy which does not take sides, but introduces the student objectively to the problems of the subject. This is, however, not the case. To illustrate why it is not the case, let me take as an example the basic question of the differences between classical and modern philosophy. Professor Long's book is based on the presupposition that the assumptions of nineteenth century philosophy are true in a way that implies that those of classical philosophy are not. As an obvious example, the book is prefaced by a quotation from Lessing which is taken as true and which implies that Plato and Aristotle largely wrote untruth. It is, of course, not my purpose here to debate the very vexed and difficult question of the quarrel between the ancients and the moderns, but simply to say that one hardly has an objective textbook when it is based on such an assumption. What makes these assumptions particularly unobjective is that they are not made explicit in the work. (b) When I say that Professor Long's book is based on an implied assumption of the truth of modern philosophy, I do not mean contemporary philosophy, but the philosophy of the late nineteenth century in Great Britain and the early twentieth in the U.S.A. His book is oblivious to nearly all contemporary philosophy. For instance, there is no mention of Wittgenstein in his book – certainly the most influential modern philosopher in professional philosophic circles in the English-speaking world. (c) Apart from the assumptions of the book, its very method seems to me inimical to the proper teaching of philosophy. It is about philosophy; it is not philosophy. The result of this approach is to encourage sophism among youngsters – that is, it encourages them to say here are a lot of opinions about this subject and that, but it does not encourage them in the real task of trying to make true judgments about those matters.

I would like to include a paragraph about Professor Long's relation to religion and my own, because I am sure you have heard it said that I confuse religion and philosophy and that you will now hear it said that my objection to Professor Long's book comes from my religion. Let me make it clear that I consider the practice of religion and the practice of philosophy two distinct human activities. I do not think that philosophy can prove or disprove Christian doctrine. My position on this matter is illustrated by the fact that the philosopher I admire the most in North America is Leo Strauss at Chicago. He is a practising Jew and I would have no hesitation in saying that he is a better philosopher than any practising Christian I know on this continent. Some of my best graduate students have been practising Jews and I have had no difficulties with them on this score. Of course, although religion and philosophy are distinct activities, their relation is a philosophic question of magnitude and Professor Long inevitably deals with it. Unfortunately he does not deal with it accurately. If, for instance, you turn to what Professor Long says about the relation between philosophy and the idea of revelation in certain religions on p. 23 of this book, I do not think one could find any trained philosophers who are either believing Protestants or Catholics or Jews who would say that it is an accurate or adequate account of the matter. I did not ask that the textbooks I use should be directed towards the spread of my religion (I suggested the works of Plato and Russell neither of whom are in any way identified with the Christian church and neither of whom are in any way identified with the true). But I could hardly be expected to use a textbook which misrepresents the religion of my allegiance. I would also point out that, although Professor Long deplores the influence of faith on certain philosophers, he has no hesitation in closely identifying the claims of his faith with the facts of the case. It is in my opinion just this which above all makes Professor Long's book so poor an instrument for introducing youngsters to philosophy most of whom will have been born since 1940 in modern industrial Canada. Professor Long's faith was obviously formed by the experience of his break with a limited Calvinism in the light of certain philosophic and scientific ideas. This was a very moving and formative experience for the English of the 1890's, for the Americans of the early 1900's and for Canadians in the 1920's, but it has little bearing on the situation of Canadians growing up in Ontario at the moment.

Some of my friends have suggested that I should get up in class and quietly say where I think the required textbook is inadequate. This would indeed be fun; but it would also be unjust. It would leave the beginners with two conflicting accounts and an exam to be faced. This might be good for the clever, but it would be radically unfair for the weaker brethren. Also I would hope that if my teaching were good the better students would understand the inadequacy of the book. Then they would surely ask (if I had the right relation with them) why I employed it as a textbook. To that question I would have no just answer – beyond appealing to the necessity of earning my living, my liking for my home town, etc. Such considerations would not stand up against the unflinching moral judgments of which youngsters are capable.

Professor Anderson told Professor Long to write to me about details, where his own letter covered the matter unequivocally in terms of general policy. Professor Long told me I could use other textbooks. He included a list of these which Professor Anderson would consider suitable. I do not see, however, that this makes possible any solution because if the York students have to write Toronto exams, marked by Toronto examiners, the use of an alternative textbook would cause an unfair burden on York students. Professor Long's textbook is sufficiently idiosyncratic that I do not see how students could answer questions chosen from it by studying from some other textbooks. The burden here would particularly fall on the marginal student, of which there are bound to be some at York.

I am sorry that this resignation has been left so long, but it has only become clear to me gradually in the last months the degree to which York is going to be tied to the U of T and the consequences that this would have on my teaching at York.

Would you ask Mr Small to get in touch with me about the loan which has been guaranteed by York so that I can make the proper arrangements about it.

If you consider there is any need for a statement about my resignation in the newspapers and if you consider that such a statement should go beyond a simple one of fact, I think that we should work it out together.

I regret that we will not be working together in the same institution.

With all best wishes,
George Grant

1 Marcus Long, *The Spirit of Philosophy* (1953)

Grant, now unemployed, began to look for other jobs. One of the more interesting was to work for Mortimer Adler's Institute for Philosophical Research. He flew to San Francisco to investigate the possibility. When he was told that he could do his work from Toronto, he accepted.

135/ To Derek Bedson　　　　　　　　　　　　　　Dalhousie University
　　　　　　　　　　　　　　　　　　　　　　　　　　　5 June 1960

Dear, dear Derek,

Sheila and I were so touched at your letters and at your phone call and at your speaking to Archbishop Barfoot.[1] Loyalty to persons is a lovely quality; but even more at the moment what concerns me is what you also have with us a common sharing about the problem of the church and its rightful place in education. The reason I wrote to you about this whole business is not only to help me get a job, but because I want Christians outside the universities to know what gates of evil these secular universities can be. Educated Christians have a traditional respect for universities because they founded them and it is therefore hard for them to recognise that universities can be sources of evil as well as good. I am sure that the church has to face this problem and that above all the Anglican church has a tremendous role in facing this in a Catholic way and yet not in the exclusive way that the Roman church so often does. This is why I am particularly glad that you spoke to Barfoot and so glad to hear of his concern for St John's.

As for my own plans; a foundation in California has asked me to apply for a grant to do full time writing next year. As we have bought a house in Toronto we will probably go there for a year and next year wait and see what comes up in the academic world. (This is private as this foundation is very strict about never mentioning its help.) The other possibility is through Robert Hutchins of the Fund for the Republic.[2] He is chairman of the editorial board of the *Encyclopedia Britannica* and has been trying to persuade the board to make me editor and to make an entirely new encyclopedia which synthesises all knowledge. He is going to get in touch with me next week again and if he offers me the right kind of job I would work for him because he is a great man, and his purposes and mine in the educational world are closely similar. But I will let you know when he lets me know. This also is confidential as there are forces very much opposed to my appointment.

As for St John's it would interest me greatly – much more than the possibility you mentioned over the phone. My reason is the following: in the body of Christ there are many functions all necessary to that body, but mine is theory-theology and philosophy and I am determined to stick to that function rather than to go into administration. I would be willing to do administration in a theological college because that would be serving an end which is related to my thought, but this administration of large secular institutions is largely having to pander to the pushing aims of the boom world. I will write to Archbishop Barfoot setting out my qualifications and I will not write it till Wednesday when I will have heard from Hutchins.

One thing I would also ask you is not to believe any stories you hear that my resignation was not necessary without checking the facts. The people at Toronto were angry about me questioning them and obviously have their story. As in all these practical matters the details are long and boring and not worth repeating. Luckily I have many good and able friends who will present the story, as I see it, at Kingston.

I am just immensely grateful to you for your friendship and concern. I knew from the second time I met you that God had blessed me with an unflinching friend. This present letter was written just to make clear that you do not have to worry about employment for the eight of us. The best thing that this has done for me has been to purge me of the silly desire I had to live in Toronto – a quite unnecessary desire which had become really foolishly idolatrous. The whole business has freed me from self-pity – a miserable vice which you got over years before myself. It still comes back like a disease, but I now see it for what it is. So I can thank God for the whole incident.

Have you seen Farrer's new book of Sermons titled *Said or Sung*[3] – very fine for the mature Christian. Did you notice that he has been appointed Warden of Keeble? What was true at Oxford still remains – nobody can explain to me what the Christian faith means as well as he.

We have an election here[4] this week. Stanfield will probably win. He is a decent and just man, but a singularly ungenerous one who is not a real conservative because he instinctively identifies himself with the privileged economically. I would not like to see him leader of the national party because of this narrowness.

Again so many thanks and please forgive an egocentric letter.

Love,
George

1 Most Rev. W.F. Barfoot (1893–1978), Anglican primate of all Canada, 1951–8
2 R.M. Hutchins (1899–1977), president of the University of Chicago and an edu-

cational reformer. In 1954 Hutchins founded the Center for the Study of Democratic Institutions.

3 Austin Farrer, *Said or Sung: An Arrangement of Homily and Verse* (1960)

4 Nova Scotia provincial election, won by Stanfield

136/ To Derek Bedson   Farnham Ave, Toronto

Dear Derek,

It will be simply lovely for us to see you and you must stay here whatever
days you can. We will be more organised physically and mentally than
when you were here last. There will be a dear old soul here from Halifax,
but she just potters about in a pleasant way and will not disturb you. We
will expect to hear from you when you arrive and I will meet you if there
is not a snow storm which means our little car is immobile.

Our plans for the future are up in the air. I turned down Brandon
because of the children. If it had been a real evangelical job the sacrifice
would have been worth it, but although Robbins is a fine man and a religious man it is of a vague Protestant mysticism. He will do a splendid job,
but it is not one I want to give my life to. Bill Kilbourn[1] has been introducing my name at McMaster and there may be a job there. He says silence
about this is absolutely necessary. The York people had me down the
other day and the president said he wanted me but the U of T are ada-
mant and he has to OK his appointments with them. He is looking for
something to tide me over till he can appoint. A very confused business. I
went to Trinity the other day. Except for the theological college I would
gather their relation with Christianity is pretty threadbare and very much
directed towards teaching a gentlemanly religion to the wealthy. This was
quite a good purpose in an era where Christianity was the inevitable public religion, but today it is not good enough.

What has struck me in the last months is how little people see any relation between Christianity and education. The secularists are quite clear.
The unbelieving Christians think the cult is a pleasant and useful relic.
Many of the believing Christians should not be concerned with this
because they are simple people. But many of the leaders of the church
don't seem to be aware of how deeply the principles of modernity (at certain points) make the believing of Christianity an impossibility and that
therefore these principles have to be shown to be false. To speak personally, I would not have missed the last months of my life for anything
because they have made me pull myself together and realise how sloppy
and wishy washy I had become and above all how intellectually lazy and

content with an idolatry of erudition. Both you and Sheila had faced certain things much earlier and clearly.

I imagine your mother (if she is coming east) will want to go direct to Joy's, but if not you and she will know how welcome she would be here.

Ever,
George

1 W.L. Kilbourn (1926–95), writer and university professor. Kilbourn was one of the people instrumental in bringing Grant to McMaster.

1961

The expansion of the Ontario universities was accompanied by a process of secularization. Religiously based institutions, such as McMaster, which had Baptist ties, were forced to move religion from the mainstream of the curriculum. McMaster chose to create a secular religion department so that the study of religion would continue in a way acceptable to the Ontario government. Grant increasingly saw this new department as a great opportunity to carry on his work in a sympathetic environment.

137/ To Derek Bedson   Farnham Ave, Toronto
19 January 1961

Dear Derek,
This is just to say that I have accepted the appointment at McMaster University. As you may or may not know, Sibley[1] of Manitoba wrote offering me an appointment as associate professor in Manitoba.

As you can imagine the chief reason against going to McMaster was Sheila's and my love for you. The reason we decided not to was because of the kind of job it was at McMaster. What I will be doing is to teach Christian doctrine to non-divinity undergraduates. This dept. of religion is really introducing the faculty of theology back into the university in a big way in a Canadian university – the very thing that has always been my dream. Paul Clifford who is Dean of Men and heading the new department is a very pleasant man – Balliol '38. More than his pleasantness, he and I are in substantial agreement as to what we should be doing. Although I was very grateful that Sibley offered me a job I was much less close to him as far as the religious ends of education and would have had to teach within the kind of limits he lays down. I have had too long at Dalhousie been careful to draw the line between philosophy and Christianity

– and I want now to be able to speak directly. It has not been philosophy but Xian doctrine that has got me through the necessitudes of life – and I think there is a crying need for young people to know what Xian doctrine is. The choice was between doing that and being near you and after long debate we chose the former.

I hope your mother is going on satisfactorily and that she is not trying to do too much. Do let us know and also let us know when you will be here.

Love and as always thanks for your friendship,

George

P.S. I can only turn Sibley down tomorrow; so would you not mention this. Also the McMaster appointment they want to announce next week.

1 William Sibley (1919–), chairman, Department of Philosophy, University of Manitoba

138/ To Rhoda and Douglas Hall[1]

80 South St, Dundas
5 September 1961

Dear Rhoda and Douglas,
We have been poor correspondents, but have just kept our emotional heads above water this year and didn't want to bore you with gloom. Thanks so much for your letter. It was lovely to hear about Kate; we do not know how you spell it as your letter is in some packing case. We were sorry to hear of your difficulties with ecclesiastical order and with universities. I know little of the former, but a lot of the latter and know how difficult they can be. There is probably nothing I can do, but if there is please tell me.

We have fallen on good times. McMaster has been awfully good and it will be interesting to see what comes of a department of religion. We have got a simply gorgeous place to live. An old Ontario farmhouse in the midst of a beautiful garden and ravine. The boys are in ecstasy and all Sheila's Englishness has come out in her yen for gardening. We have lots of space; so if you ever come Hamilton-wards you could stay with us.

I have seen little of the SCM[2] this year except for talks with Miller[3] in his bookshop. I have also seen Miss Pelton who is a sweetie ... I do not accept the RC solution to the problem, but it is much nearer the truth than the fuzzy solution of most Protestants. They at least see that the heart of the matter is the curriculum and that the curriculum as it is based in our modern secular universities is radically at odds with Christianity. I will admit to you that the SCM does a useful job in a difficult situation within limits. But [blocked out] woolly stop gap method can in the long run prejudice the relation of Christianity to education deeply. Of course, it all hinges around the terribly difficult question of the place of the intellect in the Xian life. One has to agree that love and faith are the heart of the matter, but this control principle can't be left completely unqualified. Luckily the SCM does not exist at McMaster; so I won't have to have anything to do with it. But last year I found myself just entirely unable to speak to the SCM leadership because of these matters. I would not write this way to people who did not have the interest of the Xian church centrally in them. If the Xian church surrenders at the level of curriculum it will be a sad day for generations of students. I think this is the very grave error that Bultmann and Barth lead to. I hope we can talk about this someday.

Love to you both. I hope the world goes well for you.

George and Sheila

P.S. What I am saying is that the SCM cannot depend for its success solely on great human beings such as yourself.
P.P.S. I wrote this letter several weeks ago, but it is hopelessly inadequate, but one must communicate with one's friends, however inadequately.

Have you read H. Kraemer's latest, *World Cultures and World Religions*[4] – such a tonic after the vague liberalism of so many about the dialogue between religions?

The exclusion of all Greek wisdom from modern Protestant thought is driving me to distraction. I cannot understand it. One does not have to be a liberal to see wisdom outside biblical categories. The new biblical theologians I often find identify biblicism with the modern world. But I can't take it as given that some modern assumptions may not be radically wrong and that the antique men of nature may be more nearly Xian than the modern ones.

1 D.J. Hall (1928–), principal of St Paul's University College, University of Waterloo. Rhoda (Palfrey) Hall was a friend from Halifax.
2 Student Christian Movement
3 Bob Miller, manager of the SCM Bookroom, a Toronto bookstore
4 Hendrik Kraemer (1888–1965), *World Cultures and World Religions: The Coming Dialogue* (1960)

139/ To Murray and Anne Tolmie   McMaster University
6 November 1961

Dear Murray and Anne,
I have been meaning to write for about two weeks. I think Bill K[ilbourn]
has written. When I heard that K was going to York, I suggested to him
that it would be glorious to have you here and what could we do about it?
As I am now here he was urging away the history people and I am just
writing (a) to say the obvious that it would be wonderful to have you here
and (b) to give you some impressions of the place, as I see it now. Of
course, such impressions are not much use because I do not know how
you see your life at the moment. It would be lovely to see you because the
last year has forced me to define myself much more clearly and it is good
to meet old friends again, in the light of their and one's own definitions.
      I, of course, am glad to be at McMaster (a) because central Ontario
presents more varied opportunities for the youngsters than Halifax (b)
because we have a gorgeous place to live (c) because the last year made
me realise I was too old to become an American (d) because I admire the
man who is head of the dept of religion and agree with him educationally.
None of these are reasons for you and Anne. Apart from these reasons I
think there is a good chance to do good things here. But, to be honest,
there are also sides here like all Canadian universities that scare me. I
admire K greatly and owe him *much*, but I am much less optimistic about
what is happening in our society than he is. Therefore, I expect less of the
universities. I think also I have less of the plain old virtue of courage than
K. It seems highly likely that we will spend the rest of our days here.
      This is a poor letter, but it brings you both much love from us both and
again the reiteration that it would be wonderful if you move here.

Ever,
George G.

1962

140/ To Derek Bedson   Dundas, Ontario
5 April 1962

Dear Derek,
Thanks for your letter and for the enclosed tentative rules of order. They
seem to me eminently sensible and should be a structure in which good
work can be done. I like particularly their moderation. Clarity and abso-

luteness at the level of doctrine needs to be mixed with moderation and relativeness at the level of the day-to-day. (I say this because I have just spent a weekend with a group of left-wing Christians who wanted to take absoluteness into the realm of the political in a way that seemed to me foolish.)

To speak subjectively, Byfield is in the best sense a challenge to people like Sheila and myself in the sense that one recognises the limitations of one's love in the difficulty we would have in living in a community. It is not enough to say that the church needs different kinds of vocations.

How good that you are going to Europe and I hope you have a gorgeous time. If in any sense it is possible or convenient for you to stop over in Malton, do remember that we can easily drive over there to see you or to bring you back here.

As to the election,[1] I agree with what you say. But, of course, it does not do to say in public that the NDP is going to split the Liberal vote – because that is what the Liberals are using as their chief attack on the NDP and it can only do both the PCs and NDP harm. I really could not bear for the Liberals to win but we must be ready for anything as in an era [in which] we cannot expect much. I simply cannot bear the hypocrisy of Mitchell Sharp[2] when he speaks of planning when he doesn't really mean planning. Nor the *hypocrisy* of Walter Gordon[3] who piously says that the NDP is a class party. My hope is that the PM will be smart enough to hurt Pearson and that the NDP will get a decent number of seats. What I would fear is the reverse of 1957-58: that 110-110-40 in the first election would bring a second election with the Liberals gobbling up the NDP. But I think Douglas[4] is in the best sense a political realist and will see that that is avoided. As you once said if Sauvé[5] had not died the election would be certain. [I] hope the NDP is not smashed because that would be an end of restraint on capitalism. Between ourselves I was asked to stand but did not consider it for it seemed as my job is to be a theologian.

McMaster is so A.1 that I fear, because of my Presbyterian imagination, some disaster. There is a real chance to do what I have always wanted to do and difficulties are not now external but being a [more] disciplined person. Again in private, we have a chance of working in a most intimate way at M. with the RCs but the negotiations have to be secret and will take six months.

I put this down and now send it off. I'll await your arrival back. I hope you will not be too busy during the election and sometime this summer we may meet.

Ever,
George

1 Federal general election, 18 June 1962, in which Diefenbaker was reduced to a minority government.
2 M.W. Sharp (1911–), civil servant and businessman, a leading figure in Pearson's government. He ran against Donald Fleming in Eglinton in Toronto in 1962 and was defeated, but he was elected in 1963. He resigned from the House of Commons in 1978. See Mitchell Sharp, *Which Reminds Me ...: A Memoir* (1994), 93–103.
3 W.L. Gordon (1906–87), president of the privy council and writer
4 T.C. Douglas (1904–86), Baptist minister, CCF premier of Saskatchewan, 1944–61, federal leader of the NDP, 1961–71
5 J.-M.-P. Sauvé (1907–60), premier of Quebec, 1959–60. Sauvé succeeded Maurice Duplessis as Union Nationale leader and premier. Many federal Conservatives believed that he might have been able to rescue the fortunes of their party in Quebec had he lived.

141/ To Derek Bedson   McMaster University
                                                       18 June 1962

Dear Derek,
Just a note before the election to say how worried I am that the old gang is coming back in. In the last weeks I have been seeing a lot of the Ontario establishment and have been staggered by their venom against Dief. They seem to think they have a divine right to run Canada. If they get in they plan to sell us to the U.S.A. lock, stock, and barrel.

I am hoping the NDP gets a real contingent with the Conservatives a majority so that the Liberals can't get in and then do what Dief did in 1958. I guess it centrally depends on whether rural Ontario stands firm. If it does then you people are in; so that won't be too bad if we have a good representation.

You have been so much in our minds in the last weeks – because if the Liberals become the right wing party in Canada I am worried for you. My objection to Dief is that he has not laid deep roots for your party.

Always our love,
George and Sheila

P.S. We hope hope hope to see you etc., etc.

142/ To Derek Bedson   McMaster University
                                                      20 June 1962

Dear Derek,
I am sorry to bombard you with letters. This is a letter of congratulations
on how well the PCs did in Manitoba and to say that I hope that some
people in your party at the top recognise that what happened in Ontario
was *chiefly* caused by the fact that the business community openly
espoused the Liberal party. Also I think that in an election that came soon
the Liberal party would do even better in Ontario.

I had the pitiable and boring task of being an agent in a constituency
for the NDP. At least we are now clearly an urban socialist party and there
is going to be great need of that.

Love,
George

I hope Diefenbaker will now recognise that the big capitalists are not his
supporters and that you can't count on the Bassetts[1] of this world.

I hope Dief read *Time* during the election and saw what they tried to do
to him.[2]

1 John Bassett (1915–), newspaper and television station owner, Conservative
   candidate in Toronto in the 1962 election
2 Conservative supporters saw *Time*'s coverage as aggressively pro-Liberal.

143/ To Derek Bedson   McMaster University
                                                      [late autumn 1962]

Dear Derek,
Just a note to wish your party well in the election.[1] I am sure that the elec-
torate can't be so foolish as not to recognize the quality of your chief.

Life goes well for us here and Dundas is by and large not a bad place to
raise children. There is much competition (that is, blatant secularism)
but there are parts of the old and more dignified Ontario bourgeoisie
around. There is a first-rate rector and you will be glad to hear that
Rachel is offended if we ever miss church. She is a devoted member of
the choir. Next time we meet I must speak with you about where for university. Do you think Laval is out of the question? I am not impressed by
the woman in charge at Trinity – an English gamesmistress.[2]

The best thing as far as work goes is that my main outside activity is working with Creal[3] and the priests around him. They are by and large an impressive crowd and see the present existence of the church in a far deeper way than the old Toronto established Anglicanism. Creal is a big person.

If you are this way at Xmas it would of course be very good to see you and I could drive you or pick you up if it was a question of motion – or come across and see you. I have got more used to the constant mobility of modern society than previously.

You would have been amused to hear Forsey[4] and I talking the other day. Two socialists whose main political interest was that the Conservatives hold off the Liberal threat. As I know you know, I wish the Conservatives (federally) were wiser in their relations with the academic community.

The Cuban crisis[5] did not make me optimistic about the relations of N. America with the rest of the world in the future. But it made S. and I grateful that we had not gone to the U.S.A. and grateful once more to you who were our only friend who ever expressed to us that it made any difference to stay in Canada. It is an extraordinary world in which to bring up children – as the folly in the opinions which surround them is great.

Again all the very best for the 14th. I mark the envelope 'personal' because you are a civil servant.

Ever,
George

1 Manitoba provincial general election
2 K.M Daroch was dean of women at Trinity College, University of Toronto, 1953–63.
3 Rev. Canon K.H.M. Creal (1927–), general secretary of the general board of religious education, Anglican Church of Canada
4 E.A. Forsey (1904–90), labour historian and constitutional expert
5 John F. Kennedy ordered a military blockade of Cuba in retaliation for the stationing of Soviet missiles on the island in October 1962. The blockade ended 20 November.

1963

John Diefenbaker's government was defeated in the House of Commons by a combined vote of the opposition parties. The issue was his desire to reconsider the entry of nuclear weapons into Canada. Grant thought that Diefenbaker was defending Canadian sovereignty, and he was outraged that the NDP would bring his government down on an issue relating to nuclear weapons.

144/ To Derek Bedson   McMaster University
                                                  [February 1963]

Dear Derek,
I know you must be busy, but you are the only person I can turn to for
advice. Just *dictate* a quick answer.

I have never felt such political loyalty as I feel for Green[1] and Dief.
Whatever the PM lacks, he spoke unequivocally for Canadian independence. When Macmillan purred while he was being raped, Dief fought.
And of course Green has deeply cared for the most important political
cause of all – disarmament – and has been willing to risk the wrath of big
business on this issue. Whatever Dief's failings, he has in the clinch spoken for Canada. All this leads me to loyalty to the Conservatives.

On the other hand, I know it is not right to expect the Conservatives to
be a part of the kind that will ultimately agree with me about disengagement. For years I was immobilized after the war by the fact that I saw my
pacifism had been wrong, but that there was no feasible alternative. Catholic doctrine in the first war has convinced me, but now most Catholic
theologians are saying that the use of modern weapons is 'intrinsically
wicked' for the Xian. The upshot of this, of course, is that one hopes for
disengagement for the alliance.

As you know, my life in politics will never be important to anybody else
but myself. My one influence is a strong one over students. What do you
think one should do? Should I remain loyal to the NDP although I *greatly*
disapprove of their voting against the government on this issue or should
I tell people to vote Conservative and do so myself. Once I do so I am out
of the NDP for good and all. The Conservatives in Hamilton are a tawdry
bunch. I happened to be speaking at a young PC meeting (a large one)
on the night of dissolution and all the young and slick were out cutting
Dief's throat saying he had been wrong not to back Harkness[2] and the
Americans.

I am asking your advice not as a Conservative, but as the friend whose
judgment I trust more than any other.

I rang Douglas on Tuesday to try and persuade him not to vote the government out – but failed. I was late in doing so because my dear mother
died over the weekend[3] and I was full of personal arrangements. A great
blessing for her – although clearly one misses her as she once was.

                                                            Ever,
                                                            George

1 H.C. Green (1895–1989), secretary of state for external affairs in Diefenbaker's government
2 D.S. Harkness (1903–), minister of defence in Diefenbaker's government, who resigned over the prime minister's handling of the crisis
3 Maude Grant died 1 February 1963, aged eighty-two.

145/ To André Weil[1]   [McMaster University]
                                                        22 April 1963

Dear Professor Weil:
I write in English because my written French is not always accurate. I hope that if you reply you will reply in French.

Thank you for your letter of last month expressing your willingness to see me in Princeton. Six months ago I wrote to M. Maurice Schumann[2] who spoke to your mother about my letter to him. Very generously your mother said that she would be willing to show me your sister's unpublished manuscripts if I came to Paris. I find that I can get away from Canada in June of this year and I wonder whether I could see you and your mother at that time? I could, of course, come to any place in Europe to meet your mother at that time. It will be a very great honour because, as I said in my earlier letter, your sister's writings have for me the very highest authority.

My sister and her family are in Paris and I plan to arrive to see them on 3 June. Could I drop you a note when I arrive in Paris, or are you sufficiently influenced by your life in North America to allow me to telephone you at the address to which this letter is addressed? I would be very grateful if you could let me know whether some time in the first two weeks of June would be a possible time to see you and possibly to see your mother.

It would be of great interest if we are able to meet if you could tell me the names of other of yours sister's friends whom I might speak with in other parts of France. For example, in writing of your sister, Alain[3] once said that as a student she had written brilliantly about Spinoza. Obviously in her notebooks she has come to recognise the fuller truth of ancient philosophy over modern. Yet, in her published writings there are no direct marks of the movement of her mind in that direction. It is this kind of question, which I am inevitably concerned with, both as a philosopher and because of my knowledge of her greatness.

I am writing to M. Schumann under separate cover to see whether it would be possible to see him while I am in France.

With many thanks for your kind letter.

Yours sincerely,
George Grant

1 André Weil (1906–), one of the most brilliant mathematicians of the twentieth century and older brother of Simone Weil
2 Maurice Schumann (1911–), French philosopher, journalist, and politician. During the war he was chief official broadcaster on the BBC French Service.
3 Emile Auguste Chartier ('Alain') (1868–1951), French philosopher and one of Simone Weil's teachers

146/ To Sheila Grant 9 Rue de Chaillot, Paris 16e
13 June 1963

Dearest,

I am here and Alison is being marvellous; I really feel like Strether in [Henry James's] *The Ambassadors,* and need a gentle hand and she gives it. Do write to her and say that I have said how much I appreciate it.

The trip was a trip. I arrived here, slept in the morning. It is a very beautiful and elegant place. Had lunch with Mrs Donald Fleming – then the Bank – and the Greeks at the Louvre – home to dinner – then to bed. Alison Andrew and her husband are here ... I like Alison's young husband very much.

Mademoiselle Pétrement[1] can't drive, but I see her this afternoon for an hour – so here goes. Your advice about the day was, as usual, *right.* I should always do what you say, because nobody knows my folly better than yourself.

I think of your beautiful face all the time, lying on the bed. What a lovely and happy destiny to be married to you. Every year I feel I have sloughed off so much unhappiness by pouring it over you.

Paris is very very expensive and the people look tough as nails. I would not like to live here. We are pretty lucky where we are. The great public places are magnificent. I really think that mass society is much the same in its drive whether it be capitalist or Gaullist planning. It will be hard to hold things from the past. Strauss has really seen this.

My love to each one of the children. They will have a hard row ahead in this very highly geared world of the American Empire. What can one teach them?

Look after yourself, for my selfish sake because I love you & as you love [ill.].

Love,
George

1 Simone Pétrement, Simone Weil's biographer and friend

147/ To Sheila Grant   Délégation du Canada
9 rue de Chaillot
Paris 16e
16 June 1963

Dearest [Sheila],
Well, here is a report. I have seen Mlle Pétrement and Madame Weil[1] several times, but not the brother or others.

S. Pétrement is about 55 but seems younger. She is short, an absolute blue-stocking, but of a French kind. She walks with a cane and has bad TB. She has a smile *like an angel.* She is a person of obviously the highest beauty of character and she has loved S.W. most intensely. Unfortunately I can see her only in the late afternoon for an hour at a time because she looks after her mother (who is as mother was) and has to return to the suburbs. It is also difficult because we talk in French and as always with the French they think that nobody but the French know anything. But we are beginning to communicate. I think she is a person I could be friends with all my life, but it is difficult to understand people of another civilization. And also it is not possible to raise any questions which say that S.W. was not perhaps right on a certain point – because it was the centre of her life. The great impression one gets is that S.W. was very greatly loved.

Mme Weil is quite remarkable. A very ancient, very small, very amusing Jewish matriarch who lives in the same flat and sits in the room of S.W. with a maternal love which still blazes forth. It has been very much worthwhile to talk with her and I go nearly every day. I have so much to tell you. S.W. a dit 'Le plus grand plaisir est de rester en lit dans le matin avec le café et un Agatha Christie.'[2]

She has copies of articles on science without which I could not have written the book. They are going to come out soon, I hope, but there is a colossal fight going on between the mother and the brother. The mother lives alone, has had strokes and lay on the floor for 20 hours. The son lives in the same building, but the mother has never seen the grandchildren. And I think that the brother does not want the manuscripts on mathematics and science to be published. The mother does not want me to see the brother and, at the moment, I am contemplating the whole matter. It is all very complicated.

A. and G.[3] and I went to Chartres. Yesterday A. and I went to Vezelay. It is in my opinion much greater. We must go there and spend several weeks when the children are grown up. It is interesting that the great Romanesque doorway is about Christ and the zodiac. Tomorrow I meet some woman who is going to instruct me in the études catharistes[4] and perhaps next week I will go to Toulouse and Albi. I am not sure ...

Embrace all the children for me & give them all my love.

To you a long embrace,
George

1 Simone Weil's mother
2 The greatest pleasure is to stay in bed in the morning with a coffee and an Agatha Christie.
3 Alison and George Ignatieff
4 Studies of the Cathars

148/ To Sheila Grant   Paris

[postcard:]
This is one of the great places of the world. Romanesque is for me more the incarnation than Gothic. I am learning a lot of S.W. and it is very moving. I hope we will meet soon because there is lots to say of 'notre pauvre pays.'[1] Paris is the Hobbesian model made absolute.

See you soon,
George

1 Our poor country

149/ To Derek Bedson   McMaster University
                                               13 November 1963

Dear Derek,
It was so good of you to ring me up. It was so good to talk to you because the atmosphere of complete sell out to the Americans is so nasty around here. The news columns are just as dirty about Dief as the editorials. I am afraid Pearson is going to do very well in Ontario. The line he will take is – only we will provide 'decisive' government.

Mr Camp[1] has not called. He must be up to his ears and I only want him to call, if any good is served by anything I could do. He is the best judge of that – so don't bother the man. In the meantime I am writing letters to the Quebec papers.

Again thanks,

Ever,
George

P.S. Do you know Humbert Wolfe's[2] poem which the Toronto journals remind me of?

'You cannot hope to bribe or twist
Thank God, the British journalist.
But seeing what unbribed he'll do
There's really no occasion to.'

1 Dalton Camp (1920–), journalist and Conservative organizer. As national president of the Progressive Conservative party during 1964–9, Camp led the forces trying to oust Diefenbaker from the leadership.
2 Humbert Wolfe (1885–1940)

1964

150/ To Rhoda and Douglas Hall   McMaster University, Hamilton
24 January 1964

Dear Rhoda and Doug:
Just a note of ill-typed greeting from the battlefields of McMaster. Your depressed note of December met such a responding note in our hearts. What a queer era it is to live in and how much queerer it is going to get. I see your point about the United Church and its residence, but I am sure that the first thing is that people such as yourselves be in them, but then such people are hard to find. As for the great big, mass universities, God knows. They are going to be fantastic places and hard for youngsters to survive humanly within them. I sit on the colleges division of the Anglican offices and, except for a few young people, the church has no idea what is happening in the world, which is the first step before it decides what it should do. The sheer failure to see what is happening is staggering. And I think the basis among the Anglican leaders is really their worship of progress (how hard it dies) and their expectation that Canada and North

America are moving forward to better things. In last year's federal election we had the eucharist dedicated the Sunday before to 'stable government' – in other words vote Liberal, etc. You may consider this a lack of faith, but I am really scared for our children going out into what is coming.

I have spent the last months writing a long piece called *A Lament for a Country*, which is just about Canada becoming part of the universal and homogeneous state. It is finally true that one's hope must lie in the transcendent, but what a business it is putting off one's finite hopes.

Otherwise life goes on for us quite pleasantly day by day. McMaster is no worse (and is some respects better) than many of the tough new places. Clifford is a dear delight. This year we have a very fine Jesuit on our staff and we are going to expand our relations and work with the RC world. I would love to talk to you about departments of religion – strange things, but perhaps not bad in this era.

I hope someday we see your children and indeed yourselves. In the meantime all sorts of love and I hope the winter goes well.

Ever,
George

151/ To Francess Halpenny[1]   [McMaster University]
25 February 1964

Dear Miss Halpenny:
I have written a piece called *A Lament for a Nation* of about 25,000 words. It is, therefore, too long to publish in a quarterly. I write to know whether there is any monographic publication in Canada for pieces this length. It would be better to publish it in Canada than the United States as it is entirely about Canadian life.

Its content may be such as to exclude it from your press, because it is the Canadian established classes (particularly the Liberal party) who are considered most responsible in what I consider Canada's demise. Diefenbaker is criticized, but not from within Liberal assumptions. Neither will it be favourably received by any socialist as it does not presume the world is getting better and better. It may be, therefore, that it is just too direct a publication for your press, but I write to ask.

I would be very grateful if you have any alternative suggestions. Please give my regards to your mother.

Yours sincerely,
George Grant

1 F.G. Halpenny (1919–), editor-in-chief, University of Toronto Press, 1957–69

152/ To J.M. Campsie[1]   [McMaster University]
                                                              3 March 1964

Dear Mr Campsie:
Paul Clifford has passed to me your kind letter about the possibility of
Dent's publishing this piece I have written, which I call *A Lament for a
Nation*.

   I wonder if it is the kind of thing you would be interested in publishing;
(a) It would not make a long book as it should not be much over 25,000
words. I thought of it as the kind of book that McClelland and Stewart have
brought out in their series 'Canadian Issues,' or a lengthy pamphlet in
paperback such as the Ryerson Press published in Scott Gordon's *Economists versus the Bank of Canada.*[2] As it won't be ready for about three weeks,
I had not got in touch with these publishers yet. I would, of course, be just
delighted for Dent's to publish it, but its interest is so concentratedly
Canadian that I wonder whether you would be interested. (b) I do not
intend in any way that it should be an easily read book, like the kind of gossip that Peter Newman made about Diefenbaker.[3] This is a closely written
book and full of passion and regret about Canada. It starts with a lot of factual material about Canadian history, but ends with a logic, which is
deeper, about the age of progress. Its conclusions are, therefore, not likely
to appeal to many people. I say all this not, I hope, to scare you off, but to
say that although I would be obviously willing to change wordings, etc., I
would not be willing to turn it into a popular book, either in style or
content.

   You mention in your letter to Dean Clifford that I might have some
relation to Copp Clark's. I think I promised them that if I wrote a textbook they could publish it, but I am sure I have no other relation with
them than that. It never entered my head that Rex Williams[4] would be
particularly interested.

   If, in the light of what I have said, you are seriously interested in publishing this, I will send along the manuscript when it is completed in
about three weeks. If you think the possibility of publishing it is remote, I
hope you will say so, as I will have to get in touch with McClelland & Stewart, The Ryerson Press, etc. I am very green about this kind of thing as
most of what I write appears in journals.

   It is nice to write to somebody who knows Paul Clifford. He has been a
wonderful friend to me and it is a great pleasure to work in the same
department with him.

                                                   Yours sincerely,
                                                   George Grant

1 Editor, J.M. Dent and Sons
2 Scott Gordon (1924–), *Economists versus the Bank of Canada* (1961)
3 P.C. Newman (1929–), *Renegade in Power: The Diefenbaker Years* (1963)
4 Rex Williams, who was instrumental in the original publication of *Philosophy in the Mass Age*, later persuaded University of Toronto Press to reissue it.

153/ To Derek Bedson

McMaster University
2 July 1964

Dear Derek,
I hope you had a lovely time in Europe and that the summer passes delightfully.

I write about the Conservative thinkers' conference, or what have you. I have not gone to see Camp because I don't think there is much point in my going. He was down here at McMaster at a young PC conference and didn't see me; so presumably he doesn't think there is much point to my going. I think the PCs will be more and more in the image of George Hogan[1] – a pleasant wing of the Republican party. I might easily vote for the Republicans if I lived in the U.S.A. but my only interest in the Canadian scene is in nationalism. Once they get rid of Dief and co. they will have a party which I will prefer aesthetically to the Liberals but in which there won't be much interest. Also I have written out a book which will be published called 'A Lament for a Nation' which ends with a thoroughgoing attack on the age of progress and liberalism and I wouldn't want to do any harm to the Conservatives by any identification of that with them. The extraordinary thing about the Conservatives in Canada is their inability to make any connection with the academic community – not that they aren't better off for having no connection with modern intellectuals. I greatly admire your boss and many of the old conservatives (in many ways Dief included) but I think at this stage in the world my job is to attack the roots of modernity rather than be with the people who are decently trying to cope with the world. I have no doubt that I would never vote any way but PC in the future. Dief is right the NDP are a kind of vacuous extension of the Liberals and I heartily regret ever having written anything for them. The last four years have cleared my head greatly and I am now an unequivocal anti-progressive.

By the way will you mind if I dedicate this book on Canada to yourself and Judith Robinson? The dedication will be in Latin and you and she are the two people who have been most formative on my political opinions. But if you object to your name being connected to such a savage attack please let me know. It is a difficult book and therefore it is not written for the many. I might otherwise dedicate it to de Gaulle who is my favourite living politician.

This is the seventeenth anniversary of our marriage – a lucky day for me. We both remember with such gratitude your sweetness to us on that day as well as many others. Rachel is down staying with a French Canadian family for a few weeks. Otherwise we patter round from thing to thing while I try and learn something and write something. Did you hear that Charity is the new dean of women at University College in Toronto? I think it is just the thing for her. I wonder if you will be east at all during the summer – if so it would be lovely to see you – it is very easy for us to get into Toronto, although it is always a delight to have you at our place.

Love as ever,
George

1 George Hogan, Toronto businessman, journalist, and Diefenbaker aide

154/ To Jack McClelland[1]   McMaster University
                                                          1 September 1964

Dear Mr McClelland,
About a month ago I sent you the manuscript of a book on Canadian politics called *A Lament for a Nation.* I hope it is not rushing you when I write now to ask if you are interested in publishing it, as I would like to send it elsewhere if you are not. I am sorry to bother you.

Yours sincerely,
George P. Grant

1 J.G. McClelland (1922–), president of McClelland and Stewart until 1982

155/ To S.J. Totton[1]   McMaster University
                                                          29 October 1964

Dear Mr Totton:
I am sorry to keep bothering you, but I wonder when we could meet about the manuscript on Canadian affairs. I am a slow worker and would like to get going at any changes you suggest, as well as with some changes I have in my mind.

Yours sincerely,
George Grant

1 S.J. Totton, editor-in-chief, McClelland and Stewart

156/ To Derek Bedson   McMaster University
                                                           12 December 1964

Dear Derek,
Just a note to say how splendid your boss's speech in Quebec was. I have
been so afraid that the Conservatives were going to try some opposite
tack – and what he said was so clear and eloquent. Such talk from a public
figure revives one's hope that Canada is not a lost cause. The wealthy in
Toronto are now so totally Americanized – as in Hamilton – that hope is
not easy around here.

If there is a chance to see you over Xmas we would love it. Instead of
you driving, I could do the driving.

I am in the midst of a long piece called 'A Lament for a Country' which
is an attack on the Liberals which I will send when it comes out.

All goes well for us. McM. is a good place and going to be better. We
have an SJ[1] on our staff this year from Campion Hall[2] and hope to get an
orthodox. If you hear of people who want to do graduate studies in theology – outside a denominational setting – send them here.

Hope all goes well chez vous. How wonderful to be working for and
with D.R.[3]

                                                                    Ever,
                                                                  George

1 A member of the Society of Jesus, that is, a Jesuit priest
2 The Jesuit house in Oxford
3 Dufferin ('Duff') Roblin (1917–), premier of Manitoba, 1958–67; resigned to
   run against Robert Stanfield for the leadership of the Conservative party in
   1967

1965

157/ To Leo Strauss   21 January 1965

Dear Professor Strauss,
I hope you will excuse me writing on a practical matter. Would you please
feel free to pass the letter to anybody who is close to you intellectually.

The department of religion is looking for staff under two categories,
which might be possible to combine in one man:
(a) A person who could introduce students to the thought of the Enlightenment, etc. Most of the young students are a strange mixture of empiri-

cism and existentialism, even though they do not know that this is what they believe. In introducing them to the tradition of the Bible and of Greek philosophy we have also to introduce them to modernity. I would like it to be done by somebody who has studied with you.

(b) We would like somebody in the department who lives within Judaism. As we are a very new and experimental department, and because of the circumstances here, we are not going to proceed to teach Judaism for two years, but in the meantime we would like somebody in the department who lives within Judaism. We have people in our department who, in their own lives, live within various Western and Eastern traditions, but as we have only been going for four years, we have not yet a member of our department who lives within Judaism. Indeed, it remains to be seen whether the conception of a religion department is a valid one to face the very intense secularism of a university such as this.

We are looking for somebody at the lecturer or assistant professor level. This is, somebody who is finishing or has just finished his doctorate. If he was finishing his doctorate, we would give him lots of time for that activity. Perhaps the union of the two categories is impossible. I am sending a copy of this letter to Emil Fackenheim,[1] who did me the incomparable service of first telling me about your writings.

I have read and re-read *The City and Man.*[2] I wonder if sometime you were free I could come to Chicago and take a very short bit of your time to ask you two questions. It would not be in the immediate future, as the questions about Socrates and the Christian tradition I have not yet properly formulated. The other question is concerning Aristotle and Plato's dialogues.

I must express to you again my enormous sense of gratitude for every word you have written.

Please pass this practical question on to anybody who is in your trust. Thank you in advance.

Yours sincerely,
George Grant

1 E.L. Fackenheim (1916–), German-born philosopher and theologian who taught at the University of Toronto from 1948 to 1984
2 Leo Strauss, *The City and Man* (1964)

158/ To Rod Crook[1]   22 April 1965

Dear Rod,
It was very good to see you.

It would be lovely if you lived in our house at Terrence Bay, the place I like best on earth. In thinking about it, I am sure that we should charge nothing. The cabin has not been lived in for four years, and I have no idea how you will find it. Everything may be wet and soggy inside. Mrs Henry Hicks[2] has the keys and, if she hasn't, she will know who has them. Even if you find you cannot live there, I would be immensely glad for you to look at the place and tell me. It is only nineteen miles from Halifax and, therefore, not a hard jaunt. Gene Hicks or Nita can tell you exactly how to get there. About 200 yards away is Mr J.H. Jollimore, who is the lighthouse keeper. The whole family lives in an amazing rural slum. But Mr Jollimore himself is a thoroughly honest man, although he doesn't mind getting a buck or two occasionally. (I once went to a party at his house which ended with six counter-accusations of incest.) I love the man dearly. He will do anything for you.

Dear Joan and Rod, Sheila and I are, of course, thrilled to be the god-parents of Makaela Jill Crook. We understand the responsibilities and, if the worst happened, you may be sure that Sheila would be a wonderfully reliable person. I wish I could say the same for myself. Gene Hicks is in the same relation to our children.

I do hope we see you on the way through. If possible, let us know when you are arriving. Best love to you both,

George

1 R.K. Crook, professor of sociology at Dalhousie University
2 Wife of the president of Dalhousie and an old friend

159/ To George Hogan   [McMaster University]
                                              26 April 1965

Dear Mr Hogan:
It was most kind of you to write to me about my book, and especially kind to send me the extremely interesting articles from the *Telegram.*[1]

In the light of these, I am sorry for my identification of yourself either with the *Globe* or with Goldwaterism.[2] Indeed, after the book had gone to press an old student told me things about yourself that showed me that I had been entirely mistaken. I think the remark was a product of confused anger, the worst motive for saying anything. I remember that at one stage you came out for a new leadership for the Conservative party at the same time as the *Globe* was quoting you about the new economic circumstances. From this I deduced, quite falsely, the inferred remark I made in the book. It is the only remark in the book that I am ashamed of now. I never know if any good is done by retracting something in public once one has said it, but if you would think any good purpose was served by me writing a letter anywhere I would be only too delighted to do so.

I think this confusion goes even deeper in my thought. As a Canadian I have always believed in the use of the national state as a means of protecting Canadian independence. On the other hand, in the general economic situation of North America I dislike the concentration of power that is taking place in the hands of Washington. I would not have found it impossible as an American to have voted for Senator Goldwater on domestic, but not on international issues. I unequivocally would have voted for General Eisenhower in both elections. Yet, again, as a Canadian, I would have in the past believed in a strong federal government to maintain our independence. This is a contradiction that I find difficult to reconcile as far as practical Canadian politics go at the moment.

It would be extremely pleasant to talk about these issues some time, as I hardly know anything about the practical immediacy of politics, and know that I could learn a great deal from yourself. The articles you sent me seemed to me admirable, and I hope you will soon run for federal office and be elected. My great friend is Derek Bedson, who works for Roblin, and sometime when he is east we might have lunch together.

What seems to me more important than any immediate issue is your unequivocal identification of the Conservative tradition with God. In the light of what the *Globe* has been saying in the last days about religion in the schools, I can see that all other definitions between conservatives are as nothing compared to the ultimate questions of human destiny. I enclose a theoretical article on the matter which I wrote for the *Queen's Quarterly* a year ago.[3] I quite agree with your comments about the *Globe*.

Thank you very much again for your letter and for the articles. I will ring you up next time Derek is in the east. But if anything ever brings you to Hamilton, it would be delightful for my wife and I to entertain you and your family. (We have lots of children.) Our address is 80 South Street West, Dundas, Ontario, and the telephone number is Mayfair 7-1958.

Yours sincerely,
George Grant

1 Defunct Toronto newspaper
2 Barry Goldwater (1909–) was the Republican candidate for president in the 1964 American elections. He was a strong anti-communist and critical of interventionist government.
3 George Grant, 'Religion and the State,' *Queen's Quarterly* 70, no. 2 (1963), 183–97

160/ To Derek Bedson   McMaster University
                                                          31 May 1965

Dear Derek,
I write in haste about the potential union of the Anglican and United churches.[1] It would almost certainly lead me to seek admission in the Roman Catholic Church and I would deeply regret that. But I know what the United Church is too well (it is essential immanentism) to be able to sit in it. There is much in the Roman Church which appears to me totalitarian but it does not fail in guarding the pearl of great price.

What is the best way of dealing with this situation? I am in a very sensitive position over this as I am chairman of a department with members of many faiths and which is committed to the objective study of religion. It would therefore be of some cost to this department for me to enter this battle and yet I feel some of our optimistic clerics should know what the response of some of its laity will be. Surely they have to answer the question 'what gain is there for the Anglican church in such a union?' Do tell me what you think would be the effective thing for me to do.

Yours ever,
George Grant

1 Anglican Church of Canada and the United Church of Canada, *The Principles of Union between the Anglican Church of Canada and the United Church of Canada* (1965)

161/ To Robin Mathews[1]   14 July 1965

Dear Mr Mathews,
Thank you for your letter and poem.[2] The poem is indeed insulting, as it accuses me of lack of courage, and what is worse, valetudinarianism. I do not think I lack hope, because in the Christian sense I interpret hope as a supernatural virtue, and courage is what is necessary in the world.

Yours sincerely,
George Grant

1 R.D.M. Mathews (1931–), one of the leading opponents of the Americanization of Canadian universities and co-editor of *The Struggle for Canadian Universities: A Dossier* (1969)
2 Sent in response to *Lament for a Nation*

162/ To Rod Crook[1]   [McMaster University]
                                            19 July 1965

Dear Rod,
Does the distinction between necessity and good really lead to the fact-value distinction?

This seems to me the question: are all dualistic ways of thought the same?

I think we can best start from what one thinks the moral judgment to be. My immediate difficulty is that I do not understand how Weber analyzed the making of moral judgments. (You could help me here with an account and with references.) I do think I understand what Kant says. What is the difficulty in that account for me (and with as great a thinker as Kant, one has to say that the difficulty may be that one has not grasped the doctrine) is that I do not understand the relation between freedom and reason in his teaching. On the one hand, the very idea of reason presents itself to us so that we know directly that certain actions contradict that very idea. It presents itself to us in the imperative mood; he indeed expresses that presentation with the word *Achtung*.[2] Yet, at the same time, we self-legislate this commanding law of reason, and are capable of disobedience, that is, we are free in the sense that Weber means (?). Did Weber take from Kant the idea of freedom without the idea of reason?

As I see it, the great advantage of any dualistic system (Kant's e.g.) is that it squarely faces the problem of suffering and does not swallow it up in any easy explanation. By this I mean that any position must start from a recognition that to exist is to suffer and in human terms it is to learn that we cannot have what we want. (See Plato, Christ, Freud, etc.) In other words, from the human standpoint the first thing a philosopher must try and understand is what is the purpose (if any) in the fact that our immediate desires are broken and trampled on from the earliest age. Kant's answer of duty, that is of putting aside one's immediate desires in the name of universal purpose seems to me a very great answer, and, of course, puts him in some sense squarely in the Christian tradition, the overwhelming power of which was to bring suffering into the Godhead, to be in fact the religion of slaves.

(Let me say in parenthesis that your very wise criticism of a debauched Protestantism could, it seems to me, lead you off certain tracks, important for the truth, if it leads you away from understanding the strength of Christianity as the religion of suffering. For, not only Christianity, but all the great religions, have great insights about the negation of desire as part of the human condition.)

Of course, this account of the moral judgment for Kant had to go with the possibility of science, and that for Kant meant a nature freed from purpose. Therefore, reason commanded us rather than nature giving us the law.

Now it is at this point that I would like to write down why I cannot give a satisfactory answer to your question. I hope that it will not simply be of interest as my stage, but raising some important questions.

Looking back from Kant to Plato and Aristotle (for reasons part of which will be evident in the foregoing, but part of which would take too long in a letter) I am faced with an ambiguity. I think (but am not sure) that there is in Plato a much greater understanding of the suffering of man than in Aristotle. The transcendence of the forms (the criticism of which in Aristotle is badly parroted by nearly every modern student of philosophy with one year's training – 'Plato hypostatized concepts, etc., etc.') does appear to me very similar to Kant in the sense that the good by which we act comes to us somehow from beyond nature – call it if you will by that hated word supernaturally – and demands the death of worldly desires. All the psychological or sociological reductions of that position in the name of accusing it of repression, aberration and perversion does not seem to me to get around its appeal for two reasons: (a) the meaning of the whole does not seem to be understandable in the light of evil in an immanent way; (b) the question of the meaning of the whole cannot easily be put aside either existentially or scientifically.

The ambiguity this presents to me may be put historically in two ways: (a) I am not sure I am interpreting Plato correctly; (b) I am at last realising that there are certain arguments on the Aristotelian side, which I have not met and which mean that I have to study at a more than student level A's *Ethics* and *Politics*.

(a) The interpretation of Plato. At the beginning of the *Republic* there is the statement of Glaucon about the sufferings of the just man; I have always taken that to be a straight affirmation of the transcendence of the Good. Yet, in a recent book of Strauss's he mentions (and he has some weight with me) that this is in Glaucon's mouth and is an exaggeration because we must not say that absolute justice and suffering go together. I presume he is speaking as an Aristotelian and that he implies that for them to go together would mean that there would not be an immanent political science of A's variety and that it leads to that sharp distinction between law and right, which is so characteristic of Kant and indeed of

Protestantism. I see the point, but consider it a more important point to repeat in the light of the human condition the ultimate purpose must be transcendent. In other words, the traditional interpretation that Plato was concerned with was the justice of the wise man, while Aristotle was concerned with the justice of the wise man and the natural justice of common sense, I can see.

This is, of course, very closely related to the fact that seems to me indubitable, (however one interprets the ambiguous dialogues), that Plato differs from Aristotle in believing that theory can never be detached from the moral life, while Aristotle affirms the independence of theory from moral virtue. In a rather different way this same distinction seems to me possible to make between Kant and Hegel; and, of course, I am on the Platonic and Kantian side. Why? Because I do not think it is comprehensible that one could come to understand the ultimate purpose of things except in this way; otherwise is one not shallow about evil? A circle? Yet, at the same time I am at the moment very much held by the argument 'how can one have political philosophy, if you take the Platonic side – that is transcendence?' I would recognize the terrible tendencies towards obscurantism in any doctrines of transcendence. Yet, once again, without such a doctrine I do not see that one is not led by the facts of evil to give up the idea of ultimate purpose.

Now, in terms of an acceptance of what I take to be the Platonic position, when one speaks of the separation of good and necessity one is speaking of that separation as it must appear to us here below. It does not imply that the order of necessity and the order of morality do not both proceed from the Good. Presumably, the beauty of the world which is manifested both in the order of necessity and in the order of morality may to the follower of Plato teach us more about the ultimate unity of those orders than Kant (in his wonderful *Critique of Judgment*) would say we are vouchsafed. But if my interpretation of Plato is right, he stands quite close to Kant as an agnostic. Socrates 'the philosopher is the man who knows that he knows not.' Also Pascal: 'We know too much to be sceptics; we know too little to be dogmatists.' Kant certainly says that in the preface to the 2nd edition of the 1st Critique. Beyond this – and here I know nothing; it is evidently possible according to the mystics to come to an understanding of the beauty of necessity as we submit to its afflictions and love others who are so submitted. But about that I must repeat that I know nothing. In my book (which was a popular book) I make clear that I spoke simply from the position of the person who must proceed in the practical life, from the position that the order of morality and the order of necessity cannot be known as proceeding from the Good.

This is a poor answer, but the best I can quickly do at the minute.

Ever,

George Grant

1 Crook was author of a substantial review of *Lament*: 'Modernization and Nostal-gia, a Note on the Sociology of Pessimism,' *Queen's Quarterly* 73, no. 3 (1966) 269–84.

2 Attention

163/ To Derek Bedson   McMaster University
                                              21 September 1965

Dear Derek,

Thanks for your letter and for the extremely clear article which was absolutely to the point. I think the chief motive which moves these priests is that they want to communicate with the world and they find that in the world they move in they can only communicate by being liberals. They are foolish ill-educated men who don't recognize that, when they get into bed with liberalism, it won't be they who do the impregnating – but that they will be utterly seduced. Creal is as foolish on this as any of them. I am afraid we are living in an era in which western Xianity is going to be eaten up. Some of the Roman liberals are as foolish as ours. I do not mean by this anything to do with the truth of Xianity – just its western manifestations. Nor do I mean that this is a reason not to fight. A comedy. Sheila had a sermon preached against her because she opposed as a Sunday school teacher the wild liberalism of the new curriculum.

You can imagine the very deep disappointment felt around here because of Roblin's decision not to enter the federal field. He must have had good reasons, but what I am very afraid of is that the Liberals are going to be able to revive the King-St Laurent era in which these questions go by default. Particularly the questions of nationalism. I nominate our local PC candidate tonight. I feel great loyalty to Dief because of his courage over the last years. He may have been wrong, but he has been unmoved by the concerted attacks of the united establishment.

It would be lovely to see you at Xmas. I have become a thorough bureaucrat – by necessity – which is a great bore.

As ever from us both,

George

164/ To John Diefenbaker   McMaster University
                                                                 27 September 1965

Dear Mr Diefenbaker:

In the light of our telephone conversation of last Thursday, herewith are some notes on the Constitutional question, which you asked for by the beginning of this week. I do not know whether they are of any help at all, but it has been a great honour to write them for you.

Yours sincerely,
George Grant

[attached to letter:]

NOTES ON THE CONSTITUTIONAL QUESTION

1. The Crisis in Confederation

In two years' time we celebrate the 100th anniversary of the founding of our nation. Shall that centennial of Confederation be the occasion to offer thanks to those countless Canadians in all walks of life who have laboured to build this country? Shall it be a time for dedication to new tasks and new greatness? Or rather will it be a time of drifting and uncertainty – a time when we are filled with doubt about our country's future? This is the question that all Canadians must ask themselves in the weeks that lie ahead.

We cannot close our eyes to the fact that in the last 2 1/2 years uncertainty about our national destiny has been felt throughout the land. The chief cause of this faltering is the vacuum in the federal government at Ottawa. No nation can long exist without a national government which knows where it is going. There is a sense throughout the country that there is no hand on the tiller to direct our central government. It is strange that those who once talked so much about 'stable government' have been the very men who in the first years have abdicated the proper responsibilities of the federal government. It is strange, indeed, that we should now hear the election slogan 'strong central government' from just those men who in the last years are responsible for the vacuum that now exists in Ottawa. How can you have stable government when you abdicate your responsibility to be a national government?

2. The Conservative Party is the National Party

The Conservative party has always been the instrument for the building of a united Canadian nation. Macdonald and Cartier, Tupper and Tilley moulded Confederation in 1867 to establish a new nationality – a northern nationality. They built on the northern half of this new continent a nation friendly with our great southern neighbour, but distinct and different. They dreamed of a society in which men and women would know themselves as Canadians, something new and unique in the world. Macdonald knew what labour there was in building such a nation. He often quoted the words (of Daniel Webster):[1] 'Let our object be our country, our whole country and nothing but our country.'

Today as much as then, it is the intention of the Canadian people to be a nation. It is the role of the Conservative party to give leadership to that purpose.

3. Unity in Diversity

The party of Macdonald and Cartier did not think that in such a nation all regions, all peoples, all cultures should be the same. They knew that one great purpose of Confederation was to preserve and maintain French culture on this continent. Cartier's vision told him that only in the setting of this northern nation could the French fact be preserved in the new world. He stood for a united Canadian nation just because he knew that it was only in such a unity that the French Canadians could protect their way of life. 'Plus ça change, plus c'est la même chose.'[2] Today, just as much as a hundred years ago, Canada cannot do without Quebec; Quebec cannot do without Canada.

And this has always been the Canadian way, the Conservative party's way. As people from other lands have come to enrich this nation, they have not been required to give up their heritage. In the prairies and in the large cities of Ontario, to be a Canadian does not mean to give up your own traditions. It means to bring that heritage into a common loyalty, the loyalty to Canada as a nation. And so it is with the provinces and regions of this country. Who would want people from Nova Scotia and people from British Columbia to be exactly the same in character and culture? Yes, the Conservative party says one Canada; but one Canada which rejoices in its diversity. This is why we have built up our complex structure of federalised government. A great Canadian Conservative explained federalism clearly a hundred years ago. D'Arcy McGee[3] said:

'The principle of federation is a generous principle. It is a principle eminently favourable to liberty, because local affairs are left to be dealt with by local bodies, and cannot be interfered with by those who have no local interest in them, while matters of a general character are left to a general government.'

4. Fiscal Aid to the Provinces and Municipalities

It was because we believe in diversity that the Conservative government after 1957 substantially increased financial assistance to the provincial governments. Such a fiscal policy should continue in the years ahead. There are many things that the provincial and municipal levels of government can carry out much better than a centralised bureaucracy at Ottawa. The very basis of the Conservative idea of government is that local and individual initiative can get things done better than having things done for them from Ottawa. Leaders such as Robarts, Stanfield and Roblin know the needs of their provinces, as Ottawa cannot. Because of its control over certain sources of tax revenue, the federal government must help the provinces and the municipalities to meet [their] responsibilities in the growing fields of education and with all the difficult problems which arise from automation.

5. The Calling of a National Constitutional Convention

New circumstances require new negotiations. The federal structure of Canada is undergoing strain. It needs readjustments to meet the new technological revolution; it needs readjustments to meet the just aspirations of the people of Quebec. The Conservative government will, therefore, call a National Constitutional Convention. The Convention would be comprised of governmental leaders from the federal, provincial and municipal levels of authority. When a country is dealing with the very arteries of its lifeblood, such negotiations must be undertaken by the elected representatives of the people at all levels, not by a Commission, the members of which have no elected responsibility. Nor can we settle the future fabric of this country simply in private negotiations from which the people are shut out.

6. Essential Federal Powers must not be Compromised

But there is one principle which must not be compromised in any negotiations. The federal government cannot surrender those powers which are necessary to the preservation and strength of this northern nation. The purpose of Confederation was to build a northern nationality. Such a nationality requires that certain powers remain without question in the federal government. Therefore, no Conservative government can compromise these powers. To do so would be to betray the very purpose for which this party exists.

To compromise the fundamental prerogatives of the national government would mean that Canada would become a series of disconnected regions, rather than a nation. Gradually and inevitably these regions would lose connection with each other and would fall into the orbit of the neighbouring regions to the south. Would this be in the interests of Quebec? For a hundred years, the men of little faith have been saying that this is what must inevitably happen to Canada. It is the duty of the Conservative party to see that it does not happen to our country.

Certain national powers are obvious – external affairs and national defence. But even in these areas new questions loom in the immediate future. Canada and the United States are going to have to work out together the problems of their common North American living arrangements, particularly in such fields as our common need of fresh water for our industries and cities. This cannot be properly done without a firm and certain federal government which is determined to safeguard the interests of all parts of Canada. The federal government must be strong in the sense that it bears responsibility for the welfare of all Canadians, of each Canadian region.

7. The Abdication of Federal Power by the Present Administration

The absence of proper federal authority is what must fill us with alarm at what has been happening in Ottawa in the last 2 1/2 years. We cannot know if these essential prerogatives are going to be bargained away in secret. What we do know is that the present government shows no willingness to stand up for its own authority when that authority is questioned. The abdication of its national responsibilities in essential matters by the present administration can only lead in one direction, if it is not checked. When Federal-provincial relations take on the appearance of negotiations between foreign powers, the spectacle must surely sadden all patriotic Canadians.

There is a close connection between the scandals which have beset this administration and their abdication of proper federal authority. We have had scandals before, but these scandals are different. Never before has anything so base as the international drug trade got as close to the very seat of federal power. Corruption in the past has never been as insidious as this. When an animal is weak the vultures start to circle and to descend. And the same is true of governments. Rivard and Banks[4] are men who know instinctively where weakness is present and how to make use of it. A federal government which is afraid to exercise its authority will be open to more and more of such occurrences. Furthermore, a government that comes to power in dependence on such corrupt forces can never hold the loyalty of young Canadians.

1 Daniel Webster (1782–1852), American politician
2 The more things change, the more they stay the same.
3 Thomas D'Arcy McGee (1825–68), journalist, poet, historian, and the most eloquent father of confederation
4 Lucien Rivard and Hal Banks were two criminals whose names were associated
   with scandals connected to the Liberal party. Diefenbaker made this association
   a major theme in his 1965 campaign.

165/ To John Diefenbaker   McMaster University
                                                23 December 1965

Dear Mr Diefenbaker:
When I had the honour to interview you during the election,[1] you told me some extremely interesting things about the relations of your government with President Kennedy. I write to express the hope that you will at some time put these matters on the record in writing. I know that with all your immediate duties such questions of history must seem less important. Nevertheless, I think it is very important that this be done for the sake of your own historical reputation, and for the sake of the country. The Liberal propagandists have been so unfair in attacking you that it matters very much that the truth you know should not be left unsaid. Did you notice, for instance, how gross some of the books about Kennedy have been regarding your position? I hope that some day you will be able to take the time for this activity, which would do so much for Canadian nationalism.
    Always my admiration and regards.

                                                Yours sincerely,
                                                George Grant

1 Federal general election, 8 November 1965

A pacifist, Grant never forgot what it was to be on the receiving end of saturation bombing. He consistently and vigorously opposed American involvement in Vietnam, but he would not countenance the use of civil disobedience in Canada as a means of protest against the war. However, he was not against it absolutely, and thought that it was justified in the United States.

166/ To the Editor, *Christian Outlook*   McMaster University

Dear Sir:
In the November issue, in which you published a speech of mine,[1] you also said, 'In effect, he (G.P. Grant) seems to be suggesting that real change will only come about within the power structures of society, not over against them.' It amuses me how such a deduction could be drawn from my words. I certainly think that real change is going to take place within the power structures, but it is going to be change for the worse. I was not saying to the protesting young that they should not fight the present power structures. To imply that the present power structures will lead to change for the good is to misjudge completely their present activity in Vietnam. What seems to be implied in your editorial is that change for the good (e.g. progress) must happen. This proposition I would entirely deny.

Yours sincerely,
George Grant

1 George Grant, 'Realism in Political Protest,' *Christian Outlook* 21, no. 2 (Nov. 1965), 3–6

1966

167/ To Kenneth McNaught   McMaster University, Hamilton
                                              11 February 1966

Dear Ken,
I enclose a draft letter which has been jointly worked out by some students (members of the Student Union for Peace Action) and myself. It will be the basis for a presentation to all members of parliament in the week starting Monday, February 28. We are going to have a silent vigil of 48 hours at the beginning of that week in front of parliament for its pre-

sentation. This letter is asking you whether you would sign this document (or something very close to it) and indeed whether you would take part in that silent vigil. I am going to do both.

The reasons for doing this seem to me something like the following: (1) For whatever motives, it seems to me that the U.S.A. has got into a position where it is massacring masses of Vietnamese. Canada is more and more implicated in this, and the thought of us being implicated in a long and growing war between Asia and North America is too terrible to contemplate. (2) I think it is important that those of us of the older generation who are Canadian nationalists should join these young people and show them that there are some older people in this country who are willing to speak about this matter – and not simply the older radicals. This joint effort means that the document will be a compromise, as it already is. The older generation joining this will also mean that it can work within constitutional government. The students concerned wished to start out with civil disobedience, and they have now agreed to have a silent and legal vigil. I am not convinced that this action will accomplish much in the present ferocious circumstances, but I do not see how a Canadian nationalist cannot express himself on this matter at the moment.

I really think it is important that our generation enter this, and I do hope that Beverly and you will not turn it down without a telephone call.

It would be a great pleasure to discuss this whole business with you at any time.

Yours,
George G.

168/ To Peter Calamai[1]

McMaster University
22 February 1966

Dear Sir:
Recently, I have seen a printed document around the university in which my name is associated with the liberal doctrine of civil disobedience. I hope you will allow me to use your columns to disassociate myself from this doctrine.

In a constitutional regime, civil disobedience should be a last resort and should only be used when the government is directly responsible for an undoubted evil. It is both foolish and irresponsible to propose civil disobedience as a threat to a government with which one wants to hold rational discussions to persuade it to change its policies. The terrible events which are unfolding in Vietnam are not going to be helped by denying the principles of constitutional government in Canada.

Yours sincerely,
George Grant
Chairman

1 Peter Calamai (1943–), editor-in-chief of *Silhouette*, the McMaster student newspaper

169/ To Pierre Trudeau[1]

McMaster University
23 February 1966

Dear Mr Trudeau:
When I wrote to you last week asking you to speak at the Teach-In on Vietnam I thought that I had persuaded the Student Union for Peace Action that the planned action would not include any civil disobedience. I now find that this is not so and that they are announcing the action in terms which include such proposals. As I cannot approve of such threatening the Government, I thought I should let you know of the changed circumstances as I see them.

I am sorry to have not signed this letter, but I am in bed with the flu.

Yours sincerely,
George Grant
Chairman, Department of Religion

1 Pierre Trudeau (1919–), parliamentary secretary to Prime Minister Pearson; later prime minister and leader of the Liberal party, 1968–79, 1980–4

170/ To Leo Strauss

McMaster University
25 April 1966

Dear Professor Strauss,
In reissuing an old book of mine I tried to pay you a compliment in a new introduction. I am enclosing my words on another page because my sense of debt is so great.[1]

Yours sincerely,
George Grant

1 'Concerning the more difficult and more important theoretical questions, my debt is above all to the writings of Leo Strauss. Of Professor Strauss' books I will

mention only two: *What is Political Philosophy?*, and *Thoughts on Machiavelli*. As the greatest joy and that most difficult of attainment is any movement of the mind (however small) towards enlightenment, I count it a high blessing to have been acquainted with this man's thought' (George Grant, 'New Introduction,' in *Philosophy in the Mass Age* [1966], ix).

171/ To Most Rev. H.H. Clark[1]   20 May 1966

Dear Archbishop Clark:
I write as a layman about the new curriculum and how it has been brought into being in the Anglican church.[2]

This new curriculum was brought in by a group of clerics, and it is a kind that makes it impossible for many people, who were traditional Sunday School teachers, to go on teaching. What surprises me in the organization of the church, is that this curriculum, which was above all written by the Rev Ernest Harrison, is still accepted by clerics even when it is clear that Mr Harrison, when writing it, did not believe in God. It seems to me that only the church is sufficiently ill-organized to allow such an occurrence.

I know that it is an extremely difficult question, how the church is to communicate with the modern world, and I know that many of the clerics who adopt this modern liberalism do so because of their innocent desires to communicate. But surely it is the business of the episcopate to see that what is essential is maintained, and I cannot see that this is being done in the present circumstances. The most elementary knowledge of the history of thought would tell one that Rousseau and Nietzsche are not equivalent to Christianity. What disturbs me (and yet gladdens me) is that the United Church has done so much better on this matter.[3] It saw that there were theological issues in its new curriculum. You can perhaps explain why an episcopally organized church like our own, and one that has cared about tradition, should, on the matter of the teaching of the young, have been so careless about what it produced.

Yours sincerely,
George Grant

1 Most Rev. H.H. Clark (1903–83), primate of the Anglican Church of Canada, 1959–70
2 Anglican Church of Canada, *More than Words: A Resource Book for Parish Education* (1965)
3 A.B.B. Moore, *Jesus Christ and the Christian Life* (1965)

172/ **To John Diefenbaker**   McMaster University
                                                           18 November 1966

Dear Mr Diefenbaker:
This is to express what a great Canadian you are, and how disgusted I was
to see petty men exposing you to their bad manners.[1] Of course, it was
sadly to be expected. Only you could have upset the slow movement to
death of this country under the establishment, and they and their cohorts
will never forgive you for challenging their power. Nevertheless, it is dis-
gusting to see the man who has so cared for his country treated in such
fashion by those who think that slickness, advertising, and money is a substitute for patriotism.

                                                        Yours in admiration,
                                                           George Grant

1 At the PC convention in Ottawa

1967

173/ **To Stephen Bornstein**[1]   McMaster University
                                                           20 February 1967

Dear Stephen:
Thank you very much for your letter. I am complimented by your intelligent questions. I, of course, cannot answer them properly.
    Let me say two preliminary things. (a) I am primarily a philosopher,
and one who has decided that modern political philosophy (that is since
Machiavelli) is, at its centre, false. Much of this I have come to on my own,
but I have been enormously illuminated by the thought of Leo Strauss. To
understand what I am saying one would have to understand Strauss, and
that cannot be done easily. Of all his writings I would recommend his essay
'What is Political Philosophy?' in the book of that name.[2] The essay was
given in the city which was holy both to your ancestors and mine. (b) The
little book I wrote about Canada people have taken as more important
than it is. I wrote it because I was so angry that they had brought those horrible weapons into Canada, but it was not written as a practical political
book, but to point to what always lies beyond and is more important than
the political, namely the eternal order. Now your questions:

1. Socialism had been too often allied with a cosmopolitanism, which in practical effect led to us being swallowed up, not by an international society, but by American society. (See M.J. Coldwell[3] and Frank Underhill[4].) Most socialists were just covert liberals.

2. Obviously, my grandparents influenced me, as I am sure yours did you. I was brought up in a world in which certain British things were taken for granted, but I soon found out what had gone wrong with British imperialism. I thought Ramsay Cook's strictures on myself[5] at this point were foolish because my ancestors were very much part of the liberal establishment, which I imply did not have enough brains to save their country. My relations spent their life pushing the careers of people like Pearson and Martin.[6] I dealt with this kind of psychological determinism in the paper you heard me deliver at Toronto and which is coming out in *Canadian Dimension*.[7] If they want psychological determinism they would do far better to look at my relations with my mother.

3. I wrote the piece about the empire when I was very young[8] and when I was just first revolting from the liberalism in which I was brought up. I have found it very difficult indeed to understand the collapse of the English ruling classes since 1945.

4. Determinism and freedom is a problem which arises from the Kantian way of looking at things. As I rejected that way of looking at things and think one can understand political things better through the eyes of Plato and Aristotle, I rejected the determinist freedom controversy. No, I haven't stopped beating my wife.

5. The epithet 'red tory'[9] can only be used if you look at the practical part of my book and not at the philosophical. Horowitz[10] was only concerned with the practical. I think philosophers are more likely to have sympathy with conservatives than with liberals, but, as I say in my book, modern conservatism comes out of modern assumptions as much as modern liberalism. Much of this labelling arises because people cannot distinguish any longer between ideology and philosophy. Ideology is the permitted form that philosophy often takes in this era.

6. 'Might have been' questions are largely useless. I do think, however, that as far as English-speaking Canada went the Conservative party has cared about nationalism in a way that the Liberals have not.

These are poor answers, but I do insist that if my opinions are of any interest to anyone other than myself they must be understood in terms of philosophy.

I hope we meet again sometime.

Yours,
George Grant

1 A student who had written Grant
2 Leo Strauss, *What Is Political Philosophy? and Other Studies* (1959)
3 M.J.W. Coldwell (1888–1974), English-born leader of the CCF, 1942–60
4 F.H. Underhill (1889–1971), University of Toronto historian and political thinker
5 Ramsay Cook developed these arguments in his later article 'Loyalism, Technology and Canada's Fate,' *Journal of Canadian Studies* 5 (1970), 50–60.
6 P.J.J. Martin (1903–92), an MP from 1935 until 1968 and secretary of state for external affairs in Lester Pearson's government, 1963–8; later government leader in the Senate and high commissioner to the United Kingdom
7 George Grant, 'Canadian Fate and Imperialism,' *Canadian Dimension* 4, no. 3 (March-April 1967), 21–5
8 George Grant, *The Empire, Yes or No?* (1945)
9 The term 'red tory' was applied to Candians such as Eugene Forsey and George Grant who disliked the Liberal party and who would prefer either the CCF/NDP or the Conservatives.
10 See Gad Horowitz, *Canadian Labour in Politics* (1968), ch. 1.

174/ To Walter Gordon

McMaster University
16 May 1967

Dear Mr Gordon:
Your magnificent and courageous speech on Vietnam was wonderful.[1]
For the last years I have felt that more than any other man you have maintained the honour of Canada. It is a source of enormous optimism that a person of your integrity remains in the public sphere.

If I could ever do anything to advance any cause you are interested in it would be a high honour to do so.

Yours sincerely,
George Grant

1 'I hope Canadians in all walks of life and in all political parties – including especially Mr Pearson and Mr Martin – will continue to do everything in their power to press the Americans to stop the bombing. If we fail to do this, we must be prepared to share the responsibility of those whose policies and actions are destroying a poor but determined people. We must share the responsibility of those whose policies involve the gravest risks for all mankind' (Walter Gordon, 13 May 1967, as quoted in Denis Smith, *Gentle Patriot: A Political Biography of Walter Gordon* [1973], 323).

175/ To Duff Roblin

25 July 1967

Dear Premier Roblin,

In light of what has happened in the last weeks,[1] this letter is probably too late. Nevertheless, I wish to put into writing to you that I am sure you would make the best possible leader of the Conservative party and a great prime minister of Canada in these very difficult days for our country.

Support from a person such as myself is negligible, but I wanted to put into writing that if you were to enter your name for the leadership of the Conservative party, you could count on my active support, both privately and publicly, in any way that you deemed useful.

Yours sincerely,
George Grant

1 Roblin was under increasing public pressure to announce that he would contest the Conservative leadership.

176/ To Nita and John Graham[1]

McMaster University
30 July 1967

Dear Nita and John,

Just a note to thank you for all your kindness to us. It was so good of you. It was so nice that David[2] got to know the boys and I am getting old enough to hope that this will be a permanent relation that goes on beyond the parents.

I would like also to say that there was some deep need in me to be far away within myself and, therefore, an impossibility to speak about the most important matters. I know that a certain period of my life has come to an end and that I must reform myself to move on, but in doing that I have to retreat away from converse with people, even those who are most meaningful and most interesting to me. I am sure that such periods must occur in different ways for you both. If you were aware of this retreat in me I hope you will excuse it. For me superficiality is always easier than intimacy.

Again thanks.

As ever,
George

Sheila calls out love to all.

1 John Graham (1924–90) was a professor of economics at Dalhousie. Nita Graham (1933–), a former student of Grant's, was his wife. They were both very close friends.
2 David Grant, born 6 December 1959

1968

177/ To Derek Bedson   Dundas, Ontario

Dear Derek,
My neurosis about missing things prevented our thanking you nearly adequately at the airport for your kindness. You were so good to let me break into your days like that. It was all an enormous impression for me – strangely particularly the [Hedlums] because, at the beginning of the day, one is so alive. Thank you for a lovely time.

I have thought a lot about my difficulty of communicating with Roblin. It is, of course, that rightly or wrongly I have crossed the Rubicon of really thinking that technological society is against human excellence and, yet, where does that leave one? It is certainly not something that can be even considered by people whose vocation is public life. Yet when I speak to him within his premises I feel strangely dishonest. To say this is not to mean that all of us in our different ways should not go on with what we must do, but it precludes intimacy for me with any public man – even the best.

Douglas Scott is a young person of enormous subtlety and complicatedness. If you are to go on being near him as a friend it will take enormous patience, but such people are probably the most important. You luckily have more natural strength than I – I am inclined to retreat because I am too weak for the pain involved.

Again so many thanks.

Ever,
George

178/ To John Diefenbaker   McMaster University
                                                       10 December 1968

Dear Mr Diefenbaker:
I am sorry to have been so slow in answering, but have been ill since you were here.

You paid me a great honour when you suggested that I might be your biographer. As the whole question raises very important questions for Canadian history, I hope you will not mind my writing to you about it at length.

It seems to me that there are two separate questions involved:
(1) As soon as possible there should be brought out with your stamp of authority, an answer to a lot of the nonsense that has been put around by prejudiced and unthoughtful journalists. Particularly two questions should be clarified: (a) the account of the relations of your government with the Kennedy administration and (b) what were the forces in the Conservative party which never accepted loyalty to yourself and were determined to hurt you? I think this should include not only an account of Camp's machinations, but what had been going on for a long time before that, even when you were Prime Minister. These two questions, it seems to me should be dealt with right away because of their great impact on Canada's continued sovereignty.
(2) The biography is a different matter. I do not think it can be written for many years. In the present state of Canada, it is absolutely essential that you continue in the public realm and this will be so for many years. While this is so, the biography cannot be written. To put it quite frankly, I might easily predecease yourself. I think it is important now concerning the biography, that you make arrangements that all the papers and material are in the hands of totally reliable institutions and under the control of particular people whom you know you can trust absolutely.

This leads me to suggest the following things:
(a) If it were of any use to you I could come up to Ottawa for several weeks and sit with a tape recorder while you put the history down in your own inimitable way. These tapes could then be put in some official place and only allowed to be heard under an order with your signature. If you thought the archives at McMaster would be a good place, we can have the arrangements that any tape or paper there could only be released under a triple signature of yourself, myself and the archivist, or others whom you choose. (b) If beyond the tapes you were interested in writing something, it would be a great honour for me to do anything in assisting that process.

I think it important that you arrange that your papers for now and always are put out of the reach of irresponsible and stealing hands. I had something to do with the Whitney papers (the premier of Ontario)[1] and you would be surprised how many were stolen by the descendants of the Liberals who had fought the Ontario Hydro. We had to close them down and put them under control. I think the important thing in this matter is that you name people who you *trust*. If you chose McMaster as a suitable place, we would be greatly honoured and the arrangements whereby you and your successors could remain entirely in charge of them could be worked out.

This letter may seem to be too aware of potential dishonesty, but there are great public issues at stake and the interpretation of history always influences the future. For example, it is clear from Pearson's recent lectures in England that he does not much care about the future of Canadian sovereignty.[2]

Thank you again for so honouring me by this suggestion. Please give my best regards to Mrs Diefenbaker, whom it was such a pleasure to meet.

Hoping to hear from you in this matter.

Sincerely,
George P Grant

1 Sir James Whitney (1843–1914), premier of Ontario, 1905–14
2 L.B. Pearson, *Peace in the Family of Man* (1969), the Reith Lectures for 1968

1969

179/ To Hugh MacLennan   80 South St, Dundas, Ont.
                                               27 March 1969

Dear Hugh,

It was so good of you to write and to express affection. One thing I find hard at the immediate level is the lack of connection with any personal past or continuity between various periods of one's life. Sheila and I went the other day to see a fine old girl (the founder of the IODE)[1] who was dying at ninety. As S said afterwards it is not strange that she should find her way of life quite past, that has always happened, but that we in our late forties should find our life quite broken in two with change so rapid that there is practically no connection between our now and our past.

I hope today goes well for McGill. I have no respect for the marxist principle which Gray[2] seems to act on that you can expect support from an institution, which you desire to overturn. And as for the marxists from the U.S.A., a sudden interest in the French, all one can say to the French is *et dona ferentes*.[3] The interests of French Canadians in their own survival

will not be helped by marxists, who may scare off the small town French bourgeoisie who will have to care about their own survival on this continent if there is to be any hope for anything in Quebec surviving the American dream. I so dislike the dominant direction that English-speaking society is taking all over the world that I hope the French in Quebec keep their determination not to be slowly smoothed out of existence, but not knowing the province I do not know what should be their political instrument for achieving this end. From the outside Bertrand[4] looks pretty decent and sensible, but that may simply be lack of closeness on my part. Trudeau has always seemed to be a gentlemanly kind of person. I distrust his distrust of traditional French Canada and I fear his naivety about the nature of English-speaking society. But Stanfield seems to me a rather ungenerous Whig of extremely limited horizon.
[page missing]

1 Joan Arnoldi, not the founder, but its national president and modernizer
2 Stanley Gray, a radical graduate student, later a labour organizer
3 From Virgil's *Aeneid* 1.48: 'I fear Greeks, *even bearing gifts.*'
4 J.-J. Bertrand (1916–73); premier of Quebec, 1968–70

Although Grant and his sister Charity both opposed the war in Vietnam, Charity Grant objected to the extreme tactics employed by Grant's sons, especially Robert. This episode led to an estrangement between them that lasted for fifteen years and was never completely healed.

180/ To Charity Grant   4 April 1969

Dear Charity,
Thank you for your generous and fair letter. I am slow in answering it, because it was very slow in the mail and, then, the last two days were long at the college. You say that your letter may make things worse. As far as I am concerned, quite the contrary, because it explained things more clearly that, if I was a more aware person, I should have been able to see for myself and for that I am grateful.

I forget having said to you that you had no right to say something to Robert. As I did, I did not mean it and apologise. You have every right to say what you think wise and I am always grateful for your attention and kindness to the children. I would have to be not responsible for my actions by cutting them off from your good sense.

As for my clothes, I will try to do better when we meet. I just did not know that I offended you on that score. They come from a long, bad habit (which I think stems from my sense that my body is such a disaster that I could never present it to the world). But I will be careful to make an effort when we meet, and I am sorry that it should have annoyed you.

You say that we are very different people and I agree. Our lives have gone in very contrary ways, but not, I hope, contradictory. Without positing any determinism, it is clear that a female child and a male child would respond very differently to the family situation. There were good things and bad things in that situation for both types of child, as in every case, but those goods and bads were different.

I am very grateful to you for letting me know that it is not your intention that our relation should be broken off.

Yours,
George

1970

181/ To E.T. Williams[1]   11 February 1970

Dear Mr Williams:

In your letter (which I read with the greatest interest) I saw of the death of Austin Farrer.[2] Of all the deep debts I owe to England (other than my wife) hearing him speak was the greatest. He really made me see what Europe had been before the age of progress, something extremely difficult for a North American to see. I write to ask where you think it would be wise to send a personal tribute to him. It obviously should be published in England. I do not mean an academic assessment, because that I will do over time in the proper journals in North America, where his work is at last coming into its own. I mean rather a sheerly personal tribute of the kind one finds in the *Balliol Letter.* Were I a better poet, it should be a sonnet.

I am sorry to bother you, but I am so out of touch with English and European things. Again, let me say how much pleasure and interest your annual letter provides.

Yours sincerely,
George Grant

1 Warden, Rhodes House, Oxford
2 29 December 1968

182/ To J.A. Gonsalves[1]   31 March 1970

Dear Mr Gonsalves,
You can imagine what this letter is about. The first three of the Massey
lectures[2] are all right, but the last two really need very careful and complex changes before going into print. (I am not a person who takes print
lightly.) I find that, at the end of the teaching year, I just don't get sufficiently clear time to get a clear head to say exactly what I mean about the
complex question of Nietzsche. I write, therefore, to ask whether it would
be possible to have till May. This, I know, will be a nuisance for you, but I
would be greatly obliged.

Yours,
G.P. Grant

1 Supervisor of publications, CBC
2 George Grant, 'Time as History'

McMaster II: Beleaguered 1970–80

In April 1970 the Grants took a much needed vacation in Barbados. On their return from a May Day dance, their taxi was in an accident in which four passengers in the other car were killed. Both Grant and his wife were seriously injured. After the accident, Grant never had the same level of energy as before, and he was reinforced in his determination to withdraw, as much as was possible for him, into contemplation.

183/ To J.A. Gonsalves   3 June 1970

Dear Mr Gonsalves,[1]
I am dictating this from hospital. The doctors are at last beginning to be a little clear about the extent of my injuries and, therefore, I am writing to you about *Time as History*.
a. My writing hand has been very smashed and my hip leaves me immobile, pretty much for the next several months. During that time, I am going to try and re-write as much of *Time as History* as I can. The extent of my injuries, and their seriousness, has only gradually been made clear to me by the doctors; so I can only write now. I will try and do the very best I can.
b. If it is late, I can put in the preface that I was in a crash-up in which four people were killed. It would be an excuse.
   Again, let me say how sorry I am about this.

Yours sincerely,
George Grant

1 Unaware of Grant's accident, Gonsalves wrote on 19 May to 'enquire how you are coming along with the manuscript revisions on the Massey lectures.'

184/ To John Diefenbaker   16 November 1970

Dear Mr Diefenbaker,
My son David gave his first public speech and it was on my 'favourite
Canadian' and the subject was yourself. He did this without any prompt-
ing from his father, but you may be sure that I was glad that he had known
the right Canadian to choose.

Yours ever in admiration,
George Grant

185/ To Dennis Duffy[1]   27 December 1970

Dear Professor Duffy,
Just a note to say how fine I thought your writing[2] in the *Globe* magazine
was. To speak personally, it came to me at a time of barrenness and a foolish sense of isolation from other Xians and helped my sanity – so thank
you.

Yours,
George Grant

1 Dennis Duffy (1938–), professor of English at the University of Toronto
2 Dennis Duffy, 'Gutsy Confusion in a Windy Cave,' *Globe and Mail Magazine,* 11
   July 1970

186/ To Charity Grant   27 December 1970

Dear Charity,
Thank you for the beautiful tie you gave me for Christmas.
   I write to explain why I did not send you any presents at Christmas.
When you did not ask William to meet the Ignatieffs, along with the other
children after dinner, I took this as a sign that our long relation was at an
end. Probably it would have been better not to have come to dinner that
evening and I would not then have been so rude to you in your house,
but it was only just before coming to your place that I realised that the
other children had been invited and not William.

Yours,
George

1971

187/ To Dennis Lee[1]   4 October 1971

Dear Dennis,

Thank you for sending me *Bartleby*.[2] I found it fascinating and extraordinary – to laugh and be horrified at different moments. I cannot write about it now. My only reason to do so would be my debt of friendship to you. I have spoken to you before of how difficult it is for me to get near to the union which is poetry because of a certain deep craziness. I think I am getting beyond that and might write of *Bartleby* in a year, but I think it would be foolish to do so now.

It was good seeing you and Donna. I was dark as night when you were here, but that has nothing to do with either of you. The same thing which I spoke of over *Bartleby* came up when speaking of your *Elegies*;[3] the fear of the ruin of my own life makes me silent about that which I do not live with. It is this kind of hesitation which has not enabled me to speak with you properly about them. It would be a wonderful thing for me at the moment if I could see them in their new state.

Yours,
George Grant

1 Dennis Lee (1939–), Canadian poet and editor
2 Chris Scott (1945–), *Bartleby: A Novel* (1971)
3 Dennis Lee, *Civil Elegies* (1968), a collection of poetry

Grant's strategy for appointments to the Department of Religion was to find people who lived within the faith they taught.

188/ To Paul Younger[1]   25 October 1971

Dear Paul,

This letter is to suggest that we should appoint Stanley Weber to a position in the department. I need not enclose a copy of his curriculum vitae which is on file in the department.

My reasons for making this suggestion are the following: In working with Weber over the last years, I have become convinced that he is turning into a remarkable scholar in an area which is of great significance to this department. The central core of his studies is about the relation of modern thought to Biblical religion. His formulation of this is, of course, centrally around the question of Judaism, but he is enormously open to the way the same question presents itself in Christianity. In preparing his comprehensives and his thesis, he has dealt with the formulations of such men as Mendelssohn[2] and how the enlightenment affected his account of Judaism. But in looking at Mendelssohn, he has been moved back behind the enlightenment to think of the same formulations in Maimonides[3] and forward to where it is formulated in such moderns as Rosenzweig.[4] His thesis on the way Leo Strauss has seen the long history of the relation between philosophy and the Biblical religion has shaped up to be first class and I am sure will have to be published. Beyond the thesis and out of it, there begins to appear a series of writings which I think will guarantee Weber's place in North American scholarship. This question of the relation of the enlightenment to religion seems to me the central question with which our western area should be dealing and I think that Weber would add greatly to our strength in this area.

I think Weber is a quite remarkably fine human being which is important in any appointment we make. He has been effective in his relations with undergraduates as a graduate teacher and above all, he has had an influence on other graduate students in deepening the way they have had to look at their studies.

If I may end with a personal word, my own studies would be enormously helped by having Weber here. His extensive knowledge of Judaism plus his understanding of the philosophic tradition means he is looking at the same questions that I am but within a different context and, therefore, I think a continuing dialogue would go on in the western part of the department[5] which would be of great stimulus for undergraduate and graduate students.

Sincerely,
George Grant

1 Paul Younger (1935–), a colleague in the Department of Religion at McMaster
2 Moses Mendelssohn (1729–86), German Jewish philosopher and biblical scholar
3 Moses ben Maimon (Maimonides) (1135–1204), Jewish medieval philosopher. His *Guide to the Perplexed* (1190) attempted to synthesize Aristotle and Judaism.
4 Franz Rosenzweig (1886–1929), German Jewish theologian and existential philosopher
5 Those concerned with Western religions

Grant loved his cottage at Terrence Bay, Nova Scotia, and he was by no means hesitant to join in the family rivalries and jealousies of the locals. He eventually acquired Jollimore's property.

189/ To Mr Jollimore and William Grant   22 December 1971

Dear Mr Jollimore and William:
I am writing you a joint letter with two copies, so that you can both have it in your hands when you go over it. I would advise that you go over it when nobody else is present (I, of course, do not mean Faye).[1]

I have been thinking of what we talked about concerning your land, and I have come to the following conclusion.

Your interest, Mr Jollimore, is to see that you keep the land and that nobody can take it away from you and your successors. It is clear that you need a deed and a survey. My interest in the matter is, above all, that you, as my friend, and your successors, should be safe on this land. My second interest is that nobody should get hold of the land other than you and your immediate family, in a way that might drive me out of Terrence Bay.

For example, if either Mrs Mildred Jollimore or Colin Baker get hold of the land, it would make our position there unpleasant. I therefore suggest the following: I will pay for the survey and for the legal work which will be necessary to get you a deed. This may be quite a lot of money, because it must be done carefully and well by a good lawyer. What I would like is to have the option on your land. An option means that, if you ever want to sell it, then I have the first right to buy it. It does not mean that you ever have to sell it (and I hope that never happens, because the best thing for me is that you and your family are there). What I want to avoid is that it falls into the hands of Colin Baker or Mrs Mildred Jollimore.

What I would suggest is that you and William first discuss this carefully. You are my friend and I do not want you to do anything you do not want to do. Nothing you could do about this would affect our friendship. When you and William have discussed it, it might be wise to discuss it with Royce,[2] as clearly the option is something that will have to continue beyond you or me. But in all such matters, the fewer people that hear about it, the better, because I can imagine Mrs Mildred Jollimore making trouble. If you are agreeable to this, then I will get in touch with somebody in Halifax and get some advice on who is a good lawyer to carry it out. Of course, I do not know whether all this will be legally possible (that is why we will need a good lawyer) and it may be necessary to look for some other arrangement. But that will have to wait until we have talked with a lawyer.

After we have found out what is possible, and what is not possible, legally, then the thing will be to proceed with the survey and get a deed for you and an option for me.

Best to you both.

Sincerely,
George Grant

1 William's wife
2 Royce Jollimore, Hezron Jollimore's eldest son

1972

190/ To John Robertson[1]

McMaster University
3 January 1972

Dear John,

We will meet practically tomorrow – but apart from that and apart from any practical disagreements which we from time to time may ever have, I want to say how much your letter (from before you went away) meant to the last weeks for me. It was in itself a beautiful letter and one of the rare communications that I will reread when I am sad – but apart from that fact, it was an immense joy to me that you should have written for, indeed, if I start to doubt that you are what you are, then madness has me by the throat.

The difficulty that a person such as yourself (when I use the words 'such as' – so foolishly – it makes me admire [ill.]) has in having to live in practical dealings with a person such as myself is that I am a person who, because of the first decades of my life, has had to put himself together late in life, and that is never an achieved process. At the core of my instinctive being is a lack of trust in being itself. I do not know how accurate the modern account of this as paranoia is – and this appears in the great indirectness of my practical dealings, often masked by an apparent phoney openness. It is the great gift I owe to Plato and Christ that they have taught me to be able to live in my conscious levels in trust, but the other is always there as a recurring madness.

It has been a source of continual joy to me that, through something I had no part in, you, who (so rarely for this era) know about both the Gospels and philosophy, should have come to this department. It justifies the existence of the department to me and I am sure you know that I would do nothing that would put you in a position in which you thought the department was no longer worth your efforts.

Because of my unsettled and wild being, we must always be careful that we communicate with each other and say, in the best moments, exactly what we think about matters in which we both have interests and differing thoughts. To build a good department of religion in the midst of this very strange modern world will require that kind of adult friendship and any breakdown of that is more likely to come out of my foolish sinkings into chaos.

The Canadian-American business is [ill.] – because the opportunism of the truth of revelation and philosophy quite transcends such parochial matters. My willingness to give some time to such practical things is only as a means to the greater things.

I owe you a great debt of joy and help for your letter.

George

1 John Robertson (1936–), a colleague in the Department of Religion at McMaster

191/ To J.A. Corry[1]   17 February 1972

Dear Professor Corry,

Thank you for sending me a copy of your lectures[2] and for your letter. I thought the lectures a very sane and indeed noble account of the English-speaking tradition and, as Montesquieu pointed out, it is that tradition which expresses the political height in modern Europe (and its offshoots). What I found so attractive in your writing is the constant presence of a real empiricism rather than that doctrinaire empiricism as 'methodology' which seems to me to corrupt liberalism (e.g. David Easton).[3] I think Locke was a much more comprehensive political thinker than many of his epigones who have claimed to correct him.

It is good of you to say that 'it is highly desirable that we should understand one another.' As I would learn much from talking to you, I think it right to say that we will have to transcend the fact of what different fates have been ours. It was not easy for me to leave the Canadian academic establishment and it was not easy to face the intolerance of that establishment – particularly as that intolerance claimed for itself the name of 'liberalism.' I think the most savage words ever spoken to me by an older man I had respected were said by W.A. Mackintosh[4] and I identified his opinions with your own. For an ambitious person such as myself, it is easier to take such remarks today when one is secure than at the time they were made, when I was without a job. When English-speaking liberalism seemed to have the world at its feet in the 1950s, it was not tolerant of anything which lay outside its vision and nowhere was it more intolerant than in its academic manifestations. (In parenthesis, let me say about your lectures that your identification of lawlessness with the young has perhaps less appeal to me than for you, not only because of my different assessment of the lawlessness which established American liberalism in its empire (it is not easy to forget Rostow,[5] Schlesinger,[6] Huntington[7] and the Bundys),[8] but also because the young revolters communicated with me about Christianity in a way that had never occurred with the established liberals of academic social science. I am fearful and deplore much of the conduct of the modern young, but on the other hand personally I have had more to fear from the objects of their attack than from them. These kinds of shallow circumstances naturally influence one's judgment.)

This is all prologemena (perhaps too self-pitying, but at least direct) to saying that I did not agree with what you said in your letter, that I am 'trying to transcend the western tradition.' Since 1947 I would call myself a Christian Platonist and the deepest good fortune of my life has been to find that as I have come, even slightly, to understand Christianity and Platonism, I have found myself more deeply held by them, except in certain unimportant details. To be direct, it surely has been modern liberalism which has attempted (generally for noble reasons) to transcend the Western tradition both philosophically and religiously. The relation of English-speaking liberalism to Christianity has of course been enormously complex – but now that the latter is destroyed as a substantial social force it is surely easier to see the place of liberalism in that destruction.

Coincidentally, at the same time I received your lectures, I received a lecture from my oldest friend who has the chair of public administration at LSE [Peter Self]. Both came forth so much from what is best in the only profound tradition which continues to be operative in the English-speaking world. They have jointly forced me to the difficult task (difficult, that is, for me to do fairly) of trying to apprehend what was true in that tradition and also to gauge how much it is a continuing force to be depended on in the world we are now presented with. This is difficult and indeed dangerous because I recognize that the only decent tradition of substance in the English-speaking world is liberalism, and one must be careful in speaking against it publicly. Only a fool would think that we could not do worse. Nevertheless, this tradition is generally met by the young now only in its decadence as a public technicism and a private existentialism. Indeed, the clever young seem to feel religious, political and philosophical needs which cannot be met in that English-speaking tradition and it seems healthier that these needs be met in terms of the reminders of the ancient traditions rather than in the wilder reaches of existentialism. I am grateful to your lectures for making me try to look fairly at modern liberalism because you express it so cogently and moderately.

It is good of you to say that we might meet. I will write ahead when I am coming to Kingston to see my boy [Robert], to see if you have a spare hour. It would be so good to have a coherent conversation for the first time since the ancient days of Politics 2. Please excuse this being dictated, but my writing hand is badly broken and it is painful to write at length.

With many thanks.

Yours,
George Grant

1 J.A. Corry (1899–1985), professor of political science at Queen's
2 J.A. Corry, *The Power of the Law*, Massey Lectures (1971)
3 David Easton (1917–), American political scientist. Grant rather resented the fact that Easton was the first appointment to the Sir Edward Peacock chair at Queen's, created out of funds donated by his godfather.
4 W.A. Mackintosh (1895–1970), economist and Queen's professor. Mackintosh served with the departments of finance and reconstruction until 1947, when he returned to Queen's. He was principal, 1951–61.
5 W.W. Rostow (1916–), American economist and special adviser to presidents Kennedy (1961–3) and Johnson (1966–9); a specialist in Third World development
6 Arthur Schlesinger, Jr (1917–), American historian and political adviser to the Democrats
7 Samuel Huntington (1927–), Harvard political scientist and political adviser, specializing in defence policy
8 William Bundy (1917–) was a foreign policy adviser to Richard Nixon; McGeorge Bundy (1919–), a Kennedy and Johnson adviser who advocated the escalation of the Vietnam war. In 1968 he came out in favour of de-escalation.

192/ To John and Nita Graham   postmarked 1 August 1972

Dear John and Nita,
Just a note to say thanks for your sweetness last month. We were pretty
scattered when we saw you because the last year had pushed us back on
our haunches. The sense for both of us that we had been inadequate parents came at a time when I was having to put up or shut up about the
complicated confusion that has fallen on the western world and my
inability to see anything clearly or unequivocally drove us both into a very
bad period and we were very grateful for your gentleness to us. Getting
away from here and looking at the sea seems to have done us all good.
    We have both talked a lot about how extremely taxing and yet fascinat-
ing the next months will be for you. My favourite quotation from Simone
Weil is 'Matter is our infallible judge'[1] and it must be amazing to have to
make discriminations not only in terms of one's own life but of the direction of a society. What I think is so bad for many intellectuals' lives is that
they never have to be called for such discriminations socially and evade
them when they arise in personal life. I admire tremendously how you
keep cool and yet a coolness which does not deny concern. Isn't it strange
to watch one's friends grow up and what becomes of them? A proper
coolness has been broken in us during the spring; so it was good to see
yours.
    Thanks.

                                                                Ever,
                                                                George

P.S. Best to your beautiful four.

1 Simone Weil, *First and Last Notebooks*, ed. and trans. Richard Rees (1970), 364;
   first published in Simone Weil, *La Connaissance surnaturelle* (1950), 336

193/ To Frank Milligan[1]   [autumn 1972]

Dear Mr Milligan,
This is a report concerning what I accomplished thanks to the grant
given me by the Killam Committee of the Canada council which freed me
from teaching for the academic year 1971-1972.
    The book I am writing has now the title 'Techniques and good.'[2] This
change came about because it became clear to me in writing about 'What
is technique?' that at the heart of the coming to be of modern technique

[there] has been [a] mutual interdepend[ence] with a changed conception of goodness in the western world. What led me in that direction is that the question 'what does technical civilization portend for the future for good or evil?' – a question clearly of import for thinking people – is complicated by the fact that it is very unclear what is meant by good and evil in our modern technical civilizations. Indeed, some of the most penetrating modern thinkers say that men have, in technical civilization, passed 'beyond good and evil.'

Therefore, the main body of the work historically is an account of the relation between the arising of the modern conception of technique out of that very different classical account of technique and the arising of the modern conception of good out of the original conceptions of good from Athens and Jerusalem. The best analogy is from music. It is a contrapuntal writing in which the themes of good and technique are developed together in the hope that light is thereby thrown on the question 'What does technical civilization portend for the future of good and evil?' Because the English-speaking world is now so dominant and because this is a book to be published in Ontario, the history will concentrate on the development of the conception of good in the English-speaking tradition. This has the added advantage for my purposes that, in the English-speaking world, the meeting of philosophy with religion (in its Protestant form) allows one to discuss in terms of the clearest paradigm the relation of the modern conception of good not only to Athens but to Jerusalem. I do not want the book to exclude theology in the name of philosophy or vice versa.

It is impossible to know when the book will be finished. That depends not only on the practical considerations of how much I have to do as a teacher and organizer here, but on the much more dicey question of my ability to think through certain matters. The chief of these is to be able to put in the greatest clarity what it means to say that human beings are not 'beyond good and evil' as against certain modern philosophers who say that they are. I am not now able to think that, but am much nearer to be able to do it than eighteen months ago. What I can say to the Council is that the book is rarely out of my mind, and that if I survive and remain sane (a dubious matter) this book is what I will be working on till it is completed. I have arranged to issue sections of the book in appropriate Canadian journals and to present them at appropriate learned meetings.

This all expresses my profound sense of debt to the Council. Their very generous grant (which allowed me to do this work for the first time without going into debt) allowed me to move toward thinking in a way that I had never in the past. It is to be hoped that that generosity will not only result in my own great private gain, but that, in what I publish, there may be some assistance to others who are attempting to think through the fundamental questions about technical civilization. Obviously our present circumstances call Canadians to that activity.

This report may appear to you not sufficiently detailed and perhaps pompous. But my gratitude to the Council led me to express in theoretical terms what I have been about, thanks to your generosity. If you want anything more exact than this, I will be delighted to write more.

Yours sincerely,
George Grant

1 Associate director, the Canada Council
2 Never completed

194/ To Hilda Neatby[1]   3 October 1972

Dear Hilda,
I am honoured that you should ask me to call you Hilda, and it is a delight for you to call me George.

I would very much like to see Watson's[2] comments about my grandfather. (I was a pallbearer of Watson's through my relations with the Sweezeys of Beauharnois fame. He[3] was Watson's son in law.) Reading my dad's notebooks, I have become aware of what an extremely difficult person Principal Grant was, at least as a father.

I have talked a lot about the Neatbys recently when I have met the Hedum children. What a fascinating tradition you came out of.

Queen's is much on my mind these days because the fourth generation male Grant, my son Robert, is studying history and philosophy there. If I come down to see him I will write ahead to you and see if you are visitable.

I think what is essentially interesting about Principal Grant is the strange meeting between Protestantism and liberalism. This meeting has been so dominant in the English-speaking world and is such an ambiguous relation.

Queen's was so wise to choose you for this task.[4]

Yours sincerely,
George Grant

1 H.M. Neatby (1904–75), professor of history at Queen's

2 John Watson (1847–1939), Canada's foremost philosopher of his time. He
 began teaching at Queen's in 1872 and served under Grant's grandfather.
3 Robert Oliver Sweezey (1883–1968), president of Beauharnois Light, Heat and
 Power Corp. and a benefactor of Queen's
4 Hilda Neatby, Frederick Gibson, and Roger Graham, *Queen's University: To
 Strive, to Seek, to Find, and Not to Yield* (1978)

195/ To Derek Bedson   McMaster University
                                                          11 October 1972

Dear Derek,
Since your telephone call, I have got a letter from the University of Winnipeg. I am saying no despite my desire to see yourself. I am asked to go
away and speak so much that I have made a rule for myself not to be away
from this university except rarely, and I have accepted too much for this
year already. The rebelling students had one good part of their case, that
too many professors spent their lives in airports and I am determined not
to become one of them.
  The election is depressing,[1] but I hope Stanfield will make some good
gains.

                                                                  Ever,
                                                                George

This is quick – but it brings love.

1 Federal general election, 30 October 1972, which Stanfield narrowly lost to
 Trudeau's Liberals

196/ To Derek Bedson   20 October 1972

Dear Derek,
Forgive a letter on the wing. I had to say the following: S. and I went to
George's [Ignatieff] inauguration [as provost] at Trinity last night. A sad
mixture of tired clerics and wealthy liberals. What follows is uncharitable,
but because of your experience I thought I would say it. Sheila said at the
end of the public gathering, 'Who was that Gilbert and Sullivan character
in the chair?' I said: 'That is Archbishop Clark, our spiritual father.'
Christ's name was never mentioned except in the benediction.

The election depresses me enormously. Stanfield does not seem to know how to hit at all. So my prediction would be that Trudeau would do very well in Ontario. Oh dear!

I am just on the wing.

Ever,
George

197/ To Derek Bedson   1 November 1972

Dear Derek,

Thanks for your note. I am so delighted to have been wrong about Stanfield in Ontario. Watching the results come in was a marvellous pleasure because it told one (among other things) that more than enough people were not fooled by the slick or put off by the gentleman[1] and that, at least, is some common sense. Behind that is my certainty that, whatever the limitations of the Conservatives, I feel incomparably safer with them dealing with [U.S. president Richard] Nixon than Pepin-Turner[2] et al. I wonder above all how this may affect your life.

I do not think George I. can do much positively about Trinity – but I am sure that he will a) not do anything to hurt the proper religious life of the college in a way that some liberal clerics might have done and that b) if anyone comes along with a good base for the theological college, he would not prevent it happening (I doubt that such will come about).

After an extremely difficult year for us with children (the worst of our lives) we have come out into a period of calm and happiness. A great thing has happened to me. Having always written indirectly about theology, I have come in the past months to be able for the first time in my life to write directly of theology. It now so engrosses me that I find all external practical things I have to deal with, simply difficult distractions. Sheila and I, for the first time, are getting to be able to think theologically. That may seem boastful, but it is of course just fortune or grace, not one's own efforts. But it is wonderful. Of course, it may disappear tomorrow.

I hope the decisions in the next days go in a way that are what you really want.

Love from us both,
George

Forgive my scrawl which because of my hand makes it difficult to control the pen.

1 Robert Stanfield
2 Jean-Luc Pépin (1924–), Liberal minister of Industry, Trade and Commerce,
   and a senior Quebec politician; John Turner (1929–), Liberal finance minister
   and later prime minister (1984)

1973

198/ To Hilda Neatby   25 January 1973

Dear Hilda,
I am sorry to have been slow in answering but have had a long period of
illness.
   The things you sent me from Watson are fascinating. I think what you
are writing goes right to the heart of Canadian intellectual history and
indeed the history of the English-speaking people – the meeting of Protestantism and liberalism.
   Two comments:
(1) I think Watson's 'idealism' made him think (along with Kant and
Hegel) that he had transcended authentic Christianity.
(2) I think there is also in the papers the sense that he, as an educated
European, is dealing with 'hicks' when he deals with Canadians.
   It would be very good to have a discussion of this, as Queen's liberalism
has been something I have had to contend with all my life.
   I will be in Kingston for the Canadian Society for the Study of Religion
(CSSR) Conference in June and it would be good to meet, if this is not
too late for you.
   I will be so fascinated by what you write.

Yours sincerely,
George Grant

199/ To Dennis Lee   31 January 1973

Dear Dennis,
I have telephoned you often without success; so I am putting this in writing, which I don't want to do because of the depth of things I would like
to say about your paper, but that must wait because what I want to say
about cadence and silence[1] must be said with the greatest slowness.
   I have been ill with the result that I am very far behind here. Can we,

therefore, leave meeting until after you have recovered from the teeth business? I don't know if it is better to meet here or in Toronto , but we must meet when Sheila, yourself and myself all have time to say exactly what we mean.

Ever,
George

1 A reference to Lee's article 'Cadence, Country, Silence,' *Boundary 2* (Fall 1974)

200/ To Derek Bedson   16 February 1973

Dear Derek,
Thank you very much for the reproduction[1] which came via Ab Campion[2] (a person I like greatly). The reproduction just *hit* the spot because I have been thinking of Christianity & ruling & have always loved the lines in the hymn via Revelation[3] about 'casting down their golden crowns around the glassy sea.'[4] (I was excessively annoyed by one of our liberal clerics once saying, What could these words mean?) So many thanks – I just love it. Next time we met I had intended to have a conversation about ruling & Christianity.

Archbishop Scott[5] said some very foolish words in Toronto yesterday about pornography. It is *very* very hard for me to take these untheologically trained bishops' authority seriously. What he said was straight Kantianism & doesn't he know what that is (a fine & great philosopher, but one who was set on moving Europe away from Christianity)? I go tomorrow to an evangelical Anglican congregation & am going to take it upon myself to ridicule what our primate said. Oh dear. We must talk of this.

By the way I am going to this church for the day because the clergyman (he is Wycliff & would not like to be called a priest) is Judith Robinson's nephew.[6] There is far more to his Christianity – solid Protestant Anglican evangelicalism – than most of the Catholic-oriented ones I know & with whom I have much more agreement. What he speaks and does is real.

I have been passing through a time of the most pressing madness – in terms of our older age as if I was being assailed by devils. I am not in the nut house largely because I live with someone who combines Catholic & English common sense rationality. Thank God, I seem to be moving through it. It may be no more than the male equivalent of menopause, but it has been a trying period. Part of its manifestation comes from my impatience with the lack of shrewd ambition in William & Robert. I dislike much of the Canadian ruling class – but it would be very difficult for me to face my grandchildren as silly proletarians. Yet one must face that it is better decent proletarians than much of the corruption of the upper bourgeois. What I am saying above all is that I feel very remote from the world I live in & you are one of the rare people who make me feel I am in a world with which I have sympathy. My greatest vice, I have decided, is self-pity.

I hope all goes well with the immediacies of your life and that you are not too pressed.

Thanks so much for the beautiful picture.

Ever,
George

1 Of a painting?
2 Diefenbaker political adviser
3 'They Rest not day and night, saying, Holy, Holy, Holy, Lord God Almighty, which was, and is, and is to come' (Revelations 4.8).
4 Holy, Holy, Holy! all the saints adore Thee,
   Casting down their golden crowns around the glassy sea;
   Cherubim and seraphim falling down before Thee,
   Which wert, and art, and evermore shall be.
           – Bishop R. Heber, 'Holy, Holy, Holy! Lord God Almighty!' (1827)
5 Most Rev. Edward Walter Scott (1919–), archbishop and primate of the Anglican Church of Canada, 1971–85
6 Rev. Harry Robinson, vicar of Trinity East Anglican Church in Toronto. Grant dedicated *Lament for a Nation* to Derek Bedson and Judith Robinson, 'Two lovers of their country, one living and one dead.'

201/ To Hilda Neatby   1 March 1973

Dear Hilda,

It would be of the greatest interest to me to read your section on my grandfather before I come down to Kingston in June.

I am fascinated by this not only by family or Canadian things, but because the meeting of secularism with Protestantism seems to me central to understanding the English-speaking peoples. Our present secularism fills me with such a sense of dread.

I will write well in advance to tell you which days I will be in Kingston in the hope that you will have some time for a talk.

Yours,
George P. Grant

202/ To Alex Colville[1]   24 May 1973

Dear Alex,

I am sorry to dictate an answer to your letter, but the end of term never seems to get any easier.

It was extremely good to get your letter because I had been meaning to write to you all winter. First, because when I was at Mount Allison last fall,[2] I greatly regretted that when we met I was so nervous that we did not say a proper word to each other – or to your wife. Secondly, Sheila and I have been looking again and again at the book of your pictures[3] this winter and they have filled us with joy and wonder.

I write at length about what you propose because I am so honoured by your letter and because if I am to do it, I want to do it just right. Please answer this letter with complete candour. If the alternatives I suggest are not right, I will quite understand your judgment. If what is appropriate for this lecture or lectures is a fairly popular style, then I must say no. When my children were growing up I had to do quite a lot of popular writing and I don't want to any more. Writing comes to me harder and harder and as you will know from your own life, I now want to write in a particular way. This does not mean that I would not write as an amateur in a way that any serious person could understand (because the very name of philosophy means the amateur).[4] I would not write in a silly technical way for a few professionals. But on the other hand, I want to write very closely. If the requirement of the lecture is properly popular then at the moment I am not the right person to do it.

I have two alternatives. The first is my choice. I would like to write out at the moment the reasons why the 'contractualism' which lies at the basis of English-speaking liberal moral philosophy seems to me a failure and why one must try and understand morality as natural rather than contractual. This would be a general lecture, but it would centre around a book which is very influential in the English-speaking world at the moment. The book is called *A Theory of Justice* by John Rawls[5] – professor of philosophy at Harvard. It is a brilliant attempt to talk of moral philosophy within the analytical tradition. I would like to take this book as a starting point and move out to talk about what was good and what was inadequate in the tradition of English-speaking liberalism. Would this be an appropriate lecture?[6]

My second alternative is that I have written out a long introductory chapter to a book to be called *Technique and Good*. This would require two lectures. Why I favour this less is that it is extremely closely written and really requires people to have thought quite deeply about Heidegger[7] and Plato.

I am delighted that the lecture is to be published; but, in either case, I would have to be free to publish them elsewhere, as the second is the introduction to a book, and the first I would like to publish in the political science world. But in either case I would recognize in any other publication that they had first been published at Mount Allison.

I am sorry to write at such length, but writing comes to me now with great difficulty and I want to occupy myself carefully. Please let me know what you think about my suggestions. The first suggestion, I repeat, would be my favourite.

Again, thanks for such a nice letter.

Sincerely,
George Grant

1 D.A. Colville (1920–), Canadian painter and formerly professor of fine art at Mount Allison; chairman of the committee to select the Wood lecturer
2 Grant received an honorary degree.
3 Helen Dow, *The Art of Alex Colville* (1972)
4 Grant is referring to the Greek roots of *philo-sophia* (love of wisdom) and the Latin root of *amateur,* which is *amare* (to love).
5 John Rawls, *A Theory of Justice* (1971)
6 Zdravco Planinc later sent a copy of the published version of these lectures to Rawls. Rawls replied:

8 June 1983

Mr Planinc,
A brief note to acknowledge receiving the copy of George Grant's Wood lectures for 1974, for which many thanks. I appreciate your sending them to me. I can see that his criticisms are different from any I've seen, but not necessarily any less effective for that!

Yours,
John Rawls

7 Martin Heidegger (1889–1976), German philosopher. Grant considered him the greatest philosopher of the twentieth century.

203/ To Hilda Neatby   4 June 1973

Dear Hilda,
This is just to say how much Sheila and I loved our time with you. It was by

far the highlight of our time in Kingston. It was so sweet of you to prepare such a beautiful dinner.

Since speaking to you and walking around Kingston I have thought a lot about GMG[1] and about Canada in general. One way of putting it would be: Canada was an innocent fringe country in which people expressed their innocence in the midst of the late period of European civilization. Watson's Hegelianism, for example, was a high and complex product of secularized Christianity. When you compare this with Grant's simple training up on the Nova Scotian farm, how could Grant be aware of what was appearing in the West in general and which would break in upon the innocence of a pioneering society?

I hope you have a lovely time in England. I do not think I said sufficiently forcefully how very good your writing about Queen's appeared to me.

I enclose a copy of a quotation from Grant that I included in a little book of mine.[2]

Again, thanks.

Yours,
George Grant

1 George Monro Grant, principal of Queen's and Grant's grandfather
2 'This identification of Christianity with practicality by North American Protestants is well illustrated by a quotation from my grandfather. "Work! Honest work for and with God in Christ! This is the Gospel that is preached unto us. No form, new or old, no pet doctrine or panacea, no institution or catechism can take the place of that." G.M. Grant to the Synod of the Presbyterian Church in Nova Scotia, 1866' (George Grant, *Philosophy in the Mass Age*, footnote 15).

1974

204/ To James Doull   24 January 1974

Dear James,
It is an honour to be asked and a delight to accept your invitation to be an advisor on the committee for *Diotima*.[1] It seems to me a very fine idea, and I am proud to have even a small part in it. Let me congratulate the person responsible for the title. Also, it seems to me in such very good hands. As you know, you were my first philosopher teacher and remain the person to whom my philosophic debt is the greatest. Could you tell

Prof. Armstrong how much I admire his writing. I always introduce students to Plato by asking them to read an article he wrote called 'Platonism.'

I will be honoured to submit writings of my own for consideration. As you know, my greatest weakness at this point is my poor philosophical education. But clearly, the interest of the journal makes it possible to send you modern articles which seem appropriate. My greatest joy would be sometime to be able to write out a criticism of Heidegger's criticism of Plato.

Sheila and I are coming to Nova Scotia in February and hope we meet. Our son William is married in Halifax and takes Nova Scotia as his home. We go to Terrence Bay for a couple of weeks in the summer, and this year we have the great advantage of doing it sans family; so we hope we meet. Sheila sends her love.

Above all, it would be great for me to discuss Heidegger with you. I am not a Heideggerian, but he has taught me much in the last years.

Yours ever,
George

1 The journal was finally known as *Dionysius*.

205/ To Mr Fitchen[1]   10 April 1974

Dear Mr Fitchen,
Re: Comments on [Leo Strauss's] 'The Argument and Action of Plato's *Laws*'[2]
1. This book is exactly what it says it is in its title. It is an account of what Plato is saying in his last great political book. Strauss, on writing, brings out with the greatest care and fullness what is being done by Plato. Obviously from reading the book, S. has spent many years studying it and has thought deeply about the relation of its parts to the whole. What was particularly illuminating for me was how he brought out, time and again, the meaning of details (both arguments and action) which I, who have taught the book, previously never saw.
2. I do not know if in North American academic life Plato's *Laws* will continue to be studied. (Of course it should.) But if it is, this writing of S.'s about it will be of enormous help to those who are teaching it. I am sure it would also be of great help to graduate students who are studying the *Laws*. (I know I will use it for a graduate course I give every few years on the *Laws*.) For undergraduates, I think it could be a help if they were given help in reading it by their teacher. It is, in the finest sense of the

word, an austere book and, therefore, one that undergraduates need help in reading.

3. In the English-speaking world there has not been a commentary of this kind on the *Laws* since we moved from reading Latin. Works such as C.C.J. Webb's[3] only concentrated on the tenth book of the *Laws* while A.E. Taylor's book[4] is much sketchier than Strauss's. My knowledge of the American world is much less than of the English world, but I am sure I would have heard of any commentary on the *Laws* and do not know if there are any.

4. The writing is quite clear. It is readable for one who wants to read something difficult, but it is, of course, not readable in any easy sense of that word. I do not think it contains any unnecessary repetition and I do not see how it could be cut without amputating an essential limb as it describes the action and the argument book by book and that is its purpose.

5. I think the manuscript could do with a short crisp introduction relating it to Strauss's other work. Let me say in suggesting this, I am not asking for a job because clearly such an introduction should be written by somebody much closer to Strauss than I was; but I think such an introduction (short) would put the manuscript into relation with his other works on Plato.

I hope these remarks are helpful.

Let me say again that this is an austere work, but one which I think any university press should be proud to publish.

I enclose on a separate sheet a list of books in answer to your kind offer.

Sincerely,
George Grant

1 Humanities editor, University of Chicago Press
2 Leo Strauss, *The Argument and the Action of 'Plato's Laws'* (1975)
3 C.C.J. Webb (1865–1954), author of *Studies in the History of Natural Theology* (1915)
4 Plato, *The Laws,* translated with an introduction by A.E. Taylor (1869–1945)

206/ To Dennis Lee   10 June 1974

Dear Dennis,
Herewith my comments on 'Savage Fields.'[1]

I cannot be an editor because I am not good at that and, therefore, send along more general comments.

I speak about Cohen rather than Ondaatje[2] because I have thought so much more deeply about the former and also because your analysis of *Beautiful Losers*[3] is so much longer and more detailed. I think the way you bring out the enormously complex layers of BL is fine and was of great help to a person like myself who finds that kind of enucleation helpful and who knows the book is sufficiently important to warrant it.

As I see the question you asked me in your letter, it is made difficult by the following matter. Your purpose is to show that these novels are as a new form of *poiesis*[4] to distinguish them from other forms of *poiesis*. At the same time, Cohen (as you so brilliantly show) is saying things of the most universal character about being. Cohen's apprehension of *poiesis* is within a particular modern account of being which is modern in its very account of the horror of modernity. Therefore, when you ask me for theoretical books about *poiesis* I am in a difficulty. There is no doubt that, for Plato, the only rival to philosophy to be taken seriously is tragic and comic poetry and the very heart of his writings is trying to show that philosophy takes you to the heart beyond tragic and comic poetry. In the modern era, it seems that the rival to philosophy becomes modern physics, but it is the supreme genius of Nietzsche to see that in what he considers the death of philosophy, what arises in its place for the greatest men is a new kind of tragic and comic poetry.

What I am saying, in short, is that Cohen's greatness is only a partaking in the prodigious greatness of Nietzsche and that the questions about the relation of poetry to philosophy are just beyond me. I see BL as an attempt (wonderful) to express this. It would take me hours to try to say why I have turned my back on this, which is modernity at its height.

I don't really understand why you use the phrase 'noetic realism' about this new kind of art. You would have to say to me much more about each of the words, because to me the modern in this form is both a denial of the noetic (because there is nothing eternal which is loveable) and the denial of realism in the name of subjectivity. As you make so clear, the love of Isis sounds as if there is something eternal which is loveable and we would have to discuss that at great length. What I find difficult in Cohen is the use of the novel to show forth truths about being which are essentially philosophical within the account of being which denies that there are such truths. This is all very general and unhelpful and I am afraid of these broad statements of mine which take away from the concreteness of BL which you so well have enucleated. If you are going in for theory, I do not see how you can turn away from the prodigious western problem of philosophy and poetry, and yet I have no doubt that it is about the most difficult question and it is the question which, because of scientific technology, is largely closed down in our era. In short, I am saying to you that I think BL is enormously worth analyzing in the way you have done, but that it takes you theoretically, when you enter the question of what it is as a form of *poiesis*, into questions of the most prodigious difficulty.

I do not know the other books you are going to analyze in the same way I know BL. It may simply be my own interest that makes me wonder whether you can do all these books and deal with the prodigious questions raised by Cohen.

One practical thing about Cohen, and your relation to him. I think you have to distinguish between describing what he says and things you are going to assent, and not assent, to. For example, he makes all kinds of crazy mistakes about the tradition. Tertullian[5] broke with Christianity, or again, concerning koans, contradictions do not exist in Buddhism. The biggest here is, of course, that Catherine's destruction is by Catholics, that modern history could only start once Catholicism had been destroyed, for Catholicism was the only ferocious enemy of progress in the West. I [don't] mean by this that you should get into all these very complex questions because clearly your task is to show forth a particular kind of art. But I think you should carefully distinguish between describing what Cohen says and seeming to give assent to his obvious errors. At the deepest level, what does he mean by the body and what is the opposite of the body?

For example, in both Ondaatje and Cohen you draw out the distinction between the ecstatic and the civil, but that is a distinction which is absolutely part of modernity – particularly brought into the west by Rousseau. It is not a truth about the way things are, but a modern account of the way things are. It is as much up for questioning as a basic question you are asking about the nature of art.

At a lesser level, I think you have to be very clear in your own mind as to whom you are addressing. Sometimes you are addressing the Canadian young (rather as Miss Atwood did in *Survival*).[6] But at other times you are raising questions of the most prodigious difficulty which takes you away beyond the young Canadians. I think either kind of book is worthwhile, but I think you have to be clear which it is. As you know, I am not a democrat.

Two pages, 28 on Ondaatje, and a later page are missing. I did not lose them.

One of the most complex and undiscussable aspects of Cohen is the deep Jewish ambiguity, almost hatred, of Christianity in it. One cannot discuss this because one would have such ghastly allies if one even discussed the matter.

This is an unuseful letter for your purposes, but you can see how deeply moved I was by what you wrote about Cohen, and took it at the most serious level. I am sorry my comments are so general, but we must talk about it.

I hope you both had a lovely time in England. Give my love to Linda.

Ever,

George

1 Dennis Lee (1939–), *Savage Fields: An Essay in Literature and Cosmology* (1977)
2 Michael Ondaatje (1943–), Canadian writer
3 Leonard Cohen (1934–), *Beautiful Losers* (1966)
4 Greek for 'making.' Grant used it in Heidegger's sense of a leading forth into being.
5 Tertullian (c. 160-c. 225), philosopher and theologian
6 Margaret Atwood (1934–), *Survival: A Thematic Guide to Canadian Literature* (1972)

207/ To Derek Bedson   26 July 1974

Dear Derek,
I have been wanting to write about the election[1] – but have been quite ill and am only today able to lift myself around a bit. This part of the world was not going to have anything to do with anything that required any discipline of any kind and, when the openness was combined with a more stern leader[2] as against a dull gentleman,[3] it was too much. There really is no continuing sense of community in southern Ontario and there was clearly a great fear of what would be required of people with the incomes policy. D'Arcy Luxton[4] said a week before the election that the incomes policy was going to hurt the party in this area. But what it comes down to is that Toronto and its environs are really at the heart totally Americanized. The [forces] of independence – whether traditional or radical – are really little waves on the surface. Trudeau is a kind of Canadian Kennedy – a shallow politician who makes people think this vulgar society has a slick patina to it.

I was sorry above all not so much about policy – but because they are just more decent people with the Conservatives. I never know whether you would really like to have moved to Ottawa – but it is very sad for Canada that you should not be there – that was what seems saddest to me.

This is a poor letter because I am hardly in the world (it is a depressing comment how much one's mind is dependent on one's inside). But it brings much love from us both.

Ever,
George

I will write more clearly at another time.

1 Federal general election, 8 July 1974
2 Pierre Trudeau
3 Robert Stanfield
4 The Grants' lawyer and a close friend

208/ To William Christian[1]   4 October 1974

Dear Prof. Christian,
Thank you very much for your letter about the chair in Canadian Studies. I have thought a long time about your letter and certainly one of the best things about being at Mount Allison would be the chance of talking with yourself. However, I have written back today to Arthur Motyer[2] saying not to continue the possibilities.

As you have been so kind about this I give you my reasons. (1) I have spent a great deal of my life organizing things and don't regret it, but I have come now to the point where I want to write one thing out as well as I can. It concerns what is Christianity now that Western Christianity has so much come to an end. I cannot do that and think about Canadian Studies at the same time. I would have to keep abreast of recent things in Canada and so much of it I don't understand. Also, I would have to pull together what I think a Canadian Studies program should be and I have done that kind of thing three times in my life and don't feel now I can do it again.

I also think that the university should get a younger man full of energy. Universities often make great mistakes by appointing people who have made their reputations and then rest on it.

I am very complimented that you should want me at Mount Allison.

Yours,
George Grant

1 William Christian (1945–), professor of political science at Mount Allison University, 1970–8; University of Guelph, 1978–

2 A.J. Motyer (1925–), vice-president (academic), Mount Allison University

209/ To Patrick Atherton[1]   28 November 1974

Dear Patrick,

Thank you for your very nice letter. It was kind of you to write so clearly.

Let me say at the beginning that what you are talking about seems to me rather different from what I heard from Wilfred Smith, when you speak of 'The Study by Canadians of the American Intellectual Tradition and our Relation to it.' It is clear to me that I know almost nothing of that subject and do not intend to study it. In my opinion there is nothing very much to the American intellectual tradition which takes one very far beyond Hobbes and Locke with perhaps a dash of Rousseau. This has, of course, been carried on above all within a rather shallow account of Protestantism. (I gather that Jonathan Edwards[2] may be a very good Protestant theologian, but I am not that interested.) Putting these complex matters very quickly, I think the Americans have taken 'technical reason' (your words) in a very shallow form although a very dynamic one. My interests are in two related things: a) to understand 'technical reason' which I think has been done at its greatest philosophically by Nietzsche and his chief epigone Heidegger and which has been done also best by German scientists, e.g. Heisenberg.[3] b) I am interested in explicating the truth of Christianity in relation to this height of modernity. That is, I am interested in understanding technique in a philosophic way and am only interested in American civilization in so far as it gives examples of the unfolding and of the meeting of that unfolding with Christianity. When Wilfred Smith spoke to me, he spoke much more about 'technique' than about the American intellectual tradition. I know practically nothing about the latter in detail and would not be interested in teaching myself about it so that I could teach it.

The two practical things I should mention are: (1) I have become a solitary in the sense that the only things that really interest me (other than my family) are teaching the young and trying to write down what I am thinking about technique and Christianity. I am not a solitary vis-à-vis students or necessary details of organization, but I am a solitary in so far as not allowing anything to stand in the way of my thinking. (2) I would expect to take a cut in salary if I came to King's to do something which seemed to me important. But I am very highly paid here and that cut could not go beyond a certain point because I am still responsible for some of the education of six children.

These latter points of course can be easily worked out.

What concerns me much the most is the intellectual matter I raised in the first paragraph. There is no point in carrying the matter any further unless both sides are quite clear as to what is the content of what I would be teaching and writing about. For example, I have been offered in the last years a lot of jobs in 'Canadian Studies.' None of them have had any interest for me because my thoughts are on the basic crisis of Christianity in the light of 'technical reason,' which is a world-wide crisis and essentially a theoretical one and, therefore, not limited to immediacies.

I write clearly and hope you will show this letter to James Doull, Wilfred Smith and President Morgan,[4] and then in terms of yours and their reaction to it, we could mutually decide if there is any point in proceeding with the matter.

I would be very grateful if everybody would take this letter as confidential, above all for the following reasons: Mrs Henry Hicks is one of my wife's and my oldest friends. I would not like her to hear of this matter except from myself. If we were jointly proceeding with this and I came down to talk about it, I would like her to hear of the matter from my own lips rather than indirectly.

Tell James Doull that Gadamer[5] showed his wisdom in his great admiration for James.

Sincerely,
George Grant

1 A friend and classics professor at Dalhousie
2 Jonathan Edwards (1703–58), American Protestant theologian
3 Werner Heisenberg (1901–76), one of the most important physicists of the twentieth century. Famous for his 'uncertainty principle,' he formulated a variant of quantum physics known as matrix mechanics.
4 J.D. Morgan (1933–), philosopher and principal of King's College
5 Hans-Georg Gadamer (1900–), German philosopher. Gadamer had travelled to Halifax to meet Doull at Grant's suggestion and was impressed by Doull's great philosophic learning.

1975

210/ To Raleigh Parkin   19 February 1975

Dear Raleigh,

You must be very sad about Aunt Marjorie, but glad that her difficult times were at an end. I always remember her for being so sweet to Sheila when she first came to Canada and always very sweet to our children when they were in Toronto.

I wanted to write to you and Louise about 'the roll, the rise, the carol, the creation.'[1] It is part of an answer that Manley Hopkins wrote to Robert Bridges.[2] I consider Hopkins one of the supreme poets and always find it difficult that absurd political gentlemen have their pictures in Balliol Hall while this great product of Balliol does not. I know you were a friend of Bridges's son, as I knew his granddaughter and, therefore, the ambiguous relation between Bridges and Hopkins is of interest. Bridges at least kept in touch with Hopkins when the latter had gone to Ireland as a Jesuit,[3] but had the folly of patronizing greatness (an act much like Goethe's refusal to meet Hölderlin). Bridges was Hopkins's contact with the old world of established England. Hopkins sent him his last terrific black poems (e.g. 'No worst, there is none').[4] Bridges wrote patronizingly about them and Hopkins wrote back this little poem which includes the line I quoted. I always think of this incident in my teaching in case I ever meet a genius of the first order, I don't want not to recognize him. One of the most beautiful stories I think is when Haydn was just Mr Music for Europe and came across Mozart, really unknown, and said that this was genius which utterly transcended his own music.

Love to you both.

Ever,
George

1 Sweet fire the sire of muse, my soul needs this;
   I want the one rapture of an inspiration.
   O then if in my lagging lines you miss
   The roll, the rise, the carol, the creation,
   My winter world, that scarcely breathes that bliss
   Now, yields you, with some sighs, our explanation.
   Gerard Manley Hopkins (1844–89), 'To R.B.,' from *Gerard Manley Hopkins: A Selection of His Poems and Prose,* ed. W.H. Gardner (1953, 1961), 68

2 R.S. Bridges (1844–1930), a friend of Hopkins in their youth; later poet laureate

3 In 1884 Hopkins was appointed to the chair of classics at University College, Dublin, which was then managed and partly funded by the Society of Jesus.

4 No worst, there is none. Pitched past pitch of grief,
    More pangs will, schooled at forepangs, wilder wring.
    Comforter, where, where is your comforting?
    Mary, mother of us, where is your relief?
    My cries heave, herds-long; huddle in a main, a chief
    Woe, wórld-sorrow; on an áge-old anvil wince and sing –
    Then lull, then leave off. Fury had shrieked 'No ling-
    ering! Let me be fell: force I must be brief.
Gerard Manley Hopkins 'No worst, there is none,' from *Gerard Manley Hopkins*, 61

211 / To Simone Pétrement   3 April 1975

Chère Mlle Pétrement,
Je regrette de ne pas pouvoir écrire assez correctement en français.[1]

This letter expresses my deep gratitude for your volumes *La vie de Simone Weil*.[2] Many people in many times and places will owe you so much for undertaking that task and for carrying it out so beautifully. There was a great need for such a book and only you could have achieved it. But in this life what one is called upon to do, one so often lets slip away and, therefore, the great sense of gratitude that you did not let slip away that to which you were called. When in the preface you say so charmingly: 'J'ai mieux aimé, dans bien des cas, laisser à de plus sage que moi le soin et la possibilité de choisir l'essentiel,'[3] your irony is refuted in the volumes because through the details you do make shine in a wonderful way a vision of the essential. Your magnificently clear expositions of her teachings are exemplars of what such exposition should be in a biography. In reading your words together with those of Simone Weil I have never had so forcibly the sense of how beautifully guarded the French language is from that sentimentality which is the plague of modern English and even more of German. The beauty of your language is that it is stripped of all exaggeration and excess of imagination which can so harm descriptions of the great – particularly descriptions of a saint. It is this absence of moderation (in the full Platonic sense of the word) which I find so distasteful in the writings of Nietzsche and Heidegger – despite their genius. Because of the presence of that restraint in your writing, the glory of Simone Weil shines forth very clearly.

It would be a great kindness if you could put on a card a reference to where you have written concerning the Resurrection of Christ. I have followed all your recent writings on gnosticism[4] and have read all that Simone Weil wrote on the Resurrection. The reason I ask for this is that Simone Weil's account of Christianity appears to me true and yet I am unable to think together clearly that account with the Resurrection. I would be unable to put aside what is given us on this matter in the Gospels. Nevertheless I have little sympathy for the major interpretations of this doctrine in the West since Augustine. If you have not written on this subject I would be grateful if you could suggest some other writing which is basically in unity with Simone Weil's teaching on the Resurrection. On this matter (although not on others) I am held by what Luther writes, although taking it in a Platonic sense:

'He is not worthy to be called a theologian who sees the invisible things of God as understood through the things that are made.

But only he who understands the visible and further things of God through the sufferings and the Cross.

The theologian of glory says that evil is good and good evil; the theologian of the Cross says that the thing is as it is.' (Luther, *Werke*, Weimar edition, Vol. I, p. 354)

I make another point concerning Kant simply for the sake of interest and in no way to take away from the genius of Simone Weil or from the nobility of your book. Kant was the thinker who first explicitly made the autonomy of the will central to western moral philosophy. Such a doctrine is clearly denied in Plato and is not even present in Aristotle. Kant says directly that Greek philosophy fails because it does not understand the autonomy of the human will. Also I can see great contradictions between Simone Weil's account of society and Kant's. Kant is unflinchingly contractualist. As he writes in the first supplement to *Perpetual Peace*: 'The problem of organising a state, however hard it may seem, can be solved even for a race of devils, if only they are intelligent.' I have had to think through the basis of European contractualism and its baneful results because no societies have so suffered from it as ours in North America. Also if one takes into account Kant's continual references to his debt to Rousseau, it becomes clear that he is entangled in all that has harmed the modern world in the conception of 'history' and which Simone Weil has so wonderfully criticised. I take it as a fact that the origin of the concept of 'history' is first clearly expounded in its modern sense in the 2nd Discourse of Rousseau. Admittedly Kant is to be preferred to Hegel who carries this way of thinking further into that strange enquiry 'the philosophy of history.' Nevertheless, the seeds of Hegel are already in Kant. He has journeyed very far from Plato. Indeed *The Critique of Pure Reason* is dedicated to Francis Bacon and ends with a section entitled 'The history of pure reason.'

It is likely that you will have forgotten who it is who writes to you. About 12 years ago I came to see you at the Bibliothèque Nationale thanks to the kindness of Mme Weil.

Again let me express my gratitude for your beautiful volume.

Yours sincerely,
George Grant

1 I am sorry that I cannot write French accurately enough.

2 Simone Pétrement, *La Vie de Simone Weil. Avec des lettres et d'autres textes inédits de Simone Weil,* 2 vols (1973). Grant reviewed the English translation. See George Grant, 'Book review of *Simone Weil* by Simone Pétrement,' *Globe and Mail,* 12 February 1977, 12.

3 I would have preferred, in many instances, to leave to those wiser than I the opportunity to choose what was essential.

4 For a comprehensive statement of this position, see Simone Pétrement, *A Separate God: The Origins and Teachings of Gnosticism,* trans. Carol Harrison (1990), first published in French in 1984. It contains materials from some of her earlier articles. See also Simone Pétrement, *Le Dualisme dans l'histoire de la philosophie et des religions* (1946); *Le Dualisme chez Platon, les gnostiques et les manichéens* (1947).

212/ To Professor B. Meyer[1]   21 October 1975

I am sorry this is so late. Practicality has had me on the ropes this fall.

This is to request sabbatical leave for the year July 1, 1976 to June 30, 1977.

The following are my research plans:

The long term project I am engaged in has to do with the following question: How is it possible to think about good in a era when that conception has been put in darkness? In earlier books and in a book called 'Technology and good' (which is to be published next year) I have written out what I mean by technology, and how its development has put in darkness our understanding of good, particularly in the English-speaking world. It is important to insist that what I intend by the metaphor of darkness is not simply negative.

My intention is to spend the rest of my working life trying to think out and write down what it is possible to say about good at this time. This will be a long undertaking and not all the steps which appear to me necessary to that work need to be spelled out here. What I hope to accomplish towards it in the next year's leave is the following: to attempt to write down what can still be rationally maintained from the Platonic tradition concerning good, despite the objections that have been made against that teaching in our era. This will be centred around two subjects: (a) the detailed examination of Aristotle's criticism of Plato in the Ethics (book 1, ch. 6) and the attempt to state in the light of this the reasons why Plato's account of good seems preferable to Aristotle's (b) the examination of Heidegger's writing 'Plato's teaching concerning truth' and the attempt to state why this writing fails to come to grips with Plato's account of good.

Although both these writings will have to deal in detail with the particular words of Aristotle and Heidegger, and with certain words of Plato, it is intended that this exercise in the history of philosophy will move in each case towards speaking directly about the use of the language of good contemporaneously in the English-speaking world. It appears to me unlikely that I would get any further this year than this. If this is not the case, my next step will be to write a long piece on the relation between the Platonic tradition concerning good and the Christian religion, as that relation stands in this era.

As I plan to spend my time in Dundas, I will be able to look after the Ph.D. students under my supervision that year.

1 B. Meyer (1927–), chairman of the Department of Religion at McMaster

Professor Ed Sanders,[1] an important Pauline scholar and a colleague of Grant's at McMaster, had applied for a major grant from the Canada Council to pursue the historical biblical scholarship he favoured. Grant, who disliked Sanders for reasons both personal and professional, tried to block the grant, fearing that, were Sanders successful, the prestige and influence he acquired would transform the character of the Department of Religion at McMaster. Sanders was successful, and the results were as Grant had feared.

213/ To Frank Milligan   22 December 1975

Dear Mr Milligan,

I write concerning the application to the Canada Council for a program grant in Early Christianity and Judaism made by some members of the department of religion at McMaster.

My reasons for writing are that I am naturally concerned about the future of the department of religion and am very disturbed as to the effect of the success of the application on the future of the department. In the past, I have written to the Canada Council in support of the work of Professor Sanders, but now want to make clear that the earlier support should not be taken to imply support for this much larger application.

My concern over the Sanders-Meyer application turns on the issue of what a department of religion should be in a twentieth century university. Since this department was established, we have had much debate on its proper purposes. It is the conviction of a large majority in the department that it should basically be a place where students and faculty are asked to think about the great religious questions which face us in the modern age: we believe that this should be done within the context of all the great religions of the world and within the context of the openness proper to a modern university. To do that we have brought in the resources of sociology, philosophy, anthropology, history and literary studies. It seems to us that the response from the graduate and undergraduate students shows that we are on the right track.

A minority of the department who have made this application believe that the department should be a place primarily devoted to literary and historical studies and should be geared to produce highly concentrated specialists. In my language they consider the department should concentrate on 'museum culture' which they have learned in the United States. They detach this account of scholarship from any relation to the great issues of religion faced by modern human beings. The success of this application would be to move the department gradually in the direction of becoming an institute of historicist *Religionsgeschichte*. This would be a large academic loss. Our department has become a place to which many young Canadians have turned to seek an education in religion in a free setting and working with different types of scholarship. There are surely enough institutions producing 'museum' scholarship in North America without creating another one.

I am sure that, if the Canada Council gives such a large amount of money to the one side of the department, it will inevitably distort what the department will become in the future. This appears so for the following reasons. (1) As you know, university administrators are at the moment working under such financial stringency that they are unlikely to question on abstract grounds the receipt of a large sum in grants for a specific purpose, as in the case of Professors Sanders-Meyers' application. Our administrators will simply draw the conclusion from the approval of this application that this is the kind of department the Canada Council prefers and will therefore tend to give the same preference in spending of available university funds. (2) The people in support of the application are very single-minded in their conviction that the department should be dominated by their studies.

Three related points I would like to emphasize. (1) The issue at stake is not primarily a Canadian-American issue. Many of the Americans in our department see the issue as I have outlined it. That is also true of the European and Asians in the department. It is only a Canadian issue in the sense that the people who are making the application take it for granted that properly trained staff must inevitably come from the U.S.A. and that the purpose of the project is prestige in the U.S.A. In practice they have shown themselves singularly uninterested in Canadian students. (2) My appeal to you against this program has nothing to do with the part that our department plays in the East-West program grant application made by Brock University. The success or failure of that application will make little difference to the future of this department and therefore my letter is not written covertly in support of that application. (3) I may also mention that the chairmanship of our department rotates every three years among these areas of the department: the application was made when a member of the area concerned was chairman and for that reason the majority of the department's members are only now aware of the application and have not seen its details.

You know as well as anyone that dissention among academics is generally a silly and fruitless business. The issue here, however, is not simply a personal matter, but turns on the question of principle as to how departments of religion should develop. I have therefore written to you and Professor Penelum, because I am concerned about the relation of this application to that matter of principle.

If you think it would be useful to discuss this further, I would be grateful if you could telephone me.

Yours sincerely,
George Grant

1 E. Sanders (1937–), later professor of religion at Oxford and Duke

214/ To Burgon Bickersteth

Dear Burgon,
I wanted to answer right away your extremely interesting letter about
mental retardation and the Vaniers[1] and, as I have the flu, I am dictating
my answer.

I have enquired concerning the questions you raised and have discussed them with William [Grant]. Obviously, I am not an expert on
these matters, but what follows is the upshot of my enquiries.

Let me say first that the opinions which follow are by no means William's. He has just entered this activity and is watching and listening to
theories about it. He has just conveyed to me the opinions of other people. I think he would love to find out what is happening at L'Arche, particularly because he feels certain inadequacies in what is being done
locally. He, of course, has to be very careful, as he got into this at a very
low level, without any technical training, and simply has to listen to the
vast numbers of people higher up the hierarchy than himself. He works
for The Hamilton Association for the Mentally Retarded. This was an
organization first set up by parents of such children, but it is more and
more controlled by the government of Ontario, which provides the
money. In this pattern of organization, what generally happens is greater
and greater control by professional social workers, and such social workers have a very secular ideology.

From what I gather, the chief practical difference between these people
and the Vaniers' approach to the problem is that these people believe
that the mentally retarded should be directly fitted into the life of the city
and be thought of as no different from other people. This comes from a
great optimism about the life of our modern cities. Their view is that the
Vaniers, by providing communities in which the MRs live, keep the MRs
from blending into the ordinary life of the community. Of course, one
factual point on which this turns is the level of mental retardation
(because obviously people below a certain point have to be kept separate). But these people claim that a very large percentage of MRs can be
fitted back into the community and should not be kept separate.

Behind this practical difference, I think, lies a different view of human
nature. What these people criticize the Vaniers for is that the MRs are too
happy at L'Arche. The Vaniers provide the MRs with happiness and community, while their critics would say that the MRs need freedom, that is,
making free choices in the city. (I am trying to describe both positions
fairly, although, of course, I am entirely on the side of the Vaniers.) What

I heard from the social workers whom I asked was, over and over again, that the MRs were too happy at L'Arche.

Behind all this again, I have felt quite strongly that the suspicion of the Vaniers fundamentally arose from the secular social workers' dislike of Christianity. Secular people more and more in North America, have a contempt for Christianity, but that contempt becomes dislike when explicitly Christian people seem to be accomplishing something worthwhile in the world. There is a great wave in North America by liberal people to try to free all practical things from any connection with our Christian past, whether catholic or protestant. I am sure this comes into such peoples' feelings towards the Vaniers. Of course, this relates back to the view of the MRs as essentially individuals who are not much in need of communities. To repeat, I am not an expert in these matters and what I have said just reflects my impressions of the differences involved. It is really the difference between people who believe that the whole good will be achieved by organization of the secular state and these people should see very clearly that that is not enough. Let me repeat again, that William is quite outside such a controversy and just watching. Of course, Sheila and my greatest hope for him would be that he should see the truth of Christianity. But that is something that parents can do little about and one just waits and hopes.

If you see Mrs Hughs,[2] who was kind in providing us with tea, could you tell her that I rang up her sister, Mrs Hall,[3] who lives in Hamilton and that we had a very nice conversation. Mrs Hall was just in the process of moving; so we did not go to see her, but we will be in touch with her again and she was very glad of direct news of Mrs Hughs.

I will send you an account of the department of religion by another letter. Thank you again for the wonderful day, which meant so much to all five of us. I will write again by my own hand in the next week.

Ever,
George

1 Jean Vanier (1928–) established a home for handicapped men called L'Arche (Arc) in Trosly-Breuil, France, in 1964. The movement spread to Canada, the United States, and other countries.
2 Probably Burgon's housekeeper
3 Not identified

1976

215/ To Gerald Graham   17 January 1976

Dear Gerald,

Thank you for the very good card. It was so good to have. I had been
meaning to write for ages, but the vicissitudes of university and family life
seem to make each day a bother.

I hope all goes well with you both and with the children. It is such a
relief now that the 1960s are over in the sense that it is a less wild world
for youngsters. I hope it is the same in England. I hope that you have a
good place and time for writing. If I didn't so much like the comfortable
life, I would resign from the university and spend my time writing – but I
find that the desire for comfort grows each year and that keeps me at the
grindstone. By the way, you will be glad to hear that they have just named
the Arts Bldg here 'Chester New Hall.' McMaster owed him[1] much and
this was good.

The Conservatives are just in the midst of picking a new leader. I am
sorry that Stanfield was never PM as he was a very decent Whig – and that
is something these days. Who they will pick is unfathomable. I stay with
them because they may be dumb, but there is more decency among them
than the others.

We practically never go into Toronto and, therefore, do not see people
who would be mutual friends. I hate living with the nearly complete break
with one's past – but that seems the way of the world just now.

So often I think of how much I owe both you and Mary. What she did
for us at our wedding was unforgettable and all the goodness you showed
me over so many years is not forgotten. Sheila has been going to England
often to see her nanny who is 94 – but now that the children are older, I
will start coming too & I hope that it will be possible to meet.

Best love to you both from us both and thanks again for your note. I
hope 1976 will bring all the Grahams all the best of everything.

Ever,
George

1 Chester William New (1882–1960), Baptist clergyman and a popular history
teacher at McMaster until his retirement in 1951

216/ To John Robertson   McMaster University
31 March 1976

Dear John,
It is the work of a big human being to make the first step when a breach
has occurred. You may be sure I will not forget that you were the one who
made that first step.

We must inevitably both go on this Friday as we both deem best – but
you may be sure that I will not forget that it was you who were big enough
to make the first step.

Ever,
George G.

217/ To Arthur Motyer   11 June 1976

Dear Arthur:
You will be sick of hearing from me about the Wood lectures, but they are
now on their final draft and should be with you by the end of the summer
(d.v.). They have been delayed not only because I could not get them
straight, but also because we have had a difficult illness with a child and
that has taken up my mind. They are now the thing I have given more
thought to than anything I have ever written and I hope that appears in
them. They are also about 100 pages in length.

I do not know what Mount Allison will feel about publishing this, but
they are certainly, in my opinion, the deepest writing I have ever done
and I would like them to come out under the Mount Allison aegis. If this
be possible, I would then publish them with other writings in a book of
essays separately. But I would not do anything to prevent them first coming out where they belong.

I am sorry to take this so seriously, but they have been a large piece of
business and they say something I very much want to say.

My best to Mrs Motyer and as always, to yourself greetings.

Yours,
George Grant

218/ To Larry Schmidt[1]   30 June 1976

Dear Prof. Schmidt,
Just a note about Simone Weil because I thought I spoke unclearly the other day.

I agree with you that she sometimes spoke in a way which could be taken as the worst side of gnosticism. Nevertheless, when she is at the centre of Christianity, she speaks about it in a way which has illuminated it for me as no other modern writer. What I was trying to say is the things around the edges of her thought should not take one away from the beauty of the centre.

There have been many bad books written about her. The best, in my opinion, is by M. Veto, *La metaphysique religieuse de Simone Weil* (Paris, 1971).

I hope the summer goes well.

Yours sincerely,
George Grant

1 Larry Schmidt (1942–), professor of religious studies, Erindale College, University of Toronto

On 2 April 1977 Larry Schmidt organized a conference at Erindale College at the University of Toronto that included prepared papers and conversations with Grant. The conference led to the publication of the first book on Grant's thought, Larry Schmidt, ed., George Grant in Process: Essays and Conversations *(1978).*

219/ To Larry Schmidt   31 August 1976

Dear Prof. Schmidt,
I am sorry that I have not sent you, until now, a list of people for the symposium you are kindly planning. I put it off because I thought we were meeting in the first week of August, and because, as I hope you gathered from our meeting, I did not want to seem to be blowing my trumpet in this business. I don't know how long a list of people you are concerned with, but here is a tentative list under four headings, General, Theology and Philosophy, Politics, Critics. If this is not adequate do let me know. [A list of names and addresses follows.]

I hope you would understand that I would not like invitations to go to any of these people as if I had suggested their names because that puts pressure on old friends which may not suit them. If you want other names, I have a lot I can send you.

For quite other reasons, I have to say some rude things in public soon about the Canada Council and I do not want to do that until after they have accepted or refused your application for money for this. Could you let me know how the application is proceeding, as I do not want to complicate your efforts by the things that I have to do in public for perfectly valid reasons.

I am enclosing a bibliography and very shortly I am going to send along a long writing about English-speaking political liberalism which is the hardest thing I have yet written and might be of interest.

It is very good of you to take the interest in this and you know that I am grateful. I am away from the university this year.

I hope we meet soon.

Yours sincerely,
George Grant

220/ To Raleigh and Louise Parkin   3 November 1976

Dear Raleigh and Louise,
Thank you so much for sending us the introduction to the Parkin project.[1] It is extremely interesting and I intend, if ever I am in Ottawa (which must be sometime), to look carefully at the whole thing. It sounds so good and if it tells me as many new things as the introduction, it will be fascinating. I admire you so much getting it done, as I am so prone to delay and delay so nothing is ever completed. I quite agree with Smith that you should do more writing on your own life and activities. I agree with him that it should be on your public tapes, but I also hope it will include your comments on people. I have always thought you combined quite remarkably a great ability for friendship with an ability to stand back and look at people. When I was young you were so wonderfully good to me (of course I mean both of you) that I thought of you as friendship – but I have often seen you both observing with a clear eye. One of my earliest recollections is you both at the Liberal conference at Port Hope[2] and I think it would be interesting to read your account. But I think it would be also interesting to have the eye of the people concerned, such crazy old toots as King and Moley,[3] etc.

It is sad that we haven't been in Montreal. The last three years ... we have hardly been even to Toronto. I intend to make a jaunt to Montreal in the winter to just get away, but even that is provisional ...

The PQ victory certainly was a moment.[4] One finds oneself so contrarily disposed. On the one hand southern Ontario is becoming such a poor, dim, American imitation that one admires the French to want to be their own and their own in a fairly socialist direction; on the other hand one is sad for Canada as a whole. What an era it has been. I live in a great big multiversity, totally modelled on the great American universities, and what is so strange is how much the American model is the German model of research which had such dim consequences in their society. It is strange how much the German account of the modern wins in the West when they lost two wars. I have liked Lévesque and Claude Morin[5] so much when I met them and yet one feels that one just cannot contemplate the break up of Canada.

... our children flourish. Rachel is a nurse in Vancouver. William works with the retarded in Hamilton and has a daughter called Catharine. It is so nice having him close. Robert is in Kingston – unemployed and organising a left-wing mayoralty campaign. Katie is in NS but is coming home to live with Isabel. Katie is a dear and strangely a great beauty so her life of love is always moving. David is at home, 6 foot 4 and a great singer and actor ... I think it strange that Margaret Andrew who really believed in social reform should have produced intellectual children, while I who have been interested in contemplation should have produced a lot of social reformers.

It was good seeing Alison Ignatieff for a long period the other day, particularly as she passed on news of Elizabeth and Jane. Do give them our love when you write. It is so good having the Ignatieffs in Toronto. We don't see them often, but to get to know Allie after so many years is a joy, as she is a prize person.

With so much love and thanks for the introduction, and congratulations.

George

P.S. I will write ahead if I can get away to Montreal later and find out what times of day it would be good to come in and see you. I will be staying probably with clerical friends, so if I arrive with a darling French priest[6] from a CeeJep you would like him.

P.P.S. When I was a little boy A.C.P. [Lady Parkin, Raleigh's mother] taught me to put X for kisses and Os for hugs on my letter and I can't resist sending Louise an X & an O.

1 Raleigh Parkin spent much of his retirement collecting the documents which form the core of the Grant-Parkin Papers at the National Archives of Canada.

2 Organized by Vincent Massey in 1933. Massey was president of the Liberal party, and his home was just outside Port Hope. See *The Liberal Way: A Record of Opinion on Canadian Problems as Expressed and Discussed at the First Liberal Summer Conference, Port Hope, September 1933* (1933).

3 Raymond Moley (1886–1975), an adviser to Roosevelt who had resigned as assistant secretary of state to become editor of a new American national weekly, *To-day.*

4 The Parti Québécois, led by René Lévesque, won 41 per cent of the vote and 71 seats to defeat Robert Bourassa's Liberals. Their victory marked the first time an avowedly separatist party came to power in Quebec.

5 Claude Morin (1929–), university professor and PQ minister of intergovernmental affairs, 1976–82

6 Fr Jacques Langlais

221 / To Flora MacDonald, MP[1]   23 November 1976

Dear Flora,

Thank you very much for your generous letter. It was so good of you to take the time to write. All Queen's people must be glad that Kingston has you as its MP – truly worthy of a great institution.

I hope Mr Clark[2] is really getting sound advice on the Quebec situation. His statements so far have seemed very inadequate. I do not know the rights and wrongs of what happened about the Quebec organization. However, anybody with any knowledge of the past must be scared to see the name Meighen involved in Quebec questions. Mr Meighen's[3] grandfather[4] did more than anybody else to ruin Conservative hopes in that province for several generations. I think also that every Conservative should be thinking of the fact that Premier Johnson's[5] and Premier Bertrand's[6] sons are PQ MPPs and not UN MPPs. I write this as you are a supporter of Mr Stanfield and in the hope that his wise policies vis-à-vis Quebec are reaching Mr Clark's ears.

I am going to bother you someday soon with something I have written on the abortion question.[7]

Again, thank you for such a generous letter.

Yours,
George Grant

1 Flora MacDonald (1926–), MP for Kingston, 1972–88
2 Joe Clark (1939–), leader of the Progresive Conservative party, 1976–83; prime minister, 1979–80

3 Michael Meighen (1939–), national president of the Progressive Conservative
  party, 1974–7
4 Arthur Meighen (1874–1960), prime minister of Canada, 1920–2, 1926.
  Meighen's support for conscription during the First World War and his
  general pro-British political stance made him unpopular in the Province of
  Quebec.
5 Daniel Johnson (1915–1968), Union Nationale premier of Quebec, 1966–8.
  His son, Pierre-Marc Johnson, led the Parti Québécois from 1985 until 1987
  and was premier in 1985.
6 Jean-Jacques Bertrand (1916–73) succeeded Johnson as Union Nationale
  leader and premier until his defeat in 1970 at the hands of Robert Bourassa's
  Liberals.
7 Sheila Grant and George Grant, 'Abortion and Rights: The Value of Political
  Freedom,' in *The Right to Birth: Some Christian Views on Abortion,* ed. Eugene
  Fairweather and Ian Gentles (1976), 1–12

222/ To Dennis Lee   22 December 1976

Dear Dennis,
Herewith are the pieces.[1]
    On rereading them they seem to be negative and austere. I intend to
write an introduction in which the purpose of the negations is made plain
– namely that they exist to clear away the junk of the modern era and to
say how difficult it is to make positive affirmations. I hope the introduction will make clear that these essays are really an attempt in the old manner of negative theology. I also hope to make clear in the introduction
that in no sense do I imply a return to the ancients as any kind of anti-
quarianism.
    The title of a positive book worries me. I am not sure I like the title
'Technology and Good.' Somebody suggested the title 'Oblivion of Eternity.' I think it is too flashy and clever.
    There will obviously have to be changes made where I have clearly pub-
lished these for an earlier occasion, but that is easy. I can do that in a
minute.
    It is enormously good of you to look at these and to advise me. I hope
they do not seem too barren. I enclose a tentative list of order for the
pieces. Clearly 'English-Speaking Justice'[2] is the centre and, therefore, I
have put it at the centre.

                                                        Yours,
                                                        George

1 No book was published until *Technology and Justice* in 1986.

2 George Grant, *English-Speaking Justice* (1974)

1977

223/ To Derek Bedson

Dear Derek,

Just a note to say how much S and I loved the beautiful photograph. By coincidence it was most apt – because this year I have been pondering 'creation' more than anything else – indeed for the first time in my life I began to see a bit into what it meant. So it is lovely to look at that beautiful image on our mantelpiece.

This is not a proper letter because it is a driven time of year. I become more and more an old body carting myself around from place to place with less and less spontaneity.

The Anglican Church 'task force' report[1] on abortion fills me with utter disgust and indeed *contempt.* I hope contempt without pride. But its synopsis in the church paper was truly revolting. I couldn't become a Roman [Catholic] – but oh would that one could.

I hope all goes well and that you are not too pressed that you have time for some rewarding moments.

Sheila sends her love.

Again thanks for such a lovely thing to look at.

Ever, George

P.S. I have never written about the documents about R.C.-Anglican relations – because they spoke for themselves.

1 Task Force on Human Life, *Abortion: An Issue for Conscience*, ed. Phyllis Creighton (1974)

1978

224/ To Derek Bedson   2 February 1978

Dear Derek,

Since Christmas I have wanted to write to you to say something which I was too reserved to say at that time. The letter has been delayed as I was given a piece of work to do at McMaster which I couldn't not do.

What it is about is my fear of leaving the Anglican Church despite its follies and disloyalties. What I have to say is I am sure very inconclusive and is meant in no way as having any relation to your vision and action, which I am sure comes out of a much deeper partaking in the life of the Church than I am capable. My comments are only about myself and I only bother you with them because we have been friends for so long.

Practical considerations

Of our six children, Katie and David strongly take part in Anglican worship. Rachel and Robert are vague and sporadic. William and Isabel have no connection. I do not want to do anything that will cut us off from this local parish, which is the only connection that they make with ordinary Christianity when they are at home. They all inhabit a world where their friends and their education secularize them daily and, if we were cut off from our local church, I think they would simply drop away from any connection with organized worship, let alone the eucharist.

Deeper considerations

It seems to me the case that western Christianity is now going to go through a great purging of its authority because it was in the civilization where it was dominant that the worst form of secularity has arisen and is now likely to become worldwide. Both Roman Catholicism and Protestantism are going to pay terrible prices, both extrinsic and intrinsic, for the ultimate relation they maintained with that progressive materialism. This kind of historical remark has no relation at all to the truth of Christianity which is just given for me in the perfection of Christ, which to me can only be thought in terms of Trinitarianism (though through my own unclarity I never much understand what is meant by the third hypostasis). My particular function in the midst of what seems to me the evident fall of western Christianity is to try to understand just a small amount of what was at fault in this particular manifestation of Christianity, so that one plays a minute part in something that will take centuries – namely the rediscovery of authoritative Christianity. I have no doubt that that will, slowly and through very great suffering, occur – because Christianity tells the truth about the most important matter – namely the perfection of God and the affliction of human beings, and it has been given that truth in a way no other religion has.

It may be that what I am saying is that practical people,[1] in the name of clear principles, may have to break with the visible church in certain of its manifestations, e.g. the present Anglican Church – but that I do not see myself called to these particular tasks – but rather to more theoretical tasks. I do not say that any task is more important than any other. I do know that the highest task will be performed by the saints and the suffering that will fall on them, and I know with perfect clarity that I am not one of these saints.

This is a poorly phrased and incomplete statement of what I wanted to say, but it is the best I am capable of.

We are involved in certain church immediacies at the moment because our local church, St James's, which you know has been almost completely destroyed by fire just the other day. They don't know whether it was arson – but they think that it might be because there has been a lot of it in Dundas recently, including one of the new houses right next to us in the field.

A few months ago you mentioned that it might be possible to help David get a job in northern Manitoba. This may be out of the question because of changed circumstances. If it were possible, we would be very grateful – but quite understand it may not be. David is of quite a different order of responsibility than Robert when he was so foolish.

Life goes on for us pretty well ...

I say nothing about the Canadian political scene – because words fail me about Trudeau.

I hope the new government[2] has overall simplified your life and that day-to-day existence is pleasant. Love to Ian.

Ever,
George

1 As Bedson himself did
2 Sterling Lyon (1927–) was Progressive Conservative premier of Manitoba 1977–81.

225/ To Dr Harley S. Smyth[1]   24 February 1978

Dear Dr Smyth,
Your letter of last autumn has been in my mind a great deal and my answer has been slow because I have been thinking about it. I was so surprised and honoured to see you at that lecture last autumn that I didn't answer your question at all well.

Obviously, I agree with you about the centrality of creation. On a secondary point, I was very grateful for the particular reference to St Paul. As a modern, I have been late in coming to think about Paul and his greatness, because I was led to Christianity by the Johannine tradition. I have been thinking about Paul a great deal recently, and am very grateful for your reference.

It seems to me that the difficulty about the creation is not the recognition of its truth, but our ability to communicate that truth in the light of the fact that such barriers are put in the way of its understanding by two facts about modernity. The two facts are: a) the prestige of modern science which claims that it can explain everything outside any relation to final cause. b) More important as a barrier to the communication of creation seems to me the simply false account of freedom that is at the heart of modern liberalism. That is the account of freedom as autonomy which, above all, comes from Kant. The traditional world believed in freedom, but never freedom as autonomy. The omnipresent belief in freedom as autonomy simply cuts people off from knowing their dependence upon God, which seems to me the heart of the doctrine of creation. The modern accounts of freedom seem to me patently false and have to be shown to be so.

I hope all goes well with you and yours. I find university life getting tougher and tougher as they become less human places.

Again, thanks for your letter, which made me think about the issue very deeply.

Yours ever,
George Grant

1 H.S. Smyth (1939–), Toronto neurosurgeon, active in the right-to-life movement

226/ To Derek Bedson   26 February 1978

Dear Derek,
I agree *of course* with what you say in your letter that Christ's proclamation is supernatural. If it is not that, it is nothing. (parenthesis: a nice, decent, ... but solid student of mine went to teach Xian ethics at Boston College, a Jesuit place, and he came back to tell me that the dominant Jesuit strain in the college is that the purpose of the Jesuit order is now to help the victory of a humane marxism in the world. He had got the job through an old Aristotelian Jesuit. Can you believe it?) But I believe that, except for the saints who may reach the supernatural directly, most people have to glimpse the supernatural through the natural. And I find with greater and greater clarity that the concept of the natural even in our educational, economic, political and scientific systems is of a kind that excludes

the supernatural from the minds of those who are in these systems. Therefore, when you say (which I entirely agree with) that I should tell the children that Christianity is supernatural, my difficulty is simply the means of communication because the language of the supernatural has been so killed in the public realm. I am sure that there is an enormous hunger for the supernatural in the young, but it is denied by the broad outlines of the public world they inhabit. To say this may be no more than an excuse for what I feel has been my failure in teaching these children about the supernatural – but I say it because I think it is a common experience for many in this era.

It must be sad to face one of your own generation going. It is something that has not happened with me. I am glad that you are not responsible financially for your sister-in-law.

For a moment, I saw you on the TV at the conference of 1st ministers. It was strange to think of you there. One should be ready for the fact that after so many years the Liberal party is so slick and sleazy – but I am unable sufficiently to remove myself not to be angered. Nevertheless I think he [Trudeau] will probably win again.

It was very good of you to write to David. It is not the making of money that he wants, but the ability to get away to new experience.

I was out in Calgary last week and saw Byfield's son. I met him unfortunately at the end of a long period of performance – but was very taken with him. The Bishop of Calgary seems much better than most of his colleagues.

This letter is a badly written appeal – to which *no answer* is required. I feel very broken off from all my past and you are about my only link with a Canadian past. Therefore, the appeal is that we continue in friendship. I know you will perhaps think the appeal unnecessary, but it comes out of a sense of isolation from the past and a fear of that isolation.

Ever,
George

227/ To Marshall McLuhan[1]   19 April 1978

Dear Dr McLuhan,

As I have a great admiration for you, I did not want you to hear my reasons for not coming to the conference on Innis second-hand.[2] I, therefore, send you a copy of my letter to Mr Wood.

Let me say how much I admire what you have said recently about abortion and about child pornography. So many people who become well-known cease to speak on what may be an unpopular side. I very greatly admire the fact that you have not ceased to speak.

Sincerely,
George Grant

1 Marshall McLuhan (1911–81), professor of English at St Michael's College, University of Toronto, and communications theorist
2 'Culture, Technology and the Innis Tradition,' to be held at Innis College, with Eric Havelock and Marshall McLuhan as the speakers

228/ To Dennis Duffy   26 June 1978

Dear Dennis,
Thank you very much for your nice note about a book of mine.[1] It was so good of you to write, particularly as the book had not been reviewed &, therefore, it is good to get a response from somebody & particularly from somebody one respects.
   Private I was sorry that we had such a chancy meeting at my sister's last year. I have been very wary about anything to do with Trinity because my sister is my sister and yet there is at almost every point in our lives a great gulf. Our lives have taken such different directions and to such different ways of looking. This made me very nervous meeting you in her house. I just hate family differences. When they [the Ignatieffs] leave Trinity, I hope to have a less neurotic vision of Toronto.
   Again thanks for your letter.

Ever,
George

P.S. Please send me copies of your writings.

1 Grant's *English-Speaking Justice* was dated 1974, but did not actually appear until 1978.

229/ To Wilfred Smith[1]   7 December 1978

Dear Wilfred,
Belief and History[2] has required an answer for a long time, but I was determined not to write until I had read it properly and not just with the end

of my mind. Although there are many things in it of which I have no right to judge, I think I have the right to make the judgment that it is brilliantly successful. I think this is the biggest thing you have written, not in the sense that it covers as wide a field as other things of yours, but because the central thesis lays before one the looking forward to the detailed work of the longer volume, and the thesis itself appears to me central to understanding the most important matters. You can imagine that Chap. 2 particularly held me because it swept away so much of the nonsense which makes us oblivious of eternity. But obviously the negative job is only a prolegomena to the positive one of the third chapter and what lies beyond it. Apart from the like of the central thesis, at a lower level I am always in admiration of your enormous knowledge of the detail. But of course, the details are only important in the light of the central thought about them.

I had only a minor detail to question and that detail in no way affects the thesis. On page 62 you say that Hobbes 'certainly presupposed that the article was true.' I take for granted that Hobbes was an atheist. This is a minor point because it does not affect the thesis, which I take to be of very great significance.

Sheila and I go on pretty well. Love to Muriel and for you both and for the family our best for Christmas and 1978.

Ever,
George Grant

P.S. I met Ravindra[3] in San Francisco and liked him.

1 Professor of religion, Dalhousie University
2 W.C. Smith (1916–), *Belief and History* (1977), the Richard Lectures, University of Virginia, 1974–5
3 The head of the Department of Religion at Dalhousie when Grant returned there in 1980

1979

The University of Toronto offered Grant an honorary degree. He accepted it to increase his prestige at McMaster and help in local departmental political manoeuvring. His sister Charity, who felt that she had been badly treated by the University of Toronto, accused him of disloyalty in accepting the degree.

230/ To Charity Grant   7 May 1979

Dear Charity,
Thank you for your note.
   I cannot tell you why the U of T is giving me a degree. I can tell you why
I am accepting it. I am under mounting hostility from the powers that be
at McMaster and to defend myself I accept an honour that impresses
them and, therefore, lightens their pressure ... my first obligation must be
to go on saving money. In such a situation, I have to defend myself vis-à-vis
the people who pay my salary.
   We will see you and Alison and George at Mrs Gordon's.[1] Rachel, who
is coming down to see Isabel next week, may come along too. In the
meantime, my best to Alison and George, if they are with you.

                                                          Yours,
                                                          George

1 Walter Gordon's widow

231/ To Richard Doyle[1]   15 May 1979

Dear Mr Doyle,
   At our last meeting you said you would allow me to write for the *Globe*. I
have, therefore, sent this letter to the editor directly to you because there
would be no point in publishing it after the election.[2]

                                                          Sincerely,
                                                          George Grant

1 R.J. Doyle (1923–), editor-in-chief, *Globe and Mail*; now a senator
2 Federal general election, 22 May 1979

[attached:]

Dear Sir,[1]
This is to express my disagreement with Mr Geoffrey Stevens's account of
the debate between Mr Clark and Mr Trudeau.[2] He says that Mr Clark let
Mr Trudeau get the better of him.
   Mr Trudeau has consistently used the politics of confrontation and
contempt against anybody who opposed him and that has done great
harm to this country in the last decade. It has been repugnant to hear Mr

Trudeau treat such men as Mr Douglas and Mr Stanfield and Mr Ryan with shallow contempt over the years. One of the difficult truths about politics is that one cannot fight such means by employing the same means. Mr Clark was surely right not to respond when Mr Trudeau tried to talk him down contemptuously. He was surely right to go on trying to make substantive points.

Journalists sometimes may seem to have a vested interest in the politics of confrontation and theatre. However, these are dangerous instruments to employ in a country such as ours. Mr Clark was wise to eschew them in this debate.

Your sincerely,
George Grant

1 Not published
2 Geoffrey Stevens, 'Joe Clark Survived in Debate,' *Globe and Mail*, 15 May 1979, 6

232/ To Mary Ann and Dennis Duffy   29 June 1979

Dear Mary Ann & Dennis,
Sheila and I were so grateful for your wonderful sweetness to us a week ago. You gave us a lovely day and thanks to you both it was a day which was an enjoyment and not a trial as so many public occasions are.

Also thank you Dennis for your initiative in getting me the degree. I am very grateful because it came at a time when I am rather under attack by the administration at McMaster. The words you introduced me with at the convocation were very well composed and much too generous, but I was grateful for them.

It was so good to hear about Innis.[1] HAI[2] would have been so glad that a person was appointed who combines intellect and practical wisdom. He was a person who had to break with the narrowness of the particular Baptist tradition of his youth, but was in his last works so clearly coming back to a participation in the eternal – a remarkable event for one of his generation, the difficulty of which is visible the more one sees the Protestant tradition. I am sure you will do the job just [brilliantly].

Sheila and I were & are so grateful for your friendship. We have both been struck down by a sense of guilt and failure by the last years ... In my case, it has taught me how shallow and uncertain is my partaking in Christ.

Best to both your wonderful daughters. Thank you both for your sweetness to us; we are very grateful.

Ever,
George

P.S. I am so confused that I do not remember whether there are one or two 'f's in Dufy – Duffy – but must send the letter

1 Dennis Duffy was principal of Innis College, University of Toronto, 1979–84.
2 Harold Adams Innis (1894–1952), Canadian economist, economic historian, and communication theorist; chairman of the political economy department at the University of Toronto, 1935–52

Ed Sanders's growing influence at McMaster confirmed Grant's fears that McMaster was becoming a research-oriented university, much like the other major universities in North America. He finally yielded to the entreaties of his friends at Dalhousie to return.

233/ To John and Nita Graham   23 July 1979

Dear John
and Nita – although a mixture of business and gratitude.
   You said last week that there was a chance of a job for me at Dalhousie. Sheila and I have now thought and think it would be wonderful. We would very much both like to be at Dalhousie, so that if there is any chance that I was offered a job, we would be very happy.
   We are both grateful to you for having suggested it and for saying that you would mention it to whomever is appropriate. For the last year, S. & I have been discussing living in NS when we could afford to retire, but had delayed because necessity made it five years away. It was so good of you to bring up this opportunity and we are very excited. We, of course, both understand that it is nothing to your part if they do not offer us a job, but will be grateful if you would mention it in the appropriate place.
   You were so good to me in Halifax last week. I do not understand why I deserve both your friendships, but I am so grateful for them. It was a particular help last week, for although I like and respect Vincent,[1] I am scared by the business of filming and it was wonderfully nice of you both to give so much of your time to seeing me.
   ...
   Anna and Andrew and James looked so beautifully radiant.

Love & so much thanks to you both for so much.

George

P.S. The post being what it is, would you drop me just a line to say this has arrived.

1 Vincent M. Tovell (1922–); his documentary on the life and thought of Grant, *The Owl and the Dynamo*, was broadcast by the CBC on 13 February 1980.

234/ To John Graham   31 August 1979

Dear John,

I write to ask whether you think it wise to mention to Jim,[1] when I write, that there is a possibility that I might be at Dalhousie. I feel hypocritical not mentioning it &, therefore, have not written. Yet, on the other hand, silence is always golden in uncertain situations.

I have not expected to hear anything from Dalhousie till the term is underway, but the whole thought of the possibility makes us happier & happier. I have less and less sympathy for life in southwestern Ontario. The decay of middle class decency is so fast here (I do not mean merely its sexual manifestations). This is indeed going to be a great difficulty for governments, either Liberal or Conservative, because the swing either way will put governments in or out. I feel this will be confounded by the swing of power to the West, which will make southern Ontario very volatile in its uncertainty. The call of my mother as home brought me back here, but I will be very glad if I can get away and am enormously grateful to you & Nita for putting even the possibility in my way. If we come, Sheila will depend greatly on Nita's friendship, as I will on yours also. I hope that will not be a burden.

I hope the summer has been good for you both & for the children ... We live from day to day.

Love to all.

Ever,
George

1 J.H. Aitchison (1908–94) taught political sciences at Dalhousie from 1947 until 1973, and was the first leader of the Nova Scotia NDP. He became one of Grant's closest friends.

235/ To John and Nita Graham   8 December 1979

Dear Nita & John,
This is a late note to thank you both for all your goodness last weekend.
You were both very dear to take such care. It was particularly great to end
the days talking to you two & James [Doull], because I was completely
confused by the time I reached you and needed to regain sanity.

It was an added blessing to see James properly for the first time in
years in such a setting. (I am always completely grateful to you Nita for
having pointed out to James that I was far from hating him – essentially
the cause of the difficulty was my proud fright, frightened of seeming a
fool, and my reaction to fright is always indirection & retreat – so foolish.) But I felt such a sense of how many things I wanted to talk about.
Except for the Indians, I am so sick of the absence of any philosophic
context to the scholarship at McMaster, most of them products of the
Ivy League.

Sheila and I are both set on coming if we get an offer, although one
may have to bargain a bit. There are some difficulties about leaving David
here if Isabel stays ..., but I think she will come with us probably.

It was so good to see you and S & I are both so grateful to you for all the
pains you have taken on our behalf.

Ever,
George

P.S. I include in the pains the vulgarity of what Hicks said to you in the
lecture I gave. I was so self-engrossed the evening at your place that I did
not get the full import of that vulgarity.

1980

236/ To John and Nita Graham   28 January 1980

Dear Nita and John,
This is just a note to say thank you for your part in getting me a job at Dalhousie. Dean Gray phoned me offering me a job and said the letter will
follow. S & I are so unthinking about things that I am particularly grateful
for you both suggesting it, because when you did I just saw how good for
us it would be.

Somebody sent me the article by Gauthier about myself[1] & your very nice letter. It was so good of you to take the time, Nita, and although I am not the person to judge the justice of your letter, it said something very nice about me.

Again thanks to you both.

Ever,
George

1 David Gauthier, 'Congratulations rather than confrontation,' *CAUT Bulletin* (October 1979)

Grant's resignation from McMaster, unlike his earlier resignation from York University, was attended by considerable controversy. Grant attempted to clarify what he meant by 'research' in his article 'The Battle between Teaching and Research,' Globe and Mail, *23 August 1980, 7.*

237/ To R.C. McIvor[1]   14 March 1980

Dear Dean McIvor,
This is just to say that I am resigning from McMaster as from the end of this academic year.

My reason for doing so is that for the last decade the Arts Departments have been developed in the light of a principle which can only lead to their increasing sterility. The dominance of 'research' is an appropriate principle for those parts of the university concerned with the progressive sciences. This principle cannot produce an account of knowledge adequate to an Arts Faculty. As there is no evidence that this principle is going to cease to be dominant, I am going to a university more open to a broader meaning of the term.

Let me express my admiration for yourself.

Yours sincerely,
George Grant

1 R.C. McIvor (1915–), dean, Faculty of Social Science, McMaster University

238/ To Charity Grant   6 August 1980

Dear Charity,
Just a note of greetings before we leave for NS.

I regret very much that our friendship has fallen apart over the last years. I hope that sometime in the future we may be able to meet under happy circumstances.

In the meantime, I hope that the world goes well for you in the next years.

Yours ever,
George

Dalhousie: Unhappy Return 1980–4

239/ To Alex Colville

Dear Alex,

It was so good of you and Rhoda to come to see us. It was extremely generous of you to bring us such a very beautiful present.[1] We have looked and looked at it and see more and more how beautiful it is. It simply takes my breath away to think what it must be to be able to make something of that beauty.

Life produces enough sadness on its own without cultivating it and there is something in the tradition which a dying Protestantism inherited which pushes in a foolish tendency to cultivate suffering. Sheila and I are determined to live here in 'jouissance' and the beauty of your generous present will continue to be a daily reminder of how good it is to be here.

Dalhousie seems a greatly expanded chaos, but some bright young people in classes makes it clearer what I am thinking about in a way that pulls one together.

Sheila also sends thanks for your coming to see us and the generosity and thought of what you brought with you. Will you thank Rhoda for us both.

Ever,
George

1 Colville, touched by Grant's dedication of *English-Speaking Justice* to him, gave him an artist's proof of his serigraph *Blue Heron*.

1981

Joan O'Donovan[1] wrote the first Ph.D. thesis on Grant, at St Michael's College, University of Toronto. University of Toronto Press published her thesis in 1984 under the title George Grant and the Twilight of Justice.

240/ To Joan O'Donovan   4 January 1981

Dear Mrs O'Donovan,

Your thesis is excellent. I am lucky that a person of your intelligence and clarity should have paid such attention to the confusion and bityness of my writing as to show so well what I was intending in various writings. You are immensely generous to my efforts and I am very honoured that a person of your calibre should have used her mind to look at my writing. As you will know, it is extremely difficult for me to read about my own efforts and it is for that reason that I am so late in writing to you. I wanted to read your work when I was free from the demands that everyday seems to bring and have a couple of days to give my complete attention to it. It was very rewarding to me to read your thesis because, as always, I am trying to get ready to write something (on Rousseau) and your writing helped me greatly to look at my own thoughts & see their contradictions more clearly.

As to the last passages in your thesis, they make me wish that I was not here and that we could spend much time discussing what is at stake. You are, of course, quite right that Simone Weil has a much greater authority for me than Strauss. Strauss has just enabled me to see what is involved in modern political philosophy and the means of rejecting it. SW seems to me at the highest level of illumination. Yet it leads to a life I am just not capable of living. But what she has convinced me of is the repugnance one must feel for certain emphases in the O.T., namely the *exclusivity* in Judaism. Yet clearly because of the events in Europe 1933-45, one just must not speak against Judaism, because it would encourage the secular gutter. The whole question of how one sorts out what was good & what bad in gnosticism is difficult: I am mightily convinced by Simone Pétrement,[2] but the whole matter is difficult.

The one point I think you should change in your thesis is the translation of Augustine's phrase *civitas terrena* as city of man. It is indeed very hard to get just the right words with clear modern import for the phrase, 'worldly city' is better, but not enough. City of man as compared with City of God leaves for me the implication men do not find themselves in the City of God.

You have hit very clearly & rightly the point that I do not understand what is meant by the fall. I have tried & tried & failed. I hate the Rousseauesque 'the fall upwards' of the liberals.

I think in the early paper on 'Two Theological Languages' [1953][3] I confused 'the authentic freedom' of the existentialists with Biblical freedom. Whether Biblical freedom can be made one with 'the liberty of indifference' which is the extent of freedom in Plato, I cannot at this point tell. One thing I am sure about is that the extreme division between eros & agape propounded by Bishop Nygren[4] & in a subtle way by C.S. Lewis,[5] does not do.

Your thesis very much clarified my thoughts & I will write you again about it when my head is clearer. In the meantime, this letter is just to say how good I considered it & how honoured I am that you should have taken such beautiful care to write it. My best to your husband.

Ever,
George Grant

1 J.E. O'Donovan (1950–). She and her husband, Oliver, lecture in theology at Oxford.
2 See Letter 211.
3 See George Grant, 'Two Theological Languages,' with 'Addendum' (written June 1988), in *Two Theological Languages by George Grant and Other Essays in Honour of His Work*, ed. Wayne Whillier (1990), 6–19.
4 Bishop Anders Nygren (1890–1978), *Agape and Eros*, trans. P.S. Watson (1953)
5 C.S. Lewis, *The Four Loves* (1960)

Grant discovered Céline's Second World War trilogy, Castle to Castle, North, *and* Rigadoon, *in 1979. The work immediately captivated him, and he began work on a book about the controversial French author, which was never finished.*

241 / To William Christian   7 January 1981

Dear William,

Yes, Céline is a mystery, just to me in the same way that Heidegger is a mystery. Both so great & yet both tied to the criminality of National Socialism. When Céline says 'Europe died at Stalingrad,' well, I am quite willing for Europe to die if it is at Stalingrad under these auspices. But nevertheless they both see so much. I am even willing to agree with them that there are bad sides to the influence of modern secularised Judaism over the West, but the idea that that can be met by extermination or persecution just puts them out of court. Indeed I think the sheer barrenness of the era is seen in the fact that this great artist & great philosopher should be driven at their heights to unspeakable political solutions. However banal [U.S. president Ronald] Reagan may be, one can live in that political ambience. Yet the mystery remains, namely, as it is imperative that we think about what our societies have become, is it necessary in that thought to have everything broken for one, so that one opts in action for such terrible extremities, or else is one just moved into impotence outside the world?

I quite agree with you about the constitutional proposals. My friend, Doull, here is so engrossed about them that he has dropped all else. It is going to be hard for Canadian C(c)onservatives in Ontario because the basis of Trudeau's package[1] seems to be to say to central Canada: 'You have the votes & if you have the votes I will give you continued cheaper driving.'[2] But it may just break the country.

It is good to be back in Halifax, less good at Dalhousie. It is a chaotic mess as a university. The political science department is pretty foolish, I think. There is no core of sense in the Arts & Science faculty. I just retreat and get on with writing and quite pleasant teaching.

Sheila has been up with our daughter for Xmas & I had a pleasant holiday here with older children. It is inevitable, I suppose, that two emotional absolutists like Sheila and myself should produce children who take romantic love so seriously, but I find it difficult. I am going to teach Plato's *Symposium* in the next weeks and want to try to reformulate what is given in 'the erotic.'

Give my best to Julie[3] when you see her. I hope she is going on with her studies.

My very best to Barbara and the children. Whatever else you or I may have done foolishly, we chose wisely in marriage.

Ever,
George

P.S. A poor and inadequate letter it brings much sense of wishing we could talk. I am engrossed in trying to understand Rousseau's 2nd Discourse.[4]

1 Pierre Trudeau proposed to repatriate the Canadian constitution and add a charter of rights and freedoms. It came into force in 1982.
2 Reference to the tax on gasoline proposed by the Conservatives in their 1979 budget

3 Julie Beatty (1948–) attended Grant's seminar on Plato at McMaster. Through her, he met her husband, Conservative MP Perrin Beatty (1950–): Conservative MP, 1972–93; cabinet minister, 1979–80, 1984–93.

4 Jean-Jacques Rousseau, *A Discourse on the Origin of Inequality* (1755)

242/ To Joan O'Donovan   25 January 1981

Dear Mrs O'Donovan,
I am slow in answering your letter because it went to the philosophy department & they put 'unknown' on it. I hope by this time you have received a letter about your thesis which I wrote before your letter. I have no secretarial help at Dalhousie & so you must put up with my scrawl & if there are complicated points we might speak on the phone.

It is good news to hear that your thesis is going to be published. I am only surprised that as bewildered a thinker as myself could interest many others, but I am glad that it is in your hands which are so firm and competent. I read your thesis at a time of distress for us &, therefore, will read it again & make comments particularly in the light of your generous last paragraph.

Now, your particular questions.

Kojève.[1] It was not Kojève, but James Doull at this university, who taught me Hegel (as I say in a piece in Schmidt's book). It was through Strauss that I came upon Kojève.[2] Let me say that I think Doull knows more about Strauss than Kojève (not having written much, Doull is only known to his friends). It was to escape Hegel I found Strauss & through Strauss I found Kojève.

Let me say also that, although my debt to Strauss is great as a teacher of what makes up modernity, Simone Weil is the being whose thought is to me the enrapturing. It is indeed true that I am scared of her, because the unequivocal saints are scaring to somebody like myself who loves comfortable self-preservation, but nevertheless her thought is, next to the Gospels the highest authority for me. Quite a different level of authority from Strauss. I can imagine being capable of writing something as perceptive & lucid as Strauss, but I cannot imagine loving God & being possessed by Christ as SW was. That is why I write of the same questions as Strauss and do not write of SW because she was divinely inspired and one can only approach that with fearful hesitation. She can be wrong about little scholarly details in a way that Strauss would not be, but on the greatest matters in the last years, she is writing out of the extraordinary event of being possessed by the second person (??) of the Trinity. If I can ever become a quite different person, I might be able to write something about her, other than just pointing to her writings.

By the way, as your writing is about 'history,' I should tell you that D.V. I am going to write a piece – a long one – called 'History and Justice,'[3] which is to go into a book called 'Technology and Justice,' which I hope to publish next year. The piece on 'history' will be about Rousseau who I now see as as great a founder of modernity as Nietzsche. I think I have at last seen with some clarity something I have never seen before as to what modern people mean by 'history.'

Because I have no help in the office, my papers are not sorted & I do not have the dates of the pieces in the Globe. Save this in April-May last year, there was in the *G & M* (a) a report by a reporter[4] (b) an editorial[5] (c) most important for my reasons, a piece by myself on the editorial page which quite expressed my opinion.[6] If & when I get my papers sorted, I will send you the date of my piece & you can go from there.

... Parenthood & one's failures are a gripping business.

Thanks again for bothering with my inadequate writings.

Best to your husband.

Ever,
George Grant

1 Alexandre Kojève (1902–68), author of *Introduction à la lecture de Hegel* (1947)
2 Leo Strauss, *What Is Political Philosophy and Other Essays* (1959)
3 Not finished
4 Kevin Marron, 'Research First, Students Second, McMaster Professor Complains,' *Globe and Mail,* 12 April 1980, 4
5 'The Bothersome Students,' *Globe and Mail,* 15 April 1980, 6
6 George Grant, 'The Battle between Teaching and Research,' *Globe and Mail,* 28 April 1980, 7

243/ To William Christian   17 March 1981

Dear William,

Nothing you could have sent would have been more what I need [i.e., a French version of Rousseau's Second Discourse], because I am just going to start my first big writing for many years & it is going to be about the 2nd Discourse & I knew I had to go to the library & check Cole's translation[1] with the French; so, many thanks.

I am sad that the PC meeting was a fiasco. There is such anger against Trudeau's proposals here as an outright attack on federalism just as NS &

Newfoundland are getting going. It has forced a weak man such as Buchanan[2] to be against them. Therefore, they should be increasing chances for the PCs here. I hope Perrin Beatty is thinking clearly about what should happen to the leadership matter.[3] Trudeau is such a slick demagogue & the willingness of Ontario to trust him often so much, Canada must now pay the price for (a bad sentence).

I don't think there is a chance for the student you mentioned here, because of departmental autonomy. The political science department would require all kinds of details from him. Doull & I are teaching Aristotle's *De Anima*[4] together next year which is far from politics. (Doull at 63 has just got married again to a dear teacher of philosophy from Memorial.[5] He is very dearly and sweetly full of romanticism & the constitution.)

All has gone well for us here altogether. Sheila broke her leg, but otherwise it is good.

All love to Barbara and to Mrs Beatty and to the children. Thanks again.

Ever,
George

1 Jean-Jacques Rousseau, *The Social Contract and the Discourses*, trans. with an introduction by G.D.H. Cole (1913)
2 John Buchanan (1931–), premier of Nova Scotia, 1978–88
3 Conservative leader Joe Clark was under constant pressure to hold a leadership review.
4 *Concerning the Soul*
5 Memorial University in Newfoundland

244/ To Gaston Laurion[1]   8 May 1981

Dear Gaston,
I am sorry there has been all this time about writing, but my eyes collapsed and I have been in the hands of the doctors & in the dark. This has delayed all my activities and am so sorry.

This is just to put in writing what I said on the phone, that it is a great delight to me that you are going to translate *Lament for a Nation*.[2] It is also to say that I am writing to the publishers in Toronto about the arrangements.

It has been emotionally harder for us to move than we thought, because Toronto so stands in my mind with my mother. But we are so glad

to be here, as Nova Scotia suits us much better for living than Ontario.
There is still some kind of real community here.

Your election[3] filled me with such joy, not only for Quebec, but for
other places as well. Trudeau's centralist policies just fill me with anger.
Why Newfoundland, Alberta, P.E.I. etc. should be run from Ottawa, I do
not know. But Ontario has continually voted for him and he has become
increasingly a simply egocentric demagogue.

I am so glad that you are having a sabbatical & I hope that you will
have time to read & think as well as the task of translating. It was very
good of you to take the time to see the lady in Longueuil.[4]

I will be writing again when I hear from Toronto. In the meantime this
is an official letter about translation.

Ever,
George Grant

(I sign it fully because it is official.)

1 A professor of French and the translator of *Lament for a Nation*
2 Gaston Laurion's translation, *Est-ce la fin du Canada: Lamentations sur l'échec du
  nationalisme canadien* was published in 1987.
3 The Parti Québécois was re-elected in Quebec.
4 Who also wanted to translate *Lament*

245/ To William Christian   24 September 1981

Dear William,
This is just to say hello and hope all is well with you and yours. Past time
rather fades for me, so I do not remember at what time you sent me the
2nd Discourse and whether I have thanked you. I use it every day at the
moment. What a subtle work & how much he has been underplayed in
the English-speaking account of the tradition.

I hope you had a good summer and got along with a new post-Innis
work. I believe in the doctrine of natures and I am sure you have that rare
thing – a philosophical nature – and should use it for the enlightenment
of Canada. You also have the enormous quality of not wanting to be the
hanger-on of a school (see your brush with the Straussians here). The tradition is too smashed at present to enter the quiet security of a school
because such security is so procrustean. I would love to see anything you
write and I will send you anything I write. Our writings (Sheila and mine)
have recently been practical, but I am now going back to theory. Practi-

cality was necessary because when North America is living in the blood of its infants, one cannot be indifferent.

One thing that depresses me greatly at the moment is how much more alive the U.S.A. is than Canada. Look at our three tiresome leaders of the parties. (They really must get rid of poor Clark.) I really think it an enormous tribute to the U.S.A. that there is a substantial possibility that they will be the first technological country to try & stop easy legal abortion. Whatever else one thinks of [U.S.] Senator [Jesse] Helms, when he says (in the circumstances that he might be beaten on abortion) 'If I have to go down on the principle of the rights of the unborn, then I'll go down,' one wished that our leaders would so stand.

We go on pretty well. Dalhousie is a vague, chaotic university compared to McMaster, but that has its advantages. NS itself has a bite to it; we were up in Cape Breton[1] and met some really wild Highland Catholics. Doull and I are giving a joint seminar on Aristotle's *De Anima* which is fun and keeps me on the bit, standing up to the extreme gnosticism with which he focuses the question.

Give my love to Barbara and the boys and best to Julie and Perrin B[eatty]. I wish he would make an unflinching stand [on abortion] as he seems to have something really strong that few of our politicians have.

Ever,
George

P.S. This is a poor letter, but it brings much felicitations. It was so good seeing you in May.

1 For a right-to-life conference, where Grant read the article he had written with Sheila Grant, 'Euthanasia,' in *Care for the Dying and the Bereaved*, ed. Ian Gentles (1982)

246/ To William Christian

Dear William,
Thanks for your letter.

I am really honoured to know that you and Perrin Beatty submitted my name for the OC;[1] so good of you and I am grateful, as it helps me here to be accepted. Of course it would be lovely to have lunch in Ottawa with Perrin Beatty. October 22nd (Thursday) would be best for us. My one hesitation is that he would have to have Sheila too. They pay her way to Ottawa too and she knows nobody in Ottawa and I would be unwilling to leave her as we travel together so rarely. Could we not take him to lunch as taking two people to the Parliamentary Restaurant is expensive. We will be staying at the Skyline Hotel over Wednesday night and will keep Thursday lunch free. We have to get back here late Thursday afternoon.

Yes, we got the book.[2] Can we keep it till Xmas? Both Sheila and I want to read it and it is going to be the centre of our Xmas holiday discussions. If you need it before, we will buy a copy. So good of you to send it.

Your piece in the *Globe* was so good, and what is so good about the Globe is that it means it is widely read. e.g. Our oldest friends here asked in detail about you because they had been so moved by your piece.

Dick Doyle[3] of the *Globe* was here for a couple of days and we talked the constitution all the time. I am in agreement with him that if it passes it may truly finish the country – not only Lévesque, but an old student is Peckford's[4] constitutional advisor and they are certainly planning getting out under certain circumstances. If a country goes on re-electing a megalomaniac and a clever one, it pays the price.

We get on pretty well here – although the university as a whole is very disorganized and scared about money – as it has grown much too fast in every technological direction and is utterly dependent on federal money in a way Ontario universities are not. Doull and I give a joint seminar on Aristotle's *De Anima* and I am learning a lot. Sheila has had to be in Toronto a lot for one of the children & I find that the separations tear me apart sexually. I feel as a lover of Plato I should be less torn by such matters, but I am still in my heart a modern in which physical love is at the core. Your generation is probably much wiser about such questions.

Best love to Barbara and the boys. My best to Julie and I will be grateful if you can give Perrin Beatty my message.

Ever,
George

P.S. I like and do not like the Guelph motto[5] on your letter – a good question. 'Causas' can mean such limited relations in the modern languages.

1 Grant was made an officer of the Order of Canada.
2 Donald C. Johanson, *Lucy: The Beginnings of Mankind* (1981)
3 Richard Doyle (1923–), editor-in-chief of the *Globe and Mail*
4 Brian Peckford (1942–), premier of Newfoundland and Labrador, 1979–89
5 'Rerum cognoscere causas' (Lucretius [99–55 B.C.], *De Rerum Natura*): 'To know the causes of things'

The new NDP government in Manitoba dismissed Bedson from his civil service position. Grant wrote a letter of protest to the Globe and Mail: *'Civil Service,' 28 December 1981.*

247/ To Derek Bedson   26 November 1981

[telegram:]
Angry and disgusted. What about constitutional government. You are very much in our thoughts.[1]

1 Letter to the editor, *Globe and Mail,* 28 December 1981
   Your story concerning the dismissal of Derek Bedson, the chief Manitoba civil servant, by the new NDP government raises a general issue about Canadian history (Ex-Activist Named to Manitoba's Top Post – 27 November).
   Since 1900 there has been a struggle in Canada to establish a top civil service that had some continuity despite the vagaries of political change. The attempt was to follow the British tradition rather than the American, where the leading civil servants were generally related to political parties.
   The point of our effort was to guarantee that people of high competence would give their careers to public service. This was not likely to happen if such people knew their jobs were at the whim of every ideological change. From the side of the civil servants, this required that they would serve loyally any government which was elected democratically. This state of affairs was not always perfectly realized in Canada, but its foundation as a principle is seen in the career of O.D. Skelton, who served loyally both Conservative and Liberal governments in Ottawa as their chief civil servant. By all accounts, Mr Bedson was a fine representative of that Canadian tradition.
   This principle is always under attack because of the exigencies of political patronage, and the premier of Manitoba has, therefore, taken a retrograde step in the establishment of an ideological civil service. Ideologies have a way of quickly changing in a technological society. The undermining of this tradition may seem palatable to the NDP, but it does not serve this country well.
                                                                  George Grant

1982

248/ To William Christian

Dear William,
I have been appalling about *Lucy.* Just after the new year I hurt my back

and the rest of January just went, with plenty of pain & what is most depressing – fear. When I think that the virtue of courage is knowing what to fear and what not, it depresses me that my ability to maintain outward calm is not equalled by one's inward state. The book will be off to you after the weekend.

One's life goes on in the round of small deeds. One interesting thing is the class on Aristotle's *De Anima* with Doull. In essentials my reaction is not unlike what I gather you said about the Straussians. The class is difficult because if I speak anything outside the Aristotle I am hushed up. Now, indeed, it is better to be in that position vis-à-vis Aristotle than Strauss and Doull knows the position magisterially. But (1) even at a very high level I find the completeness of his engrossment a kind of weakness in seeking comfort (the philosopher, knowing that he knows not, etc.) and (2) bad pedagogically for those who imitate without the talent. Nevertheless it has been good for me to have to stand up with somebody who is a master in a way nobody was at McMaster and good for me to use a language quite foreign to me in so standing up.

American politicians interest me more than Canadian at the moment. (But at my age I should be less interested in the immediate than I am.) Tell Perrin B when you see him that I liked very much what he said about the press as reported in the *G & M*. It is very hard, it seems to me at the moment, to combine practically what is true in the Toryism which came out of public control with the truth of the modern individualist conservatism which rightly sees the modern state as dangerous.

I hope you have enough freedom both to have some real time for studying and writing and for some pleasant times. One of the good things we share (although in rather different ways) is not thinking existence and its ends are simply understood, as they are in most modern political science. I long very much for you to bring out some writings that will bring out that subtlety for your own remarkable understanding of English 'empiricism' at its richest with other traditions.

I have been reading parts of Heidegger – what a master. Above all (in my own way) I would like to write like that. He seems not to be writing about things, but to summon up directly the things themselves, as if he was not thinking about what others had thought about things, but about the things themselves. (Badly put with a contradiction about 'about.')

Sheila goes into hospital next week for an operation – hopefully not too bad. But my dependence is churning on.

Love to Barbara and the boys and best to Julie and Perrin.
Soyez bien.[1]

Ever,

George

1 Take care.

249/ To Joan O'Donovan

Dear Mrs O'Donovan,
Sheila is going to Toronto and so I thought I would send this along.
There is not so much as I would have wished as I have been flat with a bad
back. I hope the last part of your pregnancy has not been too difficult. Do
look after yourself. My best to your husband.
   (1) The language of Athens and Jerusalem.[1] The difference is
important, but my difficulty is with the word Jerusalem to express the
opposition, because of our saviour's break with Jerusalem. I would agree
with SW in the extent that she condemns Jerusalem and the Jewish tradition. This is of course a difficult question and one filled with nuances. I
prefer Christ and Socrates to Athens and Jerusalem. You are of course
right how much I take SW's account of Christianity as the great modern
account. What is difficult in this for moderns is that it goes back behind
western Christianity, whether Catholic or Protestant. I am more and more
convinced that the mistakes are to be found in St A[ugustine]'s *City of
God.* It turns on the once and for allness of particular events. Of course
Christ is perfection, but I do not see the scheme that that perfection only
happens once. We are divided here intellectually, but I am sure that such
intellectual divisions, although culturally important, are unimportant
compared to what is given to us in loving Christ. I think you are quite
right to just lay down your western Christianity at the end and criticize my
thought in terms of it. I think you have to be very careful that you have
got exactly right what is implied in SW's position. Let me say two things
about that.
   (a) Gnosticism has been very foolishly used by official western Christianity. Of course there were some crazy gnostics (as some crazy western
Christians – remember how St John of the Cross was persecuted, let alone
the Cathari). Pétrement was a great gnostic scholar before she gave up
her own studies to edit SW. Read her on it. People like the Grants in Chicago are just foolish about gnosticism.[2] All Christianity is in tension
between the gnostic and the agnostic. (b) I have not written about SW

because at my best I hope what she says is true, but I am also scared that it is true because I am simply not up to it. To be personal, I am a lazy, lecherous, self-centred person who knows hardly anything about giving oneself away. It would be presumptuous of me to write of matters of which I know only indirectly. See p. 128 of thesis: 'It is truly a solution only for those who are entirely possessed by the light of grace.' Clearly my purpose in writing is to clear away those intermediate questions which prevent people from going directly to the truth of Christ. Therefore, I write about those intermediate questions. Obviously questions raised by Strauss are only intermediate, but they are more important for those of us who are not saints. I think this may be where your Protestantism would hesitate. There is much in Protestantism which holds me in a way Catholicism does not, but it seems to me true that in the West an essential part of Christianity – people such as Francis, Theresa, John of the Cross – have been preserved in Catholicism at its greatest. As Christ said about the end being knowing and loving God, there is an extremity of that which has been lost because of the very democratic nature of Protestantism. – Anyway, I hope prayer will become a more real presence in my life, but until it does it would be foolish of me to write of these the greatest matters.

To go on with egocentric talk of myself, about many of the questions about which you rightly question in your book, I am simply uncertain, because I have not a very well-trained intellect. It has taken nearly all my later life since I got interested in philosophy to learn what the great philosophers have said on the simple question of human practice, leaving aside metaphysical questions which are generally just beyond me. Those people who had a better education when they were young learnt of the philosophic tradition early; I have only learnt of it slowly and late. For example, it is only this year that I discovered that Rousseau was a greater former of the modern than even Nietzsche. The result is that at the moment I am writing a long piece called 'History and Justice' which is an attempt to understand the atheism of the left better than previously. Rousseau takes my breath away with how clever he is in destroying the old tradition by saying that reason is acquired by human beings in a way that can be explained without teleology. To try to demolish Rousseau (and, therefore, marxism) seems to me essential these days to free people from that which can hold them from ever thinking that Christianity might be true. Let me also say (in connection with what was said earlier) that I am very hesitant to write about differences between Christians in a public way. For example, however much I may find difficult the formulations of the 'moral majority,' they know clearly that abortion is murder when it is done for convenience and I do not want to confuse people who have that heart of the matter. If I get such people in classes I will try to help them formulate their Christianity, but I think knowing murder is murder is more important than the necessary subtleties of intellectual formulation. Perhaps one might say that correct formulations have something to do with knowing that murder is murder, but in the meantime I rejoice in the American fundamentalist Protestants who won't give way on this essential. For love is present in such formulations, even if it seems absent in their formulations of foreign policy.

I am grateful that somebody as well educated as yourself should have bothered to write of my formulations. It is clearly and lucidly written and makes a lot of things clear to me that were not previously clear. What I have said on earlier pages is just to emphasize that why I have written so little is that there are few things I know. I am above all grateful to you for making Christianity central because certainly my concentration on the intermediate is simply practical and has nothing to do with lack of concern for the essential. Perhaps when we meet we might talk of the eschatological side of Christianity which is the side which I less and less understand. Is Christianity fundamentally committed to the unicity of the historical process? If so, one has to give up the Platonism. I hope not, but am not sure. It would be so good for both of us to talk about it with both of you.

Ever,
George Grant

P.S. (a) 'ideal' is a word from the Hegelian tradition – 'best' is the better Xian substitute
(b) there are not words for 'nature' or 'history' in the Bible
(c) 'compassion' is the modern Rousseauesque word; 'charity' is the Xian word
(d) How can a Xian have a 'tragic' vision?

1 A term used by Leo Strauss to symbolize the conflict between reason and faith or philosophy and revelation
2 R.M. Grant (1917–), *Gnosticism and Early Christianity* (1959); *The Secret Sayings of Jesus* (1960); *Gnosticism: An Anthology* (1961). F.C. Grant (1891–1974), *The Gospels: Their Origin and Growth* (1957); *Ancient Judaism and the New Testament* (1959)

250/ To Jonathan Mills[1]   19 March 1982

Dear Mr Mills,

Thank you very much for your very good & very interesting letter (which infuriatingly I only just got because I had been involved with my wife having an operation).

As far as I am concerned I am unequivocally a Christian (though a poor one) & not a member of the R.C. church, but of the Anglican church. I think of Christianity as first & philosophy as simply the means of trying to communicate the truth of Christ to others.

Your letter raises many good points about the Straussians. Strauss was a nobler man than many of his followers who are often Jewish chauvinists of the worst kind.

I very much want to write a long letter in answer to yours, but it will have to wait because I have got ill since my wife's operation & only have the energy for a few lines, till I am recovered.

I hope I did not attack Protestantism in my review of Frye,[2] but only *secularised* Protestantism – quite another matter. I disliked the book because he was superior about the Gospels, which in my opinion are *perfect*.

I hope your studies go well. There is no nobler calling than the clergy, particularly in these strange days.

I will write again when recovered & hope you will send me another letter, because this one was so good & so to the point.

Ever,
George Grant

P.S. Simone Weil was *not* a Catholic. This is one of the rare subjects I know a lot about. Have you read Simone Pétrement's life of her?

1 J.P. Mills, who later wrote an M.A. thesis, 'The Historical Comedy of the Soul's Destiny: An Interpretation of the Presence and First Essay of Nietzsche's *Toward the Genealogy of Morality*,' Regent College (1985)
2 Review of *The Great Code: The Bible and Literature,* by Northrop Frye, *Globe and Mail,* 27 February 1982, E17

251/ To Ed Andrew[1]   31 July 1982

Dearest Eddie,

It was so good of you to phone us about Margaret['s death]. Even when you have the knowledge, it is so terrible, the world without Margaret in it.

The wonderful way she was there sustaining other people makes it so inconceivable that she is not here directly. For you who were her joy and pride, it must be so impossibly strange that she is not here.

To speak of other days, she was the woman (the girl) to whom I owe the fact that I did not hate women. All during my youth, she sustained my father and myself with a kind of girlhood which was tender in a wonderful way. It may have been that she was a Grant & not a Parkin & brought to our father that womanliness and high intelligence that he so loved. She denied in her being all the silly folly about pure intellect being essentially masculine.

You must have such [continuous] and wonderful memories over the years of your life. I remember her with you when you were six in 1947 at Otter Lake and how Geoff and she revelled in what you are. With three young children of her own, she still had time for generosity to Sheila who had just arrived from England & had to discover the world of the Grants. Margaret was so good to her.

Presence and absence are so strange. Not to have her present is [ill.] and for you inconceivable. Although I did not see her often, she was to me as to be taken for granted as the light and the wind.

I have written your father would you give [ill.] & my love and thoughts to Alison, Caroline, Joan and Katie.

I will write again soon.

All the love in the world.

George

1 Edward Andrew (1941–), Grant's nephew and a professor of political science at the University of Toronto

252/ To William Christian   19 November 1982

Dear William,
I have read the revised manuscript[1] with great interest and have learnt much from it. What is so good is that it takes Canadian politics seriously, not as if they were rather boring offshoots. Even in the present sad circumstances that is the cause for hope and hope is a great virtue. I was, of course, flattered by the remarks about myself.

On details.

I thought that the account of ideology was greatly improved and I think your account of it much better than most I have read. I would, on the long haul, like to have a conversation about it, because it seems to me a new phenomenon in the world, and one of the most corrosive that has come with the technological society. I think one difference would arise at the point of the respective places of philosophy and religion in human life and how ideology has arisen out of the displacement of that proper relation. But that must wait and in the meantime your account of it seems to me very good and deeper than the first edition.

Perhaps (and this is simply a matter of emphasis and how it could be done with the addition of a relative clause at particular points I do not know) the ambiguities of political separatism [that] there [are] could be emphasized more, e.g. I see old students of 30 years ago who are both close to Peckford and they have made me, perhaps, too aware of how deep is the separatism there in the light of the resources dispute. But there is an ambiguity in the fact that Trudeau's centralism has led to the ambiguities both in the East & in the West & in a different way in Quebec. I find it an ambiguity in myself, in so far as, on the one hand one sees the necessity for central government; & on the other, one recognizes the anger in people who don't want their oil to be used too much in the interests of central Canadian consumers. I think it would be wrong to make the book too current, but I think something about the population being in central Canada and the oil elsewhere and the effect of this on politics and the ambiguity in this might be slightly strengthened.

In so far as one has glimpses of other people, I think you have a better temperament for understanding how people live politically in the world than I do, who am ravished often by the Highland Scot side of my temperament. I think you have real sense about politics and this is essential as one attempts (as I think we both attempt) to ascend from politics to political philosophy. I think it is very good in the book the way you point to that ascent in the new edition.

These comments are not much use. But their lack of usefulness comes from the fact how good I think your revisions are.

I hope all goes well with you and yours, as it does with us here. It has taken us longer than I thought to get used to the change imaginatively; but except for missing people such as yourself, it is probably good as Sheila is much better ...

I'm sorry to have been confused about what Julie left. You must excuse the manners as arising from not having yet reached a system here because of lack of any secretary and partly because of age. It was not lack of care for your friendship by which I am honoured.

Love to Barbara and the boys. Best to Julie and Perrin.

Ever,
George

1 William Christian and Colin Campbell, *Political Parties and Ideologies in Canada*, 2d edition (1983)

253/ To William Christian   3 December 1982

Dear William,
It was much more than I deserve to have such a beautiful piece written about my writings.[1] It says, much better than I could say, what is my intention and it helps to give me the courage to try and write some more. It is so good of you to take the trouble and I am grateful.

I hope you are going to have some time for feasting and pleasure over Christmas. It is so very good for the children to have their grandparents alive so they feel they are part of a community beyond the atomic family. We missed this with ours as both our parents were people who had married late in the Edwardian way.

We have had a syndicalist revolt here from the faculty union. Its members are pretty spivy, but one can see why they are doing it. What remains to be seen is if the established bourgeois on the Board & in government are going to grant them 15% these days. Marxist syndicalism at $40,000 a year in NS is, to say the least, ambiguous, but at another level understandable. It is certainly not going to produce a sane university, but luckily apart from nice youngsters to teach, I am far from any great interest.

I hope you have a good holiday and have time to read something of interest. Love to Barbara and the boys, and I thank you very much for your beautiful piece of writing, which, I can only repeat, is much more than I deserve.

Ever,
George

P.S. I have just been teaching Bks 8 & 9 of Aristotle's *Ethics* ['On Friendship'] and thought of yourself.

1 William Christian, 'Rejoinder to Ian Box, "George Grant and the Embrace of Technology,"' *Canadian Journal of Political Science* 16 (June 1983), 349–54

1983

254/ To Ed Andrew   10 March 1983

Dear Eddie,
Thank you for your letter. I was pleased by how much its style continued the tradition of the Parkin women. It was so like my darling mother writing to some junior housemaster who had made a pass at one of the maids. As my favourite person of that generation was Alice Massey & she was the recipient of this style from many quarters, I was pleased to be playing her role.

I should not have said what I did to your father & he should not have bothered you with it. My passion for filiation as against affiliation has led me to want things that it is foolish to want. Charity is, of course, a virtuous person & that her magnanimity (in the Aristotelian sense of that virtue) tends towards self-righteousness is an inevitable product of her progressivism. My difficulty is that as Sam Johnson[1] says, Christianity turns on the ability to forgive, but my mad temperament makes it impossible. My temperament leads me to agree with Peter Self when he said 'Justice is so boring,' but my Platonism will not allow me to accept that.

Yours was a just letter & I am grateful for it.

Robert's number is 766-8782. He is in Peru at the moment. David's number is 463-7354. He goes to Seattle in May. My only interest in the present matter is David. He so likes Toronto that I would love him to catch visions of the Toronto of the past. It is bad to have favourite children, but David is so enchanting that I find it difficult not to favour him.

Best to Donna & the children.

Ever,
George

1 Samuel Johnson (1709–84), British critic and political writer

255/ To Charity Grant   25 May 1983

Dear Charity,
It was good of you to pass on the pamphlet from Italy. How nice that you were there. It is strange that two children of the same parents should be so different about travelling. You have the courage for it; I have not. Sheila is more like you.

All goes well for us here, as I hope it does for you.

Yours,
George

256/ To William Christian   [July 1983]

Dear William,

This is slow in writing to thank you for your kindness in getting in touch with Charles Taylor.[1] It was very good of you, a mark of friendship, which is a rare relation these days, and for which I am fortunate from a person of your quality.

I have not yet seen the article in question, so cannot comment on what seemed justifiable objections to my comments on your part. What would particularly interest me, either from yourself or Beatty would be the arguments in favour of the testing of cruise missiles. I, obviously, know less than either of you about such matters. Obviously, also, the USSR has a ghastly regime. But what has seemed to me dangerous is the very fact that the American print & TV is making out that the Russians are more aggressive than it seems to me they are. They will, of course, make trouble whenever they can, but I think it is worth remembering that they have been invaded from the West, twice this century & once in the 19th. They have more reasons to fear aggression than the West; over 1 million died in the defence of Stalingrad alone. But I would be very interested to hear the PCs' defence of their cruise stand, although I quite recognize that practical politicians have to want what they think is best in practical situations. I do not think political philosophers such as yourself do.

I was immensely pleased to see your wonderfully kind piece about my thought in print.[2] Box clearly thinks of political thought in a very immediate way, pragmatic perhaps better. His answer to you just missed the point.

It seems to me that political philosophy is very difficult in an era in which American society is of such vulgarity & indeed the English-speaking world as a whole. I hope Canada's innocence will do something to protect it from that vulgarity.

I hope above all that you are on to exactly what you want to write. I have always felt that you had a deep understanding and perception of the English sensualist tradition and you would write so wonderfully of what it meant politically before it degenerated into what it has become. A lot of poor books have been written about Hume, but you would write a very good one. That strange genius Heidegger goes on, in speaking about Descartes for the French, how Hume has never been properly brought out of concealment to understand the English-speaking world.

We go on pretty well. I am, in a while, to try and write out the general conclusions of my love for Céline. I hope you and the other Christians go well. Give all of them my love.

Ever,
George

P.S. Best to Julie and Perrin.

1 In an interview with Judy Steed, Grant was quoted as declining to discuss Charles Taylor's book *Radical Tories* (1982) with the words 'I don't want to hurt his feelings' (Judy Steed, 'George Grant, Philosopher, Teacher and Pessimist, Is Too Obstreperous to Fit into Any Pat Category,' *Globe and Mail* ['Fanfare'], 9 July 1983, 1, 3). William Christian had alerted Grant to this quote, and Grant telephoned Taylor to explain.
2 William Christian, 'Rejoinder to Ian Box, "George Grant and the Embrace of Technology,"' *Canadian Journal of Political Science* 16 (June 1983) 349–54; Ian Box, 'Reply: Thinking through Technology,' ibid., 355–9

257/ To William Christian   [July 1983]

Dear William,
It was very good of you to send me a copy of *Political Parties and Ideologies in Canada.* Since it arrived I have been delving to specific passages and what, above all, impresses me about the book is the way a literate and intelligent account of the matter does not prevent it from being used as a text for youngsters who are coming to the subject. This is a great feat and very difficult and yet these days if one does not think of how a book is to be used, it is just not read (unless it is simply entertainment), in Canada particularly. I think you have combined the two approaches brilliantly.

I have at last read Judy Steed's piece about myself[1] and have made the resolution *never* to give interviews. I was particularly annoyed to be identified with the NDP.[2] A charming and articulate woman got the better of me. Speaking to a friend, I can say that Hegel's writing about 'recognition' I should apply to my own character and fight it myself. It has been a good lesson and Sheila in her gentle way has been dishing it to me.

Give my love to Barbara and the boys and the best to Julie and Perrin. I hope you are learning something. I really think I am coming to terms with my love of Céline.

Ever,
George

1 See letter 256.

2 Steed suggested that Grant had warm feelings towards the NDP, but mentioned his disagreement with them on the issue of abortion.

258/ To Charity Grant   31 July 1983

Dear Charity,

I am very sorry that you were angry about my seeming disloyalty to mother.[1] I am quite unable to cope with a very charming and clever woman as Mrs Steed. It has taught me not to give interviews.

At a deeper level, Sheila is always surprised that I cannot let go of my adolescence. One difference between myself & yourself is that you did not attend school where your father was headmaster. Whether for good or ill, my life has been greatly a convalescence from that fact.

I am sorry to have angered you.

Yours,
George

1 Steed quoted Grant as saying that his mother's ambitions made his father unhappy. See letters 256–7.

259/ To Gaston Laurion   30 August 1983

Dear Gaston,

You were so very very good to me in Montreal. Generally when people are in need, others do not care about that need, but you did & I was so grateful. You really are what the English call 'a friend indeed.' Will you tell that to Geneviève also.

It was not only my passions, but my sense of how foolish the congress[1] was. The real place of philosophy has been so lost in the Babel of the modern world. It makes me feel more & more isolated &, therefore, your friendship was such a soothing balm. I am because of my childhood not easily a truster of other people, but you made me trust you by your kindness.

One thing I thought of Québec: this is a dreadful era, 'Rome with technology,' &, therefore, one cannot expect much. But at least already I felt in the city a great deal of pleasure from many simple people from the result of Bill 101.[2] They could make people speak their language. That may not be 'independence' but it is something and any political goods

are to be welcomed in such an era. You were part of that achievement &
should be proud.

I am grateful to you (indeed a friend) because I was overwhelmed with
nerves & defeat. If ever I could so the same for you, I would be glad.

Ever,
George

1 World Congress of Philosophy, held in Montreal
2 Bill 101, Charte de la langue française (1977), made French the official language of Quebec, not just in the legislature and courts, but also in the schools
and workplace, and for communications generally.

260/ To William Christian   31 August 1983

Dear William,
It was good of you to send me the stuff about the cruise [missiles]. I miss
so much your saneness because you have so much better practical judgment than myself. Let me say two things.

(1) What seems to me (of course I have not the proper technical information) so bad about the cruise is that it is such an extension of technological accuracy. Shortly, I do not see any easy solution to the whole
nuclear issue, but of one thing I am sure – that it will require not only a
limitation of warheads, but above all limitation of these new technological developments. I think Canada shouldn't be involved in these developments because they are almost a qualitative change in the whole situation.

(2) I regret the article in the *Globe* because I certainly will always vote
PC. The NDP are absolutely out for me because of abortion, apart from
my long-time dislike of their utopian politics. To put it personally, you are
at the stage in life when clearly you have more reason to touch immediate
politics in a way where my time of life requires greater retirement even if
the immediate circumstances were not so grim.

I hope Mulroney[1] is going to be sensible about the friends of Clark. I
thought Clark was a gentleman in defeat.[2] Mulroney does not disturb me
(despite the whispering campaign that the Liberals always start about a
new Conservative leader) because he is tough enough for those tricky
bastards & I would love to see them badly beaten. I hope it does not in
any way affect Perrin's life.

We are lucky to live in small towns. I had to go to Montreal to the World
Congress of Philosophy because the French Canadians who were organizing it asked me to give the big Canadian paper. What a difficult business
life in these big towns becomes. 6000 philosophers – a real supermarket

and my chief impression was how modernity has killed philosophy. The Russians and eastern Europeans there most depressing, but the French and the Austrians a good second.

Only for the ears of a friend such as yourself, and because I can only talk to Sheila of it – no masculine friend here. The Congress of Philosophy was disturbed for me by being moved by sexual passion in the streets of Montreal; elegance always arouses sexual desire in me. Christianity obviously forbids me pursuit. But what disturbs me more is that I cannot lift sexual eros into philosophical eros. The result was a lot of sleeping pills. It makes me feel such a fool at my age. What a queer business sexuality is; the whole thing made me start a rereading of *Symposium*.

Love to Barbara and the boys, and best to Perrin and Julie.

Ever,
George

P.S. I must beware of journalists and you are quite right to tell me so.

1 M.B. Mulroney (1939–), leader of the Conservative party, 1983–93, and prime minister, 1984–93
2 Brian Mulroney defeated Joe Clark for the leadership of the Progressive Conservative party.

261/ To Dennis Lee   November 1983

Dear Dennis,

It was so good to hear from you, as I had felt like writing, but had worried about all the things that must press upon you. S. and I hear little bits here and there from people and from papers, but always stuff which was you in the world and not you as being yourself and as being for us friend. Even now, when you write so kindly about my doings, it is done so that you were with us, although there is nothing about yourself, the details of your daily living, etc., which naturally hold one about people who are of that very small circle one can call friends. Both you and I have that strange distance from the world which has its good side, but when yours (I would gather) comes as much as mine from the results of a dying Protestantism it can result in pains for the self which make the friendship you have shown me a double joy. But anyway, enough; it is just to express how good it was to hear from you. Please forgive the bad typing and a bad machine.

It is just immensely good of you to care about what I write and you are the only person who really moves me to life about it and, therefore, you will now be bothered with a long account. I feel ashamed about bother-

ing you with it when what you write yourself is so good. [But] egocentri-
cally I put aside that shame ... I was enraptured by Céline's trilogy. Only
twice in my life have I been so enraptured: Mozart and Céline. So it got
me going again and I am writing a five chapter book which will be called
'Reading Céline's Trilogy.' You have seen the chapter on politics which
was not difficult to me. The two chapters on why his writing seems so
beautiful have been more difficult because I had always taken reading for
granted, never thought why it was beautiful. Another chapter will just be
about reading and try and detach the business from the lit. professors.
The last chapter will be a disquisition on beauty. I finish teaching this year
(thank God, thank God – how wise you were)[1] and this will leave me quite
free just to get on with it.

I was writing a book called 'Technology and Justice.' *English-Speaking
Justice* was to be one part; the Nietzsche thing you mention was the
national socialist part and I was working on the Marxist part, when I came
upon Rousseau (who I now take to be the founder of the Darwin-
Nietzsche part). It was a great discovery because I realised he was a
greater intellectual founder of modernity than anybody else, and it
stopped me trying to get down his greatness and his terrible results. So I
have put aside 'Technology and Justice' till I have written the Céline,
largely because I was sick of negativity and criticism and was so enraptured by Céline.

In the fall I wrote to Mrs Wall[2] as I did not want to bother you. I enclose
Polk's[3] reply. I had said that they could publish my books as people kept
writing to me about re-issuing *Philosophy in the Mass Age.* Polk's letter
drove me wild as I found nothing clear in it. I think it is a kind and sympathetic letter, but has no idea about what I am writing about. Larry
Schmidt is a nice German Catholic; Frank Flynn is a nice, but unreliable,
American Catholic, and if they do the work so much the better, but I
don't want it all mixed up with *Philosophy in the Mass Age,* nor do I think
their judgment of my pieces should determine what goes in.[4]

Of course I am proud that you should be willing for me to republish my
piece about yourself.[5] As I told you at the time, it was written at the very
lowest point of our lives, at a time when I wanted to express such love and
spontaneity and yet when other things penetrated the writing with grim-
ness. Yet it had to be written then or not go in the book. Do you think I
should re-write it or put it in with a note that it does not capture the joy of
your writing? My grandchildren simply quote your books all the time.

One thing that is confusing about the things Polk says about what I
wrote during my last years at McMaster is that I was writing things and

publishing things to keep the bastards in charge off my back as they examined each person's curriculum vitae minutely to see if they were ful-filling their job as a production machine. I even fell into writing cosy little reviews for the *Globe*. A great advantage of this chaotic place is that they do not see themselves as competing with the Ivy League production unit. Many of the pieces are repetitive and they were all prepared for a prepa-ration to what I was going to pull together into the book 'Technology and Justice.' As I say, this is delayed for Céline. I do not know what Schmidt is intending to include. I will send you what I have, although I am worried about you spending time. It may be a few days as I will have to collect them from disparate places here and at the university. The pieces about abortion and euthanasia were immediately polemical because the Angli-can church was officially backing all kinds of the sweetest liberal killing.

I will be extraordinarily grateful for any counsel and anything you can say to Polk. (He seems a nice person and my only objection was the chaos of his letter.) One of the difficulties here is that I have little secretarial help compared to Ontario. Understandable because they belong to a poor province, but a sweet one which has many advantages for retire-ment. If you decide anything I would know it was the best decision.

Sheila sends you so much love. I wish we could meet and I wish that we had more news of your daily doings. Sheila goes on in her own extraordi-nary way ... Whatever madness may be in me (and one of the reasons I so love Céline is that I so identify with the wild old man and feel myself now one) I was staggeringly lucky to spend my life with her and we continue to wander around NS in our solitary way. Canadian politics is such a mas-querade of folly and I wish I had the Aristophanean art to write of it. I hope above all that your muse is in possession and that other financial considerations do not distract you from that possession.

Much love and thanks for your generous letter and above all much shame that I respond to your letter by burdening you.

Ever,
George

Greet any mutual people. For example, where is Greensides [Lee's cur-rent address]?
P.S. McClelland & Stewart wrote saying they were interested in anything I might write.

1 Lee had resigned his university teaching position so that he could concentrate full time on writing.

2 President of House of Anansi, a Canadian publishing house
3 James Polk, then an editor at Anansi
4 They were planning an anthology of Grant's writings.
5 George Grant, 'Dennis Lee – Poetry and Philosophy,' in *Tasks of Passion: Dennis Lee at Mid-Career,* ed. Karen Mulhallen et al. (1982), 229–35 (also published in *Descant* [Dennis Lee special issue] 39 [Winter 1982], 229–35).

262/ To Dennis Lee

Dear Dennis,
I am sorry to have been slow in sending the writings you kindly said you would be willing to look at. I have been hit by an illness which left me prostrate, but will send them soon.
    The whole thing is so good of you.

Ever,
George

P.S. I can't find your new address so am sending this to Anansi.

263/ To William Christian   18 December 1983

Dear William,
I do not know whether it is age or concentration on student exams which makes me mixed up whether I wrote to you about the good piece you kindly sent. If this is a repeat, just forgive. I thought it excellently done and the point you were making important to be made. In the present state of Canada it is a hard point to insist on and to be listened to, but 'cast your bread upon the waters'[1] is the only motto and I thought it was really doughy bread compared to what is said about such matters usually. I hope *so hopingly* that you will get the grant from Ottawa and that you will be able to get to England to comfortable and efficient quarters, and proceed to begin to be able to write and read daily. You have the capacity for high style; I should perhaps say a high laconic style, but it takes time and peace to bring it to fruition.
    I feel guilty as hell writing about Céline & the beautiful while there are such terrible events in the world and one should probably be using one's pen about such issues. But I have never liked or wanted to write something so much &, therefore, am just doing it. It will end with a discussion of Plato & the poets, but that is far away yet.

I am asking Dalhousie for some money to come to Guelph, but Dalhousie is so crazy about such matters. They treated me like a greedy garbage collector asking something from Tammany Hall when I asked to go up to give a paper at the World Congress of Philosophy. I am rather worried about money because the moving here before retirement cut badly into pensions. But that is neurotic, because we will have quite enough to live gently here. Anyway I will be in Guelph in June[2] and it will be so good to see you and Barbara. When do you plan to go off to England? I hope this will not keep you back. It is so good of you to arrange it and I am grateful. When the date is certain, let me know.

Sheila has the darling quality of being ecstatic about festivals &, therefore, we move into Xmas with excitement. I have the grimmer Protestant vision of such festivals, but know she is righter than I am and, therefore, do not senselessly object to the uproar. Anyway you are in a more serious position because I am sure the boys like it and I hope that both have a very happy time. Also the very best for 1984; the ominous ring that Orwell has given that date does not change its nature.

Even if it is for a crucial cause and even if no harm will come from it, I find Trudeau's peace business[3] somehow depressing because one feels he is building up his ego and trying to delude very decent Canadians about its importance. Do you agree? I am sure you see the matter with greater clarity than I do, and I hate to carry my suspicion of him outside proper limits. I do not like Mulroney's so total endorsement of Israel, even if it is electorally wise. But we seem to be moving into a very dark political period & I very much fear what the Americans are doing in the Near East much more than their almost [wretched] responses in the Caribbean. To a person of my tradition it sounded like [*moira*][4] to hear Harrods[5] had been bombed[6] & I was glad to be in a small town, based on war & yet far from the kinds of violence which seem to be coming endemic.

Much Love to Barbara and the boys.

George

P.S. Forgive so many platitudes and above all if this be a repeat.

1 'Cast thy bread upon the waters: for thou shalt find it after many days' (Ecclesiastes 11.1).

2 For the annual meeting of the Learned Societies. The Canadian Political Science Association, the Canadian Historical Association, and the Canadian Philosophical Association held a special combined session to honour Grant on the occasion of his forthcoming retirement.

3 Pierre Trudeau, at the end of his period as prime minister, embarked on a
  worldwide trip to promote peace and nuclear disarmament.
4 Fate
5 Famous posh department store in London, England
6 As part of an Irish Republican Army terrorist campaign

264/ To Ed Andrew   27 December 1983

Dear Ed,
I thought your article about Plato *very* good.[1] You have learnt to write so
clearly & well that I am proud to be related to you. It is a difficult, difficult
subject & you hold its component parts so well together, which in itself is
a great art. I think your main part against Strauss is well taken, although I
would have to make some qualifications about the position from which you
argue, although these qualifications would not lead me away from your
overall disagreement with Strauss, in which I am sure you are in the right.

I have for quite a while believed that one of the deepest strands in
Strauss's writing about Plato has been to criticize the long hold of Xian
Platonism in the western and eastern interpretation of Plato. He has
done this wisely & with *no* foolishly polemical spirit. I have wanted to write
about this, but have been held back because I see no good purpose
served (as he did not) in emphasizing these days the difference between
Jews & Xians. As he saw clearly it stems from the deep difference concerning the nature (I mean more than the content) of divine revelation. He
was deeper & wiser about this than some of his epigones. I may write
about this someday, but fairly indirectly.

We had a pleasant & quiet Xmas. I hope all goes well with you and
yours as it does with us.

                                                            Ever,
                                                            George

1 Edward Andrew, 'Descent into the Cave,' *Review of Politics* 45, no. 4 (1983),
  510–35

1984

265/ To John Graham   2 May 1984

Dear John,
Sheila has told me that you had much to do with the lovely party of the

other night. This is just to thank you very much. It was for me a very good send off into a new stage of life. We both consider ourselves lucky to have such good friends as yourselves.

Let me add that I felt I was rather perversely rude to you at one point. When I am nervous I drink & it brings out my perversity. If it was offensive, please take it as part of my drunkenness.

Ever,
George

266/ To William Christian   12 July 1984

Dear William,

This is just to say that while I was in Guelph, I felt in myself a failure of friendship in the sense that both of us were taken up with things that made communication difficult & I so very much hope that it does not affect our friendship. I was very much taken up with uncertainties. I have a great sense of debt to you for many goodnesses & I did not think I expressed that properly. _

Life goes on here in the maelstrom of the medical profession. I would like to tell them where they can stick it & just go on, but Sheila tells me I must not & I must continually learn from them what is possible, as I still enjoy living, greatly.

Give my best to Barbara & the boys and best wishes to Perrin and Julie for the election.[1] I would love to see the Liberals out, but the system they have set up in Canada is a very strong one.

The centre of the letter is the expression of my friendship.

Ever,
George

1 Federal general election, 14 September 1984. Perrin Beatty was a Conservative candidate.

God Be Thanked: Retirement 1984–8

267/ To Dennis Lee   12 September 1984

Dear Dennis,
This is just to say that it is only now that I can say how marvellously helpful your editing of my writings has been, because it is only now that I have
got down to correcting them. I was very ill this summer & have been in
the hands of the medical establishment. But now I am seeing how very
helpful yours is, in every way. So generous.

I hope you have really good news ... Some modern ways help women,
but some are very difficult for the most sensitive & loving women. What a
strange thing being a parent is, but I wouldn't have missed it. It is all complicated for you in being an ocean away. Sheila sends her love.

I am beginning to pop around but still feel pretty frail & uncertain.

Just thanks for the editing & later as it gets into order there must be
some arrangement reached about tangible matters.

Ever,
George

P.S. The election gave me a negative boost because of my long dislike of
the Liberal party, but I cannot honestly see much positive good in it.

268/ To Derek Bedson   15 September 1984

Dear Derek,
I meant to write to you the day after that Lady Trent[1] was here, but I
became very ill and have had a long session of illness all summer.

Now this morning after yesterday's election I must write. It was so good to see the Conservatives doing well and some of the worst Lib. crooks getting theirs. Dislike is not a very good emotion but at the head of my list was John Roberts.[2] I think Mulroney did well; through all the attempts of the hostile TV people he answered very well and carefully. I think he is not a shallow man as the journalists tried to make out and that Irish R. Catholicism I think is probably in his soul. Of course, the best is Quebec and I do not think he will throw it away foolishly as Dief did. Obviously we are tied very tightly to the U.S.A. and he can do nothing about that, but I think he will keep his head. I expect very little from politics in this tragic era, but we could do much worse. The worst thing that happened actually in the election was Trudeau really ditching Turner in a very nasty way, involving him in the worst aspect of Trudeau's very poor regime. I am sure it was 'après moi le déluge'[3] etc. So egocentric.

I hope there are good rewards for you in Vienna[4] and that you are able to get to Spain and to England. I am sending this via Regina because all my papers are in confusion after my illness. I was glad that they kept saying that the Tories weren't so triumphant in Saskatchewan because the premier[5] has become so unpopular in the province. What a base fool he was not to see his need of your great experience.

It was a great pleasure seeing Lady Trent. I love those solid and sane English Anglicans and it was such a pleasure to see it is not a dead breed. She is quite free of the silliness that has so penetrated English intellectual life under liberalism.

They thought my illness was at first a stroke, but now they do not. I am in the hands of the big head experts which is rather boring. It was not death that I found disturbing but the possibility of long mindlessness in the world. I am quite hopeful now and we live quietly. Our great joy is that Isabel is ... doing brilliantly at the law school. After long worries about David, he is also doing very well; so we count ourselves very fortunate. I hope to get back to work at writing soon, but have been very out of it.

It is sad that we will move very little for financial reasons, but we are planning ... for a last trip to England next spring. I have let us get apart by very long silence, but please forgive that and let us know your plans. I do hope that Vienna has had its rewards as well as its difficulties and that you have been able to do things that please you. One thing that I greatly envy you is that you were not brought up corrupted by that progressiveness which so makes human beings so oblivious of eternity. It is so sad for men to turn away from their greater need because of the intellectual foolishness which I am afraid has so greatly corrupted the English-speaking world. Well bad eras come and go.

I very much regret that I have been a poor correspondent when you are abroad, but the last months were difficult medically and all was put aside except this poor old body.

Sheila sends her love.

And mine as always very deep.

George

We had a lovely visit from Rachel and great fun.

1 Bedson knew her husband.
2 John Roberts (1933–), political scientist and Liberal cabinet minister; defeated in 1984
3 'After me, the deluge': traditionally ascribed to Louis XIV
4 When he was fired by Howard Pawley in 1981, Bedson joined the Saskatchewan civil service as secretary to the cabinet, and then served in Vienna as trade officer of the Saskatchewan Agricultural Development Corporation.
5 Grant Devine (1944–), premier of Saskatchewan, 1982–91

269/ To Joan O'Donovan   19 December 1984

Dear Joan,

Your fine book about my writings arrived a few days ago and I write to say how honoured I am that a person of your calibre should have taken the time to write so clearly and so carefully about those writings. Your words are a great help to me in rethinking my past writing and I am sure will be a great help to anybody else who is interested in understanding what I have thought about. Vanity and embarrassment are in conflict in writing to you because, at one & the same time, I want to express to you my sense of honour that you should have used your great talents on such a subject and also a sense that in the face of the majesty and mystery of the universe, how poor my thoughts have been.

I like very much your statements at the end and they are a real help to my thinking. I *think* that I disagree with them but am not yet ready to say why. (In the same way, I am not yet ready to write to Oliver about his chapter on 'poseurs' in *Begotten or Made*.)[1] One thing that I am sure you will agree with is that where disagreement with fellow Christians is necessary it sinks into insignificance before one's common loyalty to Christ and, therefore, I want to express any disagreement with you or Oliver in the most careful way & when the issues have become clearer to me. I loved greatly in your book the words: 'Nevertheless, Adam did fall ...'[2] because it exactly expresses how I would like to write.

It is good to think of you at Westminster & of Oliver at Christ Church. Part of my 'fate' has been to love the English and it is so important that, in this complex time for them, they should be hearing the Gospel in a literate way. This is too late for Xmas, but I hope the three of you have a great 1985.

We are still unsure about seeing you in England in 1985. I had a very uncertain summer medically and that uncertainty remains with me. But our news is good. Isabel is doing very well at the law school ... Sheila goes on well in the circumstances of having to cope with [a wildy like] myself. I hope you have your life so well organized so that you have the time to write. You have such great capacity for clarity and good ordering and these are so important for the Xian church at this time.

Again, thanks for writing such a good book about my writings.

Ever to the three of you & of course from Sheila too.

George

1 Oliver O'Donovan, *Begotten or Made?* (1984)
2 Joan O'Donovan, *George Grant and the Twilight of Justice* (1984), 179

1985

270/ To William Christian   8 January 1985

Dear William,

It was so nice getting your note and even more the very sweet picture of the boys in front of the frieze.[1] It is good to hear that you are getting around and enjoying it. I hope England is still a society for fun, as it used to be, and that you and Barbara are having plenty. We soldier on, thank God in retirement. Sheila continues in her own extraordinary way, which I so greatly admire ... I am better than this summer; at least no more bad signs.

The PC government in Ottawa seems to be acting sensibly & very cautiously. I do not think it can do much or intends to do much about our relations with the Americans, but I like very much the lack of paranoia in relations to Quebec. I liked also that he chose a cabinet fair to the various segments in the PC party.

The Dalhousie faculty are taking a strike vote tomorrow. I hope they fail in getting a majority, but doubt it. The union seems dominated by two types of opinion. (a) A large number are not from here, let alone Canada, and, therefore, have little sense or care about the place they teach. (b) They are held by that kind of vague mixture of marxism and liberalism which gives them little picture of what the modern world is really like. Very unfair to the students, if they strike for salaries that are more based on competing for staff with Ontario, rather than apposite to the lower standard of living here.

It looks very likely that Sheila will be going to England solo, as I am just not well enough and that will mean I will not have the pleasure of seeing you. I have got engrossed in writing something about S. Weil, but I find it very slow, but my heart will be easier when I get back to that darling bastard Céline.

I hope your level of hedonism (one of the qualities that most enchants an old Puritan like myself) has not turned you from writing something out. You write so well and your clarity is so important for Canadians. Apart from such reasons, there is also the reason that, for most of us, our minds think they are clearer than they are, till we get down to the business of writing things out. It seem a necessary discipline even for the very heights such as Plato or (in his strangely modern confusions) Kant.

For amusement I have been rereading [Charles Dickens's] *A Tale of Two Cities*; what a genius. Do you read aloud to your boys? With proper cutting (because of ennui, not because of impropriety) that might be a marvellous book to read out loud, because it gives such a wonderful sense of 'history' which is so lacking in the education of young N. Americans.

Love to you all from us both. I hope the year is great for everybody.

Ever,
George

1 The Elgin marbles in the British Museum

271/ To Joan O'Donovan   4 February 1985

Dear Joan,

In the last weeks I have been sane enough to read your book about my thought carefully. It is so well done. My continuous reaction is the ego-centric one: how extraordinarily fortunate I am that a person of your sheer academic skill should have taken the time to expound my writings with such accuracy and skill, such perception and with such a clear style.

Till I had read it carefully, I did not see the degree of skill in the book. It embarrasses me that somebody of your obvious academic distinction would have paid such attention to my thoughts. I am a lucky being because that attention has meant that your accounts of particular pieces are so beautifully accurate and go to the heart of what I was attempting to say. So much inaccuracy has been written in the last years about my attempts (particularly inaccuracy arising from people who did not want to think that one could try and be philosophical from out of Christian certainties) that I am very grateful to you. I thought your book was quite correct (obviously) in pointing to how much I have had to change my mind about the means of expressing Christianity.

You will have to put up with more letters from me because I am not yet ready to say what I think about your extremely clear and fair disagreements at the end of your book. This particularly turns on what I have learnt from Simone Weil. At the moment I am writing for the first time why I think Christianity is the truth and it is around her writing. Do you know Crashaw's poem on Saint Teresa of Avila? It expresses what I think.[1] You and I are surely in agreement that evangelical Christianity is the heart of the matter particularly because it makes clear that the central act of the believer as a response to God is not dependent on intellectual prowess – but still there are those whom God seems to touch directly in the union of love and knowledge, and for these there does not seem to be a proper place in evangelical Protestantism. I am not one of these, but I think one must take their testimony in both eastern and western Christianity as greatly illuminating, particularly about Providence.

All goes well with us here ... I am very glad to be retired and try to write things down. I was particularly glad to be retired because the faculty union called a strike. I do not think faculty have the right to strike against students and would have gone on teaching. Luckily the strike collapsed. I would never feel this about strikers who are badly paid, but here it was a lot of greedy people, who are highly paid for NS.

I hope all is going well for the three of you and that the practical arrangements of your living have sorted themselves out, in so far as these ever do. I was very glad to hear that you were teaching. Teaching is not only good because of what is taught, but it is so good for the teacher because when he or she gets to his feet he finds out how clear or unclear he may be on the matter at hand, because he hears what he is saying in relation to the taught people. There is no bluffing in teaching because when it is present it is exposed, more so than in one's writing. Again, thank you for writing so fairly and clearly about my thoughts. I will write

again when I am ready to say clearly why I do not think Simone Weil a
gnostic in the bad sense of that word.

Love to all three,

Ever,

George Grant

P.S. I had a call from [Reginald] Stackhouse[2] about other matters and he
mentioned the Wycliffe appointment. I said only get an evangelical.

1 Richard Crashaw (1613–49), 'The Flaming Heart upon the Book of Saint
   Teresa.' In 'In Defence of Simone Weil,' *The Idler* 15 (Jan./Feb. 1988), 40,
   Grant quotes the following lines as a description of Simone Weil:
   O though undaunted daughter of desires!
   By all thy dow'r of Lights and Fires;
   By all the eagle in thee, all the dove;
   By thy lives and deaths of love,
   By thy large draughts of intellectual day,
   And by thy thirsts of love more large than they –   (93–8)
2 R.F. Stackhouse (1925–), principal of Wycliffe College, University of Toronto,
   1975–85

272/ To Frank Foley[1]   27 September 1985

Dear Mr Foley,
This is just to say that your letter of September 1985 to members of the
Coalition for the Protection of Human Life is a very unwise one.[2] This
may seem like interference with your proper duties, but my name is on
the letterhead on which your letter was sent out. What is central is that
the Coalition is a fine organization concerned with the most important
social issue in North America today and I think it cannot afford such ill-
considered letters under the signature of its president.
   The letter is unwise for the following reasons:
(1) The letter closely identifies mass foetuscide with the extremely complex issue of homosexuality. I see no reason why the Coalition should
wish to push such a large body of people into opposition with its goals. I
know that people of that sexual orientation have very different opinions
about this matter. (Let me say, in parenthesis, that your phrase 'homosexual and lesbian supporters' is a confused use of language. 'Homosexual'
is a generic term meaning literally 'the same sex' and, therefore, applies

to males and females alike. Such confusion does not inspire confidence about the writer.)

(2) Whatever the good intentions of your letter, its tone is unequivocally uncharitable. Is it not the case that we of the Coalition oppose mass foetuscide because it is radically unjust to the children who are being slaughtered? Should not the tone of our letters carry in them the same knowledge of justice from which our very cause arises?

(3) Obviously the male and female human beings who are most closely involved in having abortions have not been entirely homosexual. Also the medical professionals who carry out this mass slaughter are not solely homosexual. Therefore, it seems to me foolish to closely identify this slaughter with the homosexual community. Easy targets often lead us away from our essential goals. A coalition must stick to its central point.

I am saddened to write this letter to somebody who works hard at this central matter. However, the cause of the Coalition is too important not to insist that good causes can only be furthered by good and wise means.

Yours sincerely,
George Grant

1 President, Coalition for the Protection of Human Life
2 The letter, dated September 1985, contained the following sentence: 'There are two sides in this war. On one side, we have the promoters of baby killing with their homosexual and lesbian supporters. These same people, for the most part are anti-family and ANTI-GOD.'

273/ To Ian Angus[1]   [autumn 1985]

Dear Ian,

I hope you do not mind me addressing you thus. It is good to hear from you. I re-read your book on technology[2] just the other day when I found it when sorting out some books.

I regret *greatly* not having been able to get to the conference. I have been very ill this year and do not think I will ever be more than 20 miles from here ever again. I regret it not only because of yourself, but because I have been outraged at the way the Jews in Canada have been speaking about their fellow Canadian-Ukrainians. I would, therefore, have particularly wanted to come to the Conference. If this nasty business about the Ukrainians ever comes to the surface again & if you ever think of anything I could write from here, I would love to know. One does not want to seem racist about the Jews, but I think their attack on the Ukrainians was a perversion of eastern European history in their very particularist interests. This is a very hard thing to say in North America because of their control of the media in Toronto & NY, & one does not want to fall into gutter anti-Judaism. Please let me know anything I could do about this from here.

I am very sorry not to come, but I do not think I will move ever again. One finds how much one likes living when it is threatened.

Ever yours,
George Grant

1 Ian Angus (1949–), professor, Department of Communication, University of Massachusetts at Amherst
2 Ian Angus, *Technique and Enlightenment: Limits of Instrumental Reason* (1984)

274/ To Joan O'Donovan   8 November 1985

Dear Joan,
Forgive so early a Christmas greeting but by our age there are many greetings to be given and I simply could not bear to send you a card.

I hope all goes well for you & the other O'Donovans. Your last letter gave us a much better picture of what you are doing, but if there are things that have come to print, please send them along because we would both love to read them. I hope your day-to-day obligations are not too pushing and that life at Oxford gives you time just to look at the beautiful place. Just yesterday a student rang me up from Ontario because he is thinking of a thesis on Michael Foster.[1] As he asked me about him, I was so penetrated by the [sense?] of the cathedral where I always went with him for the Eucharist. Temporality is so strange. I wonder not only about what you are thinking about but what practical doings are most rewarding. It is hard for Sheila, who naturally loves her country, to read some of the reports in the papers about England, but the trouble with journalism is that there is a vested interest in describing the bad things & disregarding the ordinary & the sane.

We go better & easier than we have for many years. Isabel is at Yale & seems to be enjoying it ... Being by temperament a grim sort, I often imagine that something untoward may happen, but that is more temperament than evidence. Nova Scotia is good for us because we live so quietly and from day to day. We saw a lot of our children this summer & they all seemed well. We, of course, wish that there were more grandchildren, but have to be quite silent about that. I have a great spot in my heart for our eldest child, Rachel, & to see her happy is a great joy.

Canadian politics & life seems to go on in its pedestrian way. I do not think that the PCs will do anything serious about abortion. Like Reagan, Mulroney's instincts are sound on the matter, but they are both too success oriented to dare to touch something so divisive & so important. Otherwise Mulroney just carries on the state capitalist machine in the way one would expect. NS is so far from Toronto that we hardly know what forms life is taking there. What a queer place North America is. I can understand no other society and am very fearful of the self-righteous capitalism here.

In my thoughts I turn away more & more from political philosophy [to] the attempt to participate intellectually in the mystery of Christianity. I am writing a long piece about that, which goes slowly but is, at last, rewarding in its writing. I will send it to you when it is done & before it is published.

Give Sheila and my love to Oliver and Mathew. He must be growing up and be at a very sweet and strenuous age.

For all three of you a very happy Christmas and all good things for 1986.

Ever,

George

1 M.B. Foster (1903–59), tutor in philosophy at Christ Church, Oxford. Foster was a devout Christian, at odds with the mainstream of Oxford philosophy.

275/ To Joan O'Donovan

Dear Joan,

Thank you for your letter. Because I am answering it, please do not feel any need to answer this when you have so much to do and when you will need much attention to the new baby. I only answer because your letter moved me and because I want to. Look after yourself and take it easy after the birth, for that is a very tiring time. I can only say that children are a great joy and it does not diminish as they grow up. You saw us at a time – our worst time – when things were going badly ..., but the sheer joy quite holds one also. You and Oliver were certainly not brought up to be as selfish as I was, probably more like Sheila. But one of the things children have done for me (apart from their intrinsic beings) has been to teach me to be less selfish, because it is so easy to love them.

Certainly you are being exploited. I have just been reading the figures for the big American places. A vast percentage are full professors, very few assistant professors and a large number doing contract work at one place and then the next. There is no doubt that it is worse because you are a woman and even worse because you are doing it in Christian studies. Churches always expect one to do it for almost nothing. They don't make the difference between quite proper volunteer work and trained work. I have no idea what Oxford is like now and whether it has forces to resist what is coming in academia over here. But generally since 1945 England and even more Canada take on what is happening in the U.S.A. about ten years later. After all they won the war.

I read your article on the Barth-Brunner[1] controversy with great interest because (not only because) I had read this controversy years ago when Brunner came to Oxford and talked about it in 1947. I think your conclusions are clear and sound. My difficulty with this Lutheran-Calvinist modernity is where they get their systematic language from. Also Sheila and I have been reading aloud (as she has badly broken the bottom of her leg) and she read to me your very clear critical writing at the end of your book about myself. So well done. One thing I would raise. Simone Weil is certainly gnostic but she is also agnostic; all her writing is about the absence of God. Of course, one thing about her is that she never thought or knew even that reformed theology existed. The nearest thing she ever came across was Thomism and she thinks little of that.

What you write of Mathew is interesting and of course difficult in a day-to-day sense. When she was young Isabel was our easiest child, while Katie was turbulent and difficult. Now Katie is a particularly charming grown woman, Isabel the splendid but difficult driver. I hope you will find time to pay special attention to Mathew when the new baby arrives because one thing that was common to all our six was a special jealousy of the child just younger than themselves. At the moment we bask in the fact that all seems to be going externally OK for all six.

I will read Oliver's new book[2] with the greatest interest when it is announced here. What a fine title. Sheila's trip to England is still delayed. I do not think I will be coming, as at the moment anything beyond the environs of Halifax scares me. Probably this means we will not see you when you come back to Canada, but my mood of 'safety' may be gone by then.

Love to Oliver and a kiss for Mathew. Take care of yourself in the next months.

Retirement is bliss.

Sheila sends her love.

Ever,
George

1 J.E. O'Donovan, 'Man in the Image of God: The Disagreement between Barth and Brunner Reconsidered,' *Scottish Journal of Theology* 30, no. 4 (1987), 433–59. H.E. Brunner (1889–1966) was a Swiss Protestant theologian, and Karl Barth (1886–1968) also a Swiss theologian who was dismissed from his German teaching post for refusing to take an oath of loyalty to Hitler. Brunner criticized Barth's early theology in 1934, arguing that there was a limited universal revelation of God in creation.

2 Oliver O'Donovan, *Peace and Certainty* (1989)

276/ To Joan O'Donovan

Dear Joan,

Thank you for your letter.

It is lovely to hear about Paul. Apart from what children are intrinsically, for long-term sheer enjoyment I know nothing that can equal them. Also they make one part of life in a way that we all think we are, but in fact are not, & it is so important for people doing theology and philosophy to be part of life in a way that children make one.

It is strange you being on Duggan [Avenue, Toronto, near Upper Canada College]. Everyday I used to go to a candy store on Duggan, even at one bad stage, stealing a quarter off my father's table to go in for debauchery at that store. I don't know whether you are close to Helen Ignatieff[1] who is one of the sweetest of women.

It is very good of you to say you could put us [up] in Toronto. I was very ill this spring and am still tottering, so cannot move from Halifax. It would be lovely to see you in October and we could fit in any time that suited you in the days that you were here, the more the better as far as we are concerned. When I say 'we' it may be only 'I' for it looks as if Sheila may be in England then, as I have given up the hope of going and she cannot delay much longer or it will never be.

I do hope we can meet because there is so much to talk about. Just before getting ill, I finished a book & the central long essay[2] in it is really my answer to what you said so well in criticism of my thought. I would love for you to read this essay & indeed to review the book in a Christian publication, giving your answer to my description of Christianity. The book is called *Technology and Justice* and is published by Anansi (they say September but this may not be so early). Descriptions of Christianity are not primary compared to Christ Himself, but it would nonetheless be interesting to compare & try & understand why we state the matter differently.

This is a poor letter, but it brings love to all four of you. We are very free and adaptable so let us know when you will be free when you are here in October. If it's only Oliver, it would be sad, but still nice to see him.

Ever,
George

1 Nicholas Ignatieff's widow
2 George Grant, 'Faith and the Multiversity,' in *Technology and Justice* (1986)

277/ To Ed Andrew   7 December 1985

Dear Eddie,
This is just a Xmas & New Years letter to you & Donna and with greetings to three precious young ladies. How they must be growing up. May 1986 bring you all good things.

Yesterday was David's birthday & talking to him over the phone he said he had seen you. How very nice of you to keep in touch with him, as I love to think of Margaret's son seeing our son. He is in truth our Benjamin and I feel that somehow I let him down in the sense that he has felt resentment towards me. When I write 'somehow' I mean that I do not know how, but yet recognise that it occurred & probably by something in oneself that one was not ever aware of. How strange in their unfathomableness are these close relationships. On the whole, but only on the whole, I am less held by Freud than I once was.

I hope Guelph goes well. It is such a beautiful town. Do the children like their schools? Does Donna like her job? I hope she is teaching what interests her. I hope you do not tire yourself with the automobile and that you have a good one & are careful. What I said about Donna is not quite right. Sometimes it is good to teach what does not suit you, because then you are [thrown] to learn something by expanding it. This was my experience with Kant & I am always glad it happened. I do not mean that we should aspire to be polymaths, but that it is so easy to avoid certain necessary [patterns].

We go on well. It is an immense joy to be retired, because it allows me to follow my own reading pattern & not think of students. Sheila is immensely free now ... but has not yet quite found her next stage ... Isabel will be back for Xmas, but we will miss the fun of her presence as she has to have an operation. Katie is doing education & is going to be a French [-immersion] teacher. They are marking her harder this year than I think is right. These awful initiation rituals that professional places put on.

Willie is very busy, but very sweet to us. I do not know whether you have met Denise, but I find her very entrancing. People are always saying that I should not speak of racial traits, but there is a kind of rationality in her that seems to me very French, as if she had avoided the long tumult of English colonialism, a pre-Rousseauesque Frenchness.

Canadian politics are a fairly [dismal] state. I know the Tory party I cared about is largely gone, but I do not find Mulroney nearly as bad as all the old Liberal bagmen make out. I am glad the Tories were put out in Ontario and hope the Liberals will be better than to be expected in Quebec. What is so strange about the modern world is that I am totally sure that Reagan and Gorbachev are not maniacs like Hitler, but they have power to do greater evil even than him. How strange. One thing I like about NS is that we have an old fashioned 'pol' as premier who lies in the good old-fashioned way. The eternal perfection of goodness itself somehow shines forth in the midst of the evil & violence & in Canada the futility. Badly put.

My love to all five of you.

Ever,
George

1986

278/ To David Cayley[1]   12 February 1986

Dear David,

This is to say thank you for the care and lucidity with which you enucleated my thoughts on the radio.[2] They were most accurately done and must have come forth from a great deal of work on your part, for which I am very grateful and consider myself very fortunate. As soon as I met you I knew that I was in sensitive hands and, as far as I am a judge who could be fair, your program was the best account in any medium of my thought, as I see it. When you were here you gave me such confidence by the careful questions you asked to me to speak my mind. Of course on the personal parts, it was impossible for my friends to express my foolishness and craziness of character and it is of course one of God's blessings that one can think certain thoughts which are quite beyond the details of one's own messy personality It is always a mystery to me that I can hold the truth of what Simone Weil is saying, when I am totally unable to live it.

Thank you for all your care and intelligence and sensitivity. I am aware of how fortunate it was for me. It would be lovely for us, if you were in Halifax, to see you.

Many thanks
George Grant

P.S. I have a crazy sense that I may be spelling your last name wrongly.

1 Of the CBC program *Ideas*
2 David Cayley, 'The Moving Image of Eternity' (1986)

279/ To William Christian   15 February 1986

Dear William,

Just to say how good your piece in the *Globe* is.[1] Few articulate people have any sense of the 'douceur' of life any more except as cosiness. Sheila loved it because she comes from a long line of enthusiastic gardeners, not of the great or of the small, but of the medium size. I thought the style very right.

I must thank you for taking the trouble for the things you did in the CBC programs about my thought. Egocentricity made me listen nervously and I thought your piece in the third program was the best thing on the whole thing. It was very good of you. I liked the programs because they were not unkind and seemed clear. The only thing I objected to was Larry Schmidt's too close identification of myself with Simone Weil. Please do not mention this because Schmidt is a very vulnerable person, but really, to admire the saints is not to be like them; hoping to think clearly is quite a different matter. I say this intimate thing to an old friend.

I hope the world goes well for you. Why not produce something on the *Laches* or on the aporetic dialogues? What you said the other night has determined me to read *Laches* properly. One of the strange things of life is having to read things again, as if for the first time. I have just been reading *Phaedrus* and, although I taught it for years, it was as if I read it for the first time. I need it for something I am writing about 'faith.'

All goes pretty well for us here except that Sheila broke her leg quite badly but it is getting better slowly. All really goes well for us ...

I agree that [St] Paul is not a nice man. If one can say that there is Johannine & Pauline Xianity, I am certainly on the Johannine side. Of course there are wonderful things in Paul, but also very strange things. You mentioned Austin Farrer on your card. I liked him because he was philosophical when the theologians in England were not; & was interested in the tradition when the philosophers thought real philosophy started with Russell. But I do not think now that he was in any way a great thinker. His Biblical books are taken up with crazy typology; his philosophical books are better, but not very good. I like best a book he wrote called *The Glass of Vision*,[2] but I haven't read it for years. I quite liked his Gifford lectures 'On the Freedom of the Will,'[3] but only quite.

I hope all goes well for Barbara & the boys & that the year is good for you. Thanks again for your sweet comments & for the piece in the *Globe*.

Ever,
George

P.S. I simply cannot know what to think about the free trade issue &, therefore, do not write about it. I simply do not know how well the government is doing, but see no reason to be against them & like some of the things they do.

A poor letter but many greetings.

P.P.S. Dalhousie is getting one of your VPs[4] as President. I hope he is strong, because he will need to be.

1 William Christian, 'Oh, to See Flowers in Winter,' *Globe and Mail*, 15 February 1986
2 Austin Farrer, *The Glass of Vision* (1958)
3 Austin Farrer, *The Freedom of the Will* (1958), the Gifford Lectures, 1957. Grant had a copy inscribed 'To George and Sheila' in his library.
4 H.C. Clark (1929–), vice-president academic, University of Guleph, 1976–86; president of Dalhousie University, 1986–

280/ To Charity Grant   7 June 1986

Dear Charity,

Thank you for your sweet letter. What a good idea just to resume the closer relationship we once had. Let us do that right now. I am sure that when there has been a break between people who have been close, it arises from failures of understanding and the trouble with my failures of understanding is that I do not even recognize them very well. So I think your letter a very good idea and let us proceed from it.

I am hoping that your forgetfulness is not as bad as you say. You have very high standards and have been a very social being and, therefore, have many people to remember. I am sorry to hear about Alison.[1] Sheila had such a nice call from her in the spring when I was in hospital.

Thank you again for your sweet letter. I take it that we will just go on as we did in the past. Do let us have your news, as we will let you have ours, if we ever have any of interest.

Ever,
George

P.S. Please do not think too much of your own death. I am in the middle of a long convalescence & know that my thoughts of death do me no good. We are both young enough to have some happy years.

1 She was beginning to show signs of Alzheimer's disease.

281/ To David Bovenizer[1]   30 September 1986

Dear Mr Bovenizer,

The bad manners of my lateness in writing in detail about the wonderful things you so kindly sent me arose from the difficulties of ill health (from which we are both recovering) and the sheer lack of energy for anything but keeping the daily show on the road. You must forgive this, because my debt is very great for the things you sent. They were immensely illuminating to me, above all because my parents were of the generation of Canadians whose education was automatically completed in Great Britain. All my ancestors had come to Canada from the U.S.A. at the time of your revolution.[2] So you can see how little I had of any knowledge of American traditions and how grateful I am to have read what you sent me.

Particularly was I grateful to read of Tate,[3] Ransom[4] etc. because I had just no idea that there were such people. I had once read a poem by Ransom about Judith which had moved me, but had no idea that the poet was connected with something so deep and fine as you have shown me through these writings. Allen Tate was a revelation to me and I've read since you sent me these, 'Ode to the Confederate Dead'[5] – a very fine poem. *I'll Take My Stand*[6] is a noble, if sad, book.

Knowing so little of the U.S.A. I had taken 'conservatism' in the U.S.A. as simply a debate about the relation between private business and the government and had known nothing of this tradition, of the hope of the continuities and the belief that life was more than expansion.

I liked the 30th anniversary copy of *National Review* which showed me the broad spectrum of all kinds of American conservatives. I cannot imagine in any English-speaking country (since Gladstone) that the president of the country would turn up at a dinner in praise of an essentially intellectually oriented magazine. Most politicians hardly read and write in my country. What I got from that issue was the enormous energy of the U.S.A. and as energy is not good in itself, this is both for good and evil. For example, seeing the U.S.A. on television and the movies, one cannot help but see it as embodying the aspect of the age of progress which is the emancipation of the passions (I do not mean simply the sexual passions). Obviously this is true of Western Europe too, but then, I see Western Europe as decadent in a way I do not think that the U.S.A. is. One hopes that the continuing power of the Catholic Church and the new power of the Protestant fundamentalists will give the U.S.A. a shape which sees the danger in the loosing of the passions. Our family finds itself in the sad vacuity which the Anglican Church has become for Canada, a pale reflection of every passing secular cause.

As I take abortion to be the great immediate issue for the Western world, it has been a source of the greatest interest to me that the U.S.A. is the only country which has a deep and vigorous anti-abortion movement. In Canada we have some and I work for it, but it is not comparatively vigorous as in the U.S.A. My sense of the greatness of the U.S.A. has been greatly raised by the presence of this anti-abortion movement.

Of course, in the writings you sent me [which] I like best, there are the deeper meanings of technological civilization. I liked the writings of Dante Germino[7] the best, even more than Molnar's[8] writing. I thought none of the writings about Voegelin were good enough. Having learned much from Leo Strauss over the years, it has come to me lately that Voegelin is the profounder of the two writers.

In the next days as I get better I will arrange to send you and your family the copies of the books of mine that you asked for. I am sorry I am so slow but I've just been up to keeping the bare essentials going.

Later on this fall a new book of mine[9] is coming out in Toronto and I believe also at Notre Dame in the U.S.A. I will send out a copy to you when it reaches me.

It was immensely good of you to send me what you did. It was all of great interest to me and came at a wonderful time for me as I had time to lie in bed and read it. I am always in your debt. The good and yet difficult thing of having retired to dear old Nova Scotia is that it is far from the powerful places of interest in modern North America. Also by tradition I subscribe to English publications and was therefore particularly grateful to receive what you sent.

What a strange old world it is, and yet God's world. I think what is the greatest difficulty of living in the modern world is that very fast technological change means very fast moral, political and religious change; we are always being overwhelmed by the new. Keeping one's head is so important and, as I get older, I often find it difficult.

Again so many thanks for your great kindness.

Always in gratitude,
Yours,
George Grant

P.S. Forgive a poor letter but it is the best I can do. Forgive my atrocious writing but I have never mastered the typewriter.

1 An American admirer at the Ethics and Public Policy Center in Washington, DC
2 The only United Empire Loyalists in Grant's ancestry were on his mother's side of the family, and even that connection is tenuous. Both his great-grandfathers immigrated to Canada from the United Kingdom in the nineteenth century.
3 J.O.A. Tate (1899–1979), American poet, editor, and university professor
4 John Crowe Ransom (1888–1974), American poet
5   Leave now
    The shut gate and the decomposing wall:
    The gentle serpent, green in the mulberry bush,
    Riots with his tongue through the hush –
    Sentinel of the grave who counts us all!   (1928)
6 *I'll Take My Stand: The South and the Agrarian Tradition* (1930, reprinted 1977)
7 Dante Germino, 'The "Loss of the Centre" and the Disorder of Modernity'
8 Probably Thomas Steven Molnar (1931–)
9 *Technology and Justice*

282/ To David Dodds[1]   postmarked 11 November 1986

Dear Mr Dodds,
This is a slow answer to your very kind letter. I have been in hospital but am now recovered. But it delayed answering your letter because of sheer lack of energy. Your letter was so kind and so encouraging to me at a difficult time, that I feel very badly to be so slow in answering. You will just have to forgive my lack of energy.

It was so good to get a letter from the president-designate of the C.S. Lewis Society. When I returned to Oxford in 1945 I had decided to study theology rather than law, which had been my pre-war study; and I was very disappointed by the lectures on biblical scholarship of the narrowest kind on the one side & very vulgar positivist philosophy (A.J. Ayer,[2] etc.)

on the other. Somebody told me that there was a meeting in the hall of my college & I went. It was the first Socratic meeting of the year so C.S.L.[3] was speaking. What sense! What clarity! What importance! It was just what I had come back to Oxford to hear. My breath was taken away with gladness. From then on the Socratic Club was a centre for me. My wife & I courted at it as she attended and, as a student of English, had gone to Lewis before the war & had attended his English lectures. It was so good to see somebody whom one might have seen behind the counter of an old fashioned butcher's shop, speaking in his wonderful, articulate way, and without the least bit of pretension or pride. Later in life, I found I had disagreements with some of his thought, particularly as it was not very interested in the philosophical questions I became interested in. But I think I was wrong in that, because there is no point in arguing with fellow Xians who express Xianity beautifully, because the common loyalty to X is the main thing & everything else is secondary. It is important that many of us should see our vocation as trying to express Xianity with clarity, but I am sure not much good is done by arguments within that common loyalty. And, of course, one of C.S.L.'s greatnesses was to avoid polemic in this way while using it when some issue of principle was at stake.

It is very kind of you to think of having a society for the study of my work and I am grateful for your interest. I have a book coming out in the next days called 'Technology & Justice' & for the first time in my life I have tried to express Christianity [around] a wonderful sentence of Simone Weil's that 'faith is the experience that the intelligence is illuminated by love.' Luckily with my wife's great help I finished the proofs just before getting ill again. I am sorry that some of my writings have made you 'gloomy.' Hope is a great virtue but I do not think it should be concentrated on the events of this world but on the eternal order. The words 'pessimism' & 'optimism' were invented by Leibniz out of his rather easy hopes & I think that Xianity was right to say that despair was a sin. I am very guilty of that sin, but struggle to [overcome] it. But I don't think the achievement of the virtue of hope should make us pretend that the world is different than it is and we indeed live in a very difficult world at the moment (although, of course, no time is easy). Do you know Luther's great phrase 'the theology of glory says that good is evil and evil is good; the theology of the cross says that the thing is as it is.' I find it very difficult & turn away from it at all times. 'Take up your cross and follow me.' My hopeless self-indulgence makes this difficult for me, but I think it is true.

I am so glad that you are doing a D.Phil. on Charles Williams. I love his books. He is, I think, a better novelist than C.S.L. and the books are a constant source of pleasure & refreshment. I think *Many Dimensions*[4] is my favourite & the redemptive death of the girl is very beautiful. I like them all and re-read them recently when I was in bed. I really would love to read your thesis when it is done. If you are ever near Halifax, please come & see us. We could put you up here. I hope I am getting better and, if we were well, it would be great to see you.

I am of course greatly honoured that you should think of a society about philosophy & its relation to Xianity. It has been my great interest in life and I think it is an inescapable question. I would, of course, be highly honoured for it to be related to my name. It is very sweet of you to think of it. I really have no practical advice because it has not been possible to go to England for many years ... with the result that I do not know anything of modern Oxford. Therefore, my advice would be worth nothing. I just have a sense of being honoured & am very grateful.

Thank you for your [generous] & kind letter. It did me a lot of good at a difficult period. I hope we may keep in touch because it is good for Xians, older & younger, to learn from each other.

Ever,
George Grant

P.S. Forgive my appalling writing. I will try & type next time when I am better.

1 An American graduate student at Oxford
2 Sir A.J. Ayer (1910–89), analytical philosopher and student of Gilbert Ryle, author of *Language, Truth and Logic* (1936); became professor at Oxford in 1947
3 C.S. Lewis (1898–1963), Irish-born professor of English and Christian apologist; taught at Oxford, 1925–54
4 Charles Williams (1886–1945), *Many Dimensions* (1947)

1987

283/ To Gaston Laurion

Dear Gaston,
I am very sorry to be so long in writing to you about your 'avant-propos,'[1] by which I am honoured and the very good preface by Jacques-Yvan

Morin.[2] The cause is that I was *very* ill in December & could do nothing
but lie on my back.

(1) Let me say first that I like very much 'un pays perdu.' It catches very
well what I meant.

(2) I like Morin's preface & am honoured by the fact that he wrote it.
At a philosophical level (or what might be called a universal level) I do
not agree with him, but that is unimportant. He has thought deeply for
one who has so given himself to the practical world. Each language (at
least the great ones) has its particular perfections and I have always
thought that that of French is the refusal to cloud the acceptance of
reality. This may seem strange to say when I am intoxicated by Céline
who writes in Parisian patois often & often of his own madness (I can
still only read the books about the fall of Germany with a translation
present). But what is so magnificent about him finally is just the wonderful refusal to turn away from what is, which seems to me particularly
French (or rather appropriate to the French language). When I am
well again I intend to write a long book about poetry & philosophy, cen-
tring on Céline.

I am so immensely grateful to you for doing this translation and for the
fact that you have done it so beautifully. It is a deep expression of friendship which I greatly treasure.

My best to your wife & to you as always. May 1987 bring you all that you
want.

Ever,
George

P.S. I address you on the envelope with the eighteenth century English
way; it amuses me.

1 To the French translation of *Lament for a Nation*
2 Jacques-Yvan Morin (1931–), constitutional lawyer and PQ deputy prime minister of Quebec, 1976–84

284/ To Gaston Laurion

Dear Gaston,
I am sorry to have been so long about your lovely translation, but have
been ill again & this is the first thing I have done. It will necessarily be
short. As I said over the phone, the translation is excellent & makes the
book seem better than it was in English. What I so like about the transla-

tion is that it keeps the spirit of the book & yet does not sacrifice the wonderful rhythm of French.

I have read it carefully & have only one large point, which you must decide. I much prefer 'Lamentation sur un pays'[1] to 'Lamentation sur un pays défunt,'[2] above all for the following reason: Incomparably the greatest Scottish poem is 'Lament for the makers'[3] and not the 'dead makers.' I took the title from the Scots. (As you know the highland Scots were conquered by the British in 1745, just a few years before the capture of Québec.) Also, of course, Canada seemed my country when I was young in a way that it could not seem yours when you were young. I would prefer 'Lamentations sur un pays .' But I recognize that you understand French rhythms in a way I do not.

Otherwise I have no words to change, above all because of the movement of French which you have so well captured & I do not think that should be changed.

Forgive this short letter, but it is all I can do at the moment.

Much love & very many thanks.

Ever,
George

P.S. Do you want the manuscript back? I would love to keep it, but that may not be possible.

1 Lament for a native land
2 Lament for a dead land
3 William Dunbar (1465?–1530?), *Lament for the Makaris*

285/ To Peter Self

Dear Peter,

It was so good to get your new address via William[1] and so good of you to send it. I have been a terrible correspondent because I have been plagued with diabetes & it is a disease which takes one's energy. At last, it is under control.

Not knowing Canberra, it is hard to picture what either of your lives is in detail, but have above all an envy of the sun, as compared with these harsh North Atlantic winters. Do you work at home or are you at the university a lot? Our Australian friends are [in] Melbourne[2] and they love it with a passion. I liked the professor husband particularly because the University of Melbourne had given him no sense of the university as research factory which plagued so much of my life. He really had a sense of the university as a place where the young were led out of the cave. He must have learnt it there and of course it meant he got his ass kicked in Canada when he came as an adventure. 'What did he do?' my American colleagues asked, when he was a kind of Australian Socrates. But this has made me very pro-Australia & I hope you are both enjoying it.

I hope you had a lovely time in England. Sheila went for a trip to see old friends[3] recently & just thought it was great. Admittedly she was with the slightly impoverished retired in Fulham, but she was so happy about the general spirit she felt among the children of her friends. Obviously, Sheila would not like the ungenerosity of Mrs Thatcher's politics, if that be the case, but she was aware of more zest than some of the years we were there in the 1950s.

I go on in my usual divided state. 'Theoretically' I find Xianity best expressed for myself in a kind of gnostic Platonic way, but in my life I remain a very sensual bourgeois. I have had to give up some of the pleasures because of health and I regret every [foregone] drink of wine and every cigarette. Having it both ways was a great mark of my mother's failing; so perhaps I just took it in my youth.

The children go on well at the moment. William goes on in his sweet way. Robert is going to train as a nurse so that he has an income while he writes novels. Sheila went out to see Rachel in Vancouver & there is no visible degeneration in her MS. She has a very dear German boyfriend who is very much looking after her. Katie is going to the northwest of BC to teach French. Isabel is getting married to her Japanese friend and going to BC to teach law. David is finishing his Ph.D. on the late novels of Henry James. They all say that David and I are very alike, but sadly he is the child who finds me too difficult.

I spend a great deal of life reading Heidegger. He is certainly the greatest philosopher of the modern era. Perhaps with the collapse of Europe, because of the last wars, he is the last philosopher, as philosophy is so essentially a western phenomenon. He is, of course, an ultimately modern philosopher & if I can summon the courage I would like to write an account of why his criticism of Plato is not true. But I doubt that I will ever have the skill to do it. One thing that makes it so difficult is that he is such a remarkable commentator on the history of philosophy. Of all the great German philosophers he is the only one who was by origin Catholic. If you ever feel any desire to read him, I think the best way is either through his book on Leibniz, *The Principle of Reason*, or through 'The Question concerning Technique.' I don't think *Sein und Zeit*[4] is the best

because that is the classic account of existentialism & he spent the rest of
his life writing where he thought that inadequate. (Parenthetically, I find
it so sad that the English clergy are more & more existentialist without
even knowing it, because it certainly does not suit what was so pleasant
about the English bourgeois.) I agree with what you said about 'Weltge-
schichte' moving to Asia, but I am too made by Europe to be anything
else.

This is a poor externalised letter, but it is the first attempt to write since
illness and I can do no better. The real expression of all I owe to your
friendship and all the generosity you have shown me over the years is
more than I am capable of doing at the moment. Nevertheless, this letter
brings that sense, however poorly expressed. (Parenthesis: Leo Strauss
said to me that the Germans have no word for 'generosity.' He, of course,
had every reason for making such remarks.)

When I next get down to writing I am going to write to Peter Clarke.
Did you ever have the chance to see him in England? I was telling Sheila
the other day why I was so entranced with him when we first met in 1939.

All the best to Sandra and to yourself.

As ever, always,
George

P.S. I also want to write a translation & commentary on Rousseau's *Discourse on the origin of inequality*, another task that will not get done.

1 William Christian
2 Ian Weeks, a colleague from McMaster
3 Two friends from school
4 Martin Heidegger, *Sein und Zeit* (Being and Time; 1927)

286/ To Ed Andrew   19 January 1987

Dear Eddie,
Thank you for your letter, although it brought the sad news of how poorly
your father is. What has been so fine is not simply that your father survived, but that he had such zest for life. A year and a half ago he took William & Denise, Sheila and me out to dinner & was more full of fun than
any of the rest of us. I am sorry to hear of Elaine,[1] whom I knew in Montreal 1938–39 and who had a [love] for living which seemed never to have
been fulfilled.

I am truly sorry that I am just not well enough to answer the more general remarks in your letter, as this is the first letter I have attempted since the new wave of illness that overtook me in December. It would require a long answer because my disagreement is largely about the facts & it is very hard to argue about facts. What I would beseech you is not to write anything about Sheila which proceeds from an account of femininity which she thought was quite false from your letter. She is very fond of you & of your family (Donna & the girls) and would find it difficult to be described within an account of the male-female difference which is repugnant to her. To describe her in terms of tradition, Sheila comes on her mother's side from Catholics of the recusant tradition. They were musicians who performed the music for the mass in the Arundel family. Her father's side was the blandest of Anglican bourgeois who lived above all in the theatre. These produce very different forms of femininity from either the secularised Protestantism of the Grants or the Judaism of Donna. (Let me say in parenthesis that it is to be taken for granted that I greatly admired what your mother stood for & admire what Donna stands for; I am just expressing differences.) The great event in my life has been living with Sheila. She is incomparably more philosophic than myself. Obviously I do not mind you writing of my debt to her, but not within an account of femininity which she would abhor.

As to Platonism & Xianity. I certainly would never call Plato – a pagan. Do you know Strauss's last 'official' book, *Studies in Platonic Political Philosophy*?[2] In that he has a masterly chapter 'Jerusalem & Athens.' He wrote clearly elsewhere of the difference between Judaism & Xianity in their relation to philosophy; I accept the difference as he described it. But remember that Strauss thought no political good was served by stressing the differences between Xianity & Judaism in modern North America. I thoroughly agree with him &, therefore, have not written explicitly about that difference & would consider it a sad day if it were ever necessary.

This is a poor letter, but I can do no more & want this to go off. My love to Donna and the girls.

Ever,
George

1 Elaine Andrew, Geoff Andrew's sister
2 Leo Strauss, *Studies in Platonic Political Philosophy* (1983)

287/ To Ed Andrew

Dear Eddie,

Thank you for your letter & the present (unopened till Isabel arrives). Her 'to be' is Masaru Kohno. He was here a lot last summer & is a very sweet person. Next week we will have a large delegation from Yokahama, not made easier by the fact that Mrs Kohno does not speak English & we know no Japanese.

It is strange that Margaret's children went to Ontario while ours go to BC.[1] Katie will be in northern BC teaching French next year; so all our girls will be there. Rachel is coming to the wedding, but not [Franz] who has to be working. William & Robert are here. William's wife Denise is a very delightful Acadian; Robert's Pamela is also charming and a very formidable addition. It has been very good of you to see David. He seems to be flourishing; but, as you probably know, he is the child that finds me very difficult and, therefore, I keep distant, although all our other children particularly adore him. I hope you will see him occasionally. The wedding here will be a great celebration, conducted in this house by the present minister of your great-grandfather's church here, St Matthew's. I pass every day on the way to the park the manse where darling daddy was born. Your mother was very wise to love him because he had much of her sweet irony. I am sure Katie Andrew's marriage will be great and your girls sweet in their attendance. (Sheila goes out today to buy a dress for the wedding here.) Give your Katie our best. When you write tell us the name & something about her husband. We have heard that we will see the Szantos[2] this summer – so nice.

It was good of you to write to me about the seminar you arranged at McMaster. I am above all glad that Barry Cooper[3] was not there. At a seminar a few years ago at Guelph, he got up & accused me of snobbery (*in re* an introduction I had once written for a book on Canadian furniture).[4] Among the vices I find snobbery particularly unpleasant & and as you can imagine Sheila having been brought up in Blackheath detests it. I am generally not incensed by what people say I have said (it is part of the price of admission) but I was so incensed by this that I held onto Howard Brotz's[5] hand all the time he was saying it. Snobbery is an endemic human vice, but one that must be fought – particularly necessary to be fought in Xianity &, therefore, I was incensed to be accused of it in a large public meeting. It is one of those accusations like 'Have you stopped beating your wife?' which it is impossible to answer publicly. Just at the moment (when this is the longest piece of writing I have done since my illness a year and a half ago) I find it hard to answer important questions. There was another seminar at McMaster on myself & religion & at it there was a paper on my relation to Strauss[6] (*not quite* accurate are always the most difficult to answer). But I will have to pull myself together to answer this because, despite all the silliness of some of his epigones, he had some great things to say as a Jew & a philosopher, and I owe him too much for having broken me from the grip of Hegel, not to answer this paper. But I feel very little up to such matters. One negative attraction of Isabel's wedding is that it puts off much activity. (I also have to correct the mistakes that a professor of psychiatry at Harvard made in a book about Simone Weil.)[7]

How lovely to have been to Italy. I haven't been there since 1937 but remember it as very beautiful. Where else did you go? Did you go to Perugia and Assisi? Daddy's cousin Derrick Grant had a villa between the two & I remember it as wonderfully beautiful. Sheila still has the energy for travelling & went to England, but I have not even the energy to go to Truro. 'If I mentioned Cherubino, all I said, sir, was the purest conjecture.'[8]

It was very sweet of you to have written. Forgive a poor answer, but it brings Donna and the girls much love.

Ever,
George

1 Margaret and Geoff Andrew spent most of their married life in BC.
2 The Andrews' oldest daughter, Alison (Kit), married George Szantos, a teacher of comparative literature and a writer.
3 Barry Cooper (1943–), professor of political science, University of Calgary
4 George Grant, 'Preface' to *Heritage: A Romantic Look at Early Canadian Furniture*, by Scott Symons and John de Visser (1971)
5 Professor of sociology, McMaster University
6 Wayne Whillier, 'George Grant and Leo Strauss: A Parting of the Way,' in *Two Theological Languages by George Grant and Other Essays in Honour of His Work*, ed. Wayne Whillier (1990), 63–81
7 George Grant, 'In Defence of Simone Weil,' *The Idler* 17, 36–40
8 Mozart, *Marriage of Figaro*, act 1

288/ To David Bovenizer   26 September 1987

Dear Mr Bovenizer,
It was very good of you to send me the tape of the interesting conversa-

tion. I learnt much from it and it is, of course, fascinating to hear what young conservatives in the U.S.A. are thinking these days.

I thought it very good what Gottfried said about keeping the roots of scholarship clean. If you see him, would you tell him how much I liked his example from 17th century British history. For postgraduate work I went to an Oxford college whose master [Christopher Hill] became a stalinist whose life work it was to show that Charles I and the Protestants were both entirely guided by class interests, whatever they thought they were really arguing & fighting about.

Tell him also that I am truly tired of being called a 'pessimist.' Leibniz invented the terms 'optimist' and 'pessimist' & used them about what human beings thought of being as a whole. Clearly as a Christian believer & philosophic Platonist I am clear that 'being qua being' is good, and that as part of that, evil is conceived as the absence not the opposite of good.

But apart from that rather personalized hesitation, I thought the conversation very good. It is clearly important to have thought of how young American conservatism is to face its great responsibilities. I was naturally interested in the parts about Allan Bloom[1] who is an old and close friend. The difficulty you so wisely raised is my difficulty about Bloom's recent book about American university education.[2] I admire the fact that Bloom so loves his country. I think it is good to love your own and not to hate it. But I think this love in him makes it impossible for him to see clearly what the modern North American position is in terms of what is arising domestically and the possibilities of change in the Aristotelian direction he truly believes in. Of course, it is extremely difficult for Bloom to turn to admiration because, although he is a loyal Jew, he is not a believing Jew. Apart from the truth of Christianity, there is a wonderful joy in Christianity which is a sustenance beyond any political sustenance.

This is a poor letter of thanks, but I am just getting to my feet after a long summer of illness. But happily I am better for the first time since the onset of diabetes. But it does not leave me with the strength to say many of the things about your very good tape. It was so good of you to send it.

As I progress in health, I will write again as it means a lot to have a connection with you & what you stand for.

Ever,
George Grant

1 Allan Bloom (1930–94), student of Leo Strauss and an American political philosopher and social critic
2 Allan Bloom, *The Closing of the American Mind* (1987)

289/ To Charity Grant   8 November 1987

Dear Charity,
I was very sorry to hear that you had been in hospital in Rome. Apart
from the anxiety caused by your symptoms, being in hospital far away
from here must greatly add to the burden. I hope you are in good medical hands and that you are taking every care. So many people (including
myself) need you.

   This is badly written because I am doing it flat on my back, as I have just
come back from a stay in the hospital. My trouble is what they call
osteoarthritis which means that your back hurts a lot.

   I hope you will really take care of yourself & not do a lot in other
people's interests, but take chief care of yourself.

   It was lovely having Sue [Wild] in town. Shelley [Wild] and her husband are very dear people. Shelley has been so good to us.

   Sheila joins me in,

                                                      As ever love,
                                                      George

290/ To Gaston Laurion   11 November 1987

Dear Gaston,
Librarians have been trying to search out where I could get *L'Oeuf
Transparent*[1] & have only been able to find it in one place in Canada – the
parliamentary library – and they will not let it go. I write, therefore, to ask
whether you could lend me your copy for a week. We would promise
faithfully to return it in one week. I would very much like to read it
before writing my paper for these lawyers.

   I wonder what you think of Johnson's resignation.[2] I hope Parizeau[3]
will be able to raise that sense of French unity. You would have been disgusted by the English media over Lévesque's death. Praising him to the
skies by people who had tried to cut his throat while he lived. His biography given without mention of the imposition of the War Measures
Act.[4] Romanow[5] the leader of the NDP in Saskatchewan who had
openly betrayed him over the Constitution praising him to the skies. I
hope that Quebec will remember 'Timeo Danaos et dona ferentes'[6]
when it comes to the NDP & maintain the Parti Québécois because the
NDP stands for assimilation as much as the Liberals or for that matter
the PCs. But we must put little trust in politics, except that in the case

of Quebec there is the hope of non-assimilation. I now so detest the Americans in Nicaragua (& even more in the Persian Gulf) that I even prefer the Russians.

The great joy of my life at the moment is reading Heidegger – what a genius. It is the greatest expression I have ever [read] of the world thought without God, and that is modernity; without 'transcendence' is probably a better way of putting it.

I can never thank you enough for your act of friendship in translating my political book. I am so glad that it is to appear in French and so grateful to you. The homogenization is almost complete as far as the English-speaking people is concerned, but I hope enough people in Quebec will see its consequences for themselves.

My best to your wife and, as always to yourself, my friendship and gratitude.

Ever,
George

1 J. Testart, *L'Oeuf transparent* (1986)
2 As leader of the Parti Québécois
3 Jacques Parizeau (1930–), economist and leader of the Parti Québécois, 1987–; premier of Quebec, 1994–6
4 During the October Crisis, 1970
5 Roy Romanow was minister for intergovernmental affairs for Saskatchewan, 1979–82, and a key figure in the negotiations that led to the repatriation of the British North America Act in 1982.
6 'I fear Greeks, even when they bring gifts' (Virgil, *Aeneid* 2.48).

291 / To John Arapura[1]   12 November 1987

Dear Dr Arapura,
Your book[2] is wonderfully illuminating. This is not, of course, to say that there are not many things in it that are quite beyond me, but it opened for me things that I had dimly grasped in our conversations, and which now I thought about having before me your lucid words, so that I could try to hold certain key sentences before me and try to think what was said in them. Obviously the book is for those who already have certain primary preparations in what must be read, but I say what I have said so that you will know that your book is immensely helpful to one who has not any of those primary preparations. For example, having tried to read the

Bhagavadgita, I find Chapter III very illuminating in leading me away from some of the unwise interpretations that I had reached on reading it for myself. Of course, your conclusion was wonderfully helpful for philosophy seen only from the western tradition, as indeed are the last sections of I & II, particularly I, because it is so immensely free from what the western tradition became, although through that conclusion (of II) I think I had a glimpse of the foundation of certain things that are very obscure to me in Plato.

This letter is a late response. But when your book first arrived, I was so unwell that I could only delay the proper reading of your book. My lack of energy led to little attention (I do not understand this phenomenon) to reading such as your book, which requires very great attention if one is to hold in the mind all the various approaches which you so wonderfully hold together in your writing. I envy greatly your ability to carry on together various themes which are part of the whole, so that the attentive reader can follow these themes rather in the way one follows the polyphony of tunes held in unity in Bach.

I hope all goes well for you & Mrs Arapura and Donu.[3] Life goes well for us here, although quietly. I feel better this autumn than for years. The only thing that broke into our quietness was Isabel getting married to a boy from Yokahama. It was a sweet cross-cultural wedding.

I hope that the future will bring a meeting. If I get stronger I will come up to Ontario & let you know in advance & hope you are there.
Ever in great admiration for a very illuminating book,

George G.

1 Professor of religion, McMaster University
2 John Arapura (1920–), *Gnosis and the Question of Thought in Vedanta* (1986).
   Arapura was a colleague at McMaster and a close intellectual friend from whom Grant learned much about the Vedanta.
3 The Arapuras' son

292/ To Peter Self

Dear Peter,
I dreamt of you last night in a happy dream and it is an omen which makes me write. For a long time I have been meaning to write to say how good of you it was to come here twice and how badly I greeted you with my ill health. It was so good of you to come and how inadequate I was to that goodness.

I hope all goes well in Canberra and that your mixture of university and government allows you also time to enjoy existing and time to think. I have always hoped that you would write a book solely of philosophy because I am sure that it would be enormously subtle and I think that, at a period when Western thought is so complexly broken up just when it is influential throughout the world, it is necessary to be subtle while maintaining moral force in the practical. This was always my difficulty about doing anything about your father's book. I felt that he had not come to terms with the breakdown of Western rationalism which was internal to that very rationalism, and that I could not touch it as an editor because that lack in the book was too present for me. In the same way I always refused to turn my thesis on a great liberal theologian[1] into a book because I did not want to produce a book which patronised a tradition which is admirable but fundamentally failing, because it did not face the profound division between Christianity & progressivism (in its best, its liberal form). I tried at one point to write something about a Canadian politician of the 19th century, Joseph Howe (because once both my father & grandfather had written lives of him)[2] and yet when I came up to doing it I felt I could not write it without some ridicule of Howe's liberalism and I did not want to do that. Of course, your father went far nearer to the roots of that spirit than these simply historical writings of my ancestors.

We go on pretty well. Diabetes is kept back in me by pills not injections which is good, but for somebody who thinks he cares about eternity, it is strange how much I resent doing without alcohol, dieting and restraining smoking. (I should put alcohol in the centre as the worst deprival because that is the way that Plato writes, putting what is most important in the centre of a list.) Sheila is pretty well although she would put limitation on eating at the centre.

I am trying to write down quite a long piece on Heidegger's 4 vol. commentary on Nietzsche.[3] It has at last been well translated into English and, as my German is negligible, I had only read it in French & with that I miss certain meanings. It is a staggeringly accomplished book, certainly the best commentary by one philosopher about another that I have ever read. Yet I also have to be able to say, despite its genius, where it is wrong, because of its assailing of Plato & worse its contempt for what Christianity is.

Give my best to Sandra. I hope all goes well with the church she described when she was here. To yourself always the sense of how much I owe you. When I was young, you gave me such a sense of confidence by

your friendship and in age I have a continual sense of what a joy to my life
your friendship has been.

Ever,
George

P.S. I refrain from a crack about how appropriate it is for an Englishman
to live on Hobbs St.

1 John Oman
2 G.M. Grant, *Joseph Howe* (1904); William Grant, *The Tribune of Nova Scotia: A
  Chronicle of Joseph Howe* (1915)
3 Martin Heidegger, *Nietzsche,* ed. David Krell (1979–82)

1988

293/ To Terry Barker[1]   2 January 1988

Dear Mr Barker,
It was an immense joy to receive your communications about socialism
and abortion. I am slow in answering because they both came while I was
in hospital, but they certainly cheered me up.

What you are doing is in itself so good, but it is, of course, also so good
in its implications. It is hard these days to see the capitalism around us as
anything but debasement; yet many people (such as myself) have turned
from the 'left' just because it is nihilistic about issues such as abortion &
does not even know that it is nihilistic. Your announcement directly faces
the 'left' from within and for people like myself means that, if we want to
express ourselves politically, we need not be thrown over to supporting
the capitalist system. Of course, in some ways, what seems to me best is
how wonderful it is to speak against nihilism to young people of the left,
because it does not so easily corrupt people completely when they are
young, but when the seeds are planted they become terrible in middle
age and later. Apart from all this, if you persuade one person to save a
child, that is a wonder.

This is a poor response to the two announcements you sent me and
your nice card, but it is written when I am still not well and, therefore,
cannot express properly how much I admire what you & your colleagues
are doing. Please send me any other announcements.

The best for 1988.

Yours ever,
George Grant

P.S. I quite agree with you about the media & the effort to break through their assumptions & try to use them for something nobler than these assumptions. But terribly difficult.

1 Barker had formed an anti-abortion group within the NDP.

294/ To Peter Self   6 January 1988

Dear Peter,

It was so good to get your letter and Sandra's. I am slow in answering because I have been in hospital (to good advantage because am much better). It is always strange to think of people one loves in worlds one has no idea what they are really like.

How good that Colin Macgregor[1] is with you and that you are looking at your father's book. I admired it greatly, but could not do anything with it for the following reason. I thought there was the great gulf between us symbolized by '1914.' I thought that your father (as the people I had been brought up with) had not seen that the events of this century had shown that there was something radically wrong with western European civilization not only with what it had become in the 19th but in its very roots since the 10th century. That is, that there was something wrong with the western expression of Christianity (obviously not with Christianity itself because what is given in the Gospels is perfect itself). It was wonderful that (in your words) 'Father was worried that theology had not developed to take account of scientific thought and philosophy,' but what if modern western science & philosophy were, in principle terms, the very enemies of any possible Christian theology? Would it not mean that coming to terms with modernity would mean the corruption of Christianity (as indeed it seems to me it was in Hegel's great attempt)? On the other hand, it is necessary that some Christians have to make the prodigious effort of trying to see the relation between thought & Christianity; they have no alternative. I think that your father's very sustained & careful effort should be published and I think now is a good time, because many English people are turning away from their limited & partial accounts of philosophy (from 1945–1970 circa) which so paralysed their intellectual life. I think your father's book should be published in England, as a mark of honour to their tradition.

I quite agree with what you say about your father's insistence that the eternal Christ must be central. What else was the doctrine of the Trinity?

– in which Gethsemane & Golgotha were not forgotten, but seen in their cosmic significance.

It is impertinent of me to say it to you, but I think if you want it done you should do it. I am sure you could do a good editorial job, in so far as it needs doing. There must be people in Canberra & encyclopedias which could [uncover] the details you have no familiarity with. But I am the last person who should say this to you, because when the man who was writing my father's life died, people wanted me to take over all his materials & do the job myself and I refused because I was too interested in my own studies.

I was so ashamed that both times when you so sweetly came to see us, I was so physically low. As de Gaulle said, 'Age is a shipwreck.' But this time, out of the hospital, I feel better than for several years & I hope for a long good period. Sheila is working hard because the Bar Association in BC has asked her to take my place speaking to them about what is at stake in the life issues such as euthanasia, abortion, surrogate motherhood, etc., etc. It is great good fortune for them as S. knows much more than myself & will do it so well.

One point I should have made earlier I return to. With intelligent people (such as yourself or to a lesser extent myself) it is always wrong to affirm, above all to themselves, anything about Christianity or lesser subjects, which they do not understand. I do not think intelligence is the supreme human quality, but I think it is something & should never be offended against by those who are intelligent. I think there are simpler people who may be much nearer to Christ and for them the whole complicated theological tradition is easily taken up as true & that is great & never to be offended against. But I think intelligence is never to be made the height or, on the other hand, to be offended against.

All the best to Sandra and as always to yourself my very best love from us both. I will try to write more intelligibly when I have more energy. It was so good of you to come & see us.

Ever,
George

1 A mutual friend, not otherwise identified

295/ To Charity Grant   3 February 1988

Dear Charity,
It was very good of you to write us such a sweet letter. We are both so sorry

that you have had such difficulty with an antibiotic. No wonder you are or have been so nervous. In my various trips to hospital in the last years, I have found them a great cause of nerves, because, even if it may be necessary, one is taken up with the total medical environment where one just does not know what is going to happen next. It is so good to hear that you feel better; please do not do too much & really look after yourself.

We go on in a vague kind of way; at least I do. Sheila is out speaking to the BC Bar Association about the Morgentaller decision of the Supreme Court.[1] I am unable to travel because of my back. I admire Sheila for doing it, because she has never much liked the public world. Sheila hopes very much to see you when she comes up to see David in April. I am sorry that I am unable to come & see you, but sitting is not easy and I am frightened of being away from home in case I become immobile again.

This brings you much much love & thanks for your letter. Do please look after yourself.

Ever love,
George

1 R. v. Morgentaler (1988)

296/ To Dennis Duffy   29 February 1988

Dear Dennis,
It was kind of you to send me your kind piece about myself.[1] I cannot use the word 'good' because it is so pleasant about myself; otherwise I would. I wish we were closer so we could talk at length about Céline. I love his writing because it so catches (for me) what life is like under difficult, [ill.] conditions and how it appears to me when one is pushed. I never tire of the three little dots. I do not like his early books comparably, because in the three about the last big war in Europe he is truly 'all passion spent.'

It was lovely to know it was your daughter at the *Idler*.[2] I just love the magazine even when one disagrees, because its ambience is just something I really sympathize with. How good that your daughter is part of it – good for them & I am sure interesting for her. Please give her my greetings.

It is hard for me to see the Tories pushing free trade. All the parties got rid of their nationalists. The NDP is absolutely out for me because of their stand about abortion; so I may have to vote Liberal. At least a few of the Tories are pushing about abortion. Something difficult to fathom (for me) is why so many of these who are unflinching about abortion are so

committed to unadulterated free enterprise. But I find that abortion
quite transcends any issue but nuclear disarmament.

Please give my best to your wife, from us both.

Ever,
George Grant

1 Dennis Duffy, 'Ancestral Journey: Travels with George Grant,' *Journal of Canadian Studies* 22, no. 3 (1987), 90–103
2 Literary and political magazine, published in Toronto

297/ To David Bovenizer   6 March 1988

Dear Mr Bovenizer,
Thank you for your letter & its awful enclosure.[1] I agree that the New
York *Times*'s comments are ghastly about such an appalling activity. It
makes one 'turn one's face to the wall,' but I think the early Christians
were correct in saying that despair was a very great sin. I am able to say
this because I have been so prone to it and know how evil it is. One of Tolstoy's stories has the title 'God sees the truth, but waits.' I also think of
Simone Weil's beautiful statement (which I can only paraphrase), 'If
there were not authentic good, what would evil deprive us of.' But I am
scared for the world my grandchildren move into.

I think the only thing is just to try to hold onto Christ in one's private
and public life. I find it sufficiently difficult and above all because I find
prayer so difficult. I can think (and that is a help) but prayer is more
important and that is for me so difficult because, although I never have
difficulty knowing that God is, God appears to me more as absence than
as presence. Of course, God is both.

It was very interesting to me that you had moved from the Foundation
[Ethics and Public Policy Center] to Regnery.[2] I used to order books for
the library at my old university from Regnery & always admired their list.
I wonder what the move means for you and your family. If it be possible,
please send me Regnery's list, because in retirement I am out of touch
with new books.

We have just had a Supreme Court decision here on abortion. The
majority was, if possible, worse than Roe v. Wade but luckily we've a health
care system where the money comes from the federal government but
where administration is in the hands of the provinces. Some of the provinces have refused to allow their hospitals to finance non-medical abortions. But you can imagine how the press is attacking them as 'rednecks'

etc. etc. What is so extraordinary about our politics is that some of the left-wing politicians who speak most often about rights are just those who speak most loudly in favour of abortion on demand.

I am trying to keep going with long-range philosophical writing, but with difficulty. I have just been reading a great, but terrible, book – Heidegger's *Nietzsche*. It has at last come out in English. I had read it in French because my German is D—. But the English helps me further than the French, because French is such a rational language that it is particularly inadequate for an account of the great [philosophy] such as existentialism. But I [like] this book because it has taken me to understand more deeply than ever before what is so frightening in the roots of modernity. It really has shown me new things about Nietzsche that I had never seen in my own studies of that thinker.

It was good of you to send me that extract from the NY *Times*. We have an obligation to look upon the worst and try to look at it as a Christian.

Some time when you have a moment, do let me know what your movement to Regnery means and what it will mean for you and your family's life.

Sincerely,
George Grant

P.S. I have been in hospital a lot, but they found out the cause of the pain & it is something they can deal with. So I am better than I have been for several years.

1 'Life Industrialized,' *Times* [New York], 22 February 1988
2 A publishing house

298/ To David Dodds   6 March 1988

Dear Mr Dodds,
I am slow in answering your letter because I have been in hospital again (but am now better).

Thank you for your interesting letter.

(1) Voegelin. He is a very fine thinker. I have certainly learned a lot from him & gave once a lecture series expounding *The New Science of Politics*.[1] As to what your friend Finnis said, I would say that I too learnt a lot from both Voegelin and Strauss, but that I am fundamentally more in Voegelin's ambience than Strauss's, because it comes out of Christianity while Strauss's comes out of Judaism. I do not think, nevertheless, that Voegelin sufficiently comes to terms with Nietzsche & Heidegger and I

think this is because he sees the threat of 'modernity' too much in terms of marxism. (Of course, what he says about marxism is very good.) I think this concentration makes him fail to see that 'modernity' is expressed even more explicitly in Nietzsche than in Marx and from this comes the 'modernity' which so terribly threatens the western world from within & not from without (as is the case with marxism).

Also I have just put a note in something I have been writing about Simone Weil (my greatest modern teacher) in which I take issue with Voegelin's use of the word 'gnosticism.'[2] I do so because I think his use of it is unfair to what is true in ancient gnosticism. Of course, as in all religious traditions, there is a lot of madness in many manifestations of ancient gnosticism, but in the greatest gnostics there is a hold on what is fundamental in Platonism. Therefore, I think it wrong of Voegelin to use 'gnosticism' as a term of abuse and to identify some of the most pernicious elements of the modern with it. I think this is related to his inability to see that intellectually there are more terrible manifestations of 'modernity' than Marx and that these undermine the western world from within, not simply from without.

Of course the tradition in the western world is so broken that in the effort to recapture it through thought, we must look to all kinds of places to try to rethink the truth of Christianity and of philosophy. At the moment I am reading Heidegger's *Nietzsche* which has been completed in 4 vols in English. (My German is very, very poor.) In some ways I think it is more his *magnum opus* than *Sein und Zeit* because in it his criticism of Plato is laid bare. It is a great but terrible read. But I am seeing 'modernity' for what it is in a way I have never yet done for all my reading & teaching & writing about Nietzsche. All Christian ways differ with the particular human being and I am sure yours will be a great one. This is an extremely difficult era to live in because we are asked to know so much so [as] not to be entrapped by it.

Of course, photocopy anything of mine you like. I am flattered that you should be interested.

I have tried to see what I can do about the footnotes in *Technology and Justice* but cannot.[3] I was in a bad patch when it was coming out & so would have been capable of anything.

I hope this winter is very good for you in England & that all goes well for you & yours. Thanks again for such a good letter.

Ever,
George Grant

1 Eric Voegelin, *The New Science of Politics: An Introduction* (1965)

2 'In our time, as good a thinker as Voegelin has wrongly used "gnosticism" as a
term of abuse in his fine book *The New Science of Politics*. Therefore it is with hesitation that I categorize Simone Weil as a "gnostic," in order to make clear that
it was more than accident that held her from becoming a Catholic' (George
Grant, 'In Defence of Simone Weil,' 37).

3 Some of the footnotes were omitted by accident.

299/ To Gaston Laurion   [late April 1988]

Mon cher Gaston,
J'ai de la chance d'avoir si bon ami, comme vous-même. Vous m'avez
montré quel bonté la semaine passée. Quand j'ai laissé Halifax j'avais
grand peur parce que je n'avais pas voyagé pour dix ans et je n'avais pas
aucun peur à Montréal parce que vous étiez si gentil.

J'ai peur que l'élection en Manitoba veut signifier que les Anglais ne
désire pas même le Meech Lake.[1] Il y a si grand passion pour le homoge-
nisation parmi les Anglophones d'Amérique du Nord. Sans d'être marx-
iste, je n'ai pas compris proprement le pouvoir du capitalisme comme
internationale.

Mes remerciements et mes salutations à Geneviève.

Pour tous mes grand remerciements pour votre bonté.

Toujours,
George

P.S. J'espère que vous viendrez nous voir. Notre maison est plus confort-
able que dans le passé.[2]

1 A proposal for constitutional reform, generally known as the Meech Lake
Accord

2 I am lucky to have such a good friend as you. You showed me such goodness
last week. When I left Halifax, I was very much afraid, since I had not travelled
for ten years, but I was not at all afraid in Montreal because you were so kind.

I am afraid that the Manitoba election indicates that the English do not want
even the Meech Lake Accord. The Anglophones of North America are so
intent on homogenization. Without being a marxist, I cannot adequately
understand the power of capitalism as something international.

My thanks, and greeting to Geneviève.

All my thanks for your kindness.

Always,
George

I hope you will come and see us. Our new house is more comfortable than the old one.

300 / To Charity Grant   28 April 1988

Dear Charity,

I am sorry to be slow in answering your sweet letter, but was called away for a few days and, as I am so scared of travelling, it required all my attention.

It is so good to hear that you are feeling better, after the time in Italy and then in Toronto with flu. I hope you will have a good summer. (Since starting this letter I have just had a horrible telephone call from a civil servant about a student, who gave my name for a student loan, & they now want his address, etc., etc. They are so rude on the phone, etc., etc. the growth of the state automatically means the growth of the bureaucracy. But the way they speak leaves me shaking with impotence & kills my letter writing ability. This is all said to state the general statement that I found it harder & harder to cope with stress as I get older &, therefore, live in retirement – end of parenthesis.)

I hope you still have your cottage & will be able to get there for some quiet. I think it is no wonder that you find it difficult in Italy. Hospitals are a strain anyway (I have been in & out in the last years) but a hospital in a foreign country must be very stress laden. I am sorry your doctor is not sympathetic & I think that you had a right to be worried. I hope your doctor is good.

Sheila is going to Toronto on May 6th for a few days to see Dave & will ring you in the hope that you are there. She had to delay her trip because she went to address the BC Bar Association on abortion. Her paper was so good that it is going to be published in the *Canadian Journal of Family Law*.[1] She accomplishes much more than myself since the children are not here. I do not know whether you have seen Katie who is teaching French in Lindsay, Ont. & often goes to Dave's for the weekend.

All the children go well except for Rachel about whose MS you will have heard. We saved our money to go there & accepted the BC Bar as a way of getting the way paid.

Forgive a poor letter and a confused one. But if I didn't get it done, I will have left it too long. I am so glad to hear that you say that Alison is a bit better. Do give her love from both of us when you see her. As also to Sue [Wild]. We see Shelley on & off here with a nice French[-Canadian] husband. Shelley is a very sweet person.

Do look after yourself as many people here need you, including myself. This is a very poor letter, but it brings you much love & the hope that you will have a lovely summer.

Always with love,
George

P.S. I am glad you watch golf. Nicklaus[2] has been for many years one of my heros & now that he is past it, I have turned to watching tennis. Nicklaus was one of the rare people who overcame my general anti-American tendency.

1 Sheila Grant, 'The Non-Human Child,' *Canadian Journal of Family Law* 7 (1988)
2 J.W. Nicklaus (1940–), considered by many the greatest golf player of the twentieth century

301/ To William Christian   30 April 1988

Dear William,
It is no exaggeration to say that I never received such immediate and great pleasure from reading anything, as this morning when I read your piece on Socrates in the *G & M*.[1] It was so wonderful in its economy of saying what needed to be said within the given space of a book review. The 'de haut en bas' tone was just right and this is a difficult achievement because it has to be *sine ira et studio*[2] if it is not to seem arrogant. It was an enormous pleasure that this should have been written by a friend.
    Much later. I have been meaning to write about your two big pieces,[3] but have been held up by a series of practical duties (boring). I am much healthier now than I have been for four years (so will be writing soon), but could not delay my sense of joy at your exactly right piece this morning, less important than the others, yet perfected in its small space.

Ever,
George

1 William Christian, 'Suspect Piece of Goods,' *Globe and Mail*, 30 April 1988, C21
2 'Calmly and dispassionately' – Tacitus
3 A journal article on Plato and a book chapter on the ideologies of Canadian political parties

302/ To Terry Barker   24 June 1988

Dear Mr Barker,
Thank you for your letter and for the enclosure from Windsor. It is great
news what you say. I so dislike the exaltation of greed (in the name of liberty) which is so widespread in the English-speaking world that I would be
glad to vote for a non-capitalist party & so feel grateful for the efforts of
you and your colleagues.

I would, of course, be honoured for my piece to be reprinted in your
two newsletters.[1] Can you let Ms Crean and Mr [Beam] know as I am not
very well & two letters are a thing for me? I am glad you liked it. It was
written hurriedly on a quick request and some of the sentences are not
quite right.

I have been meaning to write to you about the splendid writings you
sent me, but have had little energy. Let me say how good I thought them
& when the summer has brought me back, I will write at the much greater
length they deserve.

I was sorry about the telephone call & my poor dog. He was having a
queer turn. I rushed him to the vet, but he died that afternoon. He had
been a dear companion for 17 years. I was very sorry to be so quick, but I
was very confused.

Thank you again for your letter & the so encouraging enclosure. I will
write again after the summer.

The best to you & yours.

Yours,
George Grant

1 George Grant, 'The Triumph of the Will,' *Jeremiad*, 3–4 (Fall-Winter 1988–9),
3–6

303/ To Katherine Temple[1]

[extract:]

Dear Katherine,
This is also an apology for being wrapped up in Arty's death when you
were here and involving you in it. It is hard to know what place to give an
animal. Having lived in England I am suspicious of those who place them
too high. I do not quite know why, but after 17 years of sweet companion-
ship, I could not consign his remains to the incinerator. It raises the

whole question of the body. Anyway it prevented me from asking you many questions about industrial society, and that is a waste.

P.S. I used to hope that I would at least be wiser when I was old, but it seems one's madness just seems to hang about.

1 A former graduate student from McMaster. This is an excerpt from a letter transcribed from a tape-recording. The complete original remains in Dr Temple's possession.

304/ To John Siebert[1]   29 June 1988

Dear Mr Siebert,
Thank you for your interesting letter; also very much for 47 *Review Story* which I will read very soon; also for the [Charles Norris] Cochrane pages. I think it is a very good idea to bring out the whole thing for the Cochrane seminar.
   Now Heidegger.
   (a) Strauss & Heidegger. Yes, it was through Strauss that I came upon Heidegger, particularly through the passage about H. that is in the French edition of S.'s book about tyranny.[2] Strauss to his death always said that H. was the only unequivocally great philosopher of our age. He heard him first in his famous debate with Cassirer[3] at Davos and rushed back to tell Rosenzweig[4] that a genius had come in Germany. Then there was the difficulty of H.'s relation to the Nat. Socialists. But Strauss never went back on his recognition of H.'s genius.
   (b) For myself it is only in the last two decades that I have been ready to bring Heidegger into my writings. He is, after all, a very consummate thinker and also a *very* prolific writer. It took me years to find the time to read H. comprehensively. The Nietzsche book is now the catalyst to write a longer piece directly about him. Let me say clearly that H. must be for me a writer who ridicules Christianity &, therefore, to write about him is to say a great 'NO.' His criticism of Plato is related to his ridicule of Christianity, but that is not of the same centrality for me. His Nietzsche book has been a great catalyst for me as it has come out in English.
   The only thing I do not like in your letter is the phrase 'Strauss's beef.' That is surely a casual way of speaking about a great subject.
   Give my best to your wife & I hope you have a good summer.

Yours,
George Grant

1 John Siebert (1959–), who was writing an M.A. thesis on Grant, 'George Grant's Troubled Appropriation of Martin Heidegger on the Question Concerning Technology,' St Michael's College, University of Toronto (1988)
2 Leo Strauss, *De la tyrannie* (1954); Leo Strauss, *On Tyranny* (1963)
3 Ernst Cassirer (1874–1945), German philosopher
4 Franz Rosenzweig (1886–1929), German philosopher

305/ To Gaston Laurion   21 July 1988

Mon cher Gaston,
Mes remerciements pour les photos. Et Sheila me désire dire ses remerciements; elle aime beaucoup les photos.[1]

I am extremely sorry to hear of your brother and am glad that you saw him recently. It is not only the sameness of the genetic origin, but the fact that one has shared the same bringing up by the same mother and father. Two or three years ago my sister died in Vancouver and I miss her greatly because when we met we would share memories, both good & bad, amusing & sad, which nobody else could share, and memories so determinative of what one is. I am so sorry for your loss.

I owe you so much for those good days in Montreal, but I must add a special joy. When I was 15 I passed a summer at Mt. Bruno with the family of a wonderful patriarch, Victor Morin. He turns out to have been the grandfather of J.-Y. Morin. That summer was very happy for me and particularly because a Morin daughter, Marie-Huguette, arranged how I spent the day – picking raspberries, etc. She was 15 years older than myself. I knew she had married an Italian army officer and had passed her life since 1937 in Italy. J.-Y. Morin told me that she had returned to Montreal for her old age. She had been too old to come out to meet me. Since returning to Halifax she sent me a very sweet letter & a photo of myself & herself in the 1930's. I am not sure why it has filled me with such joy, but I think I have broken or the world has broken me with my past, & suddenly to receive a note which said she looked back with pleasure to that time, when it was one of the easiest and happiest summers of my life, just filled me with joy. I owe this to you not only because of the beautiful translation of the book, but because of your having me up to Montreal.

What so particularly fascinated me in Montreal was meeting people who maintained a state of being which was not determined by American capitalism. Can one imagine Mme J.-Y. Morin coming forth from the American world? The sadness of English-speaking nationalism in Canada is that so much of it wants nationalism, but wants to be the same American capitalism, with a [ill.] maple leaf flag put on top. You rarely meet people who are outside the determining power of that American dream. It is for this reason that I detest [NDP leader Ed] Broadbent's supposed nationalist rhetoric. It is just the Democratic Party North. As Mulroney is the Republican Party North.

Most people have learnt to live happily in hard political eras and we do that here. Sheila has started to write a lot about abortion & other issues like genetic transplants. I am trying (with such difficulty) to refute Heidegger's masterly criticism of Plato. I will send parts along as they are written.

My best to Geneviève (I am not sure of the accents).

To you as always my gratitude for your friendship and my hope that you will have a good time in Europe.

Ever,

George

1 Thank you for the photos. Sheila wants to send her thanks too; she just loves photos.

In September 1988, Grant discovered that he had pancreatic cancer. He died 27 September 1988 and was buried at Terrence Bay.

Index

Taylor, Charles 331, 332n
Taylor, E.P. 161, 161n
Tchaikovsky, P.I. 23
technology: and change 359–60; and
    society 328
Temple, Archbishop William 103,
    104n
Tennyson, Hallam 59, 61n
Terrence Bay 227, 257, 273
Tertullian 276, 277n
Testart, J.: *L'Oeuf transparent* 371, 372n
Thatcher, Margaret 365
theology 126, 127; and philosophy
    376; and science 127, 376
Theresa, Saint 324
Thompson, Dorothy 25, 25n
Tolmie, Anne 187n
Tolstoy, Leo 93, 105, 105n, 379; *War
    and Peace* 93, 100, 105; *Where God Is
    Love Is* 105
Toscanini, Arturo 102, 103n
Totton, S.J. 224n
Tovell, Vincent 306, 307; *The Owl and
    the Dynamo* 307n
Toynbee, Arnold 57, 57n
Trevelyan, G.O. 23, 24n
Trotter, R.A. 26, 27n, 65n, 109
Trudeau, Pierre 241n, 250, 265n, 266,
    277, 299, 304, 305, 314, 314n, 316,
    317, 318, 328, 339, 340n, 343
Truman, Harry S. 128, 128n, 152,
    154n
Turner, John 266, 267n, 343
Tylor, Sir Theodore Henry 53, 53n

Underhill, Frank 244, 245n
United Church 108, 115, 174, 188,
    220, 242; union of, with Anglican
    Church, 229, 229n
United Church Observer 173

universities: and religion 169; and
    research 306, 309
University of Manitoba 207, 208n
University of Toronto 199, 200, 205,
    254n, 306n, 327n; association of,
    with York University 199, 203; Erin-
    dale College at 292, 292n; George
    Parkin Grant's honorary degree
    from 303–4; Innis College at 302n,
    305, 306n; philosophy department
    at 200; St Michael's College at 302n,
    312, 387n; Trinity College at 206,
    213, 214n, 265, 266, 302; University
    College at 224; Wycliffe College at
    348, 348n
University of Winnipeg 265
Upper Canada College 151, 353;
    George Parkin Grant and 12; Lib-
    eral Committee at 12; Visites inter-
    provinciales of 14; William Grant
    and 3, 4n

Vanier, Jean 288, 289, 289n
Vansittart, Sir Robert 76, 77n
Venice (Italy) 31
Verona (Italy) 31
Voegelin, Eric 359, 380, 381n, 382n;
    and Christianity 380; and gnosti-
    cism, 381; *The New Science of Politics*
    380, 381n, 382n

Wade, Mason 110, 112n
Wagner, Richard 23
Wallace, Sheila 59, 62n
Wansbrough, V.C. 33, 34n
Watson, Alan 27, 28, 29n, 30
Watson, John 264, 265n, 267; and
    Hegel 272
Watteau, Antoine 46, 46n
Webb, C.C.J. 274, 274n